Study Guide

for

Kimmel and Aronson

Sociology Now

prepared by

Shelly McGrath
Southern Illinois University

PEARSON

Boston   New York   San Francisco
Mexico City   Montreal   Toronto   London   Madrid   Munich   Paris
Hong Kong   Singapore   Tokyo   Cape Town   Sydney

ISBN-13: 978-0-205-59312-5
ISBN-10:   0-205-59312-7

Printed in the United States of America

10 9 8 7 6 5 4 3 2 1   12 11 10 09 08

CONTENTS

Introduction to Using this Study Guide

Getting Started

This introductory chapter will describe for you what is included in the study guide, how to use the material provided, and will give you important tips on studying for tests or quizzes. This study guide has been prepared to accompany Michael Kimmel and Amy Aronson's textbook *Sociology Now*. The study guide is intended to be a brief review and learning tool and acts as a supplement to the text. This study guide is not intended to replace the textbook; it is intended to assist you in reviewing the material after you have read the entire chapter of the text. This study guide was written to enhance student learning and help students accomplish their goals for this course.

After receiving the syllabus from your professor, you can then determine how and when to use this study guide provided to you. The study guide was designed to help you prepare for examinations and quizzes covering the concepts presented in *Sociology Now*. It should also provide you with a clearer understanding of the themes and concepts presented in the text book. Each of the chapter in the study guide corresponds with the chapters in the book.

What is in the Study Guide?

This study guide includes:
- A Chapter Outline that reviews the material covered in the chapter and gives a basis for organizing information present in each of the chapters. The chapter outline presents all of the major topics of the chapter in the order that they appear in the chapter.
- A Chapter Summary which summarizes all of the main points found in the chapter. The summary provides the most important themes and concepts discussed in the chapter.
- Learning Objectives set forth the goals of each chapter. You should be able to answer the learning objectives once you have read the textbook and learned the material. If you are unable to answer any of the objectives go back and review the material.
- Key Terms from the chapter are listed in alphabetical order. The definitions are listed next to each term. This section offers you a review of the key terms that are presented in the text.
- Key People whose work has been discussed in the chapter. In some cases these people will appear in bold print, in others they will be people who are mentioned in the chapter because of their research on the subject matter.
- Practice Test that provides you an opportunity to see how much you learned from the chapter. Each practice tests includes: 25 multiple choice questions, 10 true/false questions, 10 fill-in-the-blank questions, and 3-5 essay questions. The chapter-by-chapter Answer Key in the back of the book allows for you to check your answers. Use the practice test after you have studied the textbook material. Note the questions that you answered wrong so that you can go back and try them

again. After checking you answers return to the textbook where your comprehension was weak.

How to Use this Study Guide

Before reading the textbook, read the Learning Objectives to get an idea of what you will need to concentrate on while reading the material. As you read each chapter take notes on the major concepts and themes throughout the chapter. Being able to synthesize the material will help you learn it. While reading through the text, be sure to read the tables, figures, and boxes in the margins of the text book.

The chapter outline provides you with the major themes and concepts throughout the chapter and can be compared to the notes you have taken while reading the chapter. Reading the chapter outline and summary will provide you with the key information that you should have pulled out of the chapter. After reading the text check the key terms and key people in the study guide and make sure that you understand them and know where they are located in the text.

It is important to utilize the practice test for each chapter. The practice test can be taken as a closed book test to gage your understanding of the material. After checking your answer, go back to the pages listed by the answers to review those that you have marked incorrect or were unsure about. It is important that you go back and review the questions that you missed to fully understand the concept or theme. The page numbers in the answer key corresponds to the page numbers in the book.

Regardless of which sections you utilize, the study guide will be most valuable if you have read the textbook first.

Chapter 1
What is Sociology?

Chapter Outline

I.   Sociology as a Way of Seeing
- a. Beyond Either/Or Seeing Sociologically
- b. Making Connections: Sociological Dynamics
  - i. Sociologist interested in the connections between things getting better and things getting worse
  - ii. Social order is an intriguing as social breakdown
- c. Sociological Understanding

II.   Doing Sociology
- a. Sociology and Science
  - i. Sociology does not have the predictive power of the natural sciences
    1. People do not behave as predictably as rocks or planets
    2. Sociologists create hypotheses based on empirical observations of social phenomena
    3. Looking for scientific facts
  - ii. Social phenomena objectivity
    1. Quantitative methods
       - a. social phenomena as real as natural phenomena
       - b. studied objectively
    2. Qualitative methods
       - a. Social phenomena exists only through human interaction
       - b. Can not studied it objectively
  - iii. Questions sociology poses distinguishes itself from other social sciences
- b. Getting Beyond "Common Sense"
  - i. Common sense assumes that such patterns are universal and timeless
  - ii. Common sense explanations have no room for variation
  - iii. Sociological perspective helps you to see how events and problems that pre-occupy us today are not timeless

III.   Where did Sociology Come From?
- a. Before "Sociology"
  - i. Philosophers were attempting to understand the relationship of the individual and society
  - ii. John Locke- individual liberty
  - iii. Jean-Jacques Rousseau- society enhanced freedom
- b. The Invention of Sociology
  - i. Enlightenment 1776-1838
    1. Nature of Community
    2. Nature of Government
    3. Nature of the Economy
    4. Meaning of Individualism
    5. Rise of Secularism
    6. Nature and Direction of Change
  - ii. Sociologists praised and criticized these new developments
- c. Classical Sociological Thinkers
  - i. Auguste Comte (1798-1857)
    1. Believed that each society passed through three stages of development based on the form of knowledge that provided its foundation.
    2. Sociology must rely on science to explain social facts.
  - ii. Alexis de Tocquevill (1805-1859)
    1. He saw the United States as the embodiment of democracy.

          2. His greatest insight is that democracy can either enhance or erode individual liberty.

   iii. Karl Marx (1818-1883)

          1. His greatest sociological insight was that class was the organizing principle of social life.

          2. He initially believed that capitalism was a revolutionary system itself, destroying all older, more traditional forms of social life and replacing them with one's position being dependent on wealth, property, and class.

   iv. Emile Durkheim (1858-1917)

          1. He searched for distinctly social origins of even the most individual and personal of issues.

          2. Society is held together by "solidarity," moral bond that connect us to the social collectivity.

   v. Max Weber (1864-1920)

          1. His chief interest in all his studies was the extraordinary importance of "rationality."

          2. He developed a sociology that was both "interpretive" and "value free."

   vi. Georg Simmel (1858-1918)

          1. The special task of sociology is to study the forms of social interaction apart from their content.

          2. His major concern was about individualism.

d. American Sociological Thinkers

   i. Thorstein Veblen (1857-1929)

          1. He is best known for his satirical work, *The Theory of the Leisure Class*.

          2. He argued that America was split in two, those who work and those who have money.

   ii. Lester Ward (1841-1913)

          1. Ward stressed the need for social planning and reform.

          2. He welcomed the many popular reform movements because he saw enlightened government as the key to social evolution.

   iii. George Herbert Mead (1863-1931)

          1. Studied the development of individual identity through social processes.

          2. He argued that what gave us our identity was the product of our interactions with ourselves and with others.

e. The "Other" Cannon

   i. Mary Wollstonecraft (1759-1797)

          1. Many of her ideas included equal education for the sexes, the opening of the professions to women, and her critique of marriage as a form of legal prostitution.

          2. She argued that society could not progress if half its members are kept backward.

   ii. Margaret Fuller (1810-1850)

          1. Her book, *Woman in the nineteenth Century*, become the foundation for the women's movement.

          2. The book called for complete freedom and equality.

   iii. Frederick Douglass (1817-1895)

          1. He was the most important African American intellectual of the nineteenth century.

          2. His work stands as an impassioned testament to the cruelty and illogical of slavery, claiming that all human beings were equally capable of being full individuals.

   iv. W. E. B. Du Bois (1868-1963)

          1. He was the most articulate, original, and widely read spokesman for the civil rights of black people for a period of more than 30 years.

          2. Du Bois believed that race was a defining feature of American society.

   v. Charlotte Perkins Gilman (1860-1935)

1. In her groundbreaking book, *Women and Economics*, she explores the origins of women's subordination and its function in evolution.
2. She was the first to see the need for innovations in child rearing and home maintenance that would ease the burdens of working women.

IV.   Contemporary Sociology
    a.   Symbolic Interactionism and the Sociology of Self
        i.   This examines how an individual's interactions with their environment help people develop a sense of "self."
        ii.   Erving Goffman used what he called dramaturgical model to understand social interaction.
    b.   Structural Functionalism and Social Order
        i.   This is a theory that states that social life consisted of several distinct integrated levels that enable the world to find stability, order, and meaning.
        ii.   According to Talcott Parsons, every institution has a function.
        iii.   Robert K. Merton clarified functionalism and extended its analysis.
            1.   Manifest functions are overt and obvious.
            2.   Latent functions are hidden or unintended.
    c.   Conflict Theories: An Alternative Paradigm
        i.   This theory suggests that they dynamics of society were the result of the conflict among different groups.
        ii.   The constant struggle between the haves and the have-nots was the organizing principle of society.
    d.   Globalization and Multiculturalism: New Lenses, New Issues
        i.   Globalization and Multiculturalism: Interrelated Forces
            1.   Globalization is the interconnections- economic, political, cultural, and social- among different groups of people all over the world, the dynamic webs that connect us to one another and the ways these connections also create cleavages among different groups of people.
            2.   Multiculturalism is the understanding of many different cultures; we come to understand the very different ways that different groups of people approach issues, construct identities, and create institutions that express their needs.
        ii.   Global Tensions
            1.   McDonaldization- homogenizing spread of consumerism around the globe.
            2.   Globalization and multiculturalism express both the forces that hold us together and the forces that drive us apart.
    e.   Sociology and Modernism
        i.   Modernism- expressed as the passage from religious to scientific forms of knowledge
        ii.   Postmodernism- suggests that the meaning of social life may not be found in conforming to rigid patterns of deveo9pment but rather in the creative assembling of interactions and interpretations that enable us to negotiate our way in the world.

V.   Sociology in the 21st Century, Sociology and You

Chapter Summary

- Sociology sets for itself the task of trying to answer certain basic questions about our lives: the nature of identity, the relationship of the individual to society, and our relationships with others.
- Sociologists don't see "either/or"; they usually think in "both/and."
- Sociologists are interested in making the connections between things between things getting better and things getting worse.
- Sociologists are interested in both social order and breakdown.
- Sociology is a way of organizing all the seemingly contradictory tends.
- Sociology is a science although it cannot match the predictive power of the natural sciences; however sociologists do base their hypotheses on empirical observations of social phenomena and then test them.
- C. Wright Mill's definition of sociology, the connection between history and biography, is as compelling today.
- The American Revolution of 1776 and the French Revolution of 1789 lead to economic and political changes that inspired the thinkers of the Enlightenment era.
- The study of sociology emerged in the mid-1800s in Western Europe. Early sociologists focused on the changes occurring in Europe and they included Auguste Comte, Karl Marx, Emile Durkheim, Max Weber, Georg Simmel, and Alexis de Tocqueville.
- The early American sociologists took the ideas of the European sociologists and translated them into a more American version. The early American sociologists included Thorstein Veblen, Lester Ward, and George Herbert Mead.
- In the early years of the discipline few women and African Americans received attention for their work. Mary Wollstonecraft, Margaret Fuller, Charlotte Perkins Gilman, W. E. B. Du Bois, and Fredrick Douglas were denounced because of their views that challenged the status quo of the time.
- In the United States sociology developed as an academic field between 1930 and 1960.
- Sociology has three major paradigms: symbolic interactionsim, structural functionalism, and conflict theories.
- Symbolic interactionism focuses on the micro level and examines how an individual's interactions with their environment help people develop a sense of "self."
- Structural functionalism focuses on the macro level and explores how social life consists of several distinct integrated levels that enable the world to find stability, order, and meaning.
- Conflict theories focuses on the macro level and suggest that the dynamics of society, both social order and social resistance, were the result of the conflict among different groups.
- In the past few decades new lenses through which to view sociological issues emerged: Globalization and Multiculturalism. Globalization is a macro level analysis of the interconnections among different groups of people all over the world. Multiculturalism stresses both the macro and micro level of analysis and focuses on the ways in which different groups of people and even individuals construct their identities based on their membership in those groups.
- The idea that society is move from a less developed to a more developed state is a hallmark of the idea of modernism.
- Sociologists reflect and embody the processes we study, and the changes in the field of sociology are a microcosm of the changes we observe in the society in which we live.

Learning Objective

After completing the reading of Chapter 1, you should be able to answer the following objectives.

- Understand what sociology is and how it helps us understand the world and our place in it.
- Explain the sociological perspective, what it is and why C. Wright Mills referred to it as the intersection of history and biography.
- Identify and understand the difference between tradition and science.
- To understand that sociology is not just "common sense," but uses science to understand social phenomena.
- Identify the major social changes that were especially important to the development of sociology in Europe and the United States.

- Understand the main sociological themes that emerged from the major social changes in Europe and the United States.
- Identify and understand the sociological contributions of the early European and American sociologists.
- Understand how Emile Durkheim's study of suicide helped demonstrate how social forces affect people's behaviors and why social integration may affect the rates of suicide.
- Discuss why female and African-American sociologists were largely ignored in the early years and what their contributions during this time period were.
- Discuss each of the three major sociological paradigms- symbolic interactionism, structural functionalism, and conflict- and describe their level of analysis and what each believes holds society together.
- Define globalization and multiculturalism, and how these new lenses view sociological issues.
- Understand the differences between modernism and postmodernism.

Key Terms

Canon: White, male pioneers of sociology.

Conflict theory: a theory that suggests that the dynamics of society, both social order and social resistance, were the result of the conflict among different groups.

Generalized other: person's notion of the common values, norms, and expectations of other people in society.

Globalization: interconnections among different groups of people all over the world, the dynamic webs that connect us to one another and the ways these connections also create cleavages among different groups of people.

Latent functions: hidden, unintended, but nonetheless important functions.

Macro level analysis: examines large scale institutional processes such as the global marketplace, corporations, and transnational institutions.

Manifest functions: overt and obvious, the intended functions

McDonaldization: the homogenizing spread of consumerism around the globe.

Mechanical solidarity: life is uniform and people are similar; they share a common culture and sense of morality.

Microlevel analysis: focuses on the ways in which different groups of people and even individuals construct their identities based on their membership in those groups.

Modernism: the belief in evolutionary progress, though the application of science.

Multiculturalism: understanding of many different cultures.

Organic solidarity: with the division of labor and diverse and conflicting interests, common values are present but less obvious; people are interconnected.

Paradigm: coherent model of how society works and how individuals are socialized into their roles within it.

Postmodernism: suggests that the meaning of social life may not be found in conforming to rigid patterns of development, but rather in the creative assembling of interactions and interpretations that enable us to negotiate our way in the world.

Social Darwinism: saw each succeeding society as improving on the one before it.

Sociological imagination: sees our lives as contextual lives- out individual identities are sensible only in the social contexts in which we find ourselves.

Sociology: the study of human behavior in society.

Structural functionalism: a theory that social life consisted of several distinct integrated levels that enable the world to find stability, order, and meaning.

Symbolic interactionism: examines how an individual's interactions with his or her environment help people develop a sense of "self".

Key People

Fredrick Douglas: Douglas was the most influential African-American intellectual of the nineteenth century. His work claimed that all human beings were equally capable of being full individuals.

W. E. B. Du Bois: He believed that race was a defining feature of American society. Du Bois was concerned with the social injustices in American and was one of the cofounders of the NAACP.

Auguste Comte: Comte was the first to suggest that the scientific method be applied to the study of the social world.

Alexis de Tocqueville: French social theorist studied American democracy and the French Revolution. His greatest insight was that democracy can either enhance or erode individual liberty.

Emile Durkheim: Durkheim's interest was in searching for the social origins of even the most individual and personal of issues. Most famous work, *Suicide*, illustrated his central insight: that society is held together by moral bonds that connect us to the social collectivity.

Margaret Fuller: Her book *Women of the Nineteenth Century* became the intellectual foundation of the American women's movement.

Charlotte Perkins Gilman: She is best known for her book *Women and Economics*, in which she explores the origin of women's subordination and its function in evolution. Gilman was one of the first to see a need for innovations in child rearing and home maintenance to ease the burden of working women.

John Locke: Locke believed that society was formed though the rational decisions of free individuals, who join together though a "social contract" to form society. He emphasized individual liberty.

Karl Marx: Marx's greatest insight was that class was the organizing principle of all social life and that all other divisions would become class divisions. He believed that under capitalism, the class divisions would lead to conflict between the proletariat (mass of workers) and the bourgeoisie (those who owned the means to produce wealth). His work is associated with the conflict paradigm.

George Herbert Mead: Mead studied the development of individual identity through social processes. He emphasized the role of play in developing a "self" that is fully able to interact with others. His work is the foundation for much of the research done by interactionists.

Robert K. Merton: Merton argued that society tends toward balance and those that facilitate the balance are functional while those that undermine it are dysfunctional.

C. Wright Mills: Mills wrote that sociology is an "imagination", a way of seeing, a way of "connecting biography to history.

Talcott Parsons: He was a central figure of structural-functionalist analysis and believed that most natural societies tend toward balance.

Jean-Jacquess Rousseau: Rousseau believed that people were basically good, but that private property creates inequality, and, with it unhappiness and immorality. He believed that a collective spirit would replace individual greed and though social life people could be free. For him freedom was only obtainable if people were equal.

Georg Simmel: Simmel is responsible for finding the special task of sociology, to study the forms of social interaction apart from their content. What mattered most to Simmel in his studies was the ways in which forms of domination or competition had specific, distinctive properties.

Thorstein Veblem: Veblem is best knows for his work, *The Theory of the Leisure Class*, in which he argued that America was split between those who work (productive) and those who have money (pecuniary).

Lester Ward: Ward was one of the founders of American sociology and rebelled against social Darwinism. He instead stressed the need for social planning and reform, for a "sociocratic" society that later generations now call the welfare state.

Max Weber: His main interest was in "rationality" in the modern world. Weber's most famous work, *The Protestant Ethic and the Spirit of Capitalism*, was a study of the relationship between the emergence of the Protestant belief system and the rise of capitalism.

Mary Wollstonecraft: She was an advocate of equality of the sexes and was the first major feminist.

Additional Learning Resources with MySocLab

Read

The Last Sociologist (pg 1)
Sociology is one of the younger scientific disciplines in academia. Its founders held it in the highest esteem as a discipline uniquely suited to solve many of the social ills of their day. Some have argued that sociology has abandoned its ideals of social application in the search for legitimacy as a true scientifically based discipline.

Explore

The Sociological Tour (pg 35)
This website allows you to explore different aspects of the sociological imagination including general sociological resources, sociological theory, data resources, guide to writing a research paper, etc.

Watch

Gender in Sociology (pg 23)
This video discusses the evolution of the field of gender in sociology.

Culture (pg 24)
This video clip allows one to see how to apply the functionalist paradigm to the evetns shown in the video.

Understanding Society and Social Behavior (pg 27)
George Ritzer discusses the importance of sociological theory and how it is used to understand society and social behavior.

Visualize

Major Specialties of Sociology (pg 34)
Gives an overview of what one can focus on when studying sociology.

Practice Test
After completing the practice test, check your answers in the Answer Key of this Study Guide.

Multiple Choice Questions

1. The _____ sees our lives as contextual lives in which we find ourselves.
   a. sociological perspective
   b. social location
   c. social placement
   d. sociological imagination

2. Sociology is a _____
   a. natural science.
   b. social science.
   c. a field of secondary education.
   d. a humanities department.

3. Which of the following is not a chief theme that emerged from the rise of the "modern" system in the middle of the 19th century?
   a. The nature of community
   b. The nature of government
   c. The rise of communism
   d. The meaning of individualism

4. Who was the most important of all socialist thinkers?
   a. Emile Durkheim
   b. Auguste Comte
   c. Karl Marx
   d. Max Weber

5. Emile Durkheim's greatest work was_____
   a. *Suicide*.
   b. *The Communist Manifesto*.
   c. *Capital*.
   d. *Democracy in America*.

6. According to Durkheim, the degree to which people are tied to their social group is:
   a. symbolic interaction.
   b. social integration.
   c. positivism.
   d. survival of the fittest.

7. According to Weber, the key factor in the rise of capitalism was:
   a. social upheaval.
   b. technology.
   c. monetary power
   d. religion
8. Which theorists first applied the ideas of the Enlightenment to the position of women?
   a. Charlotte Perkins Gilman
   b. Mary Wollstonecraft
   c. Margaret Fuller
   d. Frederick Douglas

9. Which theory suggests that social life consists of several distinct integrated levels that enable the world to find stability and order?
  a. Symbolic Interactionism
  b. Structural Functionalism
  c. Conflict
  d. Globalization

10. A latent function of going to college would include:
  a. being more productive citizen.
  b. getting a good job.
  c. finding a spouse.
  d. none of the above.

11. If you were to conduct a research project focusing on large-scale patterns of society, what type of analysis would you be doing?
  a. a micro level analysis
  b. a social interaction level analysis
  c. a global level analysis
  d. a macro level analysis

12. Too little social integration led to _____ suicide, in which the individual kills him or herself because they do not feel connected to the group.
  a. Egoistic
  b. Altruistic
  c. Anomic
  d. Fatalistic

13. The map that shows an "Alternate View of the World" shows the economically poorest region of the world is:
  a. Japan and South Korea.
  b. Africa.
  c. Australia.
  d. United States.

14. Making use of the sociological perspective encourages:
  a. accepting conventional wisdom.
  b. people to be happier with their lives as they are.
  c. challenging commonly held beliefs.
  d. the belief that society is always the same.

15. Sociology helps us to:
  a. understand our place in the world.
  b. be satisfied with the opportunities in our lives
  c. be less active participants in society.
  d. all of the above.

16. Which of the following historical changes in one of the factors that stimulated the development of sociology as a discipline?
  a. the founding of the Catholic church
  b. the rise of the industrial economy
  c. the women's movement of the 1960s
  d. none of the above

17. In which of the following countries did sociology first appear?
    a. Canada
    b. Germany
    c. France
    d. United States

18. What was the major goal of the founders of sociology?
    a. to control people
    b. to help form the ideal society
    c. to prevent change in society
    d. to discover how society actually operates

19. According to Auguste Comte, what stage of societal development would the earliest human societies belong to?
    a. theological stage
    b. metaphysical stage
    c. scientific stage
    d. postmodern stage

20. _____ was expressed as the passage from religious to scientific forms of knowledge, from feudal to capitalist to communist modes of production, from traditional to legal forms of authority.
    a. Positivism
    b. Free will
    c. Modernism
    d. Postmodernism

21. The sociologist who served as one of the founding members of the National Association for the Advancement of Colored People (NAACP) and has been recently voted to have the annual award for the most influential book after him was:
    a. Frederick Douglas
    b. Martin Luther King Jr.
    c. W. E. B. Du Bois
    d. Herbert Spencer

22. The theoretical paradigm that assumes that the dynamics of society are a result of the conflict among different groups is the:
    a. Symbolic interactionist theory.
    b. Structural functionalist theory.
    c. Conflict theory.
    d. Multicultural theory.

23. Social structures sometimes have negative consequences for the operation of society. What is the term for these functions that undermine the equilibrium and balance of society?
    a. social structure
    b. social functions
    c. social order
    d. social dysfunctions

24. The social conflict paradigm might lead a sociologist to highlight:
    a. gender inequality in sports
    b. racial inequality in a company's hiring process
    c. class differences in a school's population
    d. all of the above

25. Encouraging competition and aspiring to success are tow of the _____ of sports.
    a. latent functions
    b. dysfunctions
    c. manifest functions
    d. none of the above

True-False Questions

True   False   1. Neither side of the "nature"/ "nurture" debate sees the interaction between the two as decisive.

True   False   2. Science requires systematic research to testing theories that have been developed.

True   False   3. Postmodernism is the belief in evolutionary progress, through the application of science.

True   False   4. According to Durkheim's findings, Catholics are more likely to commit suicide than Protestants.

True   False   5. Auguste Comte was the founder of sociology.

True   False   6. Both women and African-Americans were kept out of the classical canon.

True   False   7. According to conflict theory, individuals connect to others symbolically.

True   False   8. George Ritzer called the increasing homogeneity around the world "McDonaldization."

True   False   9. Postmodernists believe that the meaning of social life is found in conforming to rigid patterns of development.

True   False   10. Lester Ward rebelled against social Darwinism.

Fill-in-the-Blank Questions

1. For Simmel the special task of sociology is to study the _____ of social interaction apart from their content.

2. _____ believed that society was formed though the rational decisions of free individuals, who join together through a social contract to form society.

3. Society is held together by _____, moral bonds that connect us tot eh social collectivity.

4. _____ are overt and obvious, the intended function.

5. _____ analysis is a theoretical framework in which society is viewed as composed of many different parts that each has a function that contributes to society's stability.

6. In sociology, _____ suggests that the meaning of social life may be in the creative assembling of interactions and interpretations that enable us to negotiate our way in the world.

7. _____ argued that the wealthy were not productive and instead engaged in what he coined "conspicuous consumption."

8. Max Weber expanded on Marx's analysis of social stratification by adding _____ and _____ to social class as determinants of social status.

9. Using _____, sociologists understand the different ways that people see the world, construct selves, and create institutions.

10. _____ is a coherent model of how society works and how individuals are socialized into their roles within it.

Essay Questions

1. What are the three major sociological perspectives? What level of analysis are they and what do they believe holds society together?

2. Name three major figures from the history of sociology (one classical, one American, and one from the "other" canon) and briefly describe their contributions to the field of sociology.

3. How are societies across the globe becoming increasingly connected and what are the positive and negatives outcomes of these links?

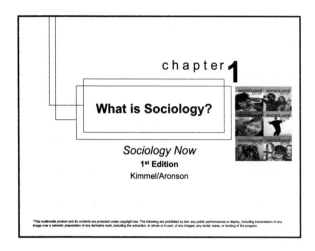

chapter 1

What is Sociology?

Sociology Now
1st Edition
Kimmel/Aronson

This multimedia product and its contents are protected under copyright law. The following are prohibited by law: any public performances or display, including transmission of any image over a network; preparation of any derivative work, including the extraction, in whole or in part, of any images; any rental, lease, or lending of the program.

Sociology As a Way of Seeing

- study of human behavior in society
- attempts to answer basic questions
  - nature of identity
  - relationship of individual to society
  - relationships between individuals
- **sociological imagination** (Mills)

Copyright © Allyn & Bacon 2009

Sociology As a Way of Seeing

- **Beyond Either/Or: Seeing Sociologically**
  - Is society getting better or worse?
  - Is the glass half full or half empty?
  - sociologists see *both* sides at once
    - "both/and" as opposed to "either/or"

Copyright © Allyn & Bacon 2009

Sociology As a Way of Seeing

- **Making Connections: Sociological Dynamics**
  - integration and disintegration
  - social *order* and breakdown

- **Sociological Understanding**
  - societal changes over time
  - cross-country comparisons

Copyright © Allyn & Bacon 2009

_____

_____

_____

_____

_____

_____

_____

Doing Sociology

- theory *and* perspective
- Sociology of
  - Art
  - Crime
  - Culture
  - Delinquency
  - Drugs
  - Gender, etc.
- social complexity of problems
- "parts" make up the entire "picture"

Copyright © Allyn & Bacon 2009

_____

_____

_____

_____

_____

_____

_____

Doing Sociology

- **Sociology and Science**
  - empirical data vs. human spirit

"When the object of study is intelligent and aware, you need different techniques and different propositions"

- **Getting Beyond "Common Sense"**
  - human behavior results from *both* nature and nurture
  - humans adapt to social contexts

Copyright © Allyn & Bacon 2009

_____

_____

_____

_____

_____

_____

_____

Where Did Sociology Come From?

- **Before "Sociology"**
  - "The Age of Reason"; "Enlightenment"
    - "social contract"/individuality (Locke)
    - the "general will"/community (Rousseau)
  - *Declaration of Independence* (Jefferson)

Copyright © Allyn & Bacon 2009

Where Did Sociology Come From?

- **The Invention of Sociology**
  - *The nature of community*
  - *The nature of government*
  - *The nature of the economy*
  - *The meaning of individualism*
  - *The rise of secularism*
  - *The nature and direction of change*

Copyright © Allyn & Bacon 2009

Where Did Sociology Come From?

- **Classic Sociological Thinkers**
  - *modernism*
  - **Auguste Comte**
    - founder of sociology
    - social statics and dynamics
  - **Alexis de Tocqueville**
    - Democracies
  - **Karl Marx**
    - *The Communist Manifesto*
    - capitalism and worker rebellion

Copyright © Allyn & Bacon 2009

Where Did Sociology Come From?

– **Emile Durkheim**
- *Suicide*
- Integration and regulation
- social *solidarity*
  - **mechanical** and **organic**

– **Max Weber** (VAY-bur)
- interpretive and value free
- *class* most significant division
  - *status* and *party*

Where Did Sociology Come From?

– **George Simmel** (ZIM-mel)
- *forms* of social interaction
- individuality
  - discovery and expression

• **American Sociological Thinkers**
– **Thorstein Veblen**
- the "productive" (workers)
- the "pecuniary" (owners)
– **Lester Ward**
- against **social Darwinism**
- "social telesis"

Where Did Sociology Come From?

– **George Herbert Mead**
- the "I" and the "me"
- **generalized other**

• **The "Other" Canon**
– **Mary Wollstonecraft**
– **Margaret Fuller**
– **Frederick Douglas**
– **W.E.B. DuBois**
– **Charlotte Perkins Gillman**

Contemporary Sociology

- What could sociology contribute to
  the study of the self?
- What processes ensure social
  order?

- **Symbolic Interaction and the
  Sociology of the Self**
  - development of the self through
    interactions with others
  - **dramaturgical model** (Goffman)
    - *backstage and frontstage*

Copyright © Allyn & Bacon 2009

Contemporary Sociology

- **Structural Functionalism and
  Social Order**
  - stability, order and meaning (Parsons)
  - **paradigm** of how society works
  - **manifest** and **latent** functions (Merton)
  - . . . *"if it exists it serves a purpose
    and shouldn't be changed"*

Copyright © Allyn & Bacon 2009

Contemporary Sociology

- **Conflict Theories: An Alternative
  Paradigm**
  - the dynamics of society resulted from conflict
    among different groups
  - **conflict theory**

The three dominant sociological theories
addressed similar sorts of questions:

- *What holds society together?*
- *How are individuals connected to larger social
  processes and institutions?*
- *What are the chief tensions that pull society apart?*
- *What causes social change?*

Copyright © Allyn & Bacon 2009

Contemporary Sociology

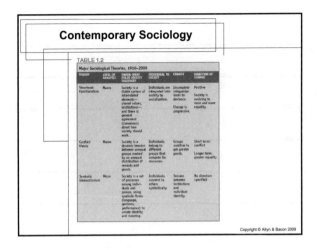

TABLE 1.2
Major Sociological Theories, 1950–2000

THEORY	LEVEL OF ANALYSIS	ORDER: WHAT HOLDS SOCIETY TOGETHER?	INDIVIDUAL TO SOCIETY	CHANGE	DIRECTION OF CHANGE
Structural-functionalism	Macro	Society is a stable system of interrelated elements—shared values, institutions—and there is general agreement (consensus) about how society should work.	Individuals are integrated into society by socialization.	Incomplete integration leads to deviance. Change is progressive.	Positive. Society is evolving to more and more equality.
Conflict theory	Macro	Society is a dynamic tension between unequal groups marked by an unequal distribution of rewards and goods.	Individuals belong to different groups that compete for resources.	Groups mobilize to get greater goods.	Short term: conflict. Longer term: greater equality.
Symbolic interactionism	Micro	Society is a set of processes among individuals and groups, using symbolic forms (language, gestures, performance) to create identity and meaning.	Individuals connect to others symbolically.	Tension between institutions and individual identity.	No direction specified.

Copyright © Allyn & Bacon 2009

Contemporary Sociology

- **Globalization and Multiculturalism: New Lenses, New Issues**
  - **globalization** (macro) - *interconnections*
  - **multiculturalism** (micro) – *understanding*
  - **macrolevel analysis**
  - **microlevel analysis**
  - **Globalization and Multiculturalism: Interrelated Forces**
    - *forces that hold us together and that drive us apart*
  - **Global Tensions**
    - **McDonaldization (Ritzer)**

Copyright © Allyn & Bacon 2009

Contemporary Sociology

- **Sociology and Modernism**
  - **modernism**
    - religion to science
    - mechanical to organic
    - feudal to capitalist

    no society ever passes from one stage fully into the next
  - **postmodernism**

- **Sociology and the Future, Sociology and You**

Copyright © Allyn & Bacon 2009

What Does America Think?

1.1 How Religious Are People?

This is actual survey data from the General Social Survey, 2004.

1. About how often do you pray? Almost 60 percent of respondents reported praying at least once a day. Women were more likely than men to pray several times a day or once a day. Results for examining by race were also striking, with 55 percent of Black respondents praying several times a day as compared to 27 percent of White respondents.

CRITICAL THINKING | DISCUSSION QUESTION

1. What social and cultural factors do you think account for the gender differences in reports of prayer frequency? What about the race difference?

Copyright © Allyn & Bacon 2009

What Does America Think?

1.2 Your Outlook on Life: Are People Basically Fair?

This is actual survey data from the General Social Survey, 2004.

1. Do you think most people would try to take advantage of you if they got a chance, or would they try to be fair? Half of all respondents thought most people would try to be fair, and 40 percent thought they would try to take advantage of others. Nine percent said it depended. Social class differences in responses were striking, with those in the lower class being most likely to think people would try to take advantage and least likely to think people would try to be fair. Those in the middle class were most likely to think people would try to be fair. When examined by sex, the range in responses was small, but when examined by race, Black respondents (58.8 percent) were far more likely than White respondents (34.4 percent) to say people would try to take advantage of others.

CRITICAL THINKING | DISCUSSION QUESTIONS

1. Half of all respondents thought most people would be fair. Is that more or less than what you expected? How do you explain these results?
2. While gender did not appear to have an effect on respondents' perceptions of others, social class and race had a striking effect. Looking at these differences and thinking about positions, why do you think these differences exist?

Copyright © Allyn & Bacon 2009

What Does America Think?

> Go to this website to look further at the data. You can run your own statistics and crosstabs here: http://sda.berkeley.edu/cgi-bin/hsda?harcsda+gss04

REFERENCES: Davis, James A., Tom W. Smith, and Peter V. Marsden. General Social Surveys 1972-2004: [Cumulative File] [Computer file]. 2nd ICPSR version. Chicago, IL: National Opinion Research Center [producer], 2005; Storrs, CT: Roper Center for Public Opinion Research, University of Connecticut; Ann Arbor, MI: Inter-University Consortium for Political and Social Research; Berkeley, CA: Computer-Assisted Survey Methods Program, University of California [distributors], 2005.

Copyright © Allyn & Bacon 2009

Chapter 2
Culture and Society

Chapter Outline

I.   Culture- set of values and ideals that we understand to define morality, good and evil, and appropriate and inappropriate
   a.   Material culture- consists of things people make, and the things they use to make them
   b.   Nonmaterial culture- ideas and beliefs that people develop about their lives and world
   c.   Cultural Diversity- world's cultures are vastly different from each other
      i.   Culture shock is the feeling of disorientation, because the cultural markers that we rely on to help us know where we are and how to act have suddenly changed.
      ii. Ethnocentrism
         1.   Often use our culture as a reference point.
         2.   Can be benign or pernicious.
      iii. Cultural relativism is the position that all cultures are equally valid in the experience of their own members.
   d.   Subcultures and Countercultures
      i.   Subcultures
         1.   Arise when a group has two characteristics.
            a.   Prejudice from main stream.
            b.   Social power.
         2.   Membership enables you to feel "one" with others and "different" from others at the same time.
      ii. Countercultures
         1.   Offer grounding identity by opposition.
         2.   Perceived as a threat to the official culture.
         3.   They are oppositional.
II.   Elements of Culture
   a.   Material cultures
   b.   Symbols are anything that carries additional meanings beyond itself to others who share in the culture.
      i.   Come to mean what they do only in a culture.
      ii. Represent ideas or feelings.
   c.   Language is the organized set of symbols by which we are able to think and communicate with each other.
      i.   Chief vehicle by which humans create a sense of self.
      ii. Language shapes our perceptions of things- Sapir-Whorf hypothesis.
      iii. Language is also political.
   d.   Rituals are the processes by which members of a culture engage in routine behavior to express their sense of belonging to the culture.
      i.   Symbolize the culture's coherence by expressing our unity.
      ii. Creates coherence by enabling each member to feel connected to culture.
   e.   Norms are the rules a culture develops that define how people should act and the consequences of failure to act in specified ways.
      i.   Prescribe behavior within the culture.
      ii. Tell us how to behave.
      iii. Vary between and within cultures.
      iv. Folkways are relatively weak and informal norms that are the result of patterns of action.
         1.   Manners or etiquette
         2.   People notice when we break them, but infractions are seldom punished.
      v.   Mores are stronger norms that are informally enforced.
         1.   These are perceived as more than simple violations of etiquette.

                2. Moral attitudes seen as serious even if there are no actual laws that prohibit them.

         vi. Laws are norms that have been organized and written down.

                1. Charged and punished by the state for this norm-breaking behavior.

                2. Enforced by local, state, and federal agencies.

    f. Values

         i. Ethical foundations of a culture

         ii. Foundations for norms

         iii. Changes in our laws are often expected to produce a change in values over time.

         iv. American Values

                1. Achievement and success

                2. Individualism

                3. Activity and work

                4. Efficiency and practicality

                5. Science and technology

                6. Progress

                7. Material comfort

                8. Humanitarianism

                9. Freedom

                10. Democracy

                11. Equality

                12. Racism and group superiority

         v. Emerging values

                1. Values have history.

                2. Some values that are emerging now as new values.

         vi. Changing and contradictory values

III.   Cultural Expressions

    a. Universality and Localism

         i. Universal and local

         ii. Every culture has families, legal systems, and religion

         iii. Cultural universals

                1. Rituals, customs, and symbols that are evident in all societies.

                2. Permit the society to function smoothly and continuously.

    b. High Culture and Popular Culture

         i. High culture attracts audiences drawn from more affluent groups

         ii. Popular culture includes a wide variety of popular music, non-highbrow forms of literature, any form of spectator sports, television, movies, and video games

         iii. Sociologists are interested in the relationships between high and low culture

         iv. Cultural capital

                1. Any "piece" of culture that a group can use as a symbolic resource to exchange with others.

                2. "Exchange" access to capital.

    c. Forms of Popular Culture

         i. Fads

                1. Short lived, highly popular, and widespread behaviors, styles, or modes of thought.

                2. Can be enormously profitable.

         ii. Fashion

                1. Behavior, style, or idea that is more permanent than a fad.

                2. There is widespread acceptance of the activity.

                3. Involved cultural institutions that mediate our relationship with culture.

    d. The Politics of Popular Culture

         i. Most cultural elites are culturally conservative

         ii. The status quo reproduces their cultural dominance

    e. The Globalization of Popular Culture

         i. Sometimes culture is exported deliberately

                         ii.   Cultural imperialism
                              1.   Deliberate imposition of one's country's culture on another.
                              2.   Global spread of American fashion, media, and language.
                      iii. Cultural transfer is not nearly as one directional as many critics contend
                              1.   Many cultural trends in America that originated in other countries.
                              2.   Imported luxury cars become associated with exotic lifestyles elsewhere.
        f.   Culture as a Tool Kit
                i.   Culture is not a thing one does or does not have.
                ii.   It is a complex set of behaviors, attitudes, and symbols that individuals use in their daily relationships with others.

IV.   Cultural Change
        a.   Culture lag
                i.   Gap between technology and material culture and it social beliefs and institutions.
                ii.   Beliefs and values of a society have to catch up to the changes in technology.
        b.   Cultural diffusion
                i.   The spreading of new ideas through a society, independent of population movement.
                ii.   Impact of the technological innovation ripples though the rest of society, eventually a new equilibrium will be reached.

V.   Culture in the 21st Century
        a.   Concepts such as culture, values, and norms help orient the sociologist, providing a way to understand the world he or she is trying to study.
        b.   Cultures are constantly changing.
        c.   Cultural diversity that defines most industrialized societies also defines American society, and that diversity will continue to provide moments of both combination and collision.

Chapter Summary

- Culture refers to the language, values, norms, and objects that are passed down in society.
- Culture is made up of material culture (things people make, and things they use to make them) and nonmaterial culture (ideas and beliefs)
- Cultural diversity refers to the world's cultures being vastly different from one another. Culture shock is when one feels disoriented, because the cultural markers we rely on help us know where we are and how to act have been suddenly changed.
- Subcultures are groups of people within a culture who share some distinguishing characteristic, belief, value, or attribute that sets them apart from the dominant culture. Subcultures are communities that constitute themselves through a relationship of difference to the dominant culture. Unlike subcultures, countercultures identify themselves through their difference and opposition to the dominant culture.
- There are six basic elements of culture: material culture, symbols, language, rituals, norms, and values. Material culture consists of what people make and what they make it with. A symbol is anything that carries additional meanings beyond itself to others who share in the culture. Language is the main vehicle for which humans create a sense of self; it allows us to think and communicate with others. Symbols and language are most important for enabling a culture to persist over time. Rituals are where members of a culture engage in a routine behavior to express their sense of belonging to their culture. Norms are the rules a culture develops that define how people should act and include folkways, mores, and laws. Values are the ideas about what is right and wrong or good and bad.
- There are twelve core American values, however some of them are contradictory to each other.
- George Murdock used the term cultural universals to describe the rituals, customs, and symbols that are evident in all societies.
- High culture attracts mostly affluent audiences while popular culture is available to everyone. Popular culture includes popular music, spectator sports, television, movies, and video games. Sociologists are interested in the way in how cultural forms can shift from high to low and from low to high.
- Fad and fashions are form of popular culture. Fads are short lived, highly popular, and widespread behaviors, styles, or modes of thought, whereas fashion is more permanent, more widespread, and more acceptable.
- Popular culture is the second largest export of the United States. Some see this trend as cultural imperialism, which is the deliberate imposition of one's country's culture on another. Some see this culture transfer as not necessarily one directional since there are many American trends that originated in other countries.
- William Ogburn used the term cultural lag to refer to the gap between technology and material culture and its social beliefs and institutions. Today technology makes cultural diffusion occur more rapidly and eventually an equilibrium will be reached.
- Concepts such as culture, norms, and values help orient sociologists and provide a way to understand the world he or she is trying to study.
- Cultures are constantly changing and a global culture is emerging.

Learning Objectives

After completing the reading of Chapter 2, you should be able to answer the following objectives.

- Define culture and differentiate between material and nonmaterial culture.
- Know what is meant by cultural diversity and culture shock. Provide examples of each and explain how they force people to challenge their own cultural assumptions.
- Define ethnocentrism and cultural relativism. Be able to give examples of both and describe the positive and negative consequences of viewing other cultures with these points of view.
- Understand the differences between subcultures and countercultures and provide examples of each.
- Know what the six elements of culture are, what their definitions are and why they are a crucial part of culture.
- Understand the Sapir-Whorf hypothesis and how language shapes or perceptions of the world.
- List the core values held by Americans and their opposites.

- Define and discuss cultural universals.
- Define high culture and popular culture and what types of activities are associated with each.
- Define fads and fashion and understand the difference between the two. Know the different types of fads.
- Define cultural imperialism and how it is imposed on people.
- Know what cultural lag and cultural diffusion are and how technology affects each.

Key Terms

Countercultures: identify themselves through their difference and opposition to the dominant culture.

Cultural capital: is any "piece" of culture- an idea, an artistic expression, a form of music or literature- that a group can use as a symbolic resource to exchange with others.

Cultural diffusion: the spreading of new ideas through a society, independent of population movement.

Cultural diversity: means that the world's cultures are vastly different from each other.

Cultural imperialism: the deliberate imposition of one's country's culture on another country.

Cultural relativism: position that all cultures are equally valid in the experience of their own members.

Cultural universals: rituals, customs, and symbols that are evident in all societies.

Culture: refers to the sets of values and ideals that we understand to define morality, good and evil, appropriate and inappropriate.

Culture lag: gap between technology and material culture and its social beliefs and institutions.

Culture shock: feeling of disorientation, because the cultural markers that we rely on to help us know where we are and how to act have suddenly changed.

Ethnocentrism: belief that one's culture is superior to others.

Fads: defined by short lived, highly popular, and widespread behaviors, styles, or modes of thought.

Fashion: is a behavior, style, or idea that is more permanent than a fad.

Folkways: relatively weak and informal norms that are the result of patterns of action.

Language: organized set of symbols by which we are able to think and communicate with others.

Laws: norms that have been organized and written down.

Material culture: consists of things people make, and the things they use to make them.

Mores: stronger norms that are informally enforced.

Nonmaterial culture: consists of the ideas and beliefs that people develop about their lives and world.

Norms: the rules a culture develops that define how people should act and the consequences of failure to act in the specified ways.

Popular culture: includes a wide variety of popular music, nonhighborw forms of literature, any forms of spectator sports, and other popular forms of entertainment, like television, movies, and video games.

Rituals: processes by which members of a culture engage in a routine behavior to express their sense of belonging to the culture.

Sapir-Whorf hypothesis: states that language shapes our perceptions.

Subculture: group of people within a culture who share some distinguishing characteristics, beliefs, values, or attributes that set them apart from the dominant culture.

Symbols: anything that carries additional meanings beyond itself to others who share in the culture.

Values: ethical foundations of a culture, its ideas about right and wrong, good and bad.

Key People

John Lofland: identified four types of fads.

George Murdock: identified 67 cultural universals that are evident in all societies.

William Ogburn: used the term culture lag to define the gap between technology and material culture and its social beliefs and institutions.

A. R. Radcliffe-Brown: cultural universals permit societies to function smoothly and continuously.

Edward Sapir and Benjamin Whorf: noticed that language actually shapes people's perceptions. Studied Hopi Indians and concluded that language provides a culture lens though which people perceive their world.

William Graham Sumner: coined the term ethnocentrism.

Ann Swidler: calls culture a "tool kit" from which people construct their identities.

Eviatar Zerubavel: noted the differences in languages.

Additional Learning with MySocLab

Read
> **Mutilation Seen as Risk For the Girls Of Immigrants (pg 41)**
> Sociologists pay careful attention to a society's values, norms, traditions, and history as they relate to its culture. Many societies have cultural traits which most members can't trace back to their origins.
> **Books of the Times; Pop Culture Conjures a Transracial American Dream (pg 58)**
> Article on Leon E. Wynter's book that discusses the "browning of mainstream commercial culture" in America.

Explore
> **Web Activity: Culture (pg 42)**
> Read the article Body Ritual Among the Nacirema to learn about their rituals and culture. After reading the article there is a series of questions to answer.

Listen
> **New Yorker in Japan (pg 41)**
> The NPR clip reports on how one American citizen became a Japanese citizen and the discrimination he faced.

Watch
> **Culture: Making Meaning (pg 40)**
> The video clip shows Lynette Spillman discussing what sociologists mean by culture and the ways in which we make meaning of the world around us.

STUDY GUIDE

Visualize

> **Differing Explanations of Cultural Variation (pg 40)**
> Gives an explanation of how different sociological perspective would view culture.
> **Personal Space (pg 48)**
> Shows an example of interaction style and the variation from culture to culture.

Practice Test

After completing the practice test, check your answers in the Answer Key of this Study Guide.

Multiple Choice Questions

1. Religion is an example of what type of culture in human society?
   a. Human society
   b. Culture lag
   c. Material culture
   d. Nonmaterial culture

2. Which of the following is included in culture?
   a. Language
   b. Values
   c. Norms
   d. All of the Above

3. The intangible things, such as ideas, values, and beliefs are known as:
   a. Material culture
   b. Non-material culture
   c. High culture
   d. Popular culture

4. The disorientation that people feel because the cultural markers they rely on to help them know where they are and how to act have suddenly changed is known as:
   a. Cultural lag
   b. Cultural diffusion
   c. Culture shock
   d. Counterculture

5. The trend in which there is a deliberate imposition of one's country's culture on another country is:
   a. Cultural diffusion
   b. Cultural relativism
   c. Cultural imperialism
   d. Culture shock

6. Which of the following is not a "core" value of U.S. society?
   a. Individualism
   b. Material discomfort
   c. Progress
   d. Equality

7. Which type of norm is punishable by the agents of the state?
   a. Norms
   b. Mores
   c. Laws
   d. Values

8. Opera singers, classical pianists, and those who know fine wines all display _____ patterns.
   a. High cultural
   b. Popular cultural
   c. Subcultural
   d. Low cultural

9. A person who criticizes the traditional Amish lifestyle for living without electricity is exhibiting:
    a. Ethnocentrism
    b. Culture shock
    c. Cultural universals
    d. Cultural relativism

10. Which of the following has not been identified by anthropologists as a category of cultural universals?
    a. Education
    b. Social Organization
    c. Social Control
    d. High culture

11. Value contradictions occur when:
    a. A society lacks social change.
    b. No one can successfully obtain ideal culture.
    c. A value such as hard work to gain upward mobility, comes into direct conflict with other values, such as cheating on you taxes and stealing.
    d. A value such as helping your neighbors, comes into direct conflict with another value, such as giving to charity.

12. In American culture, if a person intentionally robs someone, the behavior violates:
    a. Ritual.
    b. Folkway.
    c. Law.
    d. None of the above.

13. The sociological hypothesis that concluded that language provides a cultural lens through which people perceive the world is:
    a. The Sapir- Whorf hypothesis.
    b. The Davis-Moore hypothesis.
    c. The language hypothesis.
    d. They symbolic hypothesis.

14. Mores:
    a. Are relatively weak and informal norms that are the result of patterns of action.
    b. Are rules a culture develops that define how people should act.
    c. Are norms that have been organized and written down.
    d. Are perceived as more than a simple violation of etiquette.

15. The norms and values that people actually follow are:
    a. Real culture
    b. Ideal culture
    c. Normal culture
    d. High culture

16. Cultural universals:
    a. Are evident in every society.
    b. Are broad categories
    c. Connect us to groups
    d. All of the above

17. According to George Murdock, All But Which, of the following is an example of cultural universals?
    a. Informal education
    b. Division of labor
    c. Kinship systems
    d. Violent religious beliefs

18. Sociologist John Lofland identified four types of fads. Which of the following is not one of those fads?
    a. Objects
    b. Fashions
    c. Activities
    d. Personalities

19. Spreading culture from one society to another is called:
    a. Integration
    b. Imperialism
    c. Diffusion
    d. Immigration

20. The term cultural lag refers to:
    a. Societies advancing faster than other in terms of technology.
    b. All people in the society being high cultured.
    c. The gap between technology and social beliefs.
    d. The overall rate of cultural change slowing in recent decades.

21. The practice of a person judging another culture based on their own culture is an example of:
    a. Cultural diffusion.
    b. Ethnocentrism.
    c. Culture relativism.
    d. Cultural shock.

22. Which of the following would not be considered a subculture?
    a. Homosexuals
    b. White supremacist survivalists
    c. Jazz musicians
    d. Computer nerds

23. The standards by which people who share culture define what is good and bad, right and wrong are called:
    a. Values.
    b. Mores.
    c. Norms.
    d. Folkways.

24. The core cultural values in the United States are:
    a. The same over long periods of time
    b. Shared by everyone in the society
    c. Always consistent with one another
    d. Contradictory to each other

25. High culture and popular culture are distinctly different based primarily on:
    a. How long the cultural pattern has existed.
    b. How traditional the pattern is.
    c. The social standing of the people who display the cultural pattern.
    d. The moral values of the people displaying the cultural pattern.

True/False Questions

True   False   1. Symbolic meaning never changes over time.

True   False   2. Cultural universals are cultural traits that are part of every known culture.

True   False   3. An example of nonmaterial culture would include the clothes people wear.

True   False   4. The Sapir-Whorf hypothesis states that language, rituals, and norms shape our perceptions.

True   False   5. The cultural values of Americans are consistent with one another.

True   False   6. Subcultures have more opposition to the dominant culture than countercultures.

True   False   7. Cultural relativism is the position that every culture is equally valid in the experiences of its own members.

True   False   8. The United States does not have high culture, it only has a popular culture.

True   False   9. Mores are norms that are strictly enforces.

True   False   10. Ogburn referred to the condition of the beliefs of society having to catch up to the changes in technology as cultural lag.

Fill-in-the-Blank Questions

1. _____ is a group of people within a culture who share some distinguishing characteristics, beliefs, values, or attribute that sets them apart from the dominant culture.

2. The term _____ came into widespread use during the 1960s to describe an emerging subculture based on age, behaviors, and political sensibilities.

3. The term _____ refers to a shared way of life.

4. _____ is an organized set of symbols by which we are able to communicate with others.

5. _____ symbolize the culture's coherence by expressing our unity.

6. Norms that are strictly enforced are _____.

7. _____ are defined by being short live, highly popular, and widespread.

8. Culture is a complex set of behaviors, attitudes, and _____ that individuals use in their daily relationships.

9. The spreading of new ideas through a society, independent of population movement is knows as _____.

10. Sociologists call the norms that people actually follow _____.

Essay Questions

1. Define subcultures and countercultures. Describe how they are different.

2. Define norms, mores, folkways, and laws and give an example of each.

3. What are the differences between norms and values and what part does each play in society?

4. Discuss six of the "core" American values and what are the opposite values that American hold?

5. Discuss cultural imperialism and how cultural transfer is not one directional.

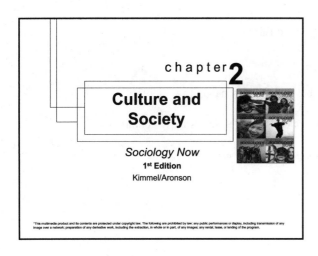

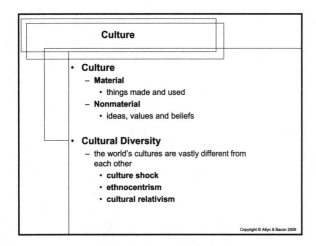

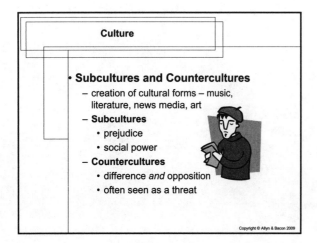

Elements of Culture

- **Material Culture**
  - Meets basic subsistence needs
  - Basic need for meaning

- **Symbols**
  - Anything that takes on additional meaning beyond itself to others
    - *can be created at anytime*
    - *meanings can change over time*
    - *not universally shared*

Elements of Culture

- **Language**
  - set of symbols
  - not solely a human trait
  - **Sapir-Whorf Hypothesis**
    - language shapes thought and perception

- **Ritual**
  - "Pledge of Allegiance"

Elements of Culture

- **Norms**
  - rules of behavior
    - **folkways**
    - **mores** (MO-rays)
    - **laws**

- **Values**
  - ethical foundations of cutlure
  - right and wrong/good and bad

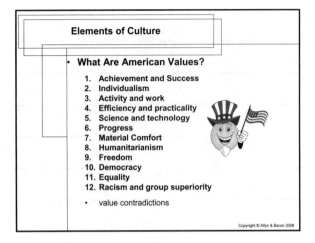

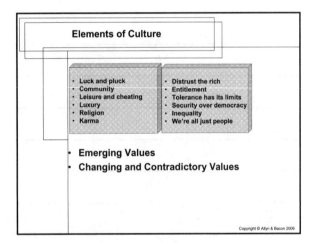

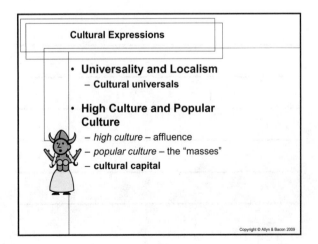

Cultural Expressions

- **Forms of Popular Culture**
  - **Fads**
    - *Objects*
    - *Activities*
    - *Ideas*
    - *Personalities*
  - **Fashion**

Cultural Expressions

- **The Politics of Popular Culture**

- **The Globalization of Popular Culture**
  - cultural imperialism

- **Culture as Tool Kit**

Cultural Change

  - culture lag
  - cultural diffusion

- **Culture in the 21st Century**

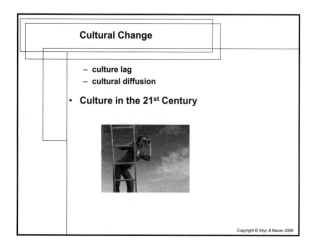

STUDY GUIDE

What Does America Think?

2.1 English as Our Official Language

This is actual survey data from the General Social Survey, 2004.

1. Do you favor or oppose making English the official language of the United States? Overall, slightly more than three-quarters of the U.S. population favors English as the official language of the United States. There are significant class differences in this, with those who identify as lower class being less likely than other groups to be in favor.

English as Official Language, by Social Class, Percent

	Lower	Working	Middle	Upper	Row Total
Favor	70.2	75.8	79.8	78.4	77.5
Oppose	29.8	24.2	20.2	21.6	22.5

CRITICAL THINKING | DISCUSSION QUESTIONS

1. How can we explain the social class differences in responses to this survey question?
2. How do you think the results might have differed had we looked at them by race or by gender?

Copyright © Allyn & Bacon 2009

What Does America Think?

2.2 Pride in Being American

This is actual survey data from the General Social Survey, 2004.

1. How proud are you of being an American? An overwhelmingly high proportion of respondents said they were very proud to be an American (89 percent). Less than 3 percent of respondents said they were not very proud or not proud at all to be American. Those who identified as working class were the least likely to say they were very proud to be American.

Pride in Being American, by Social Class, Percent

	Lower	Working	Middle	Upper	Row Total
Very proud	85.3	76.9	79.7	85.1	79.0
Somewhat proud	10.2	18.6	16.1	14.9	16.8
Not very proud	4.5	1.0	2.2	0.0	1.8
Not proud at all	0.0	0.3	0.4	0.0	0.3
Not American	0.0	3.1	1.5	0.0	2.0

CRITICAL THINKING | DISCUSSION QUESTIONS

1. While the class difference in responses was not that great, it is still interesting. Why do you think those who identify as lower class and those who identify as upper class were most likely to report being very proud to be American? Why do you think those who identified as middle class were least likely to report being very proud?
2. The number of Americans who are proud to be American is very high. Why do you think this is so? Do you think pride in country is as high in other countries? Why or why not? Give examples.

Copyright © Allyn & Bacon 2009

Chapter 3
Society: Interactions, Groups, and Organizations

Chapter Outline

I. Society: Putting Things in Context
   a. Sociology is a way of seeing that can be described as "contextualizing"- sociologists try to.
      i. Understand the social contexts in which an individual activity takes place.
      ii. The other people with who we interact.
      iii. The dynamics of the interaction.
      iv. The institutions in which that activity takes place.
   b. Society can be defined as an organized collection of individuals and institutions, bounded by space in a coherent territory, subject to the same political authority and organized through a shared et of cultural expectations and values
   c. Societies are composed of structures social interactions.
      i. Structured means our actions.
      ii. Social refers to the fact that we don't live alone.
      iii. Interaction refers to the ways we behavior in relation to others.
   d. Institutions describe more formal and stable patterns of interactions among many individuals that enable us to predict and control behavior.
   e. Social structure is a complex framework, or structure, composed of both patterned social interactions and institutions that together both organize social life and provide the context for individual action.
II. The Social Construction of Reality
   a. Social interaction- behaviors that are oriented toward other people.
   b. Cooley and the Looking-Glass Self.
      i. Describes the process by which our identity develops.
      ii. We develop our looking- glass self or mirror image self in three stages:
         1. We imagine how we appear to others around us.
         2. We draw general conclusions based on the reactions of others.
         3. Based on our evaluations of others' reactions, we develop our sense of personal identity.
   c. George Herbert Mead believed that our self arises through taking on the role of others.
   d. Goffman and the "Dramaturgical" Self
      i. Impression management- actively trying to control how others perceive me by changing my behavior to correspond to an ideal of what they will find most appealing.
      ii. We change our behavior so easily and so often, without even thinking about it- dramaturgy.
      iii. Our attempt to give the best possible performance is call face work.
   e. Nonverbal Communication
      i. Our body movements, gestures, and facial expressions, our placement in relation to others.
      ii. Most facial expressions must be interpreted depending on social situations that vary from culture to culture and era to era and must be learned though socialization.
   f. Verbal Communication
   g. Patterns of Social Interactions
      i. Five basic patterns of social interaction that links individuals in groups from the smallest to the largest:
         1. Exchange
         2. Cooperation
         3. Competition
         4. Conflict
         5. Coercion

III.   Elements of Social Structure
    a.   Status
        i.   Any social identity recognized as meaningful by the group or society.
        ii.   Ascribed status: receive involuntarily, without regard to our unique talents, skills, or accomplishments.
        iii.   Achieved status: we attain through talent, ability, effort, or other unique personal characteristic.
        iv.   Master Status: when ascribed or achieved status is presumed to important that it overshadows all of the others, dominating our lives and controlling our position in society.
    b.   Sets of behaviors that are expected of a person who occupies a certain status.
        i.   Role strain: same role has demands and expectations that contradict each other, so we cannot possibly meet them all at once.
        ii.   Role conflict: happens when we try to play different roles with extremely different or contradictory rules at the same time.
        iii.   Role exit: describes the process of adjustment that takes place when we move out of such a role.
        iv.   Rose Fucs Ebaugh notes four stages involuntarily exiting from significant social roles:
            1.   Doubt
            2.   Search Alternatives
            3.   Departure
            4.   New Role

IV.   Groups
    a.   Any assortment of people who share the same norms, values, and expectations.
        i.   Dyad- group of two.
        ii.   Crowd- aggregate of individuals who happen to be together but experience themselves as essentially independent.
        iii.   Group cohesion- degree to which the individual members identify with each other and with the group.
    b.   Group and Identity
        i.   Everyone belongs to many different groups.
        ii.   Identities based on group membership are not neutral, but hierarchically valued
    c.   Types of Group
        i.   Primary groups- friends and family that come together for expressive reasons.
        ii.   Secondary groups- co-workers or club members who come together for instrumental reasons.
        iii.   In-groups- group I feel positively toward and to which I actually belong.
        iv.   Out-groups- one to which I do not belong and do not feel very positively toward.
        v.   Reference groups- group toward which we are so strongly committed or one that we orient our actions around what we perceive that group's perceptions would be.
        vi.   Cliques are organized around inclusion and exclusion.
    d.   Group Dynamics
        i.   Every group has a structure that sociologists can analyze and study
            1.   Leader is someone in charge.
            2.   Hardcore members are those in the group with a great deal of power to make policy decisions.
        ii.   Conformity
            1.   Some groups have formal requirements.
            2.   Other times we volunteer our conformity.
            3.   Groupthink- process by which groups members try to preserve harmony and unity in spite of their individual judgments.
        iii.   Diffusion of Responsibility
            1.   Chain of command in large groups can be long enough, or authority can seem dispersed enough that any one individual may avoid taking responsibility for his or her actions.

2. This dynamic leads to the problem of bystanders.
  iv. Stereotyping- assumptions about what people are like or how they will behave based on their membership in a group.

V. Social Networks
 a. Network- type of group that is both looser and denser than a formal group.
 b. Networks and Social Experience
  i. Social connectedness of certain groups in the society can produce interaction patterns that have a lasting influence on the lives of people both within and without the network.
  ii. Social networks provide support in times of stress or illness.
  iii. Networks exert an important influence on the most crucial aspects of our lives.
 c. Networks and Globalization
  i. Message boards and chat rooms us more creativity in playing roles than we have in live interaction.
  ii. Social networks sustain us; they are what communities are made of.
  iii. Sociological consequences of such increasing isolation are significant.

VI. Organizations
 a. Large secondary groups designed to accomplish specific tasks in an efficient manner.
 b. Types of Organizations
  i. Normative Organizations: typically voluntary organization; member receive no monetary rewards and often have to pay to join.
  ii. Coercive Organizations: organizations in which membership is not voluntary.
  iii. Utilitarian Organizations: those in which we belong for a specific, instrumental purpose, a tangible material reward.
 c. Are We a Nation of Joiners?
  i. Alexis de Tocqueville called America a "nation of joiners."
  ii. How can we be so individualistic and so collective minded?
  iii. Recently it appears a nation of joiners has been changing over time.
 d. Organizations: Race and Gender and Inequality?
  i. Rules of organizations may favor some groups over other groups.
  ii. Organizational positions "carry characteristics images of the kinds of people that should occupy them."
 e. Bureaucracy: Organization and Power
  i. Bureaucracy is define as a formal organization, characterized by a division of labor, a hierarchy of authority, formal rules governing behavior, a logic of rationality, and an impersonality of criteria.
  ii. Characteristics of Bureaucracies
   1. Division of labor.
   2. Hierarchy of authority.
   3. Rules and regulations.
   4. Impersonality.
   5. Career ladders.
   6. Efficiency.
 f. Problems with Bureaucracy
  i. Bureaucracies exhibit many of their other problems of groups:
   1. Overspecialization
   2. Rigidity and inertia
   3. Ritualism
   4. Suppression of dissent
   5. The bureaucratic
  ii. Bureaucracy and Accountability
   1. Mechanism that enable bureaucracies to be efficient and formal enterprises also have the effect of reducing an individual's sense of accountability.
   2. In massive bureaucratic death camps, where processing inmates for extermination was the "business" of the organization, doctors focused on:

      a. The internal formal administrative tasks that were germane only to their position in the hierarchy.

      b. Informal culture of personal relationship among staff.

    iii. Bureaucracy and Democracy

      1. Another problem Weber identified with bureaucracies is the formal structure of accountability that is undemocratic.

      2. Officeholders in a bureaucracy tend to stay for many years, even for their entire careers.

      3. The "Iron Cage" of Bureaucracy

        a. Difference between reality and appearance of bureaucracies.

        b. Very mechanisms that make bureaucracies predictable, meaningful, efficient, and coherent and enable those of us who participate in them to see clearly all the different lines of power and control, efficiency and accountability, often lead those organization to become their opposite

        c. Organization becomes unpredictable, unwieldy, and unequal.

  g. Globalization and Organizations

    i. In large complex societies, bureaucracies are the dominant form of organization.

    ii. Groups and organizations are increasingly globalized.

      1. Global institutions are increasingly the institutional form in which people all over the world do their business.

      2. Political institutions attempt to bring different countries together under one bureaucratic organization.

    iii. The reactions against use the forms and institutions to resist it.

      1. Religious fundamentalists or political extremists who want to return to a more traditional society all use the Internet to recruit members.

      2. Globalization may change some of the dynamics of groups and organizations.

VII. Groups 'R' Us: Groups and Interaction in the 21st Century.

  a. Even though we belong to fewer groups than our parents might have, these groups may also be increasingly important in our lives.

  b. We live in a society composed of many different groups and many different cultures, subcultures, and countercultures, speaking different languages, with different kinship networks and different values and norms.

Chapter Summary

- Society is an organized collection of individuals and institutions, bounded by space in a coherent territory, subject to the same political authority and organized through a shared set of cultural expectations and values. Societies are composed of structured social interactions.

- Terms like organizations and institutions describe more formal and stable patterns of interactions among many individuals that enable us to predict and control behavior and society refers to the sum of all these other elements.

- Societies cohere through social structure which is a complex framework composed of both patterned social interactions and institutions that together both organize social life and provide the context for individual action.

- Social interactions are behaviors that are oriented toward other people that forms our identity.

- Charles Horton Cooley coined the term looking-glass self to describe the process by which our identity develops: we imagine how we appear to others around us, we draw general conclusions based on the reactions of others, and based on our evaluations of others' reactions, we develop our sense of personal identity. Goffman went beyond Cooley's concept and used the term impression management, actively controlling how others perceive us by changing behaviors to correspond to an idea of what they will find most appealing.

- Nonverbal and verbal communications are ways in which we construct our social reality.

- There are five basic patterns of social interaction, what sociologist Robert Nisbet calls the "molecular cement" that links individuals in groups from the smallest to the largest: Exchange, Cooperation, Competition, Conflict, and Coercion.

- Status and roles are used to describe the elementary forms of interaction in society. Status is any social identity recognized as meaningful by the group or society and roles are the behaviors that are expected of a person who occupies a certain status.

- A group is any assortment of people who share the same norms, values, and expectations and includes: dyads, crowds, primary groups, secondary groups, in-groups, out-groups, reference groups, and cliques.

- Groups exhibit certain predictable dynamics and have certain characteristics that include a leader who is in charge and the hardcore members who have a great deal of power to make policy decisions.

- Group dynamics include conformity, diffusion of responsibility, and stereotyping.

- Networks are types of groups that are both looser and denser than a formal group that offer us support and exert an important influence on the most crucial aspects of our lives.

- Organizations are large secondary groups designed to accomplish specific tasks in an efficient manner. One can be part of a normative organization, voluntary organizations that offer no monetary reward, coercive organization, membership is not voluntary, or utilitarian organization, have specific purposes and tangible material rewards.

- Organizations can reproduce racial and gender inequalities.

- Bureaucracies are formal organizations, characterized by a division of labor, a hierarchy of authority, formal rules governing behavior, a logic of rationality, and an impersonality of criteria.

- Max Weber's ideal bureaucracy consisted of division of labor, hierarchy of authority, rules and regulations, impersonality, career ladders, and efficiency.

- Bureaucracies, although more predictable and efficient, also exaggerate certain problems of all groups like: overspecialization, rigidity and inertia, ritualism, suppression of dissent, the bureaucratic "Catch 22" and these lead people involved in the bureaucracy to feel alienated and confused.

- Other problems with bureaucracies are that they reduce an individual's sense of accountability, are not democratic since officeholders tend to stay on for many years, and the mechanisms that make them efficient and predictable often lead those organizations to become their opposite: unpredictable and inefficient.

- Groups and organizations are increasingly globalized and political organizations are attempting to bring different countries together under one bureaucracy.

Learning Objectives

After completing the reading of Chapter 9, you should be able to answer the following objectives.

- Understand the two definitions, society and social interactions, and how their definitions complement each other.
- Discuss Charles Horton Cooley's looking-glass self and how Goffman expanded on the concept to include impression management.
- Understand how verbal and nonverbal communication influences social reality.
- Know and discuss the five basic patterns of social interaction.
- Define role performance, status, ascribed status, achieved status, and master status.
- Define role strain and role exit and discuss the stages in which people go through when voluntarily exiting a significant role.
- Distinguish between groups and aggregates and explain why they are important to society.
- Compare primary and secondary groups and explain the role they each play in our lives.
- Explain the differences between in-groups, out-groups, and reference groups.
- Discuss group dynamics in terms of conformity, diffusion of responsibility, and stereotyping.
- Define network and how social experiences and globalization effect networks.
- Define organizations, normative organizations, coercive organizations, and utilitarian organizations and give an example of each.
- State the definition of bureaucracy, explain Weber's ideal type of bureaucracy, and what the problems with bureaucracies include.

Key Terms

Achieved status: status that we attain through talent, ability, effort, or other unique characteristic.

Ascribed status: status that we receive involuntarily, without regard to our unique talents, skills, or accomplishments.

Bureaucracy: formal organization, characterized by a division of labor, a hierarchy of authority, formal rules governing behavior, a logic of rationality, and an impersonality of criteria.

Bureaucratic personality: those people who become more committed to following the correct procedures than they are in getting the job done.

Coercive organizations: organization in which membership is not voluntary.

Crowd: aggregate of individuals who happen to be together but experience themselves as essentially independent.

Dramaturgy: our performances change according to the characters on stage at the moment.

Dyad: group of two.

Ethnomethdology: researcher tries to expose the common unstated assumptions that enable such conversational shortcuts to work.

Face work: our attempt to give the best possible performance.

Group: any assortment of people who share the same norms, values, and expectations.

Group cohesion: the degree to which the individual members identify with each other and with the group.

Groupthink: process by which group members try to preserve harmony and unity in spite of their individual judgments.

Hardcore members: those with a great deal of power to make policy decisions.

Impression management: actively trying to control how others perceive me by changing my behavior to correspond to an ideal of what they will find most appealing.

In-group: group I feel positively toward and to which I actually belong.

In-group heterogeneity: awareness of the subtle differences among the individual members of your group.

Institutions: formal and stable patterns of interaction among many individuals that enable us to predict and control behavior.

Leader: someone in charge, whether elected, appointed, or just informally took control.

Looking-glass self: describes the process by which our identity develops.

Master status: status that is presumed so important that it overshadows all of the others.

Network: type of group that is both looser and denser than a formal group.

Normative organization: voluntary organization in which members receive no reward and often have to pay to join.

Organization: large secondary groups designed to accomplish specific tasks in an efficient manner.

Out-group: one to which I do not belong and do not feel very positively toward.

Out-group homogeneity: tend to believe that all members of the out-group are exactly the same.

Primary group: people who come together for expressive reasons.

Reference group: a group toward which we are so strongly committed or one that commands so much prestige that we orient our actions around what we perceive that groups perceptions would be.

Roles: set of behaviors that are expected of a person who occupies a certain status.

Role conflict: happens when we try to play different roles with extremely different or contradictory rules at the same time.

Role exit: process of adjustment that takes place when we move out of such a role.

Role performance: the particular emphasis or interpretation we give a role.

Role strain: when the same role has demands and expectations that contradict each other.

Secondary groups: people who come together for instrumental reasons.

Social interaction: behaviors that are oriented toward other people.

Social structure: complex framework, or structure, composed of both patterned social interactions and institutions that together both organize social life and provide the context for individual action.

Society: an organized collection of individuals and institutions, bounded by space in a coherent territory, subject to the same political authority, and organized through a shared set of cultural expectations and values.

Status: any social identity recognized as meaningful by the group or society.

Stereotypes: assumptions about what people are like or how they will behave based on their membership in a group.

Subordinate: individuals or groups with less social power.

Superordinate: individuals or groups with social power.

Total institutions: one that completely formally circumscribes your everyday life.

Utilitarian organization: those to which we belong for a specific, instrumental purpose, a tangible reward.

Key People

Charles Horton Cooley: argued that identity is formed through social interactions and coined the term looking-glass self.

Harold Garfinkel: developed an entire sociological tradition called ethnomethodology.

Erving Goffman: believed that our selves change not only because of other people's reaction but also because of the way we actively try to present ourselves to other people.

Irving James: psychologist who called the process by which group members try to preserve harmony and unity in spite of their individual judgments.

Rosabeth Moss Kanter: demonstrated that men's and women's behaviors had to do with the structure of the organization not with their characteristics as individuals.

George Simmel: used the term web to describe the way our collective membership in different groups constitutes our sense of identity.

Alexis de Tocqueville: called America the "nation of joiners."

Max Weber: credited with describing the essential characteristics of bureaucracies.

Additional Learning with MySocLab

Read
I Think, Therefore IM (pg 75)
The article discusses the nonverbal communication and the language used by people who IM. Teachers believe that students should know the difference between formal writing and conversational writing.
Explore
Cooley's Looking Glass Self (pg 72)
Gives a diagram of how Cooley's Looking Glass Self works.
Patterns of Alienation (pg 97)
Using data from the General Social Survey, Michael V. Miller asks the question: to what extent are Americans alienated from major social institutions? People may become alienated not only from their job, but from larger institutions within their society. Take the quiz to see how your answers compared to those of the General Social Survey's.
Visualize
The Looking Glass Self (pg 72)
This presents a diagram of Cooley's looking glass self and the path of how the concept works.
Group Size and Relationships: Student Social Structure on a Dorm Floor (pg 85)
Gives a visual representation of groups and the relationships between different members of the group.

Watch

William Roy (pg 71)

William Roy discusses how things we take as natural are socially constructed.

The McDonaldization of Society (pg 98)

George Ritzer discusses the development of his theory on the McDonaldization of Society and how it relates to Weber's "Iron Cage" of bureaucracy.

Practice Test

After completing the practice test, check your answers in the Answer Key of this Study Guide.

Multiple Choice Questions

1. All of the following are ascribed status except:
   a. sex.
   b. race.
   c. age.
   d. occupation.

2. In America, which of the following statuses would likely be your master status?
   a. Friend
   b. Student
   c. Cancer patient
   d. Mother

3. The behaviors that are expected of us when occupying a certain status are:
   a. status sets.
   b. master statuses.
   c. roles.
   d. status differentiations.

4. _____ is the term Cooley used to describe the process by which our identity develops.
   a. Dramaturgy
   b. Looking-glass self
   c. Social interaction
   d. Impression management

5. People who share the same norms, values and expectations are part of a:
   a. role.
   b. group.
   c. bureaucracy.
   d. status.

6. Which of the following group is essential in an individual's emotional well-being?
   a. Primary group
   b. Secondary group
   c. In-group
   d. Out-group

7. The groups that one uses as a standard to evaluate themselves is:
   a. primary Group.
   b. secondary group.
   c. reference group.
   d. in-group.

8. The group we do not belong to and do not feel very positively toward is:
   a. secondary group.
   b. out-group.
   c. reference group.
   d. bureaucracy.

9. Which of the following is not a negative dynamic of groups?
   a. Conformity
   b. Diffusion of Responsibility
   c. Stereotyping
   d. Divergence

10. Which of the following is not an example of a normative organization?
   a. the Sierra Club
   b. Kiwanis
   c. NRA
   d. Prison

11. What type of organization do people belong to for a specific, instrumental purpose with tangible material rewards?
   a. Normative organizations
   b. Utilitarian organizations
   c. Coercive organizations
   d. Total institutions

12. Which of the following is not a characteristic of an "ideal" bureaucracy?
   a. Division of labor
   b. Rules and regulations
   c. Inefficiency
   d. Impersonality

13. _____ refers to the degree to which the individual members identify with each other and with the group.
   a. Group cohesion
   b. Group dynamics
   c. Group identity
   d. Group association

14. Irving Janis called the process by which group members try to preserve harmony and unity in spite of their individual judgments _____.
   a. Conformity
   b. Groupthink
   c. Diffusion of Responsibility
   d. Stereotyping

15. What is the term for a status that has special importance for one's social identity that dominates or lives and controls our position in society?
   a. Ascribed status
   b. Achieved status
   c. Master status
   d. None of the above

16. _____ happens when we try to play different roles with extremely different or contradictory rules at the same time.
   a. Role conflict
   b. Role exit
   c. Role strain
   d. Role performance

17. Janet is an excellent professor at the local university but she finds that there is not enough time to devote to her children. Janet is experiencing:
    a. Role conflict
    b. Role ambiguity
    c. Roles strain
    d. Role expectation

18. Garfinkel's research method of endomethodology involves:
    a. the study of interaction in terms of nonverbal communication.
    b. tracking people's statuses and roles over the life course.
    c. studying how people interact with institutions.
    d. studying the way people make sense of their everyday surroundings.

19. According to Robert Nisbet there are five basic patterns of social interaction called "molecular cement" that links individuals in groups from the smallest to the largest. Which of the following is not one of them?
    a. Exchange
    b. Liberty
    c. Cooperation
    d. Conflict

20. What is the term used to describe the complex framework composed of both patterned social interaction and institutions that together both organize social life and provide the context for individual action?
    a. Institutions
    b. Organizations
    c. Social structure
    d. Society

21. Nonverbal communication refers to:
    a. the speech patterns of individuals.
    b. beliefs assumed to be true by everyone.
    c. body movements and gestures.
    d. the conversations that we engage in with others.

22. Which of the following is not a characteristic of a secondary group?
    a. Large size
    b. Strong emotional ties
    c. Come together for a specific purpose
    d. Impersonal interactions between members

23. Which of the following illustrates how groupthink operates?
    a. A group shares information widely and makes an effective policy recommendation
    b. A group seeks consensus, discouraging members from speaking freely, and the decision turns out to be acceptable
    c. A group shares information widely but makes no effective decision
    d. A group seeks consensus, discouraging members from speaking freely, and the decision turns out to be acceptable

24. New technology, such as the internet and text messaging has:
    a. created a global network that links people from all over the world.
    b. brought people together that have very specialized interests or uncommon beliefs.
    c. allowed more creativity for people in playing roles than we have in live interaction.
    d. all of the above.

25. In principle, bureaucracies pay little attention to:
    a. completing tasks efficiently.
    b. formal policies.
    c. marked paths for advancement.
    d. tradition.

True/False Questions

True   False   1. Ascribed statuses are attained through talent, ability, effort, or other unique personal characteristic.

True   False   2. Your master status is one that overshadows all others.

True   False   3. Primary groups usually consists of close friends and family.

True   False   4. Members of the out-group cooperate with members of the in-group.

True   False   5. A reference group is one in which we belong to.

True   False   6. Normative organization are typically voluntary.

True   False   7. The division of labor is one characteristic of a bureaucracy.

True   False   8. One problem with bureaucracies is the lose adherence to rules.

True   False   9. Subordinates can use the threat of violence, deprivation, or some other punishment to control the actions of those with less power.

True   False   10. Nonverbal communication is one of the most important ways of constructing a social reality.

Fill-in-the-Blank Questions

1. A large lecture class with 100 students is an example of a _____.

2. _____ groups are the groups that we use as the standard to evaluate ourselves.

3. Charles Horton Cooley coined the term _____.

4. If I am actively trying to control how other perceive me by changing my behavior to correspond to an ideal of what they will find most appealing. I am doing _____.

5. _____ communication includes body movements, gestures, and facial expressions.

6. Sociologists use the term _____ to refer to any social identity recognized as meaningful by the group or society.

7. Our experience of roles is a negotiation between role _____ and role _____.

8. When someone makes an assumption about what people are like or how they will behave based on their membership in a group is called a _____.

9. A _____ is a type of group that is both looser and denser than a formal group.

10. Merton used the term _____ to describe those people who become more committed to following the correct procedures than they are in getting the job done.

Essay Questions

1. Explain what is meant by the "social construction of reality and how Cooley and Goffman explained how people construct their realities.

2. What are the three most common types of organizations? How does one become a member, what is the purpose of the organization, and give an example of each.

3. Explain the traits that Max Weber considered to make the "ideal" bureaucracy.

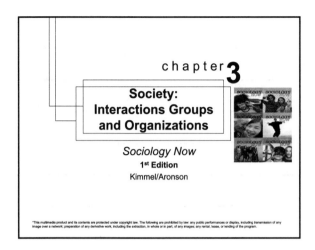

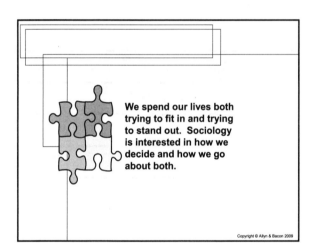

The Social Construction of Reality

    – social interaction

- **Cooley and the Looking-Glass Self**
  - imagine how we appear
  - conclusions/reactions of others
  - develop self identity

_____
_____
_____
_____
_____
_____
_____

The Social Construction of Reality

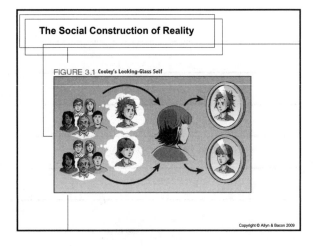

FIGURE 3.1 Cooley's Looking-Glass Self

_____
_____
_____
_____
_____
_____
_____

The Social Construction of Reality

    – "I" and "me" (Mead)

- **Goffman and the "Dramaturgical" Self**
  - presentation of self to others
  - **impression management**
  - dramaturgy
  - face work

_____
_____
_____
_____
_____
_____
_____
_____

The Social Construction of Reality

- **Nonverbal Communication**
  - body movements
  - gestures
  - facial expressions
  - placement in relation to others
  - *laughter*

- **Verbal Communication**
  - **ethnomethodology**
    - "conversational shortcuts"

The Social Construction of Reality

- **Patterns of Social Interaction**
  - *Exchange*
  - *Cooperation*
  - *Competition*
  - *Conflict*
  - *Coercion*
    - **superordinate**
    - **subordinate**

The Elements of Social Structure

- **Status**
  - **Ascribed Status**
  - **Achieved Status**
  - **Master Status**

- **Roles**
  - *expectations and performance*
  - **role strain**
  - **role conflict**
  - **role exit**
    1. *Doubt*
    2. *Search for alternatives*
    3. *Departure*
    4. *New role*

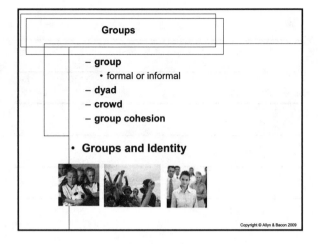

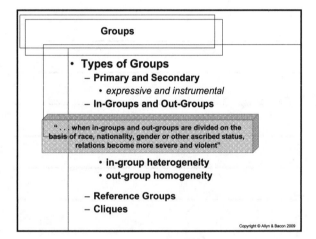

Groups

- **Group Dynamics**
  - size matters
    - **leader**
    - **hardcore members**
  - **Conformity**
  - **Diffusion of responsibility**
  - **Stereotyping** → *prejudice*

Social Networks

- **network**
  - lasting influence (Domhoff)
  - looser and denser
  - *web* (Simmel)

- **Networks and Social Experience**
  - support in times of stress or illness
  - "strength of weak ties" (Granovetter)

> ". . . online we can adopt new roles and statuses, changing not only our skills and interests, but our age, ethnicity, gender and sexuality at will."

- **Networks and Globalization**

Organizations

- **organizations**
  - size
  - purpose
  - efficiency

- **Types of Organizations**
  - Normative Organizations
  - Coercive Organizations
    - total institutions
  - Utilitarian Organizations

Organizations

- **Are We a Nation of Joiners?**
  - *Democracy in America* (de Tocqueville)
  - decrease in normative organization participation

- **Organizations: Race and Gender Inequality?**
  - rules favor some groups over others
  - criteria is not necessarily "neutral"

Organizations

- **Bureaucracy: Organization and Power**
  - *Division of labor*
  - *Hierarchy of authority*
  - *Rules and regulations*
  - *Impersonality*
  - *Career ladders*
  - *Efficiency*

FIGURE 3.3 Hierarchy of Authority

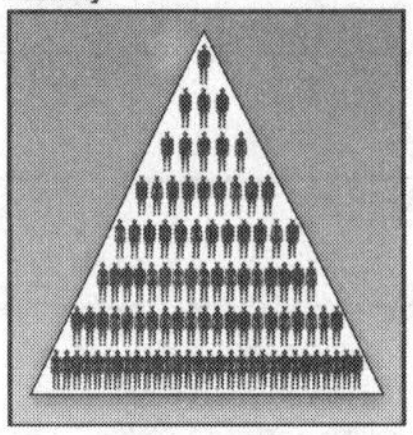

Organizations

- **Problems with Bureaucracy**
  - *Overspecialization*
  - *Rigidity and inertia*
  - *Ritualism*
  - *Suppression of dissent*
  - *The bureaucratic "Catch-22"*

Organizations

- bureaucratic personality
- Bureaucracy and Accountability
- Bureaucracy and Democracy
- The "Iron Cage" of Bureaucracy

- **Globalization and Organizations**

- **Groups 'R' Us: Groups and Interactions in the 21st Century**

What Does America Think?

3.1 Marital Status

These are actual survey data from the General Social Survey, 2004.

According to the General Social Survey, in 2004 about 60 percent of U.S. adults were married. However, this varied dramatically by social class. Those in the upper class were far more likely to be married (79 percent) than those in the lower class (36.2 percent) and the results for those who were never married were inverse, 30.1 percent for lower class and 7.9 percent for upper class. With regard to race, white respondents were far more likely to be married (63.3 percent) then were black respondents (41 percent).

CRITICAL THINKING | DISCUSSION QUESTIONS
1. Why does marital status vary by social class? What cultural values and experiences might contribute to the differences?
2. Why does marital status vary by race? What cultural values and historical experiences might contribute to the differences?

What Does America Think?

3.2 Group Membership

These are actual survey data from the General Social Survey, 2004.

Are there any activities that you do with the same group of people on a regular basis even if the group doesn't have a name, such as a bridge group, exercise group, or a group that meets to discuss individual or community problems? Almost three-quarters of respondents reported not being part of a regular informal group. White respondents (29.3 percent) were more likely than Black respondents (19.1 percent) to be part of such a group. Those who were of another racial classification were least likely to report being part of a group (14.1 percent). There was no difference in group membership by gender.

CRITICAL THINKING | DISCUSSION QUESTIONS
1. Were you surprised that so few respondents report being members of informal groups? Do you think these numbers reflect reality? Why do you think so few people belong to groups? Why do you think Black respondents were less likely to report belonging to an informal group than were White respondents?
2. What other benefits are there to group membership? Think about what kinds of groups you belong to and how you benefit from them.

What Does America Think?

▶ Go to this website to look further at the data. You can run your own statistics and crosstabs here: http://sda.berkeley.edu/cgi-bin/hsda?harcsda+gss04

REFERENCES: Davis, James A., Ton W. Smith, and Peter V. Marsden. General Social Surveys 1972–2004: [Cumulative file] [Computer file]. 2nd ICPSR version. Chicago, IL: National Opinion Research Center [producer], 2005; Storrs, CT: Roper Center for Public Opinion Research, University of Connecticut; Ann Arbor, MI: Inter-university Consortium for Political and Social Research; Berkeley, CA: Computer-Assisted Survey Methods Program, University of California [distributors], 2005.

Chapter 4
How Do We Know What We Know? The Methods of the Sociologist

Chapter Outline

I.   Why Sociological Methods Matter
- a.   Sociology is a social science attempting to study human behavior as it is lived by conscious human beings.
    - i.   People possess subjectivity- a complex of individual perceptions, motivations, ideas, and emotions.
    - ii.   Sociology uses a wide variety of methodologies.
- b.   Sociology and the Scientific Method
    - i.   As in any argument, science requires the use of evidence, or data, to demonstrate a position.
    - ii.   Some research methods use deductive reasoning in that hey logically proceed from one demonstrable fact to the next and deduce their results.
    - iii.   The feelings of our research subjects are exactly what we are trying to study, and we will need to rely on inductive reasoning, which will help us to understand a problem using our own human capacity to put ourselves in the other person's position.
- c.   The Qualitative/Quantitative Divide
    - i.   Quantitative methods use powerful statistical tools to help understand patterns in which the behaviors, attitudes, or traits under study can be translated into numerical values.
    - ii.   Qualitative methods rely on more inductive and inferential reasoning to understand the texture of social life.

II.   Doing Sociological Research
- a.   Choosing an issue
- b.   Defining the problem
- c.   Reviewing the literature
- d.   Developing a hypothesis
- e.   Designing a project
- f.   Collecting the data
- g.   Analyzing the data
- h.   Reporting the findings

III.   Types of Sociological Research Methods
- a.   Variables help use measure whether, how, and in what ways, something changes as a result of the experiment.
    - i.   Extraneous variable influence the outcome of an experiment but are not actually of interest to the researcher.
    - ii.   Confounding variables may be affecting the results of the study but for which you haven't adequately accounted.
- b.   Instead of experiments, sociologists are likely to engage in the following types of research:
    - i.   Observation
    - ii.   Interviews
    - iii.   Surveys
    - iv.   Content analysis
- c.   Observational Methods
    - i.   Experiments is a controlled form of observation in which one manipulates independent variables to observe their effects on the dependent variable.
        1. Experimental groups- group that has the changed introduced.
        2. Control group- will not experience the manipulation of the variable.
    - ii.   Field Studies
        1. Detached observation- a perspective that constrains the researcher from becoming in any way involved in the event he or she is observing.

        2. Participant observation- requires researcher to observe and participate.

        3. Ethnography- you don't pretend to be a participant, but you try to understand the world from the point of view of the people whose lives you are interested in.

     iii. Interview Studies

        1. Most typical type of qualitative study uses interviews with a small sample.

        2. These studies use a purposive sample.

           a. Respondents are not selected randomly.

           b. One problem is that the sample is not a probability sample.

           c. Enable researchers to identify common themes is data and can sensitize us to trends in attitudes and behaviors among specifically targeted groups of people.

  d. Analysis of Quantitative Data

     i. Surveys

        1. Most common method that sociologists use to collect information about attitudes and behaviors.

        2. Likert scales arrange possible responses from lowest to highest

        3. Sociologists take a sample, or subset, of the population they want to study.

           a. In a random sample people are chosen in an abstract or arbitrary method.

           b. Stratified samples divide people into different groups before constructing the sample to make sure that you get an adequate number of members of each of the groups.

           c. Cluster samples is where the researcher chooses a random sample of an area and then surveys every person in that cluster.

        4. Survey Questions

           a. The wording can change the responses.

           b. The location of the question in the survey can change the response.

     ii. Secondary analysis of existing data

        1. Involves reanalyzing data that have already been collected

        2. Replication suggests the extent to which the results of a study can be generalized to other circumstances.

  e. Content Analysis

     i. Intensive reading of certain texts.

     ii. Some involved taking random samples.

  d. Making the right connections

        a. It is always important to make sure we are comparing things that are comparable.

        b. One risks making claims that turn out not to be true.

IV. Social Science and the Problem of "Truth"

  a. Predictability and Probability

     i. Predictability refers tot eh ability to generate testable hypotheses from data and to predict the outcomes of some phenomenon or event.

     ii. Human populations have many variables.

     iii. The number of predictive variables increases dramatically as the group gets bigger and the behavior more complex.

  b. Causality

     i. Relationship of some variable to the effects it produces.

     ii. In quantitative research, variable A is supposed to have a causal impact on variable B, but it is not always easy to decide which is the cause and which is the effect.

     iii. One must always be on guard against logical fallacies that can lead you in the wrong direction.

V. Issues Conducting Research

  a. Remain Objective and Avoid Bias

     i. You must strive to make sure that your prejudices and assumptions do not contaminate the results you find.

      ii.   You must be careful to construct the research project so that you find out what is really there and not merely develop an elaborate way to confirm your stereotypes.

  b. Avoid Overstating Results
      i.   Findings are not "newsworthy" unless you find something really significant.
      ii.   Researchers must be cautious about inferring why something happens from the fact that it does happen.
      iii.   Some relationship between two phenomena does not necessarily mean that one is the cause of the other.

  c. Maintain Professional Ethics
      i.   The researcher must also be ethical.
      ii.   The most important ethical issue is that your research should not actually hurt the people you are researching.
      iii.   The psychological consequences of deceptive experiments led to significant changes in research ethics.
          1.   1970 Congress made "informed consent" a requirement for research.
          2.   All major research universities have an Institutional Review Board that oversees all research undertaken at the university.

  d. The Institutional Review Board
      i.   Research cannot begin data collection unless he or she can guarantee:
          1.   Informed consent
          2.   Continuous consent
          3.   Confidentiality
          4.   Anonymity
          5.   Deception
          6.   Harm
          7.   Protected groups
      ii.   IRBs have expanded the scope of their review to include any research that involves human subjects in any way whatever.

VI.   Social Science Methods in the 21st Century: Emergent Methodologies
  a. Social scientists are finding new methods to study human behavior.
  b. Social scientists are always trying to refine older survey techniques to obtain the most accurate data.
  c. It is often the combination of different methods that are today providing the most exciting research findings in the social science.

Chapter Summary

- Social Science attempts to study human behavior as it is lived by conscious human beings
- Science requires the use of evidence, or data, to demonstrate a position.
- Some research methods use deductive reasoning while others use inductive reasoning.
- Quantitative methods use powerful statistical tools to help understand patterns in which the behaviors, attitudes, or traits under study can be translated into numerical values. Qualitative methods rely on more inductive and inferential reasoning to understand the texture of social life.
- Research in the social sciences follows eight basic steps: choosing an issue, defining the problem, reviewing the literature, developing a hypothesis, designing a project, collecting data, analyzing data, and reporting the findings.
- There are many different types of sociological research including: observational methods (experiments, field methods, and interview studies), analysis of quantitative data (survey and secondary analysis of existing data), and content analysis.
- Predictability refers to the ability to generate testable hypotheses from data and to predict the outcome of some phenomenon or event.
- Causality refers to the relationship of some variable to the effects it produces.
- As a researcher you must strive for objectivity, to make sure that your prejudices and assumptions do not contaminate the results you find and you must be careful to construct the research project so that you find out what is really there and not merely develop an elaborate way to confirm your stereotypes.
- Overstating your research findings is a big temptation of researchers, however findings are often not "newsworthy" unless you find something really significant.
- Researchers must also be ethical. The research you conduct should not harm your subjects in any way.
- All universities have an Institutional Review Board with strict guidelines to protect test subjects.
- Social scientists are finding new methods and they are always trying to refine older survey techniques to obtain the most accurate data.

Learning Objectives
After completing the reading of Chapter 4, you should be able to answer the following objectives.

- Define what data are and what they are used for.
- Define deductive reasoning and inductive reasoning and know the difference between them
- Discuss the difference between qualitative and quantitative research.
- Know what the eight steps to doing a sociological research project are.
- Understand the differences between the types of research sociologists are likely to engage in and when to use each.
- Define purposive sample, random sample, stratified sample, and cluster sample. Know the difference between them and when it is appropriate to use each.
- Define predictability and causality.
- Understand why it is important to remain objective and unbiased when conducting research.
- Discuss why it is important to be ethical and why Institutional Review Boards are important.
- Discuss the guidelines of the Institutional Review Board.

Key Terms

Causality: relationship of some variable to the effects it produces.

Cluster sample: researcher chooses a random sample of neighborhoods and then surveys every person in that "cluster."

Content analysis: involves an intensive reading of certain "texts"- perhaps books, pieces of conversations, or a set of articles from a newspaper.

Confounding Variables: may be affecting the results of the study but for which you haven't adequately accounted.

Control Group: group that will not experience the manipulation of the variable.

Correlation: some relationship between two phenomenon, doesn't necessarily mean that one is the cause of the other.

Data: formal and systematic information, organized and coherent.

Deductive Reasoning: logically proceed from one demonstrable fact to the next and deduce their results.

Dependent Variable: depends on, or is caused by, the independent variable.

Detached Observation: perspective that constrains the researcher from becoming in any way involved in the event he or she is observing.

Ethnography: field method in which you don't pretend to be a participant, you try to understand the world from the point of view of the people whose lives you are interested in.

Experimental Group: group that will have the change introduced to see what happens.

Extraneous Variables: may influence the outcome of an experiment but are not actually of interest to the researcher.

Hypothesis: predicts a relationship between two variables.

Generalizability: extent to which the results of the study can be generalized to other circumstances.

Independent Variable: event or item in your experiment that you will manipulate to see if that difference has an impact.

Inductive Reasoning: help understand a problem using our own human capacity to put ourselves in the other person's position.

Interviews: asking a small group of people open-ended questions.

Likert scale: arranges possible responses from lowest to highest.

Literature Review: careful examination of the research already done on a topic or at least a systematic sample of that research.

Participant Observation: requires that the researcher participates and observe.

Predictability: ability to generate testable hypotheses from data and to "predict" the outcomes of some phenomenon or event.

Purposive sample: respondents are not selected randomly and not representative of the larger population, but selected precisely because he or she possesses certain characteristics that are of interest to the researcher.

Qualitative methods: rely on inductive and inferential reasoning to understand the texture of social life, the actual felt experience of social interaction.

Quantitative methods: statistical tools to help understand patterns in which the behaviors, attitudes, or traits under study can be translated into numerical numbers.

Random Sample: a number of people, chosen by an abstract and arbitrary method.

Sample: a subset of the population to be studied.

Secondary analysis: analyzing data that have already been collected.

Stratified sample: people are divided into different groups before you construct your sample and make sure that you get adequate number of members of each of the groups.

Subjectivity: complex of individual perceptions, motivations, ideas, and emotions.

Surveys: most common method used to collect information about attitudes and behaviors.

Verstehen: method that uses "intersubjective understanding."

Key People

Eric Goode: conducted research that used deceptive practices and refused to submit his research proposal to his university's Internal Review Board.

Stanley Milgram: did a study on obedience in which one subject administered "shocks" to another.

Robert Rosenthal and Lenore Jacobson: tested the "self-fulfilling prophecy" hypotheses.

Additional Learning with MySocLab

Read

On SAT, Questions Can Matter as Much as Answers

There are certain topics -- lots, actually -- that the makers of the SAT will not even consider as subjects for the reading passages on the test.

Explore

Graphing Data (pg 123)

This activity looks at how data can be presented in a pie-chart or bar graph using data from FBI Supplementary Homicide Reports: 1976-2002.

Cause, Effect, and Correlation (pg 128)

This activity explores in depth causation and the three conditions that need to be met. The activity discusses temporal priority, correlation, and spurious correlation.

Watch

Research Methodology (pg 111)

Spencer Cahill answers the question of what his preferred methodology is for his research.

Qualitative Research Methods (pg 117)

Judith Stacey discusses the qualitative methods in her research on gay men and their families.

Research Ethics (pg 132)

This video clip discusses the Tuskegee experiment and the reluctance of African Americans to participate in medical experiments.

Visualize

Methodological Terms (pg 126)

This table gives some methodological terms and their definitions.

Practice Test

After completing the practice test, check your answers in the Answer Key of this Study Guide.

Multiple Choice Questions

1. The first step in undertaking a research project is:
    a. Choosing an issue.
    b. Defining the problem.
    c. Designing the project.
    d. Collecting the data.

2. Which of the following would not be considered an observational method?
    a. Interviews
    b. Experiments
    c. Surveys
    d. Field studies

3. What type of variable is manipulated in an experiment to see if that difference matters?
    a. Dependent
    b. Independent
    c. Exogenous
    d. Confounded

4. _____ are systematically collected and organized.
    a. Data
    b. Variables
    c. Predictors
    d. Relationship

5. Which type of methods involves using statistics to understand the patterns in human behavior?
    a. Qualitative
    b. Field Studies
    c. Participant Observations
    d. Quantitative

6. In observational studies the research directly observes the behavior being studied. Which of the following is not an observational method?
    a. Experiments
    b. Field Studies
    c. Interviews
    d. Content analysis

7. Which type of quantitative method is used most commonly for sociologists to collect information about attitudes and behavior?
    a. Secondary data
    b. Surveys
    c. Content analysis
    d. Interviews

8. What type of sample involves dividing people into different groups before constructing you sample?
    a. Random sample
    b. Cluster sample
    c. Stratified sample
    d. Purposive sample

9. Analyzing "texts" such as books, pieces of conversations, newspaper articles, and magazines are considered a:
   a. Quantitative method.
   b. Qualitative method
   c. Content analysis.
   d. None of the above.

10. What type of research method includes carefully selecting a sample making it easy to identify common themes?
    a. Experiments
    b. Field studies
    c. Surveys
    d. Interview studies

11. Secondary analysis of existing data makes it easier to do what?
    a. Replicate a study
    b. Generalize about findings
    c. Monitor a study
    d. Shape social realities

12. When conducting a research project what step in the process has you state what you anticipate to find from doing the study?
    a. Literature Review
    b. Developing a Hypothesis
    c. Collecting the Data
    d. Analyzing the Data

13. Which variable may influence the outcome of an experiment but is not actually of interest to the researcher?
    a. Independent variable
    b. Dependent variable
    c. Extraneous variable
    d. Confounding variable

14. _____ are observation where the researcher is constrained from becoming involve din the event that he or she is studying.
    a. Participant observations
    b. Observation methods
    c. Field observation
    d. Detached observation

15. Which of the following prevent a researcher from getting clearance from their Institutional Review Board?
    a. Ensuring the anonymity of the subjects
    b. Clearly deceiving their subjects
    c. Providing a letter informing the subject of the project
    d. Informing the subject that they can withdraw from the study at any point in time

16. Who's study that involved subjects administering "shocks" to another.
    a. Erich Goode
    b. William F. Whyte
    c. Philippe Bourgois
    d. Stanley Milgram

17. If you wanted to conduct research looking at a group of people to fully understand certain characteristics of the group what method would you most likely use?
    a. Surveys
    b. Interviews
    c. Secondary data
    d. Content analysis

18. _____ is a field method used most often by Anthropologists.
    a. Field studies
    b. Interviewing
    c. Ethnography
    d. Participant observation

19. The research conducted on anonymous homosexual sex in public restrooms led to the development of Institutional Review Boards. Who conducted this research?
    a. Laud Humphrey
    b. Erich Goode
    c. Stanley Milgram
    d. Eric Turkheimer

20. When your data are actually able to measure what you want to measure, this is called?
    a. Predictability
    b. Validity
    c. Reliability
    d. Causality

21. Which of the following is not necessary when ensuring the results you hear about in the media are in fact correct?
    a. Who sponsored the survey
    b. What was the sample selection procedure
    c. Are some of the results based on part of the sample
    d. All of the above are necessary

22. Researchers must strive for this when conducting research to ensure that their prejudices and assumptions do not contaminate the results.
    a. Bias
    b. Subjectivity
    c. Objectivity
    d. Detachment

23. When there is a relationship between two phenomenon sociologists refer to this as:
    a. Correlation
    b. Causality
    c. Predictability
    d. Probability

24. What is one technological advancement social scientists are now using to conduct research?
    a. Random sampling of names
    b. Face-to-Face interviewing
    c. Telephone audio computer-assisted self-interviewing
    d. Mass mailing of surveys

25. What is the major draw back to using secondary analysis of existing data?
    a. Replication is easy and convenient
    b. Generalizing is not reliable because the sample group is so targeted
    c. Ethical consideration prevent many of them because of the involvement of human subjects
    d. You are completely dependent on the original source

STUDY GUIDE

True/False Questions

True   False   1. The scientific method uses objective, systematic observations to test hypotheses.

True   False   2. A variable that changes due to the effect of another variable is the dependent variable.

True   False   3. In an experiment, the experimental group does not experience the manipulation of the variable.

True   False   4. A participant observation requires a researcher to only observe the subjects they are studying.

True   False   5. A cause-and-effect relationship exists any time two variables are statistically related.

True   False   6. If you wanted to obtain a sample that had equal proportions to the actual population, a stratified sample should be used.

True   False   7. Secondary data analysis allows for replication.

True   False   8. The fact that people are aware that a researcher is observing their behavior may affect how they act.

True   False   9. Researchers should strive for subjectivity.

True   False   10. Institutional Review Boards were set up to ensure that researchers followed ethical guidelines when conducting their research.

Fill-in-the-Blank Questions

1. The means by which a research collects his or her data is _____.

2. Individuals who are selected from the larger population to participate in a research study are called a _____.

3. When conducting an experiment the researcher has the experimental group and the _____ group.

4. _____ allows the researcher to understand the texture of social life and the actual felt experience of social interaction.

5. _____ is perhaps the best method for ascertaining those larger patterns.

6. If a researcher was to look take every fifth block in a town and then surveyed every person living in those blocks, the sampling method would be considered a _____.

7. _____ is often cheaper and easier to use for research.

8. If variable A has a clear effect on variable B, we say that they are _____ related.

9. _____ is something researchers should not do unless their results are truly significant.

10. _____ is part of the Institutional Review Board's guidelines in which test subjects must be informed, in advance, of the nature of the project.

Essay Questions

1. Several different research methods are discussed in the chapter. Pick a research topic and discuss how you might try to investigate this topic using two of the different methods. How might these methods be suitable or not suitable for your particular topic?

2. Choose a research topic and explain how you would then proceed with the seven following research steps.

3. Explain in detail why it is necessary to have an Institutional Review Board.

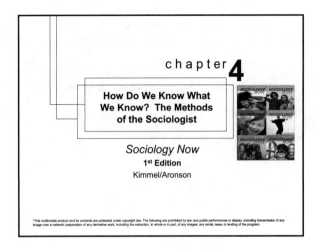

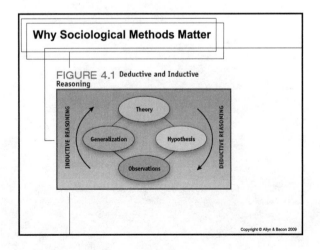

Why Sociological Methods Matter

- **verstehen** (Weber)
- emotional distance from the research process versus the human "connection"

- **The Qualitative/Quantitative Divide**
  - **quantitative methods**
    - statistical tools
    - numerical values
  - **qualitative methods**
    - understanding the texture of social life
    - less scientific

Doing Sociological Research

- *Choosing an issue*
- *Defining the problem*
- *Reviewing the literature*
- *Developing a hypothesis*
- *Designing a project*
- *Collecting data*
- *Analyzing the data*
- *Reporting the findings*

Doing Sociological Research

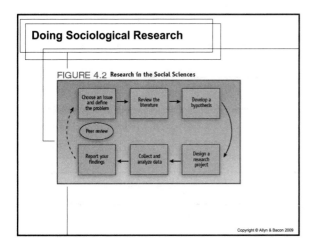

FIGURE 4.2 Research in the Social Sciences

Types of Sociological Research Methods

- *experiment*
- *variables*
  - independent – agent of change
  - **extraneous**
  - **confounding**
- sociological research methods:
  - *Observation*
  - *Interviews*
  - *Surveys*
  - *Content analysis*

Types of Sociological Research Methods

- **Observational Methods**
  - direct observation of
  - hypothesis tested against evidence

  - **Experiments** (controlled)
    - **experimental group**
    - **control group**

  - **Field studies** (social environment)
    - **detached observation**
    - **participant observation**
    - **ethnography**

Types of Sociological Research Methods

- **Interview studies**
  - **purposive sample**

- **Analysis of Quantitative Data**
  - **Surveys**
    - most commonly used methodology
    - **Likert scale**
    - types of **samples**
      - *random*
      - *stratified*
      - *cluster*

Types of Sociological Research Methods

- **Survey Questions**
  - coming up with good questions is hard
  - the wording itself can change the way people think
  - placement of questions

- **Secondary Analysis of Existing Data**
  - **secondary analysis**
  - reanalizing data that has already been collected
  - different *forms* of data may be used
  - replication

Types of Sociological Research Methods

- **Content Analysis**
  - **content analysis**
  - intensive reading of "texts"
  - snippets from television shows

- **Making the Right Comparisons**
  - things studied must be comparable

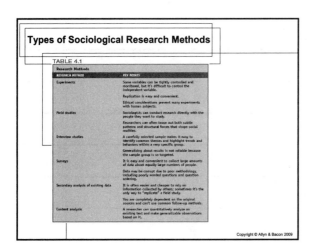

Types of Sociological Research Methods

TABLE 4.1

Research Methods	
RESEARCH METHOD	**KEY POINTS**
Experiments	Some variables can be tightly controlled and monitored, but it's difficult to control the independent variable.
	Replication is easy and convenient.
	Ethical considerations prevent many experiments with human subjects.
Field studies	Sociologists can conduct research directly with the people they want to study.
	Researchers can often tease out both subtle patterns and structural forces that shape social realities.
Interview studies	A carefully selected sample makes it easy to identify common themes and highlight trends and behaviors within a very specific group.
	Generalizing about results is not reliable because the sample group is so targeted.
Surveys	It is easy and convenient to collect large amounts of data about equally large numbers of people.
	Data may be corrupt due to poor methodology, including poorly worded questions and question ordering.
Secondary analysis of existing data	It is often easier and cheaper to rely on information collected by others; sometimes it's the only way to "replicate" a field study.
	You are completely dependent on the original sources and can't use common follow-up methods.
Content analysis	A researcher can quantitatively analyze an existing text and make generalizable observations based on it.

Social Science and the Problem of the "Truth"

- **Predictability and Probability**
  - "*social physics*" **(Comte)**
  - answers from the analysis of variables
  - value: **predict** future behaviors
    - *observer effect*
- **Causality**
  - Quantitative: **A** causes **B**
  - *Questions to consider*
    1. Does variable B come after variable A?
    2. High correlation between A and B?
    3. Extraneous variables?
    4. *Observer effect* present?

Copyright © Allyn & Bacon 2009

Issues in Conducting Research

- Academic journals
  - *American Sociological Review*
  - *Social Problems*
  - *Social Forces*
  - *American Journal of Sociology*
- Peer review

- **Remain Objective and Avoid Bias**
  - Types of Bias
    - your own assumptions and values
    - embedded within the research design itself

Copyright © Allyn & Bacon 2009

Avoid Overstating Results

- **Remain Objective and Avoid Bias**
  - prejudice/assumptions contaminate results
  - **bias**
    - *your own assumptions*
    - *the research design itself*

- **Avoid Overstating Results**
  - saying a lot about a little
  - saying a little about a lot
  - relationships between variables
    - **correlation**

Copyright © Allyn & Bacon 2009

Avoid Overstating Results

- **Maintain Professional Ethics**
  - research should not hurt participants
  - CORIHS (Committee on Research Involving Human Subjects)
- **Institutional Review Board**
  - *Informed consent*
  - *Continuous consent*
  - *Confidentiality*
  - *Anonymity*
  - *Deception*
  - *Harm*
  - *Protected groups*

Demands of Research   Rights of subjects

Copyright © Allyn & Bacon 2009

Social Science Methods in the Future: Emergent Methodologies

- *"field experiments"*
- *new survey technology*
- *virtual online communities*

Copyright © Allyn & Bacon 2009

What Does America Think?

4.1 Happiness

Taken all together, how would you say things are these days? Would you say that you are very happy, pretty happy, or not too happy? In 1971, 17 percent of respondents said they were not too happy; in 2004 it was much lower at 12 percent. Differences between Whites and Blacks were significant in 1972, with 32 percent of White respondents and 19 percent of Black respondents saying they were very happy. Black respondents were almost twice as likely to say they were not too happy than were Whites. By 2004, those differences had evened out; 34.8 percent of White respondents and 34.0 percent of Black respondents said they were very happy. In 2004, 10.5 percent of White respondents and 16.4 percent of Black respondents reported being not too happy.

CRITICAL THINKING | DISCUSSION QUESTIONS

1. What do you think the researchers were actually measuring with their survey question? If you were going to measure happiness in a survey, how would you operationalize the term, "happiness?"
2. What social and historical factors contributed to the increase in Black respondents' reported level of happiness between 1972 and 2004?

Copyright © Allyn & Bacon 2009

What Does America Think?

4.2 2000 Presidential Election

This is based on actual survey data from the General Social Survey, 2004

1. If you voted in the 2000 presidential elections, did you vote for Gore, Bush, Nader or someone else? While the numbers do not match up exactly with official vote counts, they are within an appropriate margin of error. The votes were split nearly half-and-half between Gore and Bush. What is interesting here is the differences in voting when we look at gender and race. Women were more likely to vote for Gore, and men were more likely to vote for Bush. The difference was only about 10 percent in each case. Black voters were dramatically more likely to have voted for Gore than for Bush, and White voters were more likely to have voted for Bush.

CRITICAL THINKING | DISCUSSION QUESTIONS

1. Why is there such a dramatic difference with regard to race?
2. Do you think if you broke down the results by gender and by race that you would find even more dramatic differences? What might explain the differences?

Copyright © Allyn & Bacon 2009

What Does America Think?

▶ Go to this website to look further at the data. You can run your own statistics and crosstabs here: http://sda.berkeley.edu/cgi-bin/hsda?harcsda+gss04

REFERENCES: Davis, James A., Tom W. Smith, and Peter V. Marsden. General Social Surveys 1972–2004: [Cumulative file] [Computer file]. 2nd ICPSR version. Chicago, IL: National Opinion Research Center [producer], 2005; Storrs, CT: Roper Center for Public Opinion Research, University of Connecticut; Ann Arbor, MI: Inter-University Consortium for Political and Social Research; Berkeley, CA: Computer-Assisted Survey Methods Program, University of California [distributors], 2005.

Copyright © Allyn & Bacon 2009

Chapter 5
Socialization

Chapter Outline

I. Socialization and Biology
    a. Our identity is based on the interplay of nature and nurture.
        i. Nature means our physical makeup.
        ii. Nurture means how we grow up.
    b. Socialization is the process by which we become aware of ourselves as part of a group, learn how to communicate with others in the group, and learn the behavior expected of us.
        i. Can take place through formal instruction.
        ii. Can take place informally by observing other people's behaviors and reactions.

II. Socialization in Action
    a. Some mammals are born helpless and must spend some time "growing up," learning how to find food and shelter, elude predators, and get along with others.
    b. Feral Children
        i. "Wild Boy of Aveyron."
        ii. Most feral children are probably children with mental deficiencies abandoned at a much later age.
    c. Isolated Children
        i. Some children have been isolated from almost all human contact by abusive caregivers.
        ii. "Isabelle"
            1. Was kept locked in a room with no human contact with the outside world.
            2. When she was 6 she escaped from confinement
            3. She was unable to speak.
        iii. Some can recover with effort and specialized care, but others suffer permanent damage.
    d. Primates
        i. Require the longest period of socialization other than humans.
        ii. Rhesus monkey experiment showed that the monkeys raised apart from others of their species and found severe physical and emotional problems.

III. Stages in Socialization
    a. George Herbert Mead developed a stage theory of socialization.
        i. Imitation
        ii. Play
        iii. Games
    b. Jean Piaget studied children of different ages to see how they solve problems, how they make sense of the world.
        i. Sensorimotor stage (birth to age 2)- children experience the world only through their senses.
        ii. Preoperational (2-7 years)- children are capable of understanding and articulating speech and symbols, but can not understand common concepts like weight.
        iii. Concrete operational stage (7-12 years)- children understand causal relationships and common concepts, but the can not reach conclusions through general principles.
        iv. Formal operational stage (12 years and up)- children are now capable of abstract thought and reasoning.
    c. Lawrence Kohlberg built upon the ideas of Piaget to argue that we develop moral reasoning in three stages:
        i. Preconventional (birth to age 9)- morality means avoiding punishment and gaining rewards.
        ii. Conventional (ages 9 to 20)- morality depends on children or teenagers' ability to move beyond their immediate desires to a larger social context.

        iii.   Postconventional (older than 20)- we are able to see relative morality, viewing acts as good in some situations but no others.

    d.   Sigmund Freud believed that the self consisted of three elements.

        i.   Id- inborn drive for self-gratification.

        ii.   Superego- internalizes norms and values.

        iii.   Ego- channels impulses into socially acceptable forms.

    e.   Freud also believed that each child passes through three stages of development to become a healthy adult male or female.

        i.   Oral stage- infant derives gratification from breast feeding; sensually pleasurable activity.

        ii.   Anal stage- after being weaned the baby derives gratification form urination and defecation; bodily functions are a source of pleasure.

        iii.   Oedipal stage- boy becomes "masculine" and the girl "feminine" by identifying with the parent of the same sex.

    f.   Problems with Stage Theories

        i.   The stages are rigidly defined.

        ii.   It is not clear that the failure to meet the challenges of one stage means permanent failure.

        iii.   The theorists maintain that the stages are universal.

        iv.   They assume that one passes through a stage fully and never returns to that stage.

    g.   There are two other socialization processes that are important to consider

        i.   Anticipatory socialization- when you begin to enact the behaviors and traits of the status you expect to occupy.

        ii.   Resocialization- involves learning new values, behaviors, and attitudes that are different from those you previously held.

IV.   Agents of Socialization

    a.   People, groups, or social institutions that socialize new members, either formally or informally.

        i.   Primary socialization- occurs during childhood and gives us basic behavioral patterns, but allows for adaptation and change later on.

        ii.   Secondary socialization- occurs throughout life and gives us new behavioral patterns necessary for the new situation.

    b.   Family

        i.   There are many different child rearing systems in cultures around the world.

        ii.   Our family gives us our first statuses, our definitions of ourselves as belonging to a certain class, nationality, race, ethnicity, religion, and gender.

        iii.   Studies show that different sorts of families socialize their children in different ways.

            1.   Working-class families are primarily interested in teaching the importance of outward conformity.

            2.   Middle-class families focus on developing children's curiosity, creativity, and good judgment.

    c.   Education

        i.   In modern societies we spend almost a third of our lives in school.

        ii.   Education instills social norms and values, such as the importance of competition.

        iii.   Education socializes us not only into social class, but into race, gender, and sexual identity statuses.

    d.   Religion

        i.   We are socialized into religious beliefs in many places.

            1.   Church services.

            2.   Internet.

        ii.   Religion is an important agent of socialization because it provides a divine motivation for instilling social norms in children and adults.

        iii.   In traditional societies, religion is an ascribed status.

    e.   Peers

        i.   Peer groups are friends that are usually age specific.

        ii.   Peer groups have an enormous socializing influence, especially during middle and late childhood.
1. They provide an enclave where we can learn the skills of social interaction and the importance of loyalty.
2. Peers teach social interaction through coercion, humiliation, and bullying as well as through encouragement, and group loyalty often means being condescending, mean or even violent to members of out-groups.

     f.   Mass Media
        i.   Television is probably the dominant form of mass media across the world.
1. The higher the socioeconomic status the less television viewing.
2. Women watch more than men.
3. African Americans more than Whites.
        ii.   Video games are increasingly becoming an important form of mass media.
        iii.   For teenagers, music and magazines play a great role as television in socialization.

     g.   The Workplace
        i.   In modern societies we receive specialized training and have jobs that usually require us to leave home and family and spend all day in a workplace.
        ii.   Workplaces are similar to schools in many ways.

V.   Socialization and the Life Course
   a.   Childhood (Birth to Puberty)
        i.   In modern societies we assume that they have interests, abilities, beliefs, and goals that differ from teenagers and adults.
        ii.   This notion of childhood seems like common sense, it is not universal.
        iii.   Industrialization changed the way we see childhood.
   b.   Adolescence (Roughly the Teen Years)
        i.   Biological changes that occur in puberty are universal, but the timing changes from culture to culture and over time.
        ii.   Psychologists in the early 20th century began to define adolescence as a stage of life in modern societies.
        iii.   The boundary between childhood or adolescence and adulthood is marked by many milestones, called rites of passage.
   c.   Adulthood
        i.   Most social scientists measure the transition to adulthood by the completion of five demographic markers:
1. Complete your education.
2. Get a job.
3. Get married.
4. Leave your parents' home and move into you own place.
5. Have a baby.
        ii.   Young adulthood is a social category based on the modern need to postpone full adulthood for years past adolescence.
        iii.   Middle age occurs roughly from age 30 to 60.
        iv.   Above the age of 60 has been referred to as "old age."

VI.   Gender Socialization
   a.   We are socialized into the norms and expectations of age categories.
   b.   We are also socialized into all of our roles and statuses.
   c.   Socialization into gender is one of the most profound and thorough, occupying a great deal of the time and energy of a great many agents of socialization throughout the life course.
        i.   Boys and girls undergo gender socialization to accept two entirely different sets of social norms.
        ii.   Both groups are punished for transgressions by every agent of socialization.
   d.   We are bombarded with media images every day about appropriate masculinity and femininity.

VII.   Socialization in the 21st Century
   a.   The socialization process is dynamic and continuous.

   b.   One never achieves or reaches a "true" identity but is always interacting and reacting to create what can only be a temporary or partial "self."

Chapter Summary

- Nature means our physical makeup while nurture means how we grow up.
- Humans are not born with all the information they need to survive and must spend time "growing up," learning how to find food and shelter, elude predators, and get along with others.
- Feral children are those who have never had contact with other humans and are not socialized to interact with other people and maybe a myth.
- Isolated children can overcome the lack of childhood socialization with exceptional effort and specialized care.
- George Herbert Mead developed a stage theory of socialization, stages through which children pass as they become better integrated into society that include: imitation, play, and games.
- Jean Piaget's study of children lead him to argue that children's reasoning abilities develops in four stages: sensorimotor, preoperational, concrete operational, and formal operational, each building off the previous one.
- Lawrence Kohlberg built upon Piaget's idea to argue that we develop moral reasoning in three stages: preconventional, conventional, and postconventional.
- Sigmund Freud believed the self considered three elements that are interrelated: the id, superego, and ego. He also believed that children pass through three stages of development to become a healthy adult male or female and these stages included: the oral stage, anal stage, and the oedipal stage.
- There are many problems with stage theories such as, the stages are roughly defined, they are not clear that failure to meet the challenges of one stage means permanent failure, and the theorists usually maintain that the stages are universal.
- There are two other socialization process to that are important to consider which are anticipatory socialization and resocialization.
- Agents of socialization are people, groups, or social institutions that socialize new members either formally or informally. Agents of socialization can be family, friends, education, religion, mass media, and the workplace.
- Socialization takes place over the life course.
- The stages of the life course are primarily social constructions that differ widely from culture to culture and strongly influenced by statuses like race, class, gender, and nationality and by material circumstance.
- Modern societies breaks the life course into childhood, adolescence, and adulthood. Adulthood is broken down into young adulthood, middle age, and old age.
- We are socialized into all of our roles and statuses.
- Socialization into gender is one of the most profound and thorough, occupying a great deal of the time and energy of a great many agents of socialization through the life course.
- The socialization process is dynamic and continuous.
- One never achieves or reaches a true identity but is always interaction and reacting to create what can only be a temporary or partial self.

Learning Objectives

After completing the reading of Chapter 5, you should be able to answer the following objectives.

- Discuss the nature and nurture debate and the history of this debate.
- Understand that socialization is a process and what happens when a person is not properly socialized.
- Identify the different stage theories developed by Mead, Piaget, Kohlberg, and Freud. State the strengths and limitations of each theory.
- Discuss the other two socialization processes that are important: anticipatory socialization and resocialization.
- Know the different agents of socialization in American society and how each influences people's attitudes and behaviors.

- Understand why socialization is a life long process and discuss the needs and expectations that typically accompany different stages of life.
- Know what is meant by socialization and understand how it is a life long process.

Key Terms

Agents of Socialization: people, groups, or social institutions that socialize new members, either formally or informally.

Anticipatory Socialization: when you begin to enact the behaviors and traits of the status you expect to occupy.

Ego: balancing force between the id and superego and channels impulses into socially acceptable forms.

Gender Socialization: to accept two entirely different sets of social norms for boys and girls.

Generalized other: an individual taking on the role of their group as a whole.

Groupthink: process by which group members try to preserve harmony and unity in spite of their individual judgments.

Id: pure impulse, without worrying about social rules, consequences, morality, or other people's reactions.

Peer Groups: friends that are usually age specific.

Primary Socialization: occurs during childhood and gives us basic behavioral patterns, but allows for adaptation and change later on.

Resocialization: learning new sets of values, behaviors, and attitudes that are different from those you previously held.

Secondary Socialization: occurs throughout life every time we start a new class or new job, move to a new neighborhood, make new friends, or change social roles, allowing us to abandon old, outdates, or unnecessary behavior patterns, giving us new behavior patterns necessary for the new situation.

Socialization: process by which we become aware of ourselves as part of a group, learn how to communicate with other in the groups, and learn the behavior expected of us.

Superego: internalized norms and values, the "rules" of our social group, learned from family, friends, and social institutions.

Key People

Sigmund Freud: founder of psychoanalysis and believed that the self consisted of three elements that were interrelated.

Lawrence Kohlberg: believe that people develop moral reasoning in three stages.

George Herbert Mead: developed a stage theory of socialization, stages through which children pass as they become better integrated into society.

Jean Piaget: argued that children's reasoning ability develops in four stages, each building on the last one.

Additional Learning with MySocLab

Read

Life After Home Schooling (pg 152)
The article discusses the effects of homeschooling on children's socialization process.

Explore

Different Gender Stereotypes (pg 160)
Explore this important phenomenon further, when done think about experiences that have challenged your notions of gender roles.

Piaget's Stages of Cognitive Development (pg 145)
This exercise further explains Piaget's stages of reasoning by taking you through all of the different stages.

Listen

Nature-Nurture Debate (pg 141)
Whether human behavior is a result of heredity or environment is a long running debate. As the text points out it is not nature or nurture, but both that create our identity. Listen to the audio clip to understand how framing the debate as nature vs. nurture is too narrow.

Watch

Understanding Adolescence in Our Society (pg 158)
Spencer Cahill discusses his research on notes exchanged by adolescents and how that has contributed to our understanding of being an adolescent in our society.

Visualize

Theories of Human Development (pg 148)
The chart presented lays out the different types of theories of human development, who the theories was, what the stages are, and the central principles of each theory.

Practice Test

After completing the practice test, check your answers in the Answer Key of this Study Guide.

Multiple Choice Questions

1. What is the life long process by which we become aware of ourselves as part of a group, learn how to communicate with other in the group, and learn the behavior expected of you?
   - a. Anticipatory socialization
   - b. Resocialization
   - c. Socialization
   - d. Social process

2. The case of "Isabelle," this isolated girl who was born to a unmarried, deaf-mute teenager, shows that:
   - a. humans are born socialized.
   - b. without social experience, child are incapable of interacting with others.
   - c. children can never overcome the effects of isolation.
   - d. the lack of socialization has no consequences for children.

3. Which stage in Mead's stage theory of socialization argues that children imitate others, but cannot usually put themselves into the role of other?
   - a. Imitation
   - b. Play
   - c. Game
   - d. Role playing

4. In the nature versus nurture debate, most social scientists believe:
   - a. only nurture is important.
   - b. only nature is important.
   - c. nurture is somewhat important but not as much as nature.
   - d. both nature and nurture are important.

5. The Harlow's experiments to discover the effects of social isolation on rhesus monkeys showed that:
   - a. monkey are not anxious when returned to their mother after being isolated.
   - b. isolation of six months produced the same results of being isolated for three months.
   - c. these monkeys were able to readjust to their "regular" life of living with other monkeys.
   - d. the monkeys that were isolated for six months were highly anxious when returned to their own kind.

6. Our ability to internalize norms and values of our social groups are reflected in Freud's concept of:
   - a. id.
   - b. superego.
   - c. ego.
   - d. None of the above.

7. Which stage of Piaget's cognitive theory of development believed that children are capable of understanding and articulating speech and symbols, but can not understand common concepts like weight?
   - a. Sensorimotor stage
   - b. Preoperational stage
   - c. Concrete operational stage
   - d. Formal operational stage

8. Lawrence Kohlberg's focus was on:
   - a. the generalized other.
   - b. cognition: how people think and understand.
   - c. the development of morality.
   - d. gratification.

9. Carol Gilligan expanded Kohlberg's work by showing which of the following:
    a. girls and boys typically use different standards in assessing situations as right and wrong.
    b. women tend to gravitate more toward care and men toward ethics.
    c. there are differences in the men's and women's guides for moral reasoning.
    d. All of the above.

10. Mead placed the origin of the self in:
    a. culture.
    b. social experience.
    c. the generalized other.
    d. the games children play.

11. Which of the following statements comes closest to describing Piaget's view of socialization?
    a. Personality develops over the entire life course in patterned stages.
    b. Children's reasoning ability and their ability to solve problems and makes sense of the world develops over time.
    c. Children's come to see themselves as the others see them
    d. Children's morality forms their personality from birth.

12. Which socialization process considers the idea that people begin to enact the behaviors and traits of the status that you expect to occupy?
    a. Resocialization
    b. Moral development
    c. Personality development
    d. Anticipatory

13. Which agent of socialization gives us our first statuses?
    a. Family
    b. Peer Group
    d. Media
    c. School

14. Those who reside in industrialized countries tend to define people in old age as:
    a. the most wise.
    b. the most knowledgeable about current trends.
    c. less important than young adults.
    d. All of the above.

15. Which of the following is not true about gender socialization?
    a. Boys are expected to be tough and therefore socialized as so.
    b. Girls are socialized to be passive and quiet.
    c. Boys and girls are punished if they transgress from their proper roles.
    d. This process only occurs during childhood.

16. According to several researchers including Pollack and Garbarino, boys are taught to refrain from which of the following:
    a. crying.
    b. showing vulnerability.
    c. show any emotion.
    d. all of the above.

17. In what year was the term "teenager" first used?
    a. 1944
    b. 1950
    c. 1965
    d. 1973

18. In what region of the world has the highest internet usage?
    a. South America
    b. Sub-Saharan Africa
    c. Eastern Europe
    d. North America

19. Adolescences tend to learn about love and relationships from which agent of socialization?
    a. Family
    b. Peers
    c. Media
    d. School

20. Status incongruity refers to:
    a. our skills not matching our occupations.
    b. being of one race but acting like another.
    c. living in two worlds at the same time.
    d. none of the above.

21. Freud believed that homosexuality was the result of what?
    a. Children identifying with the parent of the opposite sex
    b. Children failing to identify with the opposite-sex parent
    c. Children failing to receive gratification from urination and defecation
    d. Children being mentally unstable

22. Which stage of Piaget's cognitive theory of development states that children are capable of abstract though?
    a. Sensorimotor stage
    b. Preoperational stage
    c. Concrete operational stage
    d. Formal operational stage

23. The sociological perspective sees identity not as a possession but as a _____.
    a. Process
    b. Short term goal
    c. Socialization
    d. Initiative

24. Maternal instinct:
    a. Is natural in every woman.
    b. Occurs immediately at the birth of the child.
    c. Biological.
    d. Is part of the social expectation.

25. At what age do children go through the concrete operational stage in Jean Piaget's cognitive theory of development?
    a. Birth- 2 years
    b. 2-7 years
    c. 7-12 years
    d. 12 years and older

True/False Questions

True   False   1. Studies of primates suggest that animas react in similar ways to humans when isolated.

True   False   2. Jean Piaget introduced the concept of the generalized other to sociology.

True   False   3. During Lawrence Kohlberg's preconventional stage children are able to move beyond their immediate desires to a larger social context.

True   False   4. The assumption that effeminate men are gay and masculine women are lesbians comes from Sigmund Freud's stages of development.

True   False   5. Primary socialization occurs through family and friends.

True   False   6. Religion provides motivation for instilling social norms in children and adults.

True   False   7. Childhood is a universal notion for all cultures in the life course.

True   False   8. Men and women are socialized the same from birth through adulthood.

True   False   9. A person who switches from being a waitress to managing a clothing store will experience the process of resocialization.

True   False   10. The stage theories presented in the chapter assume that one passes through a stage fully and never returns to that stage.

Fill-in-the-Blank Questions

1. The ability to take on the role of the group as a whole is the _____.

2. The ego is developed to balance the _____ and the _____.

3. The process of learning a new set of values, behaviors, and attitudes that are different from those you previously held is _____.

4. The stage that falls after adolescence is _____.

5. In modern society old age is said to begin around age _____.

6. _____ is the stage where children experience the world only through their senses.

7. According to Kohlberg during this stage humans are able to view some acts as essentially good or bad.

8. _____ occurs throughout life giving us new behavioral patterns necessary for the new situation.

9. Television, video games, music, and magazines are all examples of _____.

10. _____ provide a cultural mechanism for members of a particular culture to pass from one developmental stage to adulthood.

Essay Questions

1. Discuss Piaget's Cognitive Theory of Development. What are the four stages, how old are people when they are in the stages, and what are the characteristics of each stage?

2. Explain the nature-nurture debate. Discuss which side of the debate Mead and Freud would be on and why.

3. How do the family, peers, school, mass media, and work contribute to the socialization process?

4. Discuss the various stages of the human life course: childhood, adolescence, and adulthood. What are the characteristics of each and how have they changed throughout time.

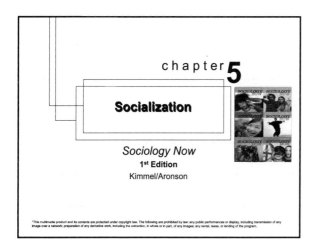

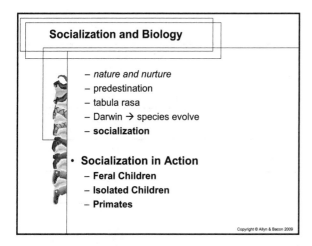

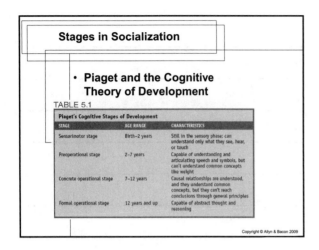

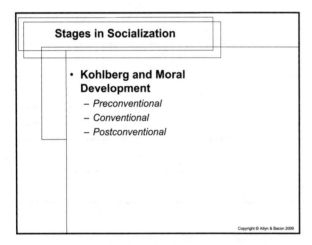

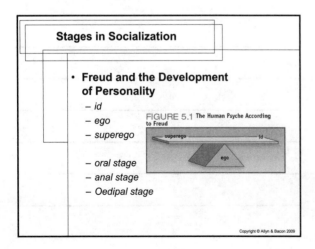

Stages in Socialization

- **Problems with Stage Theories**
  - rigidly defined
  - unfixable failure
  - stages assumed "universal"

  - **Anticipatory socialization**

  - **Resocialization**

Copyright © Allyn & Bacon 2009

Agents of Socialization

  - primary socialization
  - secondary socialization

- **Family**
- **Education**
- **Religion**
- **Peers**
- **Mass Media**
- **The Workplace**

Copyright © Allyn & Bacon 2009

Socialization and the Life Course

- **Childhood** (Birth to Puberty)
- **Adolescence** (Roughly the Teen Years)
- **Adulthood**
  - complete education
  - get a job
  - get married
  - leave parent's home
  - have a baby

Copyright © Allyn & Bacon 2009

Gender Socialization

– **gender socialization**
  - pink or blue
  - two sets of social norms
  - punishment for nonconformity

- **Socialization in the 21ˢᵗ Century**

What Does America Think?

5.1 Belief in an Afterlife

These are actual survey data from the General Social Survey, 1998.

Do you believe in life after death? Data from the General Social Survey for the 1990s show the following: More than half of the respondents definitely believed in life after death, and another one-fifth probably did. Only slightly more than 20 percent did not believe in life after death. More women than men believed in an afterlife (59.3 percent versus 53.3). Social class differences were not that marked.

CRITICAL THINKING | DISCUSSION QUESTIONS

1. From the GSS data seen above, it appears that Americans in general tend to believe in life after death. How does this reflect the character of American society and core American values?
2. Each religion has different ideas about the afterlife. How do history and culture affect how a religious group conceives its ideas about an afterlife?
3. This is one topic where there seems to be very little deviation with regard to either social class or gender. Why do you think that is?

What Does America Think?

5.2 Caring for Others

These are actual survey data from the General Social Survey, 2004.

People need not worry about others. One-quarter of respondents either agreed or strongly agreed with this statement. Another quarter was neutral. One-half disagreed or strongly disagreed. The gender differences in responses were striking. Men were far more likely to agree with the statement than were women. Almost 32 percent of the men agreed or strongly agreed, in contrast to almost 20 percent of the women.

CRITICAL THINKING | DISCUSSION QUESTIONS

1. How much we think we should care for others versus care for ourselves is heavily influenced by how we are socialized. One level of socialization is that of the larger culture. What core values do you think Americans in general hold that might help explain these survey results?
2. What do you think lies behind the variation of responses with regard to gender? What stereotypically masculine qualities might make men report that they are less worried about the needs of others than women are? What stereotypically feminine qualities might teach women that it is appropriate to care for others? Where do we learn these qualities?

What Does America Think?

▶ Go to this website to look further at the data. You can run your own statistics and cross tabs here: **http://sda.berkeley.edu/cgi-bin/hsda?harcsda+gss04**

REFERENCES: Davis, James A., Tom W. Smith, and Peter V. Marsden. General Social Surveys 1972–2004: [Cumulative file] [Computer file]. 2nd ICPSR version. Chicago, IL: National Opinion Research Center [producer], 2005; Storrs, CT: Roper Center for Public Opinion Research, University of Connecticut; Ann Arbor, MI: Inter-university Consortium for Political and Social Research; Berkeley, CA: Computer-Assisted Survey Methods Program, University of California [distributors], 2005.

Chapter 6
Deviance and Crime

Chapter Outline

I.   What is Deviance?
- a.   Breaking a social rule, or refusing to follow one.
- b.   We can be considered deviant without doing, saying, or believing anything bad or wrong just by belonging to a stigmatized minority group.
- c.   Most deviance is not illegal.

II.   Conformity and Social Control
- a.   Every culture develops different types of rules, they vary by how formalized they are.
    - i.   Folkways are routine, usually unspoken conventions of behavior.
    - ii.   Mores are norms with strong moral significance.
    - iii.   Taboos are prohibitions viewed as essential to the well-being of humanity.
- b.   Stigma
    - i.   An attribute that changes you "from a whole and usual person to a tainted and discounted one."
    - ii.   Goffman identified three strategies to neutralize stigma and save yourself from having a spoiled identity.
        1.   Minstrelization- to exaggerate the difference between the stigmatized and dominant group.
        2.   Normification- process by which one minimizes the differences between the stigmatized groups.
        3.   Militant chauvinism- maximize differences by saying that they are better.
- c.   Deviant Subculture
    - i.   Group that evolves within a dominant culture, always more or less hidden and closed to outsiders.
    - ii.   For deviant subcultures to develop they must meet three characteristics.
        1.   It must be punished but not punished too much.
        2.   It must have enough participants but not too many.
        3.   It must be complex but not too complex.
    - iii.   Youth Gangs as Deviant Subculture
        1.   Most gangs are composed of poor or working class adolescents, typically male.
        2.   Females represent a small proportion of youth gang members, but their numbers have been increasing in recent years.
        3.   Adolescents join gangs because of friends and relatives who already belong to the gang, a desire for excitement, a need for protection, and the availability of money, drugs, and alcohol.
    - iv.   Youth Gangs Today
        1.   Today youth gangs are well-armed and financed.
        2.   Gangs are now a form of organized crime.

III.   Deviance and Social Coherence
- a.   Durkheim argues that deviance is useful to society in four ways.
    - i.   It affirms cultural norms and values.
    - ii.   It clarifies moral boundaries.
    - iii.   It heightens group solidarity.
    - iv.   It encourages social change.
- b.   Explaining Deviance
    - i.   Differential Association
        1.   It is a matter of rewards and punishment.
        2.   Deviance occurs when an individual receives more prestige and less punishment by violating norms rather than by following them.

          3. Refers to the fact that we might have more than one reference group that helps us decide what we want to do.

    ii. Control Theory

        1. People do not obey lots of hidden forces.

            a. They are rational, so they decide whether or not to engage in an act by weighing the potential outcome.

            b. If there are no negative consequences you would be likely to participate in the behavior.

        2. Cost-benefit analysis

            a. Weigh the respective costs of doing something against the benefits of doing it.

            b. People who have very little to lose are most likely to become rule-breakers.

        3. People are subject to inner and outer controls; these do their job in four ways.

            a. Attachment

            b. Commitment

            c. Involvement

            d. Belief

    iii. Labeling Theory

        1. Stresses the relativity of deviance.

            a. Describes a relationship between a dominant group and the actor.

            b. For something to be deviant it has to be labeled so.

        2. It understands deviance to be a process, not a categorical difference between the deviant and the non-deviant.

        3. To become deviant you agree with the labels other people ascribe to you.

        4. Three types of deviance:

            a. Primary deviance- provokes little reaction and has little effect on your self concept.

            b. Secondary deviance- rule breaking is an indication of a permanent personality trait.

            c. Tertiary deviance- a group formerly labeled deviant attempts to redefine their acts.

  c. Deviance and Inequality

    i. Sociologists argue that deviance is also the product of the bad, wrong, and unfair social conditions of people's lives.

    ii. Relationship between inequality and deviance often leads us to see and punish the behaviors of the less fortunate and forgive the behavior of the more fortunate.

IV. Deviance and Crime

  a. Crime is any act that violates a formal normative code that has been enacted by a legally constituted body.

  b. Strain Theory

    i. Excessive deviance is a by-product of inequality.

        1. When society promotes certain goals but provides unequal means of acquiring them, the result is anomie, a conflict between accepted norms and social reality.

        2. According to Merton there are five potential reactions to the tension between widely endorsed values and limited means of achieving them.

            a. Conformist

            b. Innovators

            c. Ritualists

            d. Rebels

            e. Retreatists

    ii. Critic point out that not everyone shares the same goals.

  c. "Broken Windows" Theory

           i.   Explains how social controls can systematically weaken, and minor acts of deviance can spiral into severe crime and social decay.

          ii. Decaying houses and preexisting crime contributes to increased crime.

   d.   Criminal Subcultures

           i.   Cohen drew on Edward Sutherland's theory of differential association to propose that gang members were not being socialized with the same norms and values as non-gang members.

          ii. The five most important values for Cohen were:

                1. Nonutilitarianism

                2. Maliciousness

                3. Negativism

                4. Short-run hedonism

                5. Group autonomy

         iii. Walter B. Miller argued that there are six core values that differ from lower-class subculture and main society.

                1. Trouble

                2. Toughness

                3. Smartness

                4. Excitement

                5. Fate

                6. Autonomy

   e.   Opportunity Theory

           i.   Crime arises from opportunity to commit crime.

          ii. Revised differential association theory to propose several different types of deviant subcultures based on the opportunity to deviate:

                1. Criminal subcultures

                2. Violence subcultures

                3. Retreatist subcultures

   f.   Conflict Theory

           i.   Resemble inequality theories of deviance is that they rest on a larger structural analysis of inequalities based on class, or race, or gender, for their explanation of crime.

          ii. Quinney argued that the dominant class produces deviance by making and enforcing laws that protect its own interest and oppress the subordinate class.

V.   Types of Crime

   a.   Violent Crime- consists of four offenses: murder, forcible rape, robbery, and aggravated assault.

   b.   Property Crime- includes offenses like burglary and motor vehicle theft, where the object is the taking of money or property, but there is no force or threat of force.

   c.   Crime at Work

           i.   White-collar crime- illegal action of a corporation or people acting on its behalf.

          ii. Consumer crimes- credit card fraud.

         iii. Occupational crime- using their professional position to illegally secure something of value for themselves or the corporation.

         iv. Organizational crime- illegal actions committed in accordance with the operative goals of an organization.

   d.   Cybercrime

           i.   Use of the Internet and World Wide Web to commit a crime.

          ii. Some of these crimes involve fraudulent maneuvers to get victims to reveal personal information that can then be used to commit crimes.

   e.   Hate Crime

           i.   Criminal act committed by an offender motivated by bias against race, ethnicity, religion, sexual orientation, or disability status.

          ii. Hate crime legislation

         1.   Advocates of hate crime laws argue that hate crimes affect not only the individual but the entire community, so they should be punished more harshly.

         2.   Opponents of the law argue that they punish attitudes, not actions.

VI.   Crime in the United States

    a.   When compared to most other advanced countries, the U.S. stands out for its very high homicide rate.

    b.   Why should the crime rate be falling?

       i.   Expanding economy.

       ii.   Aging population.

      iii.   Increase in the number of police officers.

      iv.   Decrease in the number of young males.

       v.   Longer jail sentences.

      vi.   Declining sales of crack cocaine.

     vii.   Increase in immigration by females.

    viii.   Legalization of abortion.

      ix.   The "little-brother syndrome"

    c.   Crime and Guns

       i.   United States has the weakest laws on handgun ownership in the industrialized world.

       ii.   The U.S. has had difficulty passing minimal regulations to monitor the distribution of guns.

    d.   Crime and Gender

       i.   Women are significantly less likely to be arrested, less likely to be convicted, and less likely to serve sentences.

       ii.   Men commit more violent and property crimes than women.

    e.   Crime and Race

       i.   African Americans are arrested at a rate of two, three, even five times greater than statistical probability.

       ii.   Latinos are overrepresented in the U.S. criminal justice system.

      iii.   Theories that offer a perspective on this issue:

         1.   Strain Theory

         2.   Differential Opportunity

         3.   Labeling

         4.   Conflict

    f.   Crime and Age

       i.   Since the 1940s minors have been committing far more than their share of crimes.

       ii.   Sociologists point to gang activity, which has infiltrated every aspect of community life.

    g.   Crime and class

       i.   Historically, those with less power in society have been morel ikley to be arrested.

       ii.   The poorer you are the more likely that you will be arrested for a crime.

      iii.   The poorer you are the more likely that you will be a victim of a crime.

VII.   The Criminal Justice System

    a.   The Police

       i.   The number of police officers has roughly doubled over the past 30 years.

       ii.   Police officers actually spend only about 20% of their time in crime-fighting activity.

      iii.   Police have a split image

         1.   To some the police make them feel safe and secure.

         2.   To others the police are a threat.

    b.   Courts

       i.   The district attorney's office prosecutes those arrested by the police for criminal offenses.

       ii.   1990s mandatory sentencing.

         1.   Laws were supposed to be tough on crime and eliminate bias in sentencing.

         2.   Main result has been an explosion in the prison population.

    c.   Punishment and Corrections
       i.   Today the U.S. has 2.2 million people in jail or prison.
      ii.   Prisons
           1.   People convicted of crimes may be asked to pay fines and restitution to victims or to engage in community service, but for most the penalty is incarceration.
           2.   The four goals of incarceration:
               a.   Retribution
               b.   Deterrence
               c.   Protection
               d.   Rehabilitation
           3.   Prisons offer few rehab programs.
     iii.   The Death Penalty
           1.   Fewer than half of all countries in the world have the death penalty.
           2.   Most countries use capital punishment for extraordinary crimes while others use it for some business and drug-related offenses.
           3.   Who can be executed in the U.S.?
               a.   In 1989 Supreme Court decided that it was unconstitutional to execute the mentally ill.
               b.   In 1988 Supreme Court decided that it was unconstitutional to execute persons 15 years and younger.
               c.   American public generally favors the death penalty for adult offenders.

VIII.   Globalization and Crime
    a.   Global crime networks operate in every arena.
    b.   Much crime also remains "local"- an individual is assaulted or robbed in his or her own neighborhood.

IX.   Deviance and Crime in the 21st Century
    a.   Main question in deviance and crime is not why so many people break the rules but why so many people do not?
    b.   Sociological question will remain the same: How do people make the sorts of decisions about what laws to obey and which ones to break?

Chapter Summary

- Deviance refers to violations of social norms; what people consider deviant varies from one culture to another.
- Every culture has rules that prescribe what is considered appropriate behavior in that culture. They vary by how formalized they are, how central to social life, and the types of sanctions that are threatened should you break them.
- Stigma is an attribute that changes you from a whole and usual person to a tainted and discounted one. Goffman believed that stigmatized people have "spoiled identities and there are three strategies to adopt to alleviate the stigma.
- Deviant subcultures are more or less closed to outsiders and in order for a deviant subculture to develop there are three characteristics they must meet: it must be punished but not punished too much; it must have enough participants but not too many, and it must be complex but not too complex.
- Durkheim argued that deviance is useful to society in that it affirms cultural norms and values, it clarifies moral boundaries, it heightens group solidarity, and it encourages social change.
- Differential Association theory, control theory, and labeling theory all try to explain why deviance happens. According to differential association theory deviance occurs when an individual receives more prestige and less punishment by violating norms rather than following them. Control theory argues that there is a cost-benefit analysis during the decision making process and if the benefit outweighs the cost the individual is likely to engage in the behavior. Labeling theory stresses the relationship between a dominant group and the actor.
- Deviance is not solely a product of "bad" people or "wrong" behaviors but also of the bad, wrong, and unfair social conditions of people's lives.
- Crime can be defined as any act that violates a formal normative code that has been enacted by a legally constituted body.
- There are several different theories that try to explain crime. Biological theories tried to explain criminal behavior as being caused by a physical abnormality. Strain Theory argues that deviance is a by-product of inequality and our unequal means of acquiring certain goals in society. The "Broken Windows Theory" explains how the social controls of society can systematically weaken and minor acts of deviance can spiral into severe crime. Criminal subcultures form because the people belonging to them were not being socialized with the same norms and values as those who did not belong to the subcultures. Opportunity theory argues that crime actually arises from the opportunity to commit crime. Conflict theory rest of a larger structural analysis of inequalities based on race, class, or gender for their explanation of crime.
- There are several different types of crime: violent crime, property crime, white-collar crime, consumer crimes, occupational crime, organizational crime, cyber crime, and hate crimes.
- The United States has a very high rate of homicide compared to other industrialized nations.
- The United States has the weakest laws on handgun ownership in the industrialized world
- Crime varies by gender, race, age, and class. Men commit more crimes than women; African Americans and Latinos are overrepresented in the criminal justice system; young people commit more than their share of crimes; the poor are more likely to be arrested for a crime than those of higher social status.
- The criminal justice system consists of the police, courts, and prison system.
- The United States has 2.2 million people in jail or prison. Prison is the most common for of punishment and there are four goals of incarceration: retribution, deterrence, protection, and rehabilitation.
- The death penalty exists in the United States for adults who commit extraordinary crimes.
- Crime as a global enterprise has a long history, from ancient slave traders to criminal networks operating in many different countries.

Learning Objectives

After completing the reading of Chapter 6, you should be able to answer the following objectives.

- Define deviance and understand why it is relative.
- Understand the different types of social controls.
- Define stigma and understand Goffman's explanation of how people neutralize stigma.

- Know what a deviant subculture is and how they are formed.
- Discuss how Durkheim believed that deviance can be useful to society.
- Understand and discuss the theories for explaining deviance: differential association, control theory, and labeling theory.
- Know why sociologists do not believe that deviance is solely a product of bad people or wrong behaviors.
- Define crime.
- Understand and discuss the theories of crime: biological theories, strain theory, broken windows theory, criminal subcultures, opportunity theory, and conflict theory.
- Define the different types of crime (property, violent, white-collar, consumer, occupational, organizational, cyber, and hate) and understand the difference between them.
- Discuss crime in the United States and understand why the United States has such a high crime rate compared to other industrialized nations
- Discuss gender and crime, race and crime, age and crime, and class and crime. Know who is more likely to commit a crime and be incarcerated.
- Know the important parts of the criminal justice system: police, courts, and justice system.
- Discuss the four goals of the prison system.
- Talk about the death penalty in the United States and the world. Know who is eligible for the death penalty.
- Discuss globalization and crime in terms of the internet and global crime networks.

Key Terms

Broken Windows Theory: how social controls can systematically weaken, and minor acts of deviance can spiral into severe crime and social decay.

Conflict Theory: rest on a larger structural analysis of inequalities based on class, or race, or gender for their explanation of crime.

Consumer Crime: credit card fraud.

Control Theory: decision of whether or not to engage in an act by weighing the potential outcome.

Crime: any act that violates a formal normative code that has been enacted by a legally constituted body.

Cybercrime: use of the Internet and World Wide Web to commit crime.

Deviance: one who breaks a social rule or refuses to follow one.

Differential association: it is a matter of rewards an punishment.

Folkways: routine, unspoken conventions of behavior.

Hate crime: criminal act committed by an offender motivated by bias against race, ethnicity, religion, sexual orientation, or disability status.

Labeling theory: the social context that determines whether an act is considered deviant or not and how much punishment it warrants.

Mores: norms with a strong moral significance, viewed as essential to the proper functioning of the group.

Occupational Crime: using professional position to illegally secure something of value for themselves or their corporation.

Organizational Crime: illegal actions committed in accordance with the operative goals of an organization.

Primary Deviance: provoke very little reaction and have little effect on your self-concept.

Property Crime: the object is the taking of money or property, but there is no force or threat of force against the victims.

Secondary deviance: repeatedly breaking a norm and people start reacting to it in a negative way.

Social controls: rules

Stigma: attribute that changes you from a whole and usual person to a tainted and discounted one.

Strain theory: conflict between accepted norms and social reality.

Subculture: group that evolves within a dominant culture, always more or less hidden and closed to outsiders.

Taboos: subset of mores that are prohibitions viewed as essential to the well-being of humanity.

Tertiary deviance: a group formerly labeled deviant attempts to redefine their acts, attributes, or identities as normal.

Violent crime: consists of murder, forcible rape, robbery, and aggravated assault.

White-collar crime: illegal actions of a corporation or people acting on its behalf.

Key People

Howard Becker: used the term labeling theory.

Richard Cloward and Lloyd Ohlin: argued that crime arises from opportunity to commit crime.

Emile Durkheim: argued that deviance is useful to society.

Erving Goffman: used the term stigma and identified three strategies to neutralize stigma and save yourself from having a spoiled identity.

Travis Hirschi: imagined that people do a "cost-benefit analysis" during their decision making process.

Robert K. Merton: argued that some deviance puts an enormous strain on social life and there are five potential reactions to the tensions between widely endorsed values and limited means of achieving them.

Edwin H. Sutherland: used theory of differential association and argued that individuals become deviant by associating with those who are already deviant.

Additional Learning with MySocLab

Read **Census Shows Bigger Houses And Incomes, but Not for All (pg 217)**
"The rich get richer while the poor get poorer." This statement has proven to be true in the US since the 1950s. The gap between the rich and the poor grew significantly during the 1990s and continues to be wide.
Rich Nations Are Criticized for Enforcing Trade Barriers (pg 224)
Billions and billions of dollars of traded goods leave and enter the US every year. Foreign policies often make or break corporations who profit from labor, materials, and buy and sell agreements with various international businesses. Since the colonization era of world history, Western countries have consistently created policies which profited their businesses at the expense of businesses in poorer regions of the world.
In Trenches of a War on Unyielding Poverty (pg 220)
In the US about thirteen percent of the population lives below the poverty line. Another twelve percent live near poverty.

Explore
Web Activity: Social Class (pg 224)
For this activity you will read the article "Understanding Poverty in America" and "The Changing Face of Poverty" to learn more about poverty in the United States and why it is a prevalent concern for many Americans. After reading the articles there is a series of questions to answer.
Ownership of Television Sets Worldwide (pg 230)
This activity allows for you to compare poverty globally based on the number of television sets per 1,000 people.

Listen
PEW Study: Globalization (pg 231)
NPR discusses the PEW Study on globalization. The new poll shows that people find food and medicine are more easily found all over the world; however many believe there are fewer good paying jobs and the gap between the rich and the poor growing.

Watch
Understanding Social Class (pg 211)
Susan Ostrander discusses what is meant by social class and some of the important debates surrounding the definition.
World Poverty Report (pg 225)
The video clip discusses how the UN and other international institutions have failed the poor people of the world and their roles need to be reexamined. Basic rights such as food and economic opportunity are still being denied.

Visualize
Income Distribution (pg 212)
The map illustrates the median household income distribution for states.

Practice Test

After completing the practice test, check your answers in the Answer Key of this Study Guide.

Multiple Choice Questions

1. What does the term deviance refer to?
    a. the violations of serious rules
    b. crime
    c. the violations of social rules
    d. the violation of taboos

2. There are different types of rules prescribe in society. Which one is viewed as routine and usually unspoken.
    a. Folkways
    b. Mores
    c. Taboos
    d. Norms

3. According to Goffman, stigma functions to:
    a. punish people because they violated a norm.
    b. reward people for following the norms.
    c. regulate people's behavior.
    d. to identify the person who violates the norm as deviant.

4. Goffman identified three different neutralization techniques to alleviate stigma. Which of the following in not one of them?
    a. Minsterlization
    b. Nonutilitarianism
    c. Normification
    d. Militant Chauvinism

5. Why is deviance useful for society?
    a. It affirms cultural norms
    b. It clarifies moral boundaries
    c. It encourages social change
    d. All of the above

6. Differential association theory suggests that deviance is a matter of:
    a. costs and benefits.
    b. rewards and punishments.
    c. attachment and commitment.
    d. labeling the person.

7. The idea of inner and outer controls work against our tendencies toward deviance is called:
    a. Differential Association Theory.
    b. Labeling Theory.
    c. Conflict Theory.
    d. Control Theory.

8. According to Travis Hirschi, what affects the effectiveness of our inner controls?
    a. our bonds to society
    b. our socioeconomic status
    c. our social institutions
    d. our wanting to belong

9. Edwin Lemert theorized that most acts of deviance fall within three categories. Which of the following is not one of them?
    a. Primary
    b. Secondary
    c. Tertiary
    d. Mores

10. The type of deviance that violates formal normative code that has been enacted by a legally constituted body is:
    a. Folkways.
    b. Crime.
    c. Taboos.
    d. Stigma.

11. Which theory believes that criminality is caused by using alternate means to reach shared goals?
    a. Strain Theory
    b. Criminal Subcultures
    c. Biological Theory
    d. Opportunity Theory

12. Cloward and Ohlin revied the differential association theory to proposed several different types of deviant subcultures based on the opportunities to deviate. Which of the following is not one that they proposed?
    a. Retreatist subcultures
    b. Criminal subcultures
    c. Violent subcultures
    d. Aggressive subcultures

13. What types of crime consists of an illegal action of a corporation or people acting on its behalf?
    a. violent crime
    b. white-collar crime
    c. organized crime
    d. occupational crime

14. All of the following are responses to anomie, except:
    a. conformist.
    b. ritualism.
    c. retreatism.
    d. recidivism.

15. Dan lives in a high crime neighborhood with poor schools. He believes that he will never be good enough to get into college and decides to quit school. To make money he starts selling drugs and quickly makes a lot of money with which he purchases expensive clothes and a new car. Dan's behavior reflects which of Merton's reaction to strain?
    a. Innovator
    b. Ritualist
    c. Rebel
    d. Retreatist

16. According to Walter B. Miller which of the following is not an important value of lower-class subcultures?
    a. Toughness
    b. Trouble
    c. Dullness
    d. Fate

17. Which minority group is the most disproportionately represented among the prison population of the United States?
    a. whites
    b. Asians
    c. Latinos
    d. African Americans

18. A _____ crime is a crime that is motivated by bias against someone's race, religion, ethnicity, sexual orientation, or disability status.
    a. discrimination
    b. vicious
    c. hate
    d. prejudicial

19. What is not one of the factors that contributed to the drop in crime?
    a. An increase in immigration by females
    b. shorter jail sentences for hard-core criminals
    c. an aging population
    d. an expanding economy

20. Which country has the lowest firearms death rate?
    a. United States
    b. France
    c. Belgium
    d. Poland

21. Which theory would explain the high incarceration rates of blacks due to social class and not race.
    a. Strain Theory
    b. Differential Association
    c. Labeling Theory
    d. Conflict Theory

22. The part of the criminal justice system that is responsible for the criminal proceedings is the:
    a. Police
    b. Courts
    c. Corrections
    d. None of the Above

23. Which of the four proposed goals of the prison system takes the criminal off of the street so they are not able to commit further crimes?
    a. Retribution
    d. Deterrence
    c. Protection
    d. Rehabilitation

24. The United States still uses the death penalty for extraordinary crimes, however the death penalty cannot be applied to everyone. Which group of people can not have the death penalty imposed on them?
    a. Adult males
    b. Mentally ill
    c. Children between the ages of 16 and 18
    d. Adult minorities

25. Which of the following is not one of the norms and values that those who are subjected to differential association, socialized into a new set of norms and values allows them to succeed on their own terms?
- a. Nonutilitarianism
- b. Maliciousness
- c. Negativism
- d. Toughness

True/False Questions

True   False   1. Deviance is always a crime.

True   False   2. A person does not always have to commit a deviant act to be considered deviant.

True   False   3. According to Emile Durkheim deviance is useful for a society.

True   False   4. Differential Association theory explains that deviance occurs when an individual receives more prestige and less punishment by violating norms rather than by following them.

True   False   5. Deviance is solely a product of bad people and wrong behaviors.

True   False   6. Conformists accept the values and reject the means to achieving their goal.

True   False   7. Violent crime consists of murder, forcible rape, robbery, and aggravated assault.

True   False   8. The death penalty is administered evenly across all races and classes in the United States.

True   False   9. Older people are more likely to commit every type of crime.

True   False   10. White-collar crime consists of illegal actions taken by a corporation or a person acting on its behalf.

Fill-in-the-Blank Questions

1. The term _____ is used to refer to any violation of a norm.

2. _____ deviance provokes very little reaction and has very little effect on self-concept.

3. Philip Zimbardo proposed the _____ to explain how social controls can systematically weaken.

4. A _____ crime is a criminal act committed by an offender motivated by bias against race, ethnicity, religion, sexual orientation, or disability status.

5. When a society promotes certain goals but provides unequal means of acquiring them, the result is _____.

6. Cloward and Ohlin emphasize _____ in their theory explaining deviance.

7. _____ are routine, usually unspoken conventions of behavior.

8. According to the _____, a worker who earns less than a fellow worker, might make a different calculation, and risk losing their job, figuring out that at such a low wage, one can easily get a comparable job.

9. _____ refers to crimes that people of respectable and high social status commit in the course of their occupations.

10. The United States has the _____ laws on handgun ownership in the industrialized world.

Essay Questions

1. Explain why the criminal justice system is or is not biased. Provide specific examples to support your answer.

2. Define deviance and crime. Explain the differences between the two and give examples for each.

3. What are the three main types of social controls? Explain them and give examples.

4. Describe the control theory. What basic insight about deviance is offered by this approach? What are the inner and outer controls and how do they do their job?

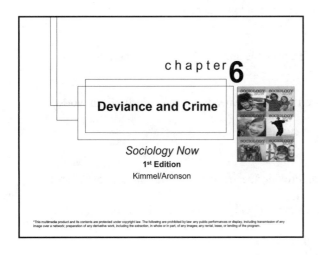

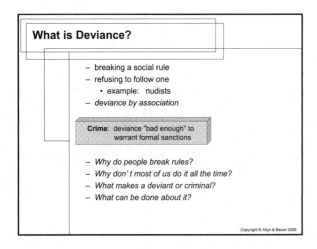

Conformity and Social Control

- **Deviant subcultures**
  - evolve within a dominant culture
  - loose association or organized
    - example: youth gangs
  - identity/ condition/activity must
    - be <u>punished</u> (but not too much)
    - have <u>participants</u> (but not too many)
    - be <u>complex</u> (but not too complex)
  - **Youth Gangs as Deviant Subcultures**
  - **Youth Gangs Today**

Deviance and Social Coherence

- deviance is useful to society **(Durkheim)**
  - *It affirms cultural norms and values*
  - *It clarifies moral boundaries*
  - *It heightens group solidarity*
  - *It encourages social change*

Deviance and Social Coherence

- **Explaining Deviance**
  - **Differential Association (Sutherland)**
    - associate with people who are deviants
    - rewarded for deviant behavior
  - **Control Theory (Hirschi)**
    - decisions through "cost-benefit analysis
    - determine punishment/reward/risks
  - **Social Controls (Reckless)**
    - outer controls ⎰ Attachment
    - inner controls ⎱ Commitment
      Involvement
      Belief

Deviance and Social Coherence

– **Labeling Theory**
- Powerful determine what is deviant
  – **primary deviance**
  – **secondary deviance**
  – **tertiary deviance**

Copyright © Allyn & Bacon 2009

Deviance and Social Coherence

- **Deviance and Inequality**
  – those who have power:
    - rules are "natural" and "good"
    - internalized by individuals
    - masks political agenda
  – justification of inequalities - *labeling actors and acts as deviant*
    - gender
    - sexual orientation
    - race/ethnicity
    - social class

Copyright © Allyn & Bacon 2009

Deviance and Crime

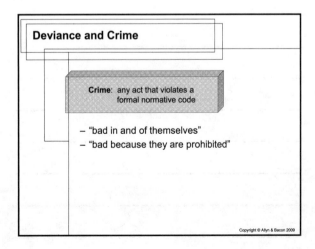

Crime: any act that violates a formal normative code

– "bad in and of themselves"
– "bad because they are prohibited"

Copyright © Allyn & Bacon 2009

Deviance and Crime

- **Strain Theory** (Merton)
  - Conformists
  - Innovators
  - Ritualists
  - Rebels
  - Retreatists

- **Broken Windows Theory**
  - minor acts of deviance can spiral into severe crime and social decay (Zimbardo)

Copyright © Allyn & Bacon 2009

Deviance and Crime

- **Criminal Subcultures**
  - youth gang member values (Cohen)
    - *Nonutilitarianism*
    - *Maliciousness*
    - *Negativism*
    - *Short-run hedonism*
    - *Group autonomy*
  - lower-class subcultural norms (Miller)
    - *Trouble*
    - *Toughness*
    - *Smartness*
    - *Excitement*
    - *Fate*
    - *Autonomy*

Copyright © Allyn & Bacon 2009

Deviance and Crime

- **Opportunity Theory** (Cloward and Ohlin)
  - crime arises from opportunity
  - emphasis on *learning*
    - **deviant subcultures**
      - criminal subcultures
      - violence subcultures
      - retreatist subcultures

- **Conflict Theory**
  - larger structural analysis of inequalities based on race, class or gender (Quinney)

Copyright © Allyn & Bacon 2009

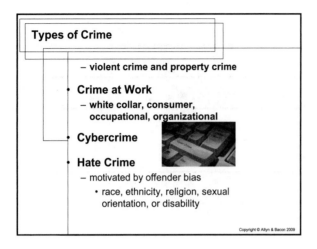

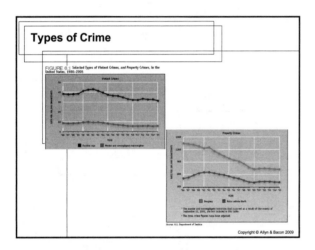

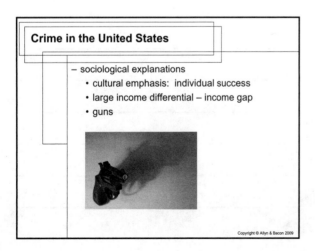

Crime in the United States

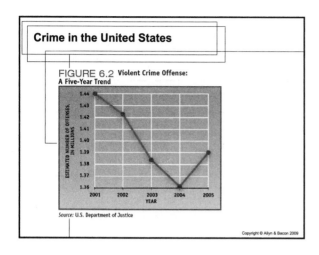

FIGURE 6.2 Violent Crime Offense: A Five-Year Trend

Source: U.S. Department of Justice

Copyright © Allyn & Bacon 2009

Crime in the United States

- **Crime and Guns**
- **Crime and Gender**
- **Crime and Race**
  - *Strain theory*
  - *Differential opportunity*
  - *Labeling*
  - *Conflict*
- **Crime and Age**
- **Crime and Class**

Copyright © Allyn & Bacon 2009

The Criminal Justice System

- **Police**
- **Courts**
- **Punishment and Corrections**
  - **Prisons**
    - *Retribution*
    - *Deterrence*
    - *Protection*
    - *Rehabilitation*
  - **The Death Penalty**

Copyright © Allyn & Bacon 2009

Globalization and Crime

- historical and contemporary
- "not just the Internet"
- Operations in every arena

You are most likely to be the victim of a crime locally

- **Deviance and Crime in the 21st Century**

Copyright © Allyn & Bacon 2009

What Does America Think?

6.1 Censoring Perceived Deviance

This is actual survey data from the General Social Survey, 1972–2004.

1. There are always some people whose ideas are considered bad or dangerous by other people. For instance, somebody who is against all churches and religion . . . Should such a person be allowed to teach in a college or university? Data from 2004 show the following: 65.1 percent said yes, 34.9 percent said no. The percentage of people saying yes has steadily increased from 1972, when data showed 41.9 percent of respondents saying yes and 58.1 percent saying no. The current percentage of 65.1 is the highest it has been since the survey started in 1972.

2. What about a man who admits that he is a homosexual? Should such a person be allowed to teach in a college or university? Data from 2004 show the following: 80.1 percent said yes, 19.9 percent said no. The percentage of people who agree that a homosexual should be allowed to teach has been steadily increasing from 1973, when 49.4 percent of the respondents said yes, and 50.6 percent said no.

3. Should a person who believes that Blacks are genetically inferior be allowed to teach in a college or university? Data from 2004 show the following: 47.8 percent said yes, 52.2 percent said no. There has been very little variation in responses since the question was first asked in the 1976 survey.

Copyright © Allyn & Bacon 2009

What Does America Think?

4. If some people in your community suggested that a book written against churches and religion should be taken out of your public library, would you favor removing this book? In 2004, the responses were 25.3 percent to remove the book and 74.7 percent to not remove it. Attitudes have changed somewhat since 1982, when 40.2 percent said to remove the book.

5. If some people in your community suggested that a book written in favor of homosexuality should be taken out of your public library, would you favor removing this book? In 2004, 26.4 percent of respondents said remove the book and 73.6 percent said don't. The percentage of people advocating removing the book has been in a steady decline since 45 percent said remove in 1973.

6. If some people in your community suggested that a book that said Blacks are inferior should be taken out of your public library, would you favor removing this book, or not? In 2004, 32.9 percent of respondents said they would be in favor of removing the book, while 67.1 percent said they would not. Although those numbers have remained pretty steady since the 1970s, the percentage of people wanting to remove the book peaked in 1982 at 40.4 percent.

CRITICAL THINKING | DISCUSSION QUESTIONS

1. It appears that American's attitudes toward censoring unpopular ideas have changed significantly in the past 30 years. How does this change reflect changes in American society and in American values?

2. Why do more Americans seem to be tolerant of books in the library having perceived deviant views than they are of college teachers having perceived deviant views?

3. What does it say about American values that more Americans would censor an antireligion point of view than a prohomosexual view?

Copyright © Allyn & Bacon 2009

What Does America Think?

6.2 **Death Penalty for Murder**
This is actual survey data from the General Social Survey, 1972–2004.

1. Do you favor or oppose the death penalty for persons convicted of murder? In 2004, almost 70 percent of respondents were in favor of the death penalty. When we look at the responses by race, though, we see a very large and significant difference. Seventy-two percent of White respondents favor the death penalty for murder, while only 40 percent of Black respondents do so.

CRITICAL THINKING | DISCUSSION QUESTION

1. How can we explain the difference in White and Black responses to the survey question?

▶ Go to this website to look further at the data. You can run your own statistics and crosstabs here: http://sda.berkeley.edu/cgi-bin/hsda?harcsda+gss04

REFERENCES: Davis, James A., Tom W. Smith, and Peter V. Marsden. General Social Surveys 1972–2004: [Cumulative File] [Computer File]. 2nd ICPSR version. Chicago, IL: National Opinion Research Center [producer], 2005; Storrs, CT: Roper Center for Public Opinion Research, University of Connecticut; Ann Arbor, MI: Inter-University Consortium for Political and Social Research; Berkeley, CA: Computer-Assisted Survey Methods Program, University of California [distributors], 2005.

Chapter 7
Stratification and Social Class

Chapter Outline

I.   What is Social Stratification?
       a.   It is a system of structured social inequality and the structure of mobility in a society.
       b.   Why do we have Social Stratification?
            i.   Durkheim believed that stratification was a necessary organizing principle of a complex society and it serves to create interdependence among society's members.
            ii.   Davis and Moore argued that as long as some degree of social mobility was possible, stratification is essential to the proper functioning of a society.
            iii.   Meritocracy- system in which those at who are the most "meritorious" will rise to the top, and those who are less so will sink to the bottom.
            iv.   Stratification divides us far more than it unites us.
       c.   System of Stratification
            i.   Caste system- fixed and permanent; you are assigned to your position at birth, without any chance of getting out.
            ii.   Feudalism- fixed and permanent system; if you were born a lord or a serf, you stayed there your whole life.
            iii.   Class system- based on economic position and people are ranked according to achieved status.

II.   Social Class
       a.   Theories of Social Class
            i.   Marx and Class
               1.   Class was the foundation of his entire theory.
               2.   How we organize ourselves to produce things, and how we distribute the rewards is called the mode of production.
               3.   Relations of production are the relationships people enter into to facilitate production and allocate it rewards.
               4.   Some people own the means of production (bourgeoisie).
               5.   Everyone else works for them (proletariat)
            ii.   Weber and Class
               1.   Weber argued that there were three components to social class
                  a.   Class position- whether you are an owner or a worker; how much money you have; your property.
                  b.   Status- based on your relationship to consumption.
                  c.   Power- ability to do what you want to do.
               2.   Sociologists after Weber have continued to postulate new components of social class.
                  a.   Your social connections.
                  b.   Your ascribe and attained statuses.
               3.   Sociologists today tend to use the term socioeconomic status instead of social class.
       b.   Socioeconomic Classes in the United States
            i.   The Upper Upper Class
               1.   Superrich with an annual income of over $1 million.
               2.   Include older established wealthy families who amassed their fortunes during the industrial boom.
               3.   Include those who have amassed their fortunes recently during the information revolution.
            ii.   Lower Upper Class
               1.   Annual income between $150,000 and $1 million.
               2.   Have advanced degrees from high-ranking colleges.

3. They are upper-level CEOs, manager, doctors, and engineers.
   iii. Upper Middle Class
      1. Annual household income between $80,000 and $150,000.
      2. High-end professionals and corporate workers.
      3. Most have college degrees.
   iv. Middle Middle Class
      1. Annual household income between $40,000 and $80,000.
      2. Most hold white-collar jobs.
      3. Have very little investment income.
   v. Working Class
      1. Annual household income between $20,000 and $40,000.
      2. They tend to be blue-collar workers.
      3. They usually have high school diplomas and may have been to college.
   vi. Lower Class
      1. Annual household income of less than $20,000.
      2. They hold unskilled and semi-skilled jobs.
      3. Most do not have a high school diploma.
      4. They usually live paycheck to paycheck.
   vii. The Underclass
      1. They have no income and no connection to the job market.
      2. Their major support comes from welfare and food stamps.
  c. America and the Myth of the Middle Class
   i. Americans believe that class is even less important than ever and that most Americans are middle class.
   ii. Since the turn of the 20th century the middle class has expanded dramatically.
   iii. Today most people in the United States classify themselves as middle class, even if they have to resort to creative redefinitions.
   iv. Economist Michael Lind argues that the middle class has always been a product of social engineering by the government.
  d. Income Inequality
   i. The United States is increasingly a nation of richer and poorer.
      1. In the United States the top 5 percent earn an average of 11 times more than the bottom 20 percent.
      2. In Sweden the top 20 percent earn less than 4 times the bottom 20 percent.
   ii. The income gap in the United States actually seems to be widening.
      1. The gap between the rich and poor more than doubled between 1980 and 2000.
      2. The richest 1 percent have more money to spend after taxes than all of the bottom 40 percent.
  e. Class and Race
   i. Class position is based on your position in the economic world.
   ii. Race is ascribed at birth.
   iii. Historical legacy of racism has enormous consequences for class position.
   iv. African Americans are overrepresented among the poor.
III. Poverty in the United States and Abroad
  a. 1964 President Lyndon Johnson declared "war on poverty' in the United States as part of his dream of a Great Society.
   i. Mollie Oshansnky devised the poverty threshold, a minimum income necessary to not be poor.
      1. The poverty line is the official measure of poverty calculated to include those whose incomes are equal to or less than three times the least expensive food budget is the
      2. Poverty line does not take into account thins beside food, shelter, and clothes.
   ii. Fred Block calculated the "dream line"

       1. This calculation includes housing, high-quality day care, full health coverage, and higher education.

       2. The American dream is out of reach for many Americans.

  b. Who is Poor in America?

    i. Not all poor people are ethnic minorities.

    ii. Not all poor people live in the inner city.

    iii. Not all poor people are unemployed.

    iv. Children are more likely than others to be poor.

    v. Mothers are more likely than others to be poor.

    vi. The elderly are less likely than others to be poor.

  c. The Feminization of Poverty

    i. Women compose an increasing number of poor people.

    ii. Of the poor over the age of 18, 61 percent are females and 39 percent are males.

    iii. In poor countries, women suffer double deprivation, the deprivation of living in a poor country and the deprivation imposed because they are women.

  d. Explaining Poverty

    i. Personal Initiative

      1. People are poor because they lack something- initiative, drive, ambition, discipline.

      2. People are poor because they are unmotivated and lazy.

      3. Sociologists see it as a structural problem.

        a. People are unmotivated because they are poor.

        b. No matter how hard they try and how motivated they are, the cards are so heavily stacked against them that they eventually give up.

    ii. The culture of poverty

      1. Poverty is not a result of individual inadequacies but of larger social and cultural factors.

      2. Poor children are socialized into believing that they have nothing to strive for.

    iii. Structures of Inequality

      1. Poverty results from nationwide and worldwide factors that no individual has any control over.

      2. Poverty also reduced life chances, limited opportunities for securing everything from health care to education, from job autonomy to leisure, from safety at home to the potential for a long life.

  e. Poverty on a World Scale

    i. Half of the world's population lives on less than $2 a day.

    ii. The gross domestic product of the poorest 48 nations in the world, is less than the wealth of the world's three richest people combined.

  f. Reducing Poverty

    i. Poverty has been a more difficult enemy than anyone originally believed.

    ii. A greater proportion of families and children in America today live in poverty than in 1973.

    iii. Different types of nations have tried different strategies to alleviate poverty.

      1. Industrial nations have implemented welfare systems.

      2. Only the United States does not provide basic structural requirements.

    iv. Global efforts to reduce poverty on a global scale have historically relied on "outside" help.

      1. The United States spends billions in direct aid to poor nations.

      2. Foundations funnel massive amounts of aid to poor nations to improve health care and education.

    v. Newer strategies are targeted at local people.

      1. Mexico and Brazil have embraced "conditional cash transfer schemes" by which the government gives direct payments to poor families.

      2. Pakistan economist Muhammad Yunus has developed "microcredit" by which the bank lends tiny amount to local poor people.

IV.   Social Mobility
    a.   It is the movement from one class to another.
        i.   Intergenerational- your parents are working class, but you became lower.
        ii.   Intragenerational- you move from working to lower or from working to middle.
    b.   Dynamics of Mobility
        i.   Structural mobility is a general upward trend of the entire society.
        ii.   Recent pattern has been downward mobility, caused by the decline in manufacturing jobs, coupled with the growth of service jobs.
        iii.   Underemployment- highly educated and qualified for positions higher than the ones they occupy.
    c.   Social Mobility today
        i.   Since the beginning of the 21st century, the United States has become less mobile than it has ever been in history.
        ii.   American levels of mobility are significantly lower than Canada and most Scandinavian countries.
V.   Global Inequality
    a.   Systematic differences in wealth and power among countries.
    b.   Classifying Global Economies
        i.   Social Scientists used to divide the world into three socioeconomic categories.
            1.   The First World
            2.   The Second World
            3.   The Third World
        ii.   Today we use the terms developed, developing, and underdeveloped.
        iii.   World Bank's classification by economic and social indicators suggests a high or low quality of life.
        iv.   High-Income Countries
            1.   Countries cover 25 percent of the world's land surface.
            2.   They are home to 17 percent of the world's population.
        v.   Middle-Income Countries
            1.   Countries cover 47 percent of the world's land surface.
            2.   They are home to over half of the world's population.
        vi.   Lower-Income Countries
            1.   Countries cover 28 percent of the world's land surface.
            2.   They are home to 28 percent of the world's population.
    c.   Explaining Global Inequality
        i.   Market Theories
            1.   These theories stress the wisdom of the capitalist market.
            2.   They assume that the best possible economic consequences will results if individuals are free to make their own economic decisions.
            3.   Modernization Theory focuses on the conditions necessary for a low-income country to develop economically and must go through four stages to break out of poverty.
                a.   Traditional Economy- starting point of impoverished countries.
                b.   Takeoff to economic growth- experience some economic growth when they start to work hard and save money to invest.
                c.   Drive to technological maturity- they gradually improve their technology, reinvest, and adopt the institutions and values of the wealthy countries.
                d.   High mass consumption- people in impoverished countries would enjoy the fruits of their labor by achieving a standard of living similar to that of the wealthy countries.
        ii.   State-Centered Theories
            1.   Perhaps the solution is not the market, operating on its own, but active intervention by the government.

        2. These theories argue that appropriate government policies do not interfere with economic development but that government plays a key role in bringing it about.

    iii. Dependency Theory

        1. Focuses on the unequal relationship between wealthy and poor countries, arguing that poverty is the result of exploitation.

           a. Exploitation began with colonialism- political-economic system under which powerful countries establish, for their own profit, rule over weaker peoples or countries.

           b. Although colonialism gradually ended, the exploitation did not.

        2. Theory has been criticized for being simplistic and for putting all blame for global poverty on high-income nations and multinational corporations.

    iv. World System Theory

        1. Draws on dependency theory but focuses on the global economy as an international network dominated by capitalism.

        2. Immanuel Wallerstein founded this theory and coined the term world economy.

        3. World system is composed of four interrelated elements:

           a. Global market of goods and labor.

           b. Division of the population in to different economic classes, based loosely on Marxian division of owners and workers.

           c. International system of formal and informal political relations among the world economy.

           d. Division of countries into three broad economic zones

               i. Core- Western Europe and where Western Europeans immigrated in large numbers.

              ii. Periphery- includes countries that were under Western European domination but did not receive many permanent settlers.

             iii. Semiperiphery- intermediate zone between the core and periphery.

        4. Global commodity chains- worldwide networks of labor and production processes, consisting of all pivotal production activities.

           a. The most profitable activities in the commodity chain are likely to be done in the core countries; least profitable activities are likely to be done in peripheral countries.

           b. The world economy makes the peripheral countries dependent on the core countries in three major ways:

               i. Narrow, export-oriented economies.

              ii. Lack of industrial capacity.

             iii. Foreign debt.

  d. Global Mobility

      i. Rich countries can become poor and poor countries can become rich.

      ii. Recently there has been a trend of newly industrializing economies, countries that move from poor to rich in a matter of a few years.

VI. Class Identity and Class Inequality in the 21st Century

  a. Class continues to have a remarkable impact in our lives.

  b. Just as class increases in importance and class inequality increases in its impact on our everyday lives and out society, so too do Americans continue to disavow its importance.

Chapter Summary

- Social stratification is concerned with the ranking of people. Your social position is a matter of birth, passed on from parents to children, from generation to generation.
- Some sociologists argue that stratification is essential to the proper functioning of society and stratification creates a meritocracy, a system in which those at who are the most meritorious are at the top and those who are less so will sink to the bottom.
- The are three general types of systems of stratification: caste systems, feudal systems, and class systems. Class is the most modern form of stratification.
- Marx was the first social scientists to make class the foundation of his entire theory. He argued that human survival depends of the production of things and how we organize ourselves as a society to do this and how we distribute the rewards is called the mode of production.
- Marx argued that there were two classes, the bourgeoisie (capitalists) who owned the means of production and the proletariat (lower classes) who were forced to become wage-laborers or go hungry.
- Weber extended Marx's two class system and argued that there were three components to social class: economic, social, and political. Whereas Marx used only economic to discuss class, Weber identified other dimensions that explained people's position in society.
- Today there are six or more socioeconomic classes in the United States and they include: the upper upper class, lower upper class, upper middle class, middle middle class, working class, lower class, and the underclass.
- Many people believe that most Americans are middle class. Economist Michael Lind argues that the middle class is a product of social engineering by the government.
- The United States is increasingly a nation of richer and poorer. The income gap is widening and the richest 1 percent have more money to spend after taxes than all of the bottom 40 percent.
- Historical legacy of racism has enormous consequences for class position given the limited mobility there actually is. African Americans are overrepresented among the poor.
- In 1964 President Lyndon Johnson declared a "war on poverty." With this came the poverty line.
- Not all of the poor people are ethnic minorities, not all of them live in the inner city, not all poor are unemployed, children are more likely to be poor than others, mothers are more likely to be poor than others, and the elderly are less likely than others to be poor.
- The feminization of poverty is the termed used to explain why women compose an increasing number of poor people.
- There are several explanations to why poor people are poor. The include the personal initiative, the culture of poverty, and the structures of inequality.
- Although there are many poor people in the United States, there is a substantial poverty problem world wide. Half of the world's population lives on less than $2 a day.
- The "War of Poverty" did not decrease the amount of poverty found in the United States. Today a greater proportion of families and children live in poverty than in 1973.
- Social mobility means the movement from one class to another and can occur in two forms: intergenerational and intragenerational.
- Global inequality is the systematic differences in wealth and power among countries and there seems to be a global class structure developing.
- Social scientists used to divide the world into three socioeconomic categories; the First World, Second World, and Third World. Today, that classification is outdated and has changed it to high-income nations, middle-income nations, and low-income nations.
- The Market Theories, State-Centered Theories, Dependency Theory, and the World System Theory are used to explain global inequality.
- Just as people can move up or down on the socioeconomic ladder, countries can also move up or down.

Learning Objectives

After completing the reading of Chapter 7, you should be able to answer the following objectives.

- Define social stratification and the different systems of stratification.
- Describe the various components of social stratification and discuss the debate between Marx and Weber over those components.
- Discuss each of the seven socioeconomic classes, what their annual income is and who is in each class.
- Understand the myth of the Middle Class in America.
- Discuss income inequality and how gender and race play a part in the inequality.
- Define the poverty line, how it is calculated, and the implications of it.
- Know who the poor are in terms of race, age, gender, employment status, and location.
- Define the feminization of poverty.
- Compare structural and individual explanations of poverty in the United States.
- Understand poverty globally and what efforts have been taken to reduce it.
- Define social mobility and know the differences between intergenerational, intragenerational mobility, and structural mobility.
- Know the trends of structural mobility.
- Define global inequality and understand the income gap on a global level.
- Know how social scientists used to divide the world into three socioeconomic categories and what those categories are today.
- Discuss how the World Bank classifies economic and social indicators that would suggest high or low quality of life.
- Compare the high income, middle income, and low income countries in terms of how much land space they take up, what percent of the population lives in each, and give examples of each type.
- Discuss the theories of global inequality: modernization theory, state-centered theories, dependency theory, and world systems theory.
- Describe global mobility and the recent trend of newly industrialized economies.

Key Terms

Bourgeoisie: capitalists that owned the means of production.

Caste system: fixed and permanent; you are assigned to your position at birth, without any chance of getting out.

Class: based on economic position- a person's occupation, income or possessions.

Class systems: systems of stratification based on economic position, and people are ranked according to achieved status.

Colonialism: political-economic system under which powerful countries establish, for their own profit, rule over weaker people or countries.

Culture of poverty: argues that poverty is not a result of individual inadequacies but of larger social and cultural factors.

Dependency Theory: focuses on the unequal relationship between wealthy countries and poor countries, arguing that poverty is the result of exploitation.

Feminization of Poverty: women compose an increasing number of poor people.

Feudalism: fixed and permanent system; if you were born a lord or a serf, you stayed there your whole life.

Global Commodity Chains: worldwide networks of labor and production processes, consisting of all pivotal production activities, that form a tightly interlocked "chain" from raw materials to finished products to retail outlet to consumer.

Global inequality: systematic differences in wealth and power among countries.

Meritocracy: system in which those at who are the most "meritorious" will rise to the top and those who are less so will sink to the bottom.

Modernization Theory: focuses on the conditions necessary for a low-income country to develop economically.

Poverty Line: poverty threshold; the minimal amount of money one could live on.

Power: ability to do what you want to do.

Proletariat: lower classes who are forced to become wage-laborers.

Social Mobility: the ability to move up or down in the rankings.

Social stratification: it is a system of structured social inequality and the structure of mobility in a society.

Socioeconomic status: emphasize that people are ranked through the intermingling of many factors, economic, social, political, cultural, and community.

Status: based on your relationship to consumption; your lifestyle.

Structural mobility: means that the entire society got wealthier.

Underclass: has no income and no connection to the job market.

World System Theory: draws on dependency theory but focuses on the global economy as an international network dominated by capitalism.

Key People

Lyndon B. Johnson: president who declared a "war on poverty."

Oscar Lewis: introduced the culture of poverty thesis.

Karl Marx: first to make social class the foundation of his entire theory.
Mollie Oshansnky: decided on the definition of poverty and developed the poverty line.

W.W. Rostow: developed modernization theory and argued that a nation's poverty is largely due to the cultural failings of its people.

Max Weber: based stratification on thee dimensions: class, status, and party.

Additional Learning with MySocLab

Read

Census Shows Bigger Houses And Incomes, but Not for All (pg 217)
"The rich get richer while the poor get poorer." This statement has proven to be true in the US since the 1950s. The gap between the rich and the poor grew significantly during the 1990s and continues to be wide.

Rich Nations Are Criticized for Enforcing Trade Barriers (pg 224)
Billions and billions of dollars of traded goods leave and enter the US every year. Foreign policies often make or break corporations who profit from labor, materials, and buy and sell agreements with various international businesses. Since the colonization era of world history, Western countries have consistently created policies which profited their businesses at the expense of businesses in poorer regions of the world.

In Trenches of a War on Unyielding Poverty (pg 220)
In the US about thirteen percent of the population lives below the poverty line. Another twelve percent live near poverty.

Explore

Web Activity: Social Class (pg 224)
For this activity you will read the article "Understanding Poverty in America" and "The Changing Face of Poverty" to learn more about poverty in the United States and why it is a prevalent concern for many Americans. After reading the articles there is a series of questions to answer.

Ownership of Television Sets Worldwide (pg 230)
This activity allows for you to compare poverty globally based on the number of television sets per 1,000 people.

Listen

PEW Study: Globalization (pg 231)
NPR discusses the PEW Study on globalization. The new poll shows that people find food and medicine are more easily found all over the world; however many believe there are fewer good paying jobs and the gap between the rich and the poor growing.

Watch

Understanding Social Class (pg 211)
Susan Ostrander discusses what is meant by social class and some of the important debates surrounding the definition.

World Poverty Report (pg 225)
The video clip discusses how the UN and other international institutions have failed the poor people of the world and their roles need to be reexamined. Basic rights such as food and economic opportunity are still being denied.

Visualize

Income Distribution (pg 212)
The map illustrates the median household income distribution for states.

Practice Test
After completing the practice test, check your answers in the Answer Key of this Study Guide.

Multiple Choice Questions

1. Which system is fixed and permanent because you are assigned to your position at birth without any chance of getting out?
   a. Class
   b. Caste
   c. Feudal
   d. None of the Above

2. What type of mobility refers to the upward or downward movement in a social class all within your lifetime.
   a. Social mobility
   b. Intergenerational mobility
   c. Intragenerational mobility
   d. Horizontal mobility

3. The official measure of poverty calculated to include those whose incomes are equal to or less than three times the least expensive food budget is the:
   a. poverty line.
   b. welfare line.
   c. poverty index.
   d. poverty rate.

4. The poverty rate for Whites is 8.3 percent compared to _____ percent for African Americans and 21.8 percent for Hispanics.
   a. 23
   b. 9.8
   c. 25.8
   d. 24.9

5. Which segment of the population is most likely to experience poverty today?
   a. middle-aged adults
   b. young adults
   c. the elderly
   d. children.

6. Which explanation of poverty is based on the assumption that people lack initiative, drive, ambition, and discipline to pull themselves out of poverty?
   a. culture of poverty
   b. personal initiative
   c. structures of inequality
   d. feminization of poverty

7. Social stratification refers to:
   a. the idea that all people are created equally.
   b. all people have an equal chance of upward mobility.
   c. ranking categories of people in a hierarchy.
   d. All of the above.

8. Which of the following is not one of India's traditional caste categories?
    a. Shudras
    b. Brahmin
    c. Kshatriyas
    d. Sanskrit

9. The term meritocracy refers to a social stratification system based on:
    a. your position at birth.
    b. your economic position.
    c. merit.
    d. weaknesses.

10. The claim that your social position reflects your work ethic is commonly made in:
    a. Class systems.
    b. Caste systems.
    c. Feudal systems.
    d. All of the above.

11. This class has an annual household income of more than $150,000 but less than $1 million and tend to have advanced degrees from high-ranking colleges.
    a. The upper upper class
    b. The lower upper class
    c. The upper middle class
    d. The middle middle class

12. Which of the following is a myth about the poor in America?
    a. Not all poor people live in the inner city
    b. Mothers are more likely to be poor than others
    c. Not all poor people are unemployed
    d. All poor people are ethnic minorities

13. Which region of the world has the highest percentage of people living on less than $1 a day?
    a. East Asia
    b. Latin America
    c. Sub-Saharan Africa
    d. Middle East

14. Max Weber based an individual's social position on:
    a. social prestige.
    b. power.
    c. economic class.
    d. All of the above.

15. The World Bank has classified countries with a new system. Which of the following is not a measure that the World Bank uses to suggest a high or low quality of life?
    a. Gross Domestic Product
    b. Political system of a nation
    c. Life expectancy
    d. Infant mortality rate.

16. What type of country has people living mostly in villages and on farms, and have only a few sustenance industries?
    a. High income
    b. Middle income
    c. Low income
    d. None of the above

17. Which explanation of global inequality focuses on the unequal relationship between the wealthy and poor countries, arguing that poverty is the result of exploitation?
    a. Market Theories
    b. State-Centered Theories
    c. Modernization Theory
    d. Dependency Theory

18. The world system is composed of four interrelated elements according to Immanuel Wallerstein. Which of the following is not one of them?
    a. a global market of goods and labor
    b. the division of the population into different economic classes
    c. an international system of formal and informal political relations among the most powerful countries
    d. the division of countries into six broad economic zones

19. The term global commodity chains refers to:
    a. a worldwide network of labor and production processes
    b. an internal network of production and labor
    c. a national network of production that controls the world
    d. an international network in which one country controls all of the production

20. At the lowest level of social stratification in the United States is the:
    a. lower class.
    b. underclass.
    c. working class.
    d. lower middle class.

21. One of the following statements in Not true. Which is it?
    a. The poverty rates for whites is much lower than African Americans
    b. The poverty rates for the elderly has decreased since 1967
    c. The United States has a higher rate of mortality than any other industrialized country
    d. The poverty rates is highest in the inner city

22. What type of social stratification system is based on race?
    a. Caste system
    b. Class system
    c. Feudal system
    d. Apartheid system

23. What is the single best predictor of people's life chances?
    a. economic gain
    b. political power
    c. class
    d. status

24. Which of the following is ranked the lowest on the occupational prestige scale?
    a. Waitress
    b. Cab Driver
    c. Accountant
    d. Police officer

25. Approximately what percentage of households make less than $40,000 a year?
    a. 22 percent
    b. 46 percent
    c. 24 percent
    d. 40 percent

STUDY GUIDE

True/False Questions

True   False   1. Feudalism is the most common class system in the world today.

True   False   2. Karl Marx's class system was based on class position, social status, and power.

True   False   3. The working class has a household income between $20,000 and $40,000 and tend to be blue-collar workers.

True   False   4. Workers' wages increase proportionately with their corporation's profit.

True   False   5. Those who are part of the underclass have no connections to the job market.

True   False   6. All poor people in the United States are ethnic minorities.

True   False   7. The culture of poverty thesis argues that poverty is not a result of the larger social and cultural factors but of individual inadequacies.

True   False   8. Intergenerational mobility is when you move up or down a class from your parents' class.

True   False   9. The income gap that is seen in the United States can also be seen worldwide.

True   False   10. Today the World Bank classify countries by economic and social indicators that suggest a high or low quality of life.

Fill-in-the-Blank Questions

1. According the Weber, there are three components to social class: _____, _____, and _____.

2. How we, as a society, organize ourselves to produce things, and how we distribute the rewards, is what Marx called the _____.

3. _____ emphasizes that people are ranked though the intermingling of many factors, economic, social, political, cultural, and community.

4. The income gap in the United States is actually _____.

5. The _____ argues that poverty is a result of larger social and cultural factors and not a result of individual inadequacies.

6. _____ refers to the movement, up or down, from one class to another.

7. _____ countries cover 47 percent of the Earth's land areas and are home to more than half of its populations.

8. W.W. Rostow's _____ focuses on the conditions necessary for a low-income country to develop economically.

9. The _____ countries of Wallerstein's World Systems Theory include Western Europe, United States, Canada, Australia, New Zealand, South Africa, and Japan.

10. Most poor families in the United States are headed by _____.

Essay Questions

1. What is social stratification and what are the three different types of stratification systems. Define and discuss them.

2. Explain the differences between Marx's and Weber's approach to social stratification. Why is Weber's more complex?

3. What are the three explanations of poverty? Discuss in detail.

4. Discuss W.W. Rostow's modernization theory. What are the four stages that countries go through to break out of poverty?

5. How do the core countries make the peripheral countries dependent on them?

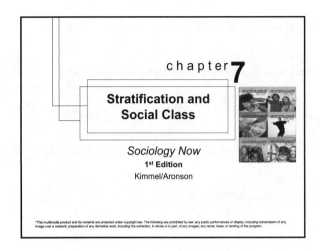

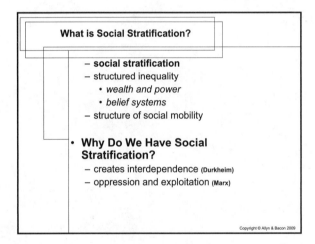

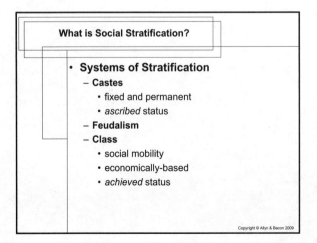

Social Class

- **Theories of Social Class**
  - Marx and Class
    - bourgeoisie
    - proletariat
  - Weber and Class
    - *Class position*
    - *Status*
    - *Power*
  - socioeconomic status ("SES")

Social Class

TABLE 7.1

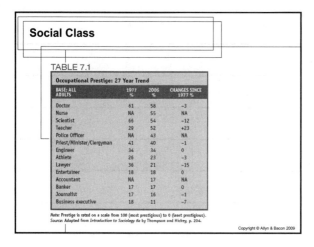

Occupational Prestige: 27 Year Trend			
BASE: ALL ADULTS	1977 %	2006 %	CHANGES SINCE 1977 %
Doctor	61	58	–3
Nurse	NA	55	NA
Scientist	66	54	–12
Teacher	29	52	+23
Police Officer	NA	43	NA
Priest/Minister/Clergyman	41	40	–1
Engineer	34	34	0
Athlete	26	23	–3
Lawyer	36	21	–15
Entertainer	18	18	0
Accountant	NA	17	NA
Banker	17	17	0
Journalist	17	16	–1
Business executive	18	11	–7

Note: Prestige is rated on a scale from 100 (most prestigious) to 0 (least prestigious).
Source: Adapted from *Introduction to Sociology 8e* by Thompson and Hickey, p. 204.

Social Class

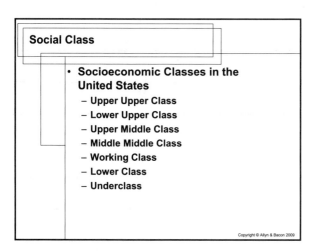

- **Socioeconomic Classes in the United States**
  - Upper Upper Class
  - Lower Upper Class
  - Upper Middle Class
  - Middle Middle Class
  - Working Class
  - Lower Class
  - Underclass

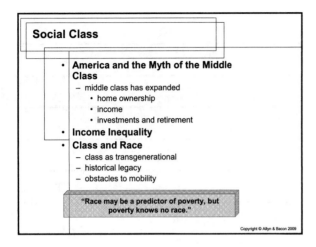

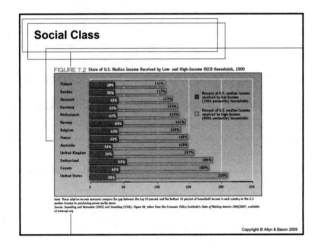

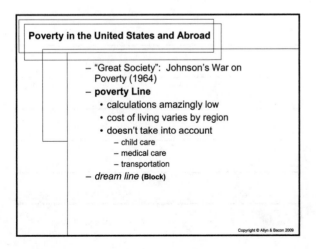

Poverty in the United States and Abroad

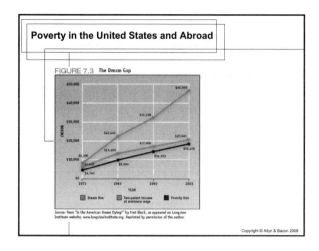

FIGURE 7.3 The Dream Gap

Source: From "Is the American Dream Dying?" by Fred Block, as appeared on Longview Institute website, www.longviewinstitute.org. Reprinted by permission of the author.

Poverty in the United States and Abroad

- **Who is Poor in America?**
  - *Not all poor people are ethnic minorities*
  - *Not all poor people are unemployed*
  - *Children more likely to be poor*
  - *Mothers more likely to be poor*
  - *Elderly are less likely to be poor*

- **Feminization of Poverty**
  - lower wages
  - childcare costs

Poverty in the United States and Abroad

- **Explaining Poverty**
  - **Personal Initiative**
  - **The Culture of Poverty**
  - **Structures of Inequality**
    - structural disadvantages of the poor
      - *Poor education*
      - *Higher rates of chronic diseases*
      - *poor or nonexistent health care*
      - *inferior housing*
      - *victim of crime/labeled as criminal*

- **Poverty on a World Scale**

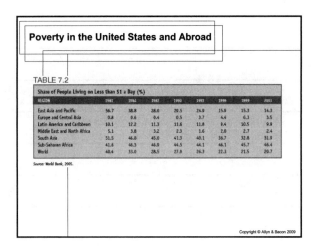

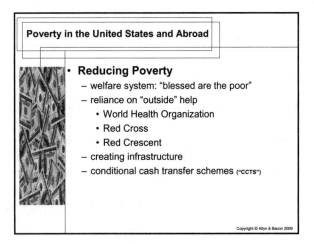

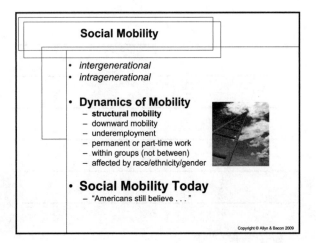

Global Inequality

– global inequality
- systematic differences
- *rich countries get richer; poor countries get poorer*

FIGURE 7.4 Where the Money Is

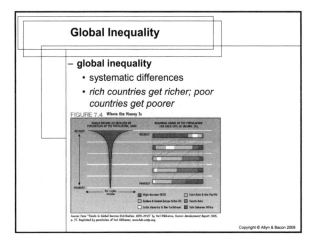

Source: From "Trends in Global Income Distribution 1970–2015" by Yuri Dikhanov, *Human Development Report 2005,* p. 37. Reprinted by permission of Yuri Dikhanov, www.hdr.undp.org.

Copyright © Allyn & Bacon 2009

Global Inequality

- **Classifying Global Economies**
  - The First World → *developed*
  - The Second World → *developing*
  - The Third World → *underdeveloped*

Copyright © Allyn & Bacon 2009

Global Inequality

- *World Bank* "Quality of Life" Indicators
  - Gross Domestic Product
  - Work
  - Life expectancy
  - Infant mortality rate
  - Literacy rate
  - Percentage of children in labor force
  - Birth rate
  - Distribution of wealth
  - Gender inequality

Copyright © Allyn & Bacon 2009

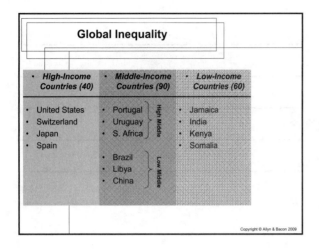

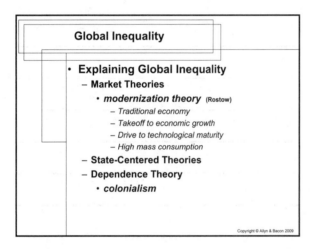

Global Inequality

- **World System Theory** (Wallerstein)
  - global market
  - population divided into economic classes
  - international political relations
  - three economic zones
    - core
    - periphery
    - semi-periphery
  } countries

- *global commodity chains*
- **Global Mobility**
- **Class Identity and Class Inequality in the 21st Century**

Copyright © Allyn & Bacon 2009

What Does America Think?

7.1 Conflict between Poor and Rich in the United States

This is actual survey data from the General Social Survey, 1972–2004.

1. In all countries, there are differences or conflicts between different social groups. In your opinion, in America, how much conflict is there between poor people and rich people? In the 2000 General Social Survey, more than half of all respondents said they thought there was either strong or very strong conflict between the rich and the poor. Those who identified as lower class were far more likely than others to say there was strong (47.1%) or very strong (39.2%) conflict. With regard to race, Blacks were far more likely than Whites to report they thought there was strong (42.9%) or very strong (27.3%) conflict.

CRITICAL THINKING | DISCUSSION QUESTIONS

1. The social class difference in responses was significant. Almost 90 percent of those who identified as lower class reported thinking there was strong or very strong conflict, while only about 60 percent of those who identified as upper class reported the same. What explains the social class differences?
2. Black Americans were far more likely than White Americans to report thinking there is strong or very strong conflict between the rich and the poor. In sociology, we study the intersections between race, class, and gender. How does the intersection of race and class help explain these survey results?

What Does America Think?

7.2 Charitable Giving

This is actual survey data from the General Social Survey, 1972–2004.

1. During the past 12 months, how often have you given money to a charity? Over the past 5 years, have you contributed your time to help the needy? Data from 2002 show that most individuals gave money to a charity in the year prior to the interview. Breakdown by social class shows the higher the social class, the greater the likelihood of giving. The responses for giving time to help the needy broke down in a similar way by social class. In addition, individuals were more likely to have given money in the past year than time in the past 5 years.

CRITICAL THINKING | DISCUSSION QUESTIONS

1. Why do you think the social class differences exist? They are easy to explain away by saying that richer people have more money to give to charity, and poor people need their money for basic necessities. What other sociological explanations can you come up with?
2. The differences among social classes for giving money to charity were much greater than the differences for contributing time to help the needy. What might explain that?
3. Many people reported not giving money and not giving time for charity. What are some commonly held stereotypes about the needy that might hold people back from giving or at least give them justification for not giving?

What Does America Think?

▶ Go to this website to look further at the data. You can run your own statistics and crosstabs here: http://sda.berkeley.edu/cgi-bin/hsda?harcsda+gss04

REFERENCES: Davis, James A., Tom W. Smith, and Peter V. Marsden. General Social Surveys 1972–2004: [Cumulative file] [Computer file]. 2nd ICPSR version. Chicago, IL: National Opinion Research Center [producer], 2005; Storrs, CT: Roper Center for Public Opinion Research, University of Connecticut; Ann Arbor, MI: Inter-University Consortium for Political and Social Research; Berkeley, CA: Computer-Assisted Survey Methods Program, University of California [distributors], 2005.

Chapter 8
Race and Ethnicity

Chapter Outline

I.   Distinguishing between Race and Ethnicity
   - a.   What is race?
     - i.   Race depends on an assumption of biological distinction.
     - ii.   Sociologically "race" is not real- there are not distinct races that are pure and clearly demarcated from others.
   - b.   Ethnicity depends on an assumption of cultural distinction.
   - c.   Biraciality and Multiraciality
     - i.   There is no such thing as a "pure" race.
     - ii.   Until 1967 biracial marriages were punishable by prison sentence in all but 9 states.
     - iii.   In 2000, 2 percent of the population was identified as biracial and multiracial.

II.   The Sociology of Race and Ethnicity
   - a.   Minority Groups
     - i.   A racial minority group is not defined strictly by being a numerical minority.
     - ii.   Minority groups need to have four characteristics:
       1. Differential power
       2. Identifiability
       3. Ascribed status
       4. Solidarity and group awareness
   - b.   Majority Groups
     - i.   These groups are often constructed in the U.S. though skin color: dark people versus light people.
     - ii.   Whiteness becomes the standard, the norm.
     - iii.   How we got white people
       1. The privilege of whiteness has a history of political positioning.
       2. During the 19th century, ethnologists, anthropologists, and sociologists traveled around the world, dividing people into races, ordering them from the most to the least intelligent and evolved.
          - a. These racial classifications was directly related to a fear of immigration.
          - b. By 1924, the door to immigration from most of Europe slammed shut.
       3. By the 1920s, racialist "science" was being taught s fact in American Universities.

III.   Prejudice
   - a.   Stereotypes- generalizations about a group that are oversimplified and exaggerated, and fail to acknowledge individual differences in a group.
   - b.   Racism- prejudice that is systematically applied to members of a group.
     - i.   It can be over racism, in speech, manifest in behaviors such as discrimination, or a refusal to associate with members of that group.
     - ii.   It can be subtle racism and even unconscious, simply a set of mental categories that we possess about the "other" based on stereotypes.

IV.   Discrimination
   - a.   Set of actions based on prejudice and stereotypes.
   - b.   Robert Merton divided prejudice and discrimination into four categories:
     - i.   All-weather bigot: are prejudice and discriminate against minority group members.
     - ii.   Fair-weather bigots: are prejudice but they do not discriminate when there may be negative consequences.
     - iii.   Fair-weather liberals: are not prejudice but discriminate when it is profitable for them to do so.

iv. All-weather liberals: are not prejudice and do not discriminate.
c. Institutional Discrimination
    i. It is deeply embedded in such institutions as the educational system, the business world, health care, criminal justice, and the mass media.
    ii. Minority groups become the victims of systematic oppression, even when only a few people, or none at all, are deliberately trying to discriminate.
    iii. Fair Housing Act of 1968- banned discrimination in housing, but institutional discrimination persists.
d. Segregation and Integration
    i. Segregation is the physical separation of different groups
        1. *Plessy vs. Ferguson*, 1896, Supreme Court decided that "separate but equal" accommodations for Blacks and Whites was not discriminatory.
        2. Usually "separate" meant "unequal."
    ii. Integration is the physical intermingling of the races, which presumably would lead to cultural intermingling and racial equality.
        1. *Brown vs. the Board of Education*, 1854, Supreme Court rules that "separate but equal" was never equal.
        2. Fifty years later, integration has not been entirely achieved.
e. Affirmative Action or "Reverse Discrimination"?
    i. Affirmative action programs ensure that minorities get fair treatment in employment applications.
        1. Opponents claim that minority applicants are "stealing jobs" from more qualified White applicants.
        2. Reverse discrimination
    ii. Sometimes affirmative action programs can lead to tokenism, in which a single member of a minority group is present in the office, workshop, or classroom.
f. Hate Groups
    i. People join hate groups to promote discrimination against ethnic and other minorities.
        1. Know-Nothing Party was formed in 1849 to promote anti-Catholic and anti-immigration legislation.
        2. The Ku Klux Klan formed shortly after the end of slavery in 1863 to try to prevent newly freed blacks from acquiring social equality.
    ii. Though membership in organized hate groups is relatively low, there is an alarming increase in violent crimes in which the victim was chosen because of his or her membership in some minority group.
V. Theories of Prejudice and Discrimination
a. Primordial theory- suggests that a conflict exists between in-groups and out-groups, without explaining how some groups come to be classified as out-group.
b. Frustration-aggression theory- people are goal direct and when they can not reach their goals, they become angry and frustrated.
    i. If they are not able to find the source of their frustration they will direct their aggression towards a scapegoat.
    ii. Sometimes people may become convinced that the scapegoat is actually the cause of their frustration.
c. Conflict theory- prejudice is a tool used by elites, people at the top of the social hierarchy, to "divide and conquer" those at the bottom, making them easier to control.
d. Feminist theory- considers how the category of race overlaps with other social categories, especially gender.
e. Doing Something about It
    i. Early social scientists argued that prejudice could be changed by exposure to members of the minority group.
        1. During the 1960s and 1970s, a huge amount of time and money was invested in busing students from segregated schools to introduce Black and White students to each other.
        2. Contact alone does not diminish prejudice.

ii. Mark Snyder found that even awareness of prejudice and desire to change were insufficient.

iii. Gordon Allport called prejudice "a self-fulfilling prophecy"; what we see fulfills our expectations and the stereotypes are confirmed.

1. Discrimination is simply a form of socialization.
2. The targets of discrimination can be socialized into believing that the stereotypes are accurate and behave accordingly.

f. Overcoming Prejudice

i. Mere contact is not enough, but when people of different groups must work together toward a common goal, most measures of prejudice decrease.

ii. Evidence suggests that many people are just learning what answers look best on surveys, regardless of how they really feel or react.

VI. Ethnic Groups in the United States

a. Ethnicity- a group that has some distinctive norms, values, beliefs, practices, outlooks, and cultural artifacts that emerge historically and tend to set the group apart from other groups, physically and culturally.

b. Ethic groups share a common ancestry, history, or culture.

c. People from Europe- 75 percent of the U.S. population was identified as White, most of European ancestry, in the 2000 Census

d. People from North America

i. Native Americans were the original inhabitants of North America.

ii. European settlers usually approached the native Americans through stereotypes: "noble savages" or "wild savages."

iii. In the 2000 Census, only about 1.5 percent of the population identified as Native American.

iv. The history of contact between European immigrants and Native Americans left many tribes destroyed, decimated, or displaced onto reservations.

e. People From Latin America

i. In 2000, 12.5 percent of the U.S. population declared they were Hispanic or Latino/Latina.

ii. Hispanics may be of any race since the regions they come from were originally settled by Native Americans, Europeans, Africans, and Asians.

iii. Latinos in the U.S. come from various countries of origin.

1. 34.3 million are from Mexico.
2. 2.3 million are from Central America, mainly from El Salvador, Guatemala, Honduras, and Nicaragua.
3. 1.7 million are from South America, mainly from Columbia, Ecuador, and Peru.
4. 1.2 million are from Cuba.
5. 912,000 are from the Dominican Republic.
6. 3.5 million are from Puerto Rico.

iv. Hispanic Americans are not only the fastest-growing minority group in the United States, they also have the fastest-growing affluence.

f. People from Sub-Saharan Africa

i. In the 2000 Census, 12.5 percent of the U.S. population was identified as Black or African American.

ii. The African American population is expected to experience modest growth.

iii. African American shave achieved some measure of political and economic success.

1. There is a sizeable middle-class.
2. They now have educational backgrounds and earnings comparable to that of middle-class Whites.

iv. African Americans still lag behind White non-Hispanic Americans.

1. Black men's median earnings are 75 percent of what White men earn.
2. Thirty percent of Black families and 9 percent of White families are below the poverty level.

g. People from East and South Asia

          i. About 3.6 percent of the U.S. population traces its ancestry to East, Southeast, or South Asia.

          ii. Even within a nationality, there are many ethnic differences.

          iii. Asian Americans are often depicted as the "model minority."

    h. People from the Middle East

          i. There are about two million people in the United States that trace their ancestry to the Middle East or North Africa.

               1. First wave between 1880 and 1920 came from the failing Ottoman Empire.

               2. After 1970, many middle class Israelis, Arabs, and Iranians immigrated to America.

          ii. Stereotypes about Middle Easterners tend to be more extreme, and more commonly believed, than stereotypes about other minority groups.

          iii. Prejudice against Middle Easterners, Arabs, and Muslims has increased significantly in the last decade, and especially after the 9/11 terrorist attacks.

  i. Ethnicity and Conflict

          i. When several different ethnic groups are present in a single nation, they often compete for power and resources.

          ii. Genocide is the planned, systematic destruction of a racial, political, or cultural group.

               1. Nazi massacre of six million Jews, Gypsies, gay, and other "undesirables."

               2. Turkish elite of the Ottoman Empire killed over one million ethnic Armenian between 1915 and 1923.

               3. In 1990s, the dominant Hutu ethnic group killed hundreds of thousands of minority Tutsi in Rwanda and Burundi.

  j. Melting Pot (Assimilation) and Multiculturalism (Pluralism)

          i. Assimilation is when a minority group nearly abandons their cultural traditions altogether and embrace the dominant culture.

          ii. Pluralism maintains that a stable society need not contain just one ethnic, cultural, or religious group.

               1. Different groups can treat each other with respect instead of competing.

               2. Minority cultures can then maintain their own distinctiveness and still participate in a greater society without discrimination.

               3. Pluralism becomes multiculturalism, in which cultural groups exist not only side by side but equally.

          iii. Bilingualism- the ability to speak two different languages fluently.

VII.   Race and Ethnicity in the 21st Century

  a. Race and ethnicity are vital elements of our identity and also the basis for discrimination and inequality.

  b. The changes in racial and ethnic identities are liable to be dramatic and lasting.

Chapter Summary

- Race depends on an assumption of biological distinction while ethnicity depends on an assumption of cultural distinction.
- Minority groups are composed of people who are singled out for unequal treatment by the dominant group. To be classified as a minority group, it need to have four characteristics: differential power, identifiability, ascribe status, and solidarity and group awareness.
- The majority group has more economic, social, and political resources than minority groups.
- The privilege of being White does not depend on your skin color, rather it has a history and is the result of political positioning.
- Prejudice is a belief that causes us to negatively prejudge people based on their social location and discrimination is the unfair treatment of people.
- Racism describes a set of attitudes. Overt racism manifests in behaviors such as discrimination or the refusal to associate with member of that group and subtle racism is a set of mental categories that we possess about the "other" based on stereotypes.
- Institutional discrimination is discrimination built into society's social institutions and can be seen in the education system, the business world, health care, criminal justice, and the mass media.
- Segregation is the physical separation of the dominant and minority group while integration in the physical intermingling of the races.
- In 1965, President Lyndon B. Johnson established the Equal Opportunity Commission, which administers many affirmative action programs to ensure that minorities get fair treatment in employment applications. Opponent to affirmative action believe that minority applicants steal jobs from more qualified White applicants, reverse discrimination.
- The hate group the Know-Nothing Party was established in 1849 to promote anti-Catholic and anti-immigrant legislation. The KKK was formed in 1963 to prevent the newly freed slaves from acquiring social equality. Hate groups still exist today although there membership is relatively slow.
- The primordial theory suggests that conflict exists between in-groups and out-groups but does not explain how some groups come to be classified as out-groups. The frustration-aggression theory believes that people are goal directed, and when they can't reach their goals, they become angry and frustrated. The conflict theory suggests that prejudice is a tool used by the elites, people at the top of the social hierarchy, to "divide and conquer" those at the bottom, making them easier to control and manipulate. The feminist theory considers how the category of race overlaps with other social categories.
- The largest ethnic group in the United States are Europeans followed by Latinos, African Americans, Asian Americans, and the Native Americans.
- There have been many ethnic conflicts throughout history resulting in genocide. The most notable are the Nazi massacring Jews, Gypsies, gays, and other "undesirables; Turkish elite of the Ottoman Empire killing ethnic Armenians; The Hutu in Rwanda and Burundi killing hundreds of thousand of Tutsi; Serbs killing the Kosovar Albanians.
- Minority groups can assimilate, abandoning their cultural traditions altogether and embrace the dominant culture. During the 1980s and 1990s pluralism became the alternative to the melting pot. Pluralism maintain that a stable society need not contain just one ethnic, cultural, or religious group; the different groups can treat each other with mutual respect instead of competing and trying to dominant each other.
- Today race and ethnicity are still vital elements of our identity and is also the basis for discrimination and inequality.

Learning Objectives
After completing the reading of Chapter 8, you should be able to answer the following objectives.

- Distinguish between race and ethnicity.
- Describe the characteristics between the minority group and the majority group.
- Understand the history of "Whiteness."
- Define prejudice and discrimination and know the difference between the two.
- Define racism and differentiate between overt racism and subtle racism.

- Explain the four categories that Robert Merton divided prejudice and discrimination into.
- Define institutional discrimination and give examples of it.
- Understand what affirmative action programs do.
- Discuss hate groups, when where they formed and what the status of them is now.
- Understand the four different theories of prejudice and discrimination that the book presents.
- Compare and contrast the experience of White Europeans, Latinos, African Americans, Native Americans, Asian Americans, and Middle Easterners in the United States.
- Discuss assimilation, pluralism, and multiculturalism.

Key Terms

Affirmative Action: programs to ensure that applicants are employed and employees are treated without regard to race, color, creed, or national origin.

Apartheid: means "separation" and was the system that mandated segregation of different racial groups.

Ascribed status: membership is something you are born with.

Assimilation: minority groups abandon their cultural traditions altogether embracing the dominant culture.

Differential power: difference in access to economic, social, and political resources.

Discrimination: set of actions based on prejudice and stereotypes.

Ethnicity: based on assumption of cultural distinctions.

Ethnic Groups: share common sense of ancestry, history, or culture.

Genocide: the planned, systematic destruction of a racial, political, or cultural group.

Indentifiability: minority group members' physical or cultural traits that distinguish from the dominant group.

Institutional Discrimination: social institutions promote discriminatory practices toward people in the minority group.

Integration: physical intermingling of the races.

Matrix of Domination: an interlocking system of control in which each type of inequality reinforces the others so that the impact of one cannot be fully understood without also considering the others.

Majority Group: the group that controls economic, social, and political resources.

Minority Group: group that has less access to social, economic, and political resources; identifiable by physical or cultural traits; has an ascribe status; and an awareness of membership in a definable category of people.

Overt racism: manifests in behaviors such as discrimination, or the refusal to associate with members of that group.

Pluralism: maintains that a stable society need not contain just one ethnic, cultural, or religious group.
Prejudice: set of beliefs and attitudes that cause us to negatively prejudge people based on their social location.

Primordial theory: conflict exists between in-groups and out-groups, but it does not explain how some groups come to be classified as out-groups.

Race: based on the assumption of biological distinction.

Racism: prejudice that is systematically applied to members of a group.

Scapegoat: weak, convenient, and socially approved target for others to direct their aggression at.

Segregation: physical separation between two groups of people based on race or ethnicity.

Stereotypes: generalization about a group that are oversimplified and exaggerated.

Subtle racism: a set of mental categories that we possess about the "other" based on stereotypes.

Tokenism: single member of a minority group present in an office, workshop, or classroom.

Key People

David Duke: former KKK Grand Wizard.

Patricia Hill Collins: coined the term "matrix of domination."

Ku Klux Klan (KKK): group formed shortly after the end of slavery in 1863 to try to prevent newly blacks from acquiring social equality.

Robert Merton: divided prejudice and discrimination into four categories.

Additional Learning with MySocLab

Read

> **Racial Tensions Lead to Student Protest at Colgate (pg 251)**
> In the US, increases in racial diversity come slowly. Caucasians comprise about seventy-five percent of the total population followed closely by Hispanics, African Americans, Asians, and Native Americans.
> **A Slaying in 1982 Maintains Its Grip on Asian-Americans (pg 253)**
> A gathering of mostly Asian-American college students mulled over programs and speaker to make their message resonate. Twenty years ago a Chinese-American was beaten to death by two auto workers who apparently believed he was Japanese.

Explore

> **Explanation of Racial Inequality (pg 254)**
> This activity explores how African Americans and white American have different views on why discrimination still persists. The data for this study is taken from the 1998 General Social Survey.
> **Web Activities: Race: Affirmative Action Remains a Controversial Issue (pg 257)**
> Read the articles "Ten Myths About Affirmative Action," "Michigan weighs ban on affirmative action," and "Michigan Voters Ban Affirmative Action" to learns more about the complex topic of affirmative action. After reading the articles there is a series of questions to answer.

Listen

> **Hispanics Now Largest Minority (pg 266)**
> Robert Siegel notes that new Census figures indicate Hispanics are now the largest minority group in the United States. The U.S. Census Bureau denotes the term Hispanic to mean an ethnicity not a race.

Watch

> **White Privilege in the U.S. (pg 249)**
> Wood Doane discusses some of the taken-for-granted privileges that whites enjoy in the United States.
> **The KKK (pg 258)**
> This video clips covers a protest of the KKK and discusses how symbolic interactionists may explain prejudice.

Visualize

> **African Americans: Continued Gains (pg 267)**
> The pie-chart helps to visualize the changes in African American's earnings from 1967 to 1994.

Practice Test

After completing the practice test, check your answers in the Answer Key of this Study Guide.

Multiple Choice Questions

1. Ethnicity:
    a. depends on an assumption of biological distinction.
    b. depends on an assumption of cultural distinction.
    c. depends of having a physical characteristic.
    d. is relatively easy to determine.

2. A minority group:
    a. is based on numerical numbers.
    b. is not identifiable.
    c. is discriminated against based on personality traits.
    d. is discriminated against because of physical traits.

3. Which of the following best describes the melting pot?
    a. a society in which groups blend into a sort of ethnic stew.
    b. a society in which each groups maintains its own characteristics.
    c. a society in which everyone adapts to a minority group's ways.
    d. a society in which different groups live separately from each other.

4. Prejudice is a set of _____ while discrimination is a set of _____.
    a. actions; beliefs
    b. beliefs; attitudes
    c. beliefs; actions
    d. None of the above

5. According to Feminist Theory, prejudice:
    a. is a tool by the elites to control those at the bottom.
    b. is directed to the scapegoat by the person who is frustrated.
    c. suggests conflict exists between in-groups.
    d. is magnified because of how the category of race overlaps with other statuses.

6. Genocide is:
    a. planned, systematic destruction of a racial group.
    b. planned, systematic destruction of a political group.
    c. planned, systematic destruction of a cultural group.
    d. All of the above.

7. Sociologists see race as:
    a. fluid.
    b. fixed.
    c. eternal.
    d. None of the above.

8. Biracial relationships that were punishable by prison sentence until 1967 were labeled:
    a. immoral.
    b. miscegenation.
    c. inferior.
    d. corrupt.

9. What is the term for a category of people, distinguished by physical or cultural traits, who are not socially disadvantaged?
  a. Minority group
  b. In-group
  c. Out-group
  d. Majority group

10. Where did the Teutonic people come from?
  a. Northern Europe
  b. Middle East
  c. Southern Europe
  d. East Asia

11. The "discovery" that Europe had inferior and superior races was directly related to what?
  a. Blacks being lynched in the south
  b. The influx of Asian immigrants to the United States
  c. Fear of immigration
  d. The relative fast integration of the German and French

12. When believing that all Asian people are very intelligent is an example of:
  a. prejudice.
  b. discrimination.
  c. racism.
  d. stereotyping.

13. Which of the following is not an example of genocide?
  a. the Nazis killing 6 million Jews and others
  b. the Hutu in Rwanda and Burundi killing thousands of Tutsi
  c. the Turkish elite killing over one million ethnic Armenians
  d. the Muslims in Bosnia killing thousands of Serbs in Bosnia

14. What type of racism includes someone having a set of mental categories that they possess about the "other" based on stereotypes?
  a. Overt racism
  b. Subtle racism
  c. Institutional racism
  d. Individual racism

15. Which category of people are not prejudice, but they do discriminate when it is profitable for them to do so?
  a. All-weather bigots
  b. Fair-weather bigots
  c. Fair-weather liberals
  d. All-weather liberals

16. Which of the following would not be included in the social distance scale?
  a. Would you make them a personal friend
  b. Would you work in the same office
  c. Would you accept them as a neighbor
  d. Would you live in the same city

17. People join what type of group to promote discrimination against ethnic and other minorities?
  a. in-groups
  b. hate groups
  c. out-groups
  d. worship groups

18. Conflict theory suggests that prejudice is a:
    a. tool used by the elites to control those at the bottom.
    b. a conflict that exists between the in-group and out-group.
    c. does not explain how some groups come to be classified as out-groups.
    d. emotional reaction when someone becomes angry and frustrated.

19. According to the book *The Bell Curve: Intelligence and Class Structure in American Life*, what is the cause of crime, poverty, and unemployment?
    a. Cultural patterns
    b. High intelligence
    c. Low intelligence
    d. Immorality of some races

20. The process of each ethnic, cultural, or religious group maintaining their own traditions is:
    a. assimilation.
    b. melting pot.
    c. pluralism.
    d. bilingualism.

21. Institutional discrimination refers to:
    a. some people holding biased attitudes.
    b. people stereotyping other groups of people.
    c. discrimination that is deeply embedded in the individual working in the business world.
    d. discrimination that is deeply embedded in the education system.

22. Multiculturalism opposes assimilation because:
    a. the United States ahs provided a better life for all categories of people.
    b. it does not happen in this country.
    c. this suggest that minorities are the ones who need to do all the changing.
    d. All of the above.

23. The overall social standing of Native Americans is:
    a. above the national average.
    b. below the national average.
    c. about the national average.
    d. the same as other ethnic groups.

24. Which of the following categories of Hispanics in the United States has the largest population?
    a. Cubans
    b. Puerto Ricans
    c. Guatemalans
    d. Mexicans

25. A national civil rights movement, which ended most lawful discrimination took place when?
    a. During the 1820s.
    b. During the 1950s.
    c. During the 1960s.
    d. There is still lawful discrimination.

True/False Questions

True   False   1. Race is defined by the biological distinction of skin color, however the concept of "race" is constructed by society.

True   False   2. Race and ethnicity mean the same thing.

STUDY GUIDE

True   False   3. Members of a minority group does not have a disadvantage in terms of access to economic, social, and political resources.

True   False   4. Prejudice is a set of actions based on stereotypes that negatively affect the group in question.

True   False   5. Stereotypes are generalizations about a group that are oversimplified and exaggerated.

True   False   6. If someone is unconscious about the set of mental categories that they posses about the other based on stereotypes is overt racism.

True   False   7. All-weathered bigot are prejudice against minority group and discriminate against them.

True   False   8. The first hate group did not appear until the late 1900s.

True   False   9. Native Americans are not disadvantaged compare to European Americans.

True   False   10. Many people believe that English should be the United States legal language.

Fill-in-the-Blank Questions

1. Prejudice is a matter of _____ while discrimination is a matter of behavior.

2. Ethnicity refers to _____ considered important by a society.

3. Minority group membership is _____ because they share physical or cultural traits that distinguish them from the dominant group.

4. _____ describes a set of attitudes.

5. According to Robert Merton people who are not prejudice but do discriminate are called _____.

6. The _____ was formed shortly after slavery was outlawed to prevent the newly freed blacks from acquiring social equality.

7. Only 1.5 percent of the population identified as _____ in the 2000 Census.

8. Asian Americans are often depicted as the _____ minority.

9. _____ maintains that a stable society need not contain just one ethnic, cultural, or religious group.

10. _____ are the largest minority group in the United States.

148

Essay Questions

1. How does each of the four theories explain prejudice and discrimination.

2. What traits does a race or ethnic group need to have to be classified as a minority group? Give details.

3. Describe the history of one or more minorities in terms of where they came from, when the migrated to the United States, and their social status.

4. Define and contrast assimilation and pluralism.

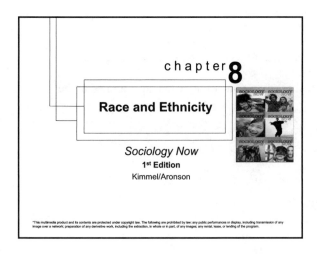

chapter **8**

Race and Ethnicity

Sociology Now
1st Edition
Kimmel/Aronson

This multimedia product and its contents are protected under copyright law. The following are prohibited by law: any public performances or display, including transmission of any image over a network; preparation of any derivative work, including the extraction, in whole or in part, of any images; any rental, lease, or lending of the program.

Distinguishing Between Race and Ethnicity

- **race** biological distinction
- **ethnicity** cultural distinction
  - both *are social constructions*
  - *neither have basis in empirical fact*

- **What is Race?**
  - a biological distinction with no basis in any empirical fact
  - division based on cultural factors
  - 18th century – physical attributes become determining factors in "race"

"... things that are perceived as real are real in their consequences."

Copyright © Allyn & Bacon 2009

Distinguishing Between Race and Ethnicity

- **Biraciality and Multiraciality**
  - every human group has mixed ancestry
  - *Miscegenation*
    - mulattos
    - mestizos
  - interracial romantic relationships are still stigmatized

Copyright © Allyn & Bacon 2009

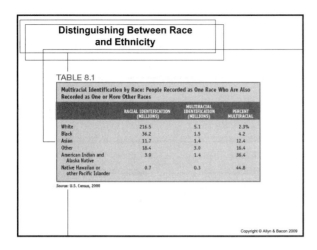

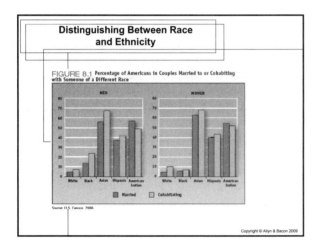

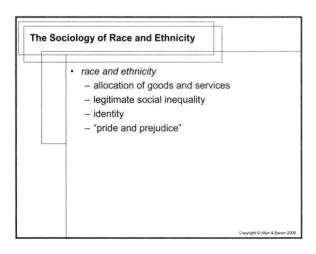

The Sociology of Race and Ethnicity

- **Minority Groups**
  - **Differential power**
  - **Identifiability**
  - **Ascribed status**
  - **Solidarity and group awareness**

- **"Majority" Groups**
  - semantics
  - whiteness as "standard"
  - light over dark *within* groups
  - **How We Got White People**

Prejudice

- **Prejudice**
  - beliefs and attitudes
  - prejudgment → social location

- **Stereotypes**
  - oversimplified and exaggerated generalizations
  - cultural "explanations" of difference have now replaced biological ones
  - people seem to believe stereotypes in light of the facts

Prejudice

- **Racism**
  - prejudice systematically applied to groups
    - *overt racism*
    - *subtle racism*
  - once race is superior

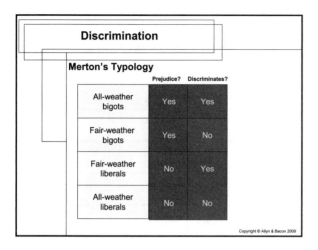

Discrimination

Merton's Typology

	Prejudice?	Discriminates?
All-weather bigots	Yes	Yes
Fair-weather bigots	Yes	No
Fair-weather liberals	No	Yes
All-weather liberals	No	No

Discrimination

- **Institutional Discrimination**
  - most subtle and pervasive type
  - deeply embedded in social institutions
  - Fair Housing Act of 1968

- **Segregation and Integration**
  - **Segregation:** physical separation
    - "Separate but equal" (1896 *Plessy vs. Ferguson)*
    - *Apartheid:* South Africa
  - **Integration:** physical intermingling
    - *Brown vs. Board of Ed.* 1954

Discrimination

- **Affirmative Action or "Reverse Discrimination"?**
  - **affirmative action** ensures fair treatment
  - only 25 of all pending EOC cases are for reverse discrimination
    - Affirmative action abolished in college admissions in CA, WA and FL
    - **tokenism**
- **Hate Groups**
  - Know-Nothing Party
  - Ku Klux Klan
  - hate crimes continue to grow

Theories of Prejudice and Discrimination

- *primordial theory*
  - Innate conflict between in-groups and out-groups
- *frustration-aggression theory*
  - Frustrated when goals are not met
  - Aggression towards **scapegoat'**
- *conflict theory*
  - "divide and conquer"
- *feminist theory*
  - Intersection of race and gender, sexual orientation, social class, religion, age and ability status
    - **matrix of domination** (Collins)

Copyright © Allyn & Bacon 2009

Theories of Prejudice and Discrimination

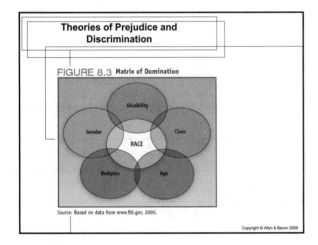

FIGURE 8.3 **Matrix of Domination**

Source: Based on data from www.fbi.gov, 2005.

Copyright © Allyn & Bacon 2009

Theories of Prejudice and Discrimination

- **Doing Something about It**
  - Exposure to people from other groups
    - busing in the 1960s and 1970s
    - contact alone does not diminish prejudice
  - Awareness and desire to change prejudice behavior patterns insufficient
  - Prejudice as "self-fulfilling prophecy" (**Allport**)
    - Discrimination as form of socialization
  - Affect of "labeling" upon students of color
    - "acting *White*"
    - "acting like girls"

- **Overcoming Prejudice**

Copyright © Allyn & Bacon 2009

Ethnic Groups in the United States

- **People from Europe**
- **People from North America**
- **People from Latin America**
- **People from Sub-Saharan Africa**
- **People from East and South Asia**
- **People from Middle East**

Ethnic Groups in the United States

- **Ethnicity and Conflict**
  - ethnicity is *fluid* and *situational*
  - **genocide**

- **Melting Pot (Assimilation) and Multiculturalism (Pluralism)**
  - Abandon Cultural traditions
  - Coexistence

- **Bilingualism**
  - Non-legalized preference for English

- **Race and Ethnicity in the 21st Century**

What Does America Think?

8.1 Neighborhood Segregation

This is based on actual survey data from the General Social Survey, 2004; cumulative data.

1. Please respond to the following statement: White people have the right to keep Black people out of their neighborhoods if they want to, and Black people should respect that right. Seventy-five percent of respondents disagreed either slightly or strongly. Almost 80 percent of Black respondents disagreed strongly, as opposed to 45 percent of White respondents. Only about 11 percent of respondents agreed strongly.

CRITICAL THINKING | DISCUSSION QUESTIONS

1. Why do you think 10 percent of black respondents agreed that White people should be allowed to keep Black people out and that Black people should respect that right? Do you think those same individuals feel that Black people should be able to keep White people out of their neighborhoods?
2. How do you think responses to this question would differ by social class? By geographical region? How would you explain those potential differences?
3. Seventy-five percent of respondents disagreed with White-imposed neighborhood segregation. What percent of respondents do you think would have disagreed had this survey been given in 1850? In 1950? Explain your answers.

What Does America Think?

8.2 The Melting Pot

This is based on actual survey data from the General Social Survey, 2004.

1. Some people say that it is better for a country if different racial and ethnic groups maintain their distinct customs and traditions. Others say that it is better if these groups adapt and blend into the larger society. Which of these views comes closer to your own? The responses to this question were split almost in half. Slightly more than 50 percent of respondents thought it was better if groups adapted and blended into the larger society. White respondents (55.4%) were more likely to think that than were Black respondents (52.8%), and those who identified as other race were least likely to feel groups should assimilate (45.7%).

CRITICAL THINKING | DISCUSSION QUESTIONS

1. Why do you think there were only very small differences in responses by racial classification?
2. In many areas of the world, the question of assimilation and group difference leads to civil war and even genocide. Why do you think that does not happen in the contemporary United States?

Copyright © Allyn & Bacon 2009

What Does America Think?

➢ Go to this website to look further at the data. You can run your own statistics and crosstabs here: http://sda.berkeley.edu/cgi-bin/hsda?harcsda+gss04

REFERENCES: Davis, James A., Tom W. Smith, and Peter V. Marsden. General Social Surveys 1972–2004: [Cumulative file] [Computer file]. 2nd ICPSR version. Chicago, IL: National Opinion Research Center [producer], 2005. Storrs, CT: Roper Center for Public Opinion Research, University of Connecticut; Ann Arbor, MI: Inter-University Consortium for Political and Social Research; Berkeley, CA: Computer-Assisted Survey Methods Program, University of California [distributors], 2005.

Copyright © Allyn & Bacon 2009

Chapter 9
Sex and Gender

Chapter Outline

I.   Sex and Gender: Nature and Nurture
   a.   Sex- biology of maleness and femaleness.
   b.   Gender refers to the meanings that societies give to the fact of biological difference.
        i.   Cultural meaning of masculinity and femininity.
        ii.   Gender varies in four crucial ways:
            1.   Gender varies from culture to culture.
            2.   Definitions of gender change over time.
            3.   Definitions of gender vary within a society.
            4.   gender varies over the life course.
   c.   Gender identity refers to our understanding of ourselves as male or female, what we think it means to be male or females.
        i.   Masculinities and Femininities
        ii.   The differences among men and among women are often greater than the differences that we imagine between women and men.
        iii.   Making the terms plural indicates how different groups of men or women might have different identities.
   d.   Gender inequalities
        i.   Domination of men over women.
        ii.   Domination of some men over other men and some women over other women.
        iii.   Patriarchy- the rule of the fathers, men hold power over women.

II.   The Biology of Sex and Gender
   a.   Evolutionary Imperatives
        i.   The chief goal is to reproduce themselves.
        ii.   Can see the origins of both gender differences and gender inequality in the different strategies males and females develop to reproduce.
        iii.   Some evolutionary psychologists go so far as to claim that rape is "natural, biological phenomenon that is a product of human evolutionary heritage."
   b.   Brain and Hormone Research
        i.   Sex hormones- the hormones that trigger the development of secondary sex characteristics.
        ii.   Sex differentiation is most pronounced at two points:
            1.   During fetal development.
            2.   At puberty.
        iii.   Much hormone research concerns the effect of testosterone on behavior, since males have much higher levels than females, and its effects seem far more noticeable.
        iv.   Biology is not necessarily destiny.

III.   Exploring Cross-Cultural Variations of Sex and Gender
   a.   Sex differences are not something deeply biological.
   b.   The Value of Cross-Cultural Research.
        i.   Explores both universality of gender difference and gender inequality.
        ii.   Contemporary anthropologists still observe two cultural universals.
            1.   A gendered division of labor.
            2.   Gender inequality.
        iii.   Prehistoric societies were far more cooperative than we earlier thought.
        iv.   Why is every contemporary society male dominated?
            1.   Engels observed that the three foundations of modern society caused male domination and helped shape all modern political institutions.
            2.   Modern nuclear family- father at the head, which established which children were his, and modern law that guaranteed the orderly transfer of property.

      v. What determines women's status?
         1. Size and Strength.
         2. Women's economic activity.
         3. Child care.
  c. Blurring the Boundaries of Gender
      i. Anthropologists suggest that there may be far more gender out there than we know.
      ii. Numerous cultures have clearly defined gender role for the berdache (member of one biological sex who takes the social role of the other sex).
  d. Rituals of Gender- And What They Tell Us
      i. Circumcision
         1. Surgical removal of the boy's foreskin.
         2. Female circumcision is the surgical removal of the clitoris.
         3. Female circumcision is designed to completely eliminate the possibility of women's sexual pleasure, while most often leaving intact their reproductive ability.
      ii. Couvade
         1. Ritual practice by men when their wives are pregnant.
         2. Men observe the same food rituals, and even seclude themselves during their wives' delivery.
      iii. All the cultures are all very highly male dominant.
         1. Male circumcision cements the bonds between father and son and ensures that the son has undergone a marking that will grant him the privileges of being a male in that culture.
         2. Female circumcision removes women's sexual agency and ability to experience pleasure is destroyed so that women will be more compliant and reliable under the control of men.

IV. Becoming Gendered: Learning Gender Identity
  a. Gender socialization- process by which males and females are taught the appropriate behaviors, attitudes, and traits for their biological sex.
      i. From infancy onward, people interact with children based at least as much on cultural expectations about gender than about the child itself.
      ii. All through childhood boys and girls are dressed differently, taught to play with different toys, read different books, and they even watch different cartoon shows.
         1. Boys play on one side of the playground and girls play on the other.
         2. Boys and girls not only learn gender differences, but they learn gender inequality.
      iii. Gender polarization to describe the male-female distinction as the organizing principle of social life.
      iv. Eleanor Maccoby and Carol Jacklin found only four areas with significant and consistent gender differences:
         1. Girls have somewhat higher verbal ability.
         2. Boys have somewhat better visual and spatial ability.
         3. Boys do somewhat better on mathematical tests.
         4. Boys were significantly more aggressive than girls.
  b. The Social Construction of Gender
      i. We construct our gender identities all through our lives, using the cultural materials we find around us.
      ii. The term gender role is used to define the bundle of traits, attitudes, and behaviors that are associated with biological males and females.
      iii. Sociologists have suggested that the gender role model ignores several important dimensions of gender identity and gender inequality.
         1. It seems to assume that the two sex roles are independent and equal.
         2. The term role does not adequately capture gender in its complexity.
      iv. Gendered Institutions
         1. Gender is a dynamic in all of our interactions.

              2.   Observing how institutional arrangement are gendered often helps explain whether more men or women occupy those positions.

V.   Gender Inequality on a Global and Local Scale
- a.   Discrimination against women is a global problem.
  - i.   Just about every country in the world treats women less well than men.
  - ii.   In developing countries the problem is more fundamental and pervasive.
- b.   The U.S. gender wage gap- the gap in average wages for women and for men.
  - i.   In the U.S. women make up nearly two-thirds of all hungry adults.
  - ii.   Feminization of poverty
- c.   Globalization has also changed the dynamics of global gender inequality.
  - i.   Global geographic mobility is extremely sex-segregated- men and women move separately.
  - ii.   Some women and girls are kidnapped into a new expanding global sex trade.

VI.   Gender Inequality in the United States
- a.   The Gendered World of Work
  - i.   The work we do is gendered
    1. We have definite ideas of what sorts of occupations are appropriate for women and which are appropriate for men.
    2. Traditional ideologies persist about women and work.
    3. Gender discrimination in the workplace was once more direct and obvious.
       - a.   Women were simply prohibited from entering certain fields.
       - b.   Until the late 1960s, classified advertising was divided into male employment and female employment.
  - ii.   Sex Segregation in the Workplace.
    1. Refers to women's and men's concentration in different occupations, industries, jobs, and levels in workplace hierarchies.
    2. Dual labor market based on gender
       - a.   Rarely do men and women compete against each other for the same job at the same rank in the same organization.
       - b.   Feminization of the professions- salaries drop as female participation increases.
  - iii.   The Wage Gap
    1. Women earn less than men.
       - a.   Gap is magnified at management level.
       - b.   Gap has been remarkably consistent over time.
    2. In recent years the wage gap has been closing.
  - iv.   Glass Ceilings and the Glass Escalator
    1. Glass ceiling- artificial barriers that prevent qualified individuals from advancing upward within their organization into management level positions.
    2. Glass Escalator- males being promoted to administrative positions much more rapidly than their female colleagues.
  - v.   Sexual Harassment at Work
    1. Creates an unequal work environment by singling out women for different treatment.
       - a.   Quid pro quo harassment- occurs when a supervisor uses his or her position to try to elicit sexual activity from a subordinate by threatening to fire or promising to promote.
       - b.   Hostile environment- occurs when a person feels threatened or unsafe because of the constant teasing or threatening by other workers.
    2. Most cases of sexual harassment happen between male supervisors and female employees.
  - vi.   Balancing Work and Family
    1. Women also face discrimination if they try to balance work and family life.

2. The second shift- the housework and child care that also need to be done after a regular working shift is over.
   a. Men's share of housework increased somewhat during the 20th century, largely in response to the increasing numbers of women working outside the home.
   b. Today North American women spend 60 percent more time on chores than men.
   c. If women are responsible for housework and childcare, they are pulled away from their workplace commitments, have less networking time and may be perceived as having less ability to relocate.

b. Gender Inequality in School
   i. From the earliest ages, our educations teach us far more than the ABCs.
      1. Hidden curriculum- all the other lessons we learn in school
      2. Subjects are often taught as gender coded.
   ii. State and local governments work to eliminate gender inequality in schools because discrimination, stereotypes, and harassments hurt both boys and girls.

c. Gender Inequality in Everyday Life
   i. Industrial Revolution drove a wedge between home and work, emotional life and rational life.
      1. Most men had to leave their homes for work that was competitive and challenging.
      2. Women's sphere remained the emotional refuge of home and hearth.
      3. Result is that women have come to be seen as the experts on love and friendship.
   ii. Marriage is a deeply gendered institution.
      1. Marriage is something she wants and he resists.
      2. Jessie Bernard identified two types of marriage.
         a. His marriage
         b. Her marriage
         c. His is better than hers

VII. The Politics of Gender
   a. Opposition to Gender Roles
      i. Men and women have bumped up against restrictive stereotypes and arbitrary rules that excluded them.
         1. Women wanted to join the labor force, seek education, and vote but found they could not do it on their own.
         2. Their opposition to gender roles become political.
      ii. Men find traditional definitions of masculinity restrictive.
         1. Men's rights groups blame women for their plight.
         2. Women's movement was so successful that now men are the victims of reverse discrimination.
   b. The Women's Movement(s)
      i. The modern women's movement was born to remove obstacles to women's full participation in modern life.
         1. First wave of the women's movement took place in the 19th century.
            a. Concern was with women's entry into the public sphere.
            b. Campaigns to allow women to vote, go to college, to serve on juries, to join a union all largely succeeded by the middle of the 20th century.
         2. Second wave of the women's movement took place in the 1960s and 1970s.
            a. Determined to continue the struggle to eliminate obstacles to women's advancement.
            b. Determined to investigate the ways that gender inequality is also part of the personal life.

          c.   Focused on men's violence against women, rape, and the denigration of women in the media.

      3.   Third wave of the women's movement has emerged among younger women.

          a.   Share the outrage at institutional discrimination and interpersonal violence.

          b.   They are more multicultural, and seek to explore and challenge the intersections of gender inequality with the other forms of inequality.

    ii.   Profeminist- men who believe that gender equality is not only a good thing for women, but that it would also transform masculinity in ways that would be positive for men.

  c. Feminism

    i.   Most young women subscribe to virtually all the tenets of feminism but they believe that they are already equal to men.

    ii.   Feminism rests on two principles:

      1.   Empirical observation that women and men are not equal.

      2.   The moral stand is that this inequality is wrong and should change.

    iii.   Liberal Feminism

      1.   Follow classical liberal political theory and focus on the individual woman's rights and opportunities.

      2.   They want to remove structural obstacles that stand in the way of individual women's entry and mobility in their occupation or profession.

    iv.   Radical Feminism

      1.   Believe that women are not just discriminated against economically and politically, but they are also oppressed and subordinated by men directly, personally, and most often through sexual relations.

      2.   Believe that patriarchy is the first and original form of domination, and that all other forms of inequality derive from it.

    v.   Multicultural Feminism

      1.   Argues that the experience as people of color cannot be extracted from the experience as women and treated separately.

      2.   Emphasize the historical context of racial and class-based inequalities.

VIII.   Gender Inequality in the 21st Century

  a. There is little doubt that around the world gender inequality is gradually being reduced.

  b. Today there is significant backlash against gender equality.

    i.   Some people believe that women's rights are simply morally wrong.

    ii.   Many men have resorted to theological or biological arguments to try to force women to return to their traditional positions.

Chapter Summary

- Sex is the biology of maleness and femaleness while gender is the meanings that societies give to the fact of biological differences.
- Gender varies in four crucial ways: gender varies from culture to culture; definitions of gender change over time; definitions of gender vary within a society; gender varies over the life course.
- Gender identities refer to our understanding of ourselves and male and female. Femininities and Masculinities refer to the interaction between class, race, and gender.
- Evolutionary Imperative says that the chief goal of all living creatures is to reproduce themselves and males and females develop different reproductive strategies to ensure that this happens and that they are able to pass on their genetic material to the next generation.
- There are differences between male and female brains and their sex hormones. Sex differentiation is most pronounced at two points: during fetal development when primary sex characteristics develop and during puberty when sex hormones trigger the development of secondary sex characteristics.
- Cultural definitions of masculinity and femininity vary significantly and develop cultural explanations that claim their way is the natural way to do things.
- Size and strength, women's economic activity, and child are determinants of women's status.
- Gender socialization is the process by which males and females are taught the appropriate behaviors, attitudes, and traits for their biological sex and society is organized to make sure of this.
- The social construction of gender means that we construct our gender identities all though our lives, using cultural materials we find around us. Gender is something we get through socialization and have for the rest of our lives.
- Discrimination against women is a global problem with developing countries having the more fundamental and pervasive discrimination.
- Sex segregation, the wage gap, the glass ceiling and escalator, sexual harassment, and the balancing of work and family are all examples of gender inequality in the workplace.
- Various movements have been organized to challenge the inequality and enhance the possibilities of gender identities including: the three waves of the women's movement and more recently the "men's rights" movement.
- There are several major strands of feminism and each has its own formula for equality. Three of the strands are liberal feminism, radical feminism, and multicultural feminism.
- Gender inequality is gradually being reduced but there is significant backlash against gender equality.

Learning Objectives
After completing the reading of Chapter 9, you should be able to answer the following objectives.

- Define sex and gender and differentiate between them.
- Understand the four crucial ways that gender varies.
- Define gender identity and how making the term indicates how groups of men and women might have different identities.
- Discuss the biology of sex and gender in terms of the evolutionary imperatives and the brain and hormone research.
- Explain why gender behavior cannot be all biological using examples of cross-cultural research.
- Define gender socialization and gender roles, and explain why gender is socially constructed.
- Discuss gender inequality on a global scale in terms of the differences in developed and developing nations.
- Explain gender relations in the workplace, including the changes in the labor force participation, sex segregation, the wage gap, the "glass ceiling", the "glass escalator", sexual harassment, and the family.
- Discuss how the education system perpetuates gender inequality.
- Discuss the different waves of the feminist movement and the men who oppose gender inequality.

- Describe the three different types of feminism present in the book, including what their political formula is and what issues are important to each,.

Key Terms

Evolutionary imperative: term used to imply that the chief goal of all living creatures is to reproduce.

Femininities: recognizes the multiple meanings female gender might contain.

Feminization of poverty: term that indicates women make up an increasing number of poor people.

Feminization of the professions: phenomenon in which salaries drop as female participation increases, revealing that it is less the intrinsic properties of the position that determines its wages and prestige, and more which sex does it.

Gender: refers to the meaning that societies give to the fact of biological difference.

Gender identity: our understanding of ourselves as male or female, what we think it means to be male or female.

Gender inequality: the domination of men over women and the domination of some men over other men, and some women over other women.

Gender polarization: describes the male-female distinction as the organizing principle of social life, toughing virtually every other aspect of human experience.

Gender roles: the bundle of traits, attributes, and behaviors that are associated with biological males and females.

Gender socialization: process by which males and females are taught the appropriate behaviors, attitudes, and traits for their biological sex.

Gender wage gap: the gap between earnings of men and women.

Intersectionality: denotes the study of the intersections of gender, race, class, age, ethnic, and sexual dimensions of inequality.

Liberal feminism: follows classical liberal political theory and focuses on the individual woman's rights and opportunities.

Masculinities: recognizes the multiple meanings male gender might contain.

Multicultural feminism: the experience as people of color cannot be extracted from the experience as women and treated separately.

Patriarchy: a system in which men hold power over women.

Primary sex characteristics: characteristics that are anatomically present at birth.

Radical Feminism: believe that women are not just discriminated against economically and politically, they are also oppressed and subordinated by men directly through sexual relations.

The second shift: housework and child care that also need to be done after a regular working shift is over.

Secondary sex characteristics: sex characteristics that occur during puberty.

Sex: biological distinction.

Sex hormones: testosterone and estrogen, the hormones that trigger development of secondary sex characteristics.

Sex segregation : women's and men's concentration in different occupations, industries, jobs, and levels in workplace hierarchies.

Sexual harassment: creates an unequal work environment by singling out women for different treatment.

Social construction of gender: construct our gender identities all though our lives, using the cultural materials we find around us.

Key People

Jessie Bernard: argued that marriage benefits men more than it does women.

Marvin Harris: argued that warfare an the preparations for war and the main cause of male domination because warfare demands that there be a core of highly valued fathers and sons to carry out its military tasks.

Ruth Hubbard: Harvard biologists questioned biological research on gender differences.

Margaret Mead: anthropologist that studied cultural differences in gender.

Additional Learning with MySocLab
Read

A Conversation with — Anne Fausto-Sterling; Exploring What Makes Us Male or Female (pg 282)
The article discusses Dr. Anne Fausto-Sterling's application of ideas about gender roles to the formal study of biology.
Want to Try Out for College Sports? Forget It (pg 304)
Sociologists consider the social structural patterns when doing research on social phenomena. The patterns of groups and the relationships within those groups guide our behaviors from day to day.

Explore

Web Activities: Gender: Women in the U.S. Still Experiencing the Glass Ceiling (pg 302)
Read the articles "Women still struggling to break the glass ceiling" and "Are Women Happy Under the Glass Ceiling to understand women's experiences in the workforce and the trends of women's employment in top corporate positions. After reading the articles there is a series of questions to answer.

Listen

Title XI (pg 304)
Despite many efforts to legally eliminate gender inequality, however, such inequality persists. The National Women's Law Center investigated vocational education and found that girls are often steered into historically female occupations that are also lower paying.

Watch

Sociological Perspective on Gender (pg 293)
This video clip discusses what it is about gender that is most interesting to sociologists. Sociologists study the way society understands what it means to be a man or a woman.

Visualize

Housework (pg 303)
The bar chart presents the breakdown of household responsibilities by gender.
Roles (305)
The chart shows the advantages and disadvantages of being male or female.

Practice Test

After completing the practice test, check your answers in the Answer Key of this Study Guide.

Multiple Choice Questions

1. Gender refers to:
   a. the biology of maleness and femaleness.
   b. the meaning that societies give to the fact of biological differences.
   c. the degree of inequality between men and women in a society.
   d. our understanding of ourselves as male or female.

2. Which of the following is not one of the ways gender varies?
   a. It varies from culture to culture
   b. Definitions of gender stay the same over time
   c. Definitions of gender vary within a society
   d. Gender varies over the life course

3. Margaret Mead's research on gender in three South Sea cultures illustrates that:
   a. all cultures believe their was is the "natural" way.
   b. all cultures define masculine the same way.
   c. all societies display changing gender definitions.
   d. all cultures define feminine the same way.

4. What is the term for a society in which males dominate females?
   a. Matriarchy
   b. Gender inequality
   c. Monarchy
   d. Patriarchy

5. The evolutionary imperative refers to:
   a. males and females developing identical reproductive strategies.
   b. males and females developing reproductive strategies based on their primary sex characteristics.
   c. males and females developing different reproductive strategies.
   d. None of the above

6. When comparing countries, women's equality is lowest in:
   a. United States.
   b. Italy.
   c. Brazil.
   d. South Korea.

7. Which of the following does not determine women's status in society?
   a. Child care
   b. Women's economic activity
   c. Size and strength
   d. All of the above

8. What is the term used that describes the male-female distinction as the organizing principle of social life?
   a. Gender roles
   b. Gender polarization
   c. Gender inequality
   d. Gender socialization

9. _____ is the term used to define the bundle of traits, attitudes, and behaviors that are associated with biological males and females.
    a. Gender
    b. Gender socialization
    c. Gender roles
    d. Gendered violence

10. Eleanor Macoby and Carol Jacklin found a surprising degree of similarities between the sexes. They found only four areas with significant and consistent gender roles, which of the following is not one of those four areas?
    a. Girls have somewhat higher verbal ability
    b. Boys have somewhat better visual ability
    c. Boys do somewhat better on mathematical tests
    d. Boys are no more aggressive than girls

11. Gender inequality is more fundamental and pervasive in which type of nation?
    a. Nonindustrialized
    b. Semi-industrialized
    c. Industrialized
    d. None of the above.

12. Approximately what percentage of women participate in the labor force today?
    a. 20 percent
    b. 40 percent
    c. 60 percent
    d. 80 percent

13. If sexual harassment makes a person feel threatened or unsafe because of constant teasing or threatening by other workers is referred to as:
    a. Quid pro quo harassment
    b. Hostile environment
    c. Violent harassment
    d. Subordinate harassment

14. The feminization of the professions means that:
    a. women are concentrated in certain professions.
    b. salaries increase as female participation increases.
    c. salaries drop as female participation increases.
    d. males are forced out of certain occupations.

15. When men are in predominately female professions and are promoted to administration more rapidly than their female colleague, sociologists would refer to this as:
    a. Glass escalator.
    b. Glass ceiling.
    c. Glass elevator.
    d. Polite discrimination.

16. Gender inequality can be seen in:
    a. the workplace.
    b. the education system.
    c. in everyday life.
    d. All of the above.

17. Which wave of feminism shared the outrage at institutional discrimination and interpersonal violence?
    a. First wave
    b. Second wave
    c. Third wave
    d. Fourth wave

18. Liberal feminists believe:
    a. that structural obstacles stand in the way of individual women's entry and mobility in their occupation.
    b. that women are oppressed through sexual relations with men.
    c. that blanket statements about men and women should be made.
    d. the experience as people of color cannot be extracted from the experience as women and treated separately.

19. Which type of feminism has been successful in bringing issues of domestic violence and rape to international attention?
    a. Liberal Feminism
    b. Radical Feminism
    c. Multicultural Feminism
    d. Profeminism

20. In the United States today, white women who are at the management level earned _____ as much as a white male at the management level.
    a. 48 percent
    b. 57 percent
    c. 59 percent
    d. 70 percent

21. Which group's median annual earnings are the lowest?
    a. Hispanic women
    b. Hispanic men
    c. Black men
    d. Black women

22. Which of the following occupation is not dominated by females?
    a. Occupational therapists
    b. Registered Nurses
    c. Machinists
    d. Dental Hygienists

23. Intersectionality shows _____ to be a source of social disadvantage.
    a. Race
    b. Religion
    c. Age
    d. All of the above

24. Friedrich Engel claimed that capitalism:
    a. reduced all forms of domination.
    b. intensified men's domination over women.
    c. had little change on men's domination over women.
    d. reduced men's domination over women.

25. The second wave of feminism started in what decade?
    a. 1890s
    b. 1920s
    c. 1960s
    d. 1990s

True/False Questions

True   False   1. Sex and gender basically mean the same thing.

True   False   2. Primary sex characteristics become clearly evident at puberty.

True   False   3. Patriarchy means men hold power over women.

True   False   4. There is no gender inequality in the work place.

True   False   5. Men who are employed in traditionally female occupations experience the glass escalator.

True   False   6. Liberal feminists believe that they are not just discriminated against economically, but are also oppressed by men through sexual relations.

True   False   7. Women earn approximately 70 percent of what men earn.

True   False   8. There is a higher percentage of women in government in the United States than in Australia.

True   False   9. The most recent research on gender differences found that there is little or no difference in characteristics or behaviors between boys and girls.

True   False   10. Circumcision is done for the same reason on boys and girls.

Fill-in-the-Blank Questions

1. _____ refers to the meaning that societies give to the fact of biological difference.

2. Biology would argue that _____ result in very different gendered behaviors for women and men.

3. At puberty hormones transform boys and girls bodies and triggers the development of _____ sex characteristics.

4. _____ is the process by which males and females are taught the appropriate behaviors, attitudes, and traits for their biological sex.

5. Sociologists speak of gender as being _____.

6. The concentration of women and men into different occupations is _____.

7. Women often hit a _____ barrier beyond which they cannot go, despite the fact that they can see others above them.

8. Women earn approximately _____ for every dollar a man earns.

9. The _____ refers to the lessons other than the ABCs learned in school.

10. _____ argues that the experience as people of color cannot be extracted from the experience as women and treated separately.

Essay Questions

1. Based on her research in the South Sea, what did Margaret Mead conclude about gender in society?

2. What is gender socialization and how are boys and girls socialized differently throughout their childhood.

3. Compare and contrast the three waves of the feminist movement in this country by identifying their political formulas and the issues that are important to each.

4. Explain how the work we do is gendered? Discuss sex segregation, the wage gap, the glass ceiling, and escalator.

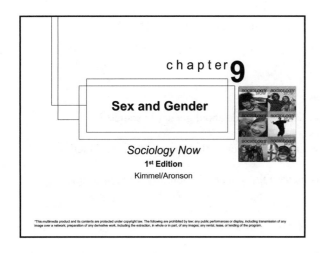

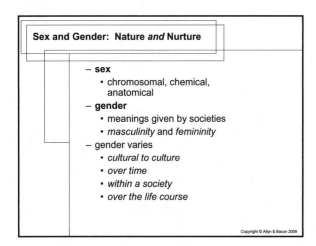

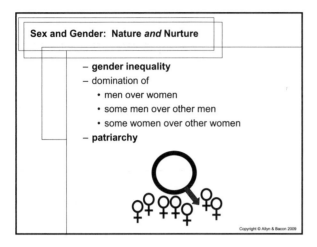

Sex and Gender: Nature *and* Nurture

- **gender inequality**
- domination of
  - men over women
  - some men over other men
  - some women over other women
- **patriarchy**

Copyright © Allyn & Bacon 2009

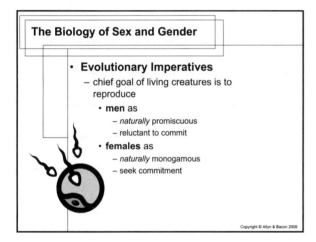

The Biology of Sex and Gender

- **Evolutionary Imperatives**
  - chief goal of living creatures is to reproduce
    - **men** as
      - *naturally* promiscuous
      - reluctant to commit
    - **females** as
      - *naturally* monogamous
      - seek commitment

Copyright © Allyn & Bacon 2009

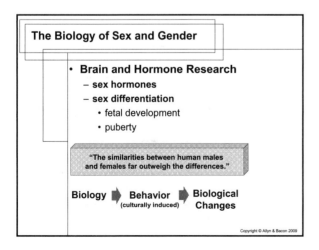

The Biology of Sex and Gender

- **Brain and Hormone Research**
  - **sex hormones**
  - **sex differentiation**
    - fetal development
    - puberty

"The similarities between human males and females far outweigh the differences."

Biology ➡ **Behavior** (culturally induced) ➡ **Biological Changes**

Copyright © Allyn & Bacon 2009

**Exploring Cross-Cultural Variations
of Sex and Gender**

- "cultural definitions of masculinity and
femininity vary significantly"
  – *Arapesh*
  – *Mundugamor*
  – *Tchambuli*

• **Value of Cross-Cultural Research**
  – Level of inequality
  – Differences between men and women
  – Room for cultural change
  – *Male dominance:* contemporary
    societies

Copyright © Allyn & Bacon 2009

**Exploring Cross-Cultural Variations
of Sex and Gender**

•determinants of women's
status
  – *Size and strength*
  – *Women's economic activity*
  – *Child care*

• **Blurring the Boundaries of
Gender**
  – *two or* more *genders?*
    • the nadle
    • berdache
    • "sworn virgin"

Copyright © Allyn & Bacon 2009

**Exploring Cross-Cultural Variations
of Sex and Gender**

• **Rituals of Gender – And
What They Tell Us**
  – circumcision
  – couvade

Copyright © Allyn & Bacon 2009

Becoming Gendered: Learning Gender Identity

- **Gender Socialization**
  - appropriate behaviors, attitudes and traits for each sex
  - differential interaction with children
  - **gender polarization**
    - organizing principle of social life
- **Social Construction of Gender**
  - gender identity as performance
  - **gender roles**
  - **gendered institutions**

Gender Inequality on a Global and Local Scale

- **gender wage gap**
- **feminization of poverty**
- **gender and race**
- **"second shift"**

Gender Inequality on a Global and Local Scale

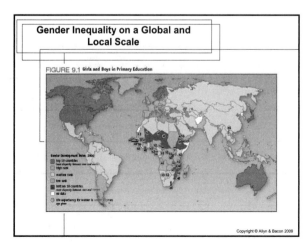

FIGURE 9.1 Girls and Boys in Primary Education

Gender Inequality on a Global and Local Scale

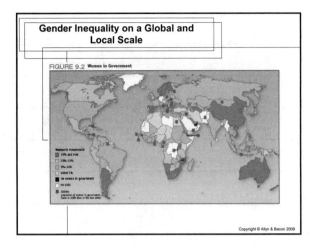

FIGURE 9.2 Women in Government

Copyright © Allyn & Bacon 2009

Gender Inequality in the United States

- **The Gendered World of Work**
  - gender and occupational choice
  - women seen as *less than*

  - **Sex Segregation in the Workplace**
    - brawn versus brains
    - "feminization of the professions"

  - **The Wage Gap**

  - **Glass Ceilings and the Glass Escalators**

  - **Sexual Harassment at Work**

  - **Balancing Work and Family**

Copyright © Allyn & Bacon 2009

Gender Inequality in the United States

- **Gender Inequality in School**
  - "hidden curriculum"
  - "chilly classroom climate"
- **Gender Inequality in Everyday Life**
  - *Industrial Revolution*
    - men: separation of love and work
    - women: experts on love and friendship
    - marriage: *she* wants, *he* resists

Copyright © Allyn & Bacon 2009

The Politics of Gender

- **Opposition to Gender Roles**
- **Women's Movement(s)**
  - First Wave: "Women, their rights and nothing less! Men, their rights and nothing more!"
  - Second Wave: "The personal is political."
  - Third Wave: "Girls rule!"
- **Feminism**
  - **Liberal Feminism**
  - **Radical Feminism**
  - **Multicultural Feminism**

- **Gender Inequality in the 21st Century**

What Does America Think?

9.1 Gender Roles
This is actual survey data from the General Social Survey, 2004.

1. A man's job is to earn money; a woman's job is to look after the home and family. In 2004, about 22 percent of respondents either agreed or strongly agreed with this statement. About 65 percent disagreed, including 35 percent who strongly disagreed. Men were more likely than women to agree with the statement.

CRITICAL THINKING | DISCUSSION QUESTIONS
1. How do you think these responses would be different if the survey were taken in the 1950s? How have historical events and social movements contributed to the greater acceptance of women working outside the home and men working in the home?
2. What do you think explains the gender differences in survey results? How might a conflict theorist explain the differences?

What Does America Think?

9.2 Women and Politics
This is actual survey data from the General Social Survey, 2004.

1. Most men are better suited emotionally for politics than are most women. In 1972, slightly more than half of respondents said they disagreed with this statement. There was virtually no gender difference in responses. In 2004, more than three-quarters of respondents disagreed, with females being slightly more likely to disagree than were males.
2. If your party nominated a woman for president, would you vote for her if she was qualified for the job? This question asks about potential voting behavior, and the responses are very different from those above. In 1974, 80 percent of all respondents said they would vote for a qualified female presidential candidate. In 1998, the latest date for which statistics are available, that number had risen to above 90 percent. In both years, there was very little gender difference.

CRITICAL THINKING | DISCUSSION QUESTIONS
1. How would you explain the responses above? Why do you think the researchers asked about emotional suitability for politics? Do you think if gender was not a factor in the question that emotions would have been considered?
2. Why do you think there was virtually no gender difference in responses? Were you expecting that finding? Why or why not?
3. More respondents said they would vote for a female president than said that women were as emotionally suited as men for politics. What do you think explains that difference?

What Does America Think?

▶ Go to this website to look further at the data. You can run your own statistics and crosstabs here: **http://sda.berkeley.edu/cgi-bin/hsda?harcsda+gss04**

REFERENCES: Davis, James A., Tom W. Smith, and Peter V. Marsden. General Social Surveys 1972–2004: [Cumulative file] [Computer file]. 2nd ICPSR version. Chicago, IL: National Opinion Research Center [producer], 2005; Storrs, CT: Roper Center for Public Opinion Research, University of Connecticut; Ann Arbor, MI: Inter-University Consortium for Political and Social Research; Berkeley, CA: Computer-Assisted Survey Methods Program, University of California [distributors], 2005.

Chapter 10
Sexuality

Chapter Outline

I.   Studying Sexuality: Bodies, Behaviors, and Identities
    a.   Scientists draw a distinction between sex and gender.
        i.   Sex is biological, standard across the human species.
        ii.   Gender is a social construction that differs from culture to culture and across time.
    b.   Sexuality refers to the identities we construct that are often based on our sexual conduct.
    c.   Sexual scripts are a set of ideas and practices that answer the basic questions about sex.
    d.   Sexual socialization is how we understand our culture's sexual scripts cohere into a preference and is socially constructed in four ways.
        i.   Sexuality varies enormously from one culture to the next.
        ii.   Sexuality varies within any one culture over time.
        iii.   Sexuality varies among different groups in society.
        iv.   Sexual behaviors change over the course of your life.
    e.   Desires and Behaviors
        i.   At first glance desires seem to be instinctive.
           1.   If desires were instinctive the standards of physical attractiveness would be the same across human cultures.
           2.   In many cases desires are a function of social class.
        ii.   Sexual behaviors are any behaviors that bring sexual pleasure or release.
           1.   Even within the same society different groups have different incidence of specific sexual activity.
           2.   Sexual behaviors are monitored and policed by social institutions.
    f.   Sexual Identities
        i.   Our sexual identities cohere around a preference for a type of person or a specific behavior.
        ii.   One does not experience sexual identity as something you fashion deliberately from the cultural norms of your society.
        iii.   Heterosexuality and Homosexuality
           1.   Sexual identity refers to an identity that is organized by the gender of the person to whom we are sexually attracted.
           2.   Heterosexuality is the sexual behavior between people of different genders
           3.   Homosexuality is the sexual behavior between people of like genders.
        iv.   Bisexuality is a sexual identity organized around attraction to both women and men.
        v.   Identities as Behaviors
           1.   There are other sexual identities based more on sexual behaviors than the gender of your partner.
           2.   Pedophilia is the erotic attraction to children who may be of either gender.
        vi.   Asexuality is a sexual identity of people that have no sexual desire.
    g.   The Interplay of Biology and Society
        i.   Orientation is pretty stable by about the age of 5 and unchangeable.
        ii.   Scientists claim that sexual orientation is the result of biology.
        iii.   Sociologists generally believe that sexual orientation is both biologically based and socially constructed.

II.   Researching Sexuality
    a.   Early Sex Research
        i.   In the late 19th century, sex research was gradually taken over by scientists, who sought to observe sex without moral condemnation.
        ii.   Richard von Krafft-Ebing who first observed and labeled fetishes and perversions and came to the conclusion that women should never experience sexual desire of any kind.

          iii. Havelock Ellis believed that sexual desire is among the great driving forces of life and thought sex was normal, natural, and good even for women.

          iv. Magnus Hirschfeld believed that people are born bisexual but as they develop they lose their same-sex desires and become exclusively heterosexual.

   b. Modern Sex Research

      i. The Kinsey Reports

         1. Studied sexual behavior, unclouded by morality.

         2. He exposed a wide gulf between American's professed morality and their actual behaviors.

            a. The higher your socioeconomic class, the more sex you have.

            b. The clients of prostitutes were not only college boys and soldiers on leave.

            c. Women enjoy sex.

            d. Extramarital affairs are not extremely rare.

         3. The most controversial findings concerned same-sex behavior.

            a. Kinsey found a great deal of variation in practices, so much that he classified his respondents along a seven-point continuum.

            b. Only 45% of men in the sample were exclusively heterosexual and 66% of women.

      ii. The National Health and Social Life Study

         1. Found huge amounts of non-procreative sexual behavior.

         2. Findings were very different from the Kinsey report.

            a. Kinsey did not draw a random sample, as NORC did.

            b. Many of the men in Kinsey's were soldiers during WWI and WWII.

III.   American Sexual Behavior and Identities

   a. The "Gender" of Sexuality

      i. The single most important organizing principle of sexuality is gender.

      ii. For many years it was assumed that only men experienced sexual desires and women were interested in romance and companionship but not sex.

      iii. Today most agree that women have sexual desires but it is inappropriate to express openly.

         1. Sexual double standard encourages men to pursue sex as an end in itself.

         2. Women are taught to consider sex with one partner and only in the context of an emotional relationship.

      iv. Masculinization of sex includes the pursuit of pleasure for its own sake, the increased attention to orgasm, increased number of sexual partners, the interest in sexual experimentation, and the separation of sexual behavior from love.

   b. Convergence on Campus: Hook Up

      i. Sexual encounter which may or may not include sexual intercourse, usually occurring on only one occasion between two people whoa re strangers or brief acquaintances.

      ii. On many campuses the sexual marketplace is organized around groups of same-sex friend who go out together to meet appropriate sexual partners in a casual setting.

   c. Convergence on Campus: Just Saying No

      i. Abstinence pledgers may represent a counterculture

      ii. The pledge encourages young people to refrain from heterosexual intercourse until marriage.

      iii. They appear to have some effect

      iv. Because abstinence-based program are often used instead of actual sex education, few people really know what counts in keeping your pledge.

   d. Rape and Sexual Assault

      i. One of the most important differences in men's and women's sexualities is in the area of nonconsensual sexual activity.

      ii. On college campuses more than half of all sexual assaults take the form of date rape.

   e. What Else Affects Sexuality

         i.   Race

        ii.   Age

      iii.   Politics

IV.   Sexual Inequality

    a.   Homophobia is an attitude, a socially approved dislike f gay men and lesbians, the presumption that they are inferior to straight people.

    b.   Heterosexism is the institutionally based inequality that may derive from homophobia.

    c.   Sexual Minority Communities

        i.   People with minority sexual orientations often band together.

        ii.   As early as the 19th century there were gay neighborhoods in some large cities.

      iii.   In 1969 the Stonewall riots led to the formation of the Gay Liberation Front.

      iv.   Gay rights movement was successful because it arose simultaneously with the youth counterculture of the late 1960s.

       v.   Gay Rights movement has been so successful that they are no longer a counter culture of subculture; it is now part of mainstream culture.

    d.   Sexuality as Politics

        i.   Sex has always been political.

        ii.   Contemporary sexual politics involved political, scientific, and religious issues.

    e.   Sex Tourism; The Globalization of Sex

        i.   For centuries, wealthy men have sought sexual adventures with exotic strangers.

        ii.   Sex tourism represents the globalization of prostitution.

           1.   Uses the internet to advertise its wares.

           2.   Some countries have well developed sex tourism industries.

           3.   Sex tourism expresses the unequal relationship between countries that sell sex and countries who can buy it.

    f.   Pornography

        i.   Visual or written depiction of sexual activity with no "redeeming social value."

        ii.   Debates about pornography have traditionally pitted conservatives against liberals.

           1.   Conservatives believe that any sexually explicit material is morally wrong and socially corrosive.

           2.   Liberals believe that adults should be able to make their own decisions about what they want to view and read.

      iii.   Experiments have found small differences of both behavior and attitudes between men who viewed significant amounts of violent heterosexual pornography in a laboratory setting than those who did not.

      iv.   In recent years it has become a global industry.

    g.   Sex Education and Birth Control

        i.   Many people believe that teaching about sex encourages young people to experiment with sex.

        ii.   Others believe young people are going to experiment anyways.

      iii.   New form of sex education has been heavily promoted by the federal government.

           1.   In 2003, the federal government devoted $117 million to abstinence education.

           2.   Some states have turned down federal money to teach sensible sex education.

      iv.   Sociological evidence is clear that information about birth control and its availability do not increase the amount of sex people have nor the onset of sexual activity among young people.

       v.   Many people have religious objections to certain types of birth control because they believe that life begins at the moment an egg is fertilized.

           1.   Opposition to abortion has transformed the global politics of birth control

           2.   Inadequate information about birth control can be a matter of life or death in some countries.

V.   Sexuality in the 21st Century

    a.   Sexuality is the foundation of identity, just as race or class or gender.

    b.   Changing attitudes will eventually lead to changed policies.

STUDY GUIDE

Chapter Summary

- Sexuality refers to the identities we construct that are often based on our sexual conduct.
- Every culture develops a sexual scripts and our understanding of our culture's sexual scripts begin to cohere into a preference is the sexual socialization.
- Sexual behavior is any behavior that brings sexual pleasure or release and is not limited to physiology.
- Sexual customs vary enormously. In some cultures people never have sex outside while others believe that having sex indoors would contaminate the food supply. In the United States kissing is a universal initiation while in others it is found to be disgusting.
- Norms about sexual behaviors govern not only our sexual conduct but also how we develop a sexual identity.
- Sexual identity refers to an identity that is organized by the gender of the person to who we are sexually attracted. Homosexuality refers to sexual desires or behaviors with members of one's own gender while heterosexuality is the sexual behavior between people of different genders. Bisexuality is organized around the principle that one can be attracted to men and women while asexual people have no sexual desires for any person, male or female.
- There are other sexual identities based more on sexual behavior than the gender of your partner, such as, partialism, fetishism, sadomasochism, exhibitionism, and pedophilia.
- The early research on sex included research on sexual perversions, masturbation, and bisexuality. Krafft-Ebing concluded that women should never experience sexual desire while Ellis found that women had a strong sex drive and believed that sex was normal, natural, and good. Hirschfeld believed people were born bisexual and when they grew up they lost the same-sex desire.
- Two important works of modern sex research include the Kinsey report and the study conducted by the National Health and Social Life Study. Kinsey found that the higher socioeconomic class the more sex you had, that clients of prostitutes were not just soldiers or college boys, women enjoyed sex, and extramarital affairs were not uncommon. The National Health and Social Life Study found far fewer men and women having extramarital affairs than Kinsey originally reported.
- The single most important organizing principle of sexuality is gender and men and women are raised to have very different attitudes toward sexual desire, behavior, and identity.
- Sexual behaviors have grown increasingly similar between men and women, which had lead to the phenomenon of "hooking-up" on college campuses and a sexual counter culture of "abstinence only" pledgers.
- More than half of all sexual assaults on campus take the form of date rape.
- Race, age, and politics also shape our sexual identities and behaviors.
- Homophobia is the attitude, a socially approved dislike of gay men and lesbians, the presumption that hey are inferior to straight people while heterosexism refers to the institutionally based inequality, a set of practices rather than an ideology.
- Sexual minorities banded together to escape the hostility of mainstream society. Over time the gay-rights movement became increasingly successful, so successful that they are seen as mainstream.
- Sex tourism represent the globalization of prostitution and expresses the unequal relationships between countries who sell sex and countries who can buy sex.
- Pornography refers to a visual or written depiction of sexual activity with no redeeming social value. The debate around pornography has traditionally pitted conservatives against liberals.
- Sex education in the United States has been heavily promoted by the federal government. Abstinence only is taught as the sole option for unmarried people in 23 percent of schools.
- The availability of birth control does not increase the amount of sex people have nor even the onset of sexual activity among young people although the debate continues still toady.
- Sexuality is the foundation of identity, just as race, class, or gender and is a basis for inequality.

Learning Objectives
After completing the reading of Chapter 9, you should be able to answer the following objectives.

- Understand the difference between sex and gender.
- Define sexuality, sexual script, and sexual socialization and how it influences our identity.
- Define sexual behavior and understand how it is monitored by social institutions.
- Discuss sexual identities in terms of heterosexuality, homosexuality, bisexuality, and asexuality.
- Discuss the early sex research and modern sex research. Know what research was conducted by Richard von Krafft-Ebing, Havelock Ellis, Magnus Hirschfeld, Kinsey, and the National Health and Social Life Study and what the results showed.
- Understand how gender affects sexuality and how it has changed over time.
- Discuss how the convergence lead to the idea of "hooking up," abstinence only programs, and the consequences of the convergence on rape and sexual assault.
- Define homosexuality and heterosexism.
- Understand how sexual minorities form their own communities and discuss how these minorities have been successful throughout the past several decades in obtaining their rights.
- Know what sex tourism is and the stratification between the countries that buy and sell sex.
- Define pornography and discuss the debate surrounding the issue.
- Understand the politics behind the sex education programs in the United States and how birth control plays a part.

Key Terms

Asexual: those who have no sexual desire.

Bisexual: sexually attracted to both men and women.

Heterosexism: institutionally based inequality that may derive from homophobia; set of practices rather than an ideology.

Heterosexuality: sexual behavior between people of different genders.

Homophobia: attitude, a socially approved dislike of gay men and lesbians, the presumption that they are inferior to straight people.

Homosexuality: refers to sexual desires or behaviors with members of one's own gender.

Hooking up: sexual encounter which may or may not include sexual intercourse, usually occurring on only one occasion between two people who are strangers or brief acquaintances.

Masculinization of Sex: numbers of sexual partners, the interest in sexual experimentation, and the separation of sexual behavior from love.

Pedophilia: erotic attraction to children.

Pornography: visual or written depiction of sexual activity with no "redeeming social value."

Sex: sexual behaviors or the things people do from which they derive sexual meaning.

Sex Tourism: globalization of prostitution.

Sexual behavior: any behavior that brings sexual pleasure or release.

Sexual identity: refers to an identity that is organized by the gender of the person to whom we are sexually attracted.

Sexual script: set of ideas and practices that answer the basic questions about sex.

Sexual socialization: our understanding of our culture's sexual scripts.

Sexuality: refers to the identity we construct hat are often based on our sexual conduct.

Key People

Alfred Kinsey- collected sexual histories from 18,000 American for his research on sexual behavior and morality.

Berl Kutchinsky- observed the effects of legalizing pornography.

Michael Rochlin- composed questionnaire to illustrate the impact of homophobia on the way heterosexuals understand sexuality.

Additional Learning with MySocLab

Read

> **Ideas & Trends: Legal License; Race, Sex and Forbidden Unions (pg 323)**
> As a political, legal and social issue, same-sex marriage seems to be now where interracial marriage was about 50 years ago.
>
> **On Sex, U.S. and France Speak Same Language (pg 330)**
> The article discusses a study that analyzed the sexual behavior of those who live in France and compared them to Americans. In most areas of sexuality the distinctions were negligible.
>
> **Passenger on Jet: Gay Hero or Hero Who Was Gay? (pg 337)**
> Since the 1980s open discussion about homosexuality has become commonplace. Yet, many stereotypes, misperceptions, prejudices, and even hate persist toward gays and lesbians.

Listen

> **Supreme Court Sodomy Ruling (pg 337)**
> This sound clip from NPR discusses the overturning of the anti-sodomy law in Texas by the Texas Supreme Court. This marked a historical moment in the gay and lesbian civil rights movement.

Watch

> **Claire Renzetti: Research on Gay and Lesbian Domestic Violence (pg 318)**
> This video clip discusses Claire Renzetti's research on domestic violence in gay and lesbian relationships. She answers the question: how much violence is there in gay and lesbian relationships.

Practice Test

After completing the practice test, check your answers in the Answer Key of this Study Guide.

Multiple Choice Questions

1. What term refers to the biological distinction between males and females?
    a. gender
    b. sexuality
    c. sex
    d. gender roles

2. Sexuality can be seen as socially constructed. Which of the following is not a way in which sexuality is socially constructed?
    a. Sexuality varies enormously from one culture to the next
    b. Sexuality varies over time
    c. Sexuality varies among different groups in society
    d. Sexual behaviors stay the same over the course of your life

3. Which researcher observed dramatic differences in sexual customs of two neighboring tribes in New Guinea?
    a. Clyde Kluckohn
    b. Ernestine Friedel
    c. Havelock Ellis
    d. Magnus Hirschfeld

4. What was the significance of Kinsey's report on sexuality in the United States?
    a. More than half the people in the United States were not exclusively heterosexual
    b. Women were interested in sex and could have orgasms
    c. That there was not an inconsistency between American's morality and their actual behaviors
    d. Extramarital affairs were indeed very rare.

5. People who are heterosexual prefer partners who are:
    a. of the opposite sex.
    b. of the same sex.
    c. neither the opposite or the same sex.
    d. of the opposite or same sex.

6. The study conducted by the National Health and Social Life Study showed that about _____ of married men and _____ of married women did not remain faithful to their spouse.
    a. 10 percent; 30 percent
    b. 30 percent; 15 percent
    c. 20 percent; 20 percent
    d. 25 percent; 10 percent

7. Sexual attraction to someone of the same sex is called:
    a. heterosexuality.
    b. homosexuality.
    c. bisexuality.
    d. asexuality.

8. What is the single most important organizing principle of sexuality?
    a. gender
    b. race
    c. age
    d. education

9. The sexual double standard in our culture encourages women to:
    a. not have sex at all.
    b. seek sex with many different partners.
    c. pursue sex as an end in itself.
    d. have sex in the context of an emotional relationship,

10. _____ includes the pursuit of pleasure for its own sake, the increased attention to orgasm, increased number of sexual partners, and the interest in sexual experimentation.
    a. Sexual convergence
    b. Feminization of sex
    c. Masculinization of sex
    d. Hooking up

11. Which racial/ethnic group is the least liberal in terms of sexual behaviors?
    a. Whites
    b. African Americans
    c. Hispanics
    d. Asians

12. _____ is the institutionally based inequality and is a set of practices.
    a. Homophobia
    b. Heterosexism
    c. Masculinization of sexuality
    d. Rape

13. During which time period did the American Psychiatric Association remove homosexuality from its list of disorders?
    a. 1940s
    b. 1950s
    c. 1970s
    d. 1990s

14. Which of the following is not a reason the gay-rights movement was successful?
    a. It arose with the counterculture of the 1960s.
    b. The connections gay people made with nongay people
    c. Politicians were faced with people who looked like other young people
    d. They embraced the label of homosexual

15. Which country is most likely to be purchasing sex?
    a. United States
    b. Vietnam
    c. Thailand
    d. Russia

16. Who tend to be the consumers of sex tourism?
    a. middle class men
    b. wealthy women
    c. men from poor nations
    d. wealthy men

17. About what proportion of women who attended high school between 1945 and 1950 who ever had intercourse?
    a. 50 percent
    b. 9 percent
    c. 20 percent
    d. 60 percent

18. According to the research, on average men report having _____ sexual partners than females.
    a. fewer
    b. more
    c. about the same
    d. None of the above

19. The term homophobia refers to:
    a. fear of one's sexuality.
    b. fear of experiencing close personal interaction with people thought to be gay.
    c. fear of experiencing sexual attraction to people of the same sex.
    d. fear of not being attracted to anyone.

20. Opponents of pornography argue that:
    a. it unfairly depicts women as sexual objects used for men's pleasure.
    b. it silences women's efforts to express their sexuality.
    c. it increases female aggression towards men.
    d. legalizing it reduced the number of sex crimes committed.

21. In a global perspective, prostitution occurs most often in what type of country?
    a. Wealthy countries where women are free to choose their occupation
    b. Middle-income countries where women can make more money in this profession
    c. Poor countries where women have few economic resources
    d. Prostitution is found evenly throughout the world.

22. In the United States, the government typically funds what type of sex education program?
    a. Those that include birth control and condom use
    d. Those that offer many options to individuals
    c. Those that focus exclusively on abortion as a form of birth control
    d. Those that teach abstinence as the preferred method of birth control

23. Increasing the availability and in developing countries would lead to:
    a. a higher standard of living.
    b. a moral decline among those living in those countries.
    c. a lower standard of living.
    d. a significant increase in sexual activity.

24. What is the type of sexual behavior in which a person is attracted to having sex in public?
    a. Fetishism
    b. Exhibitionism
    c. Pedophilia
    d. Partialism

25. Which type of sexual refers to a person who is attracted to both men and women?
    a. Homosexuality
    b. Heterosexuality
    c. Bisexuality
    d. Asexuality

True/False Questions

True   False   1. Sexuality refers to the set of ideas and practices that answer basic questions about sex.

True   False   2. Sexual behaviors do not vary from culture to culture.

True   False   3. Someone who is heterosexual practices sexual behaviors with a person of the opposite sex.

True   False   4. Bisexual people are attracted to both people of the same sex and people of the opposite sex.

True   False   5. The Kinsey report found that fewer than 20 percent of all people have extramarital affairs.

True   False   6. There is often a wide gap in our moral positions and our actual behavior.

True   False   7. The sexual behaviors of men and women have become increasingly similar.

True   False   8. Abstinence pledgers could be considered a counterculture on college campuses.

True   False   9. Homophobia is a set of practices rather than an ideology.

True   False   10. The United States is a seller in the global sex trade.

Fill-in-the-Blank Questions

1. Sexual _____ brings about sexual pleasure or release.

2. Among heterosexuals in our culture, men are the sexual _____ and women are to be sexually _____.

3. Homosexuals are attracted on to the _____.

4. When a person does not have a sexual desire for anyone, they are said to be _____.

5. _____ is defined as a sexual encounter which may or may not include sexual intercourse, usually occurring on only one occasion between two people who are strangers or brief acquaintances.

6. People who disapprove of gay men and presume straight people are superior are _____.

7. _____ represents the globalization of prostitution.

8. Because of the United State's policy on funding agencies who provide abortions in other parts of the world, _____ now deliver most of the information on birth control.

9. _____ is socially constructed and varies between cultures and over time.

10. _____ found surprising results in his study of sexual behavior.

Essay Questions

1. Explain the four ways in which sexuality is socially constructed.

2. What is homosexuality, how did they band together, and what were some major events in history that lead to the success of the gay rights movement?

3. Discuss how sex tourism reproduces unequal relationships between countries and gender inequality.

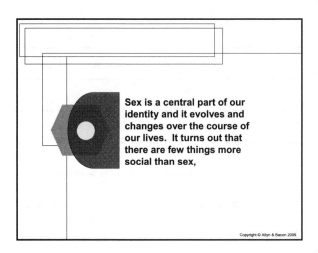

Studying Sexuality: Bodies, Behaviors, and Identities

– sexual script
– sexual socialization
– sexuality as social construction
• varies from culture to culture
• varies over time
• varies among different groups
• changes over the life course

STUDY GUIDE

Studying Sexuality: Bodies, Behaviors, and Identities

- **Desires and Behaviors**
  - "desire" as instinctual/olfactory
  - standards of physical attractiveness
  - **sexual behavior**
    - sex or something else?
    - with whom, frequency, where, etc.
    - American perspectives
      - *kissing*
      - *gender roles in sex*
      - *motivation for sex*

Copyright © Allyn & Bacon 2009

Studying Sexuality: Bodies, Behaviors, and Identities

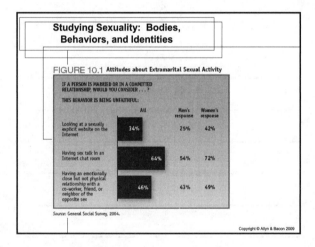

FIGURE 10.1 Attitudes about Extramarital Sexual Activity

Source: General Social Survey, 2004.

Copyright © Allyn & Bacon 2009

Studying Sexuality: Bodies, Behaviors, and Identities

- **Sexual Identities**
  - **Heterosexuality and Homosexuality**
    - nonmarital *versus* marital
    - can sexual orientation change?
  - **Bisexuality**
    - is not indiscriminate
    - few understand
    - sense of pride → character over gender
  - **Identities as Behaviors**

Copyright © Allyn & Bacon 2009

188

Studying Sexuality: Bodies, Behaviors, and Identities

  – **Identities as Behaviors**
  - *partialism*
  - *fetishism*
  - *sadomasochism*
  - *exhibitionism*
  - *voyeurism*
  - **pedophilia**
  – **Asexuality**

- **The Interplay of Biology and Society**

Researching Sexuality

- **Early Sex Research**
  – Richard von Krafft-Ebing
  – Havelock Ellis
  – Sigmund Freud
  – Magnus Hirschfield

Researching Sexuality

- **Modern Sex Research**
  – **The Kinsey Reports**
    - Higher SES – more sex
    - Full range of men clients of prostitutes
    - Women enjoy sex
    - Extramarital affairs not rare

  – **The National Health and Social Life Study**

American Sexual Behavior and Identities

– Is attitude a predictor of behavior?

- **The "Gender" of Sexuality**
  – single most organizing principle of sexuality is gender
  – "his" and "her" sexuality
  – doctors assumed women lacked sexual desire

American Sexual Behavior and Identities

"Men are socialized to express a "masculine" sexuality, and women are socialized to express a feminine sexuality regardless of their sexual orientation."

  – sexual double standard
  – Gay men and lesbians carry over gendered sexual predispositions
  – **masculinization of sex**

American Sexual Behavior and Identities

- **Convergence in Campus: Hooking Up**
  – **hooking up**
  – sex buddies
  – "friends with benefits"
  – DTR – "define the relationship"

- **Convergence in Campus: Just Saying No**
  – "abstinence pledgers"

American Sexual Behavior and Identities

- **Convergence in Campus: Just Saying No**
  - "abstinence pledgers"

- **Rape and Sexual Assualt**
  - nonconsensual sexual activity
  - intoxication of victim

- **What Else Affects Sexuality?**
  - race, age and politics/societal equality

Sexual Inequality

  - **homophobia**
  - **heterosexism**
    - gay and lesbian "invisibility"
    - discrimination
    - hate crimes
    - devaluing of same-sex desires/behavior

- **Sexual Minority Communities**
  - Stonewall Riots (1969)
  - DSM
  - media

Sexual Inequality

- **Sexuality as Politics**
  - political, scientific, and religious issues

- **Sex Tourism: The Globalization of Sex**
  - "consumer" (wealthy men);
  - "commodity" (poor men and women)

"Sex tourism thus expresses the unequal relationship between countries who "sell" sex and countries who "buy" it, as well as the inequalities between men and women, both globally and locally."

Sexual Inequality

- **Pornography**
  - no "redeeming social value"
  - global industry/Internet

- **Sex Education and Birth Control**

- **Sexuality in the 21st Century**

Copyright © Allyn & Bacon 2009

What Does America Think?

10.1 Extramarital Sex

These are actual survey data from the General Social Survey, 2004.

How wrong do you think it is to have sex with a person other than one's spouse? In 1973, 70 percent of respondents said it was always wrong to have sex with a person other than one's spouse. In 2004, those numbers were higher, at slightly over 80 percent. In both years, and in the years in between, more women than man were likely to say it was always wrong, and more men than women to say it was never wrong.

CRITICAL THINKING | DISCUSSION QUESTIONS

1. The gender difference in responses is not large, but it is interesting. What do you think explains the gender difference?
2. Why do you think the number of respondents who said extramarital sex was always wrong has increased in the past 30 years?

Copyright © Allyn & Bacon 2009

What Does America Think?

10.2 Homosexuality

These are actual survey data from the General Social Survey, 2004.

Do you think homosexual sexual relations are always wrong, almost always wrong, sometimes wrong, or not wrong at all? The majority of respondents to the General Social Survey questions from 1973 to 2004 reported that they thought homosexual relations were almost always wrong. However, those numbers have declined significantly over the past 30 years, while the number of respondents who reported thinking homosexual relations were not wrong at all increased dramatically. Gender differences were almost nonexistent, but there are interesting differences when we look at the data by social class.

CRITICAL THINKING | DISCUSSION QUESTIONS

1. Social class differences in attitudes toward homosexuality are quite striking. How do you explain these differences? What part does social location and socialization into the class structure play?

Copyright © Allyn & Bacon 2009

What Does America Think?

▶ Go to this website to look further at the data. You can run your own statistics and crosstabs here: http://sda.berkeley.edu/cgi-bin/hsda?harcsda+gss04

REFERENCES: Davis, James A., Tom W. Smith, and Peter V. Marsden. General Social Surveys 1972–2004: [Cumulative file] [Computer file]. 2nd ICPSR version. Chicago, IL: National Opinion Research Center [producer], 2005; Storrs, CT: Roper Center for Public Opinion Research, University of Connecticut; Ann Arbor, MI: Inter-University Consortium for Political and Social Research; Berkeley, CA: Computer-Assisted Survey Methods Program, University of California [distributors], 2005.

Chapter 11
Age: From Young to Old

Chapter Outline

I.   Age and Identity
- a.   Age is less a biological condition than a social construction.
- b.   Differences between chronological and functional age.
  - i.   Chronological age- a person's age determined by the actual date of birth.
  - ii.   Functional age- set of observable characteristic and attributes that are used to categorize people into different age cohorts.
  - iii.   Age cohort- group of people who are born within a specific time period.
- c.   Stages of life
  - i.   All societies have divided the life span into stages, seasons, or age groups.
    1. Adolescence- life stage between childhood and adulthood.
    2. Boundaries of life stages are subject to variation and change.
  - ii.   Childhood
    1. Medieval Europe child treated as little adults.
    2. Childhood, as a distinct stage of life, did not emerge until the Industrial Revolution.
    3. "Innocent"
    4. Concerns over childhood exposure to sex and violence began near the end of the nineteenth century.
  - iii.   Adolescence
    1. Before the eighteenth century adolescences was not seen as a distinct sociological stage.
    2. As labor become more specialized children required more specialized training and attended high school.
  - iv.   Young Adulthood
    1. Transitional stage from adolescence.
    2. Marks the beginning of our lives as fully functioning members of society.
  - v.   Middle Age
    1. People are starting middle age later, in their 50s instead of their 40s.
    2. Difficult manual labor ages one more rapidly.
    3. Developmental task of middle age is acceptance.
    4. They are the "sandwich generation"- caring for dependent children and aging parents at the same time.
  - vi.   Old Age
    1. Number of older Americans has increased dramatically in the last 100 years.
    2. Two factors have lead to the increase in the percentage of the population that is elderly.
       - a. Birth rates have declined.
       - b. Life expectancy has been going up.
    3. In poor countries, life expectancy did not rise significantly during the twentieth century.
    4. There are three life-stages among the elderly:
       - a. "Young old" ages 65-75.
       - b. "Old old" ages 75-85.
       - c. "Oldest old" ages 85 and higher.
  - vii.   Aging and Dying
    1. Myths about growing old
       - a. Living in a nursing home- only about 5% live in long-term care facilities.

    b. Losing mental abilities- less than 5% develop any type of mental lose.

    c. Being alone.

    d. Having nothing to do- characteristic of income not of age.

   2. Rates of death vary depending on race, sex, and age.

   3. Elisabeth Kubler-Ross: five stages people face with imminent death.

    a. Denial

    b. Anger

    c. Negotiation

    d. Depression

    e. Acceptance

   4. Death is a process not an event.

II. Age and Inequality

 a. Ageism- differential treatment based on age and usually affects the elderly rather than the young.

 b. Declining status of the aged is not universal.

 c. With the Industrial Revolution scientific knowledge began to advance and social norms began to change every few years.

   i. Knowledge of elderly became obsolete.

   ii. Elderly become less valuable.

 d. Age and Poverty

   i. Many elderly lack savings, investments, or pensions to be self-supportive after retirement.

   ii. Age magnifies the gender and racial inequalities.

   iii. Social security- gives retired workers a monthly stipend based on how much they contributed to the program through their lives.

 e. Social Isolation

   i. As people age they are particularly vulnerable to social isolation.

   ii. Many experience social disengagement- gradual withdrawal from feeling connected to their immediate communities or to the wider world.

 f. Retirement

   i. Mark of social status

   ii. Abrupt transition form work to leisure belongs to the past.

    1. Many elderly continue to work after retirement.

    2. Some never retire.

 g. Elder Care

   i. Before the 20th century family members were expected to take care of their elderly relatives.

   ii. Many industrialized nations now have institutionalized elder care.

III. Boomers, Busters, and Boomlets: The Generation of Youth

 a. Postwar baby boom- 1945-1964

   i. First boomers hit middle age in the early 1980s.

   ii. Baby boom lasted for 20 year so the earliest boomers are a full generation removed from the latest.

 b. Generation X (baby busters)

   i. Born after 1954.

   ii. Worse off economically than the baby boomers.

 c. Generation Y (baby boomlet)

   i. Number of baby boomers born at the end of the baby boom meant that during their young adulthood, between 1975 and 1995) a new wave of birth occurred.

   ii. Three times the size of generation X.

   iii. Sizable portion are minorities.

   iv. First generation to embrace the widening impact of the information revolution.

 d. Global Youth- A Dying Breed

   i. People are living longer and having fewer children.

   ii. Percentage of youths worldwide will continue to decline steadily.

IV.   Youth and Inequality
    a.   Aging population is composed mostly of middle-class, politically active, organized retirees.
        i.   Politically mobilized.
        ii.   Vote at high rates.
    b.   Young people are virtually powerless.
        i.   Children and adolescents cannot vote.
        ii.   Unemployment rate is nearly double that of middle-aged people.
    c.   Youth and Poverty
        i.   In 2006 the poverty rate for children under 18 in the United States was 21.9 percent.
        ii.   Parents expected to provide full financial support.
    d.   Health Care
        i.   In the United States, nearly 12 percent of children and adolescents under 18 have no health insurance.
        ii.   Having no health insurance means doing without checkups, immunizations, and necessary medical procedures.
    e.   Child Labor
        i.   Strict laws ensure that no job can be hazardous or tie consuming or interfere with their "carefree" childhood.
        ii.   In the United States teenagers seem to be working for extra money rather than to contribute to household income.
            1.   Globally, one out of every six child aged 5 to 17 is in the workforce.
            2.   Sub-Saharan Africa has largest amount of children in the workforce.
        iii.   The new slavery
            1.   global trafficking transports people far from their homes for forced, bonded, and illegitimate labor
            2.   most are seeking escape from poverty
        iv.   The worst form of child labor
            1.   Most jobs in forced and bonded labor are technically legal.
            2.   1.8 million work in the global sex trade.
            3.   Some countries permit the conscription 13-14 year olds.
V.   Getting Older and Getting Better? Youth and Age in the 21st Century
    a.   Status of elders may rise as baby boomers start hitting retirement age.
    b.   Young and old people are constantly changing the meaning of age in our society.

Chapter Summary

- Age is a social construction rather than a biological condition.
- Sociologists differentiate between chronological age- a person's age determined by actual date of birth- and functional age- a set of observable characteristics and attributes that are used to categorize people into different age cohorts.
- Gerontology is the scientific study of the biological, psychological, and sociological phenomena associated with old age and aging, however, sociologists now understand that such a study tells only half the story.
- Today the study of age and aging in sociology requires that we study both identity and inequality among both the young and old.
- The life span is broken down into stages and each stage has its own age norms.
- Children in medieval Europe were portrayed as little adults but today they are seen as innocent. We believe that children's actions do not carry the same consequences as those of adults.
- Adolescence was not seen as a distinct sociological stage until the late 1880s.
- Young adulthood is the transition between adolescence and middle adulthood. There have been five milestones that define adulthood.
- Middle adulthood now starts in a person's 50s. Middle-aged adults now find themselves in the "sandwich generation," caring for dependent children and aging parents.

- The elderly population is growing dramatically due to the birth rates declining and life expectancy going up.
- People with incurable diseases go through five stages: denial, anger, negotiation, depression, and finally acceptance.
- Death is a process not an event. It may be the end of biological life but its meaning changes dramatically cross culturally.
- Many elderly lack savings accounts, investments, and pensions to be self-supporting after retirement, however the poverty rate for the elder is about 10%.
- As people age they are vulnerable to social isolation and many experience a social disengagement.
- Retirement is a mark of social status but today many elderly continue to work and some never retire.
- Before the twentieth century families were expected to take care of their elderly relatives. Today industrialized nations elder care has become institutionalized through nursing homes, hospitals, and other institutions.
- After World War II a baby boom occurred followed by generation X, which was much smaller in cohort size, followed by generation Y, three times the size of generation X.
- Generation Y has a sizeable proportion that are minorities and 75 percent have working mothers. This is also the first generation that has embraced the widening impact of the information revolution.
- On a global level, the percentage of young people is declining. People are living longer and having fewer children.
- The elderly are more politically active, have more power, and are economically better off than the younger people in our society.
- Children and adolescence 18 under 18 years of age have the highest rates of poverty and 12 percent have no form of health insurance.
- Child labor laws ensure that no job can be hazardous or time consuming. There are both federal and state guidelines on what types of jobs and how many hours teenagers can work.
- Global trafficking transports people far from their homes for forced, bonded, and illegitimate labor. Most are forced or bonded into jobs that are technically legal, but there are over a million who work in the global sex trade and other forms of criminal activities.

Learning Objectives
After completing the reading of Chapter 11, you should be able to answer the following objectives.

- Define and understand the difference between chronological age and functional age.
- Summarize the stages of life including: childhood, adolescence; young adulthood, middle age, and old age.
- Discuss why living in a nursing home, losing mental abilities, being alone, and having nothing to do are all myths of aging.
- Know the five stages Elisabeth Kubler-Ross believes people go through when faced with imminent death.
- Define ageism and give an example.
- Discuss the poverty rate among the young and the elderly.
- Define retirement and discuss how it has changed over the years.
- Discuss how caring for the elderly has changed over time. Who used to be responsible for it and who is responsible now.
- Discuss the baby boomers generation, generation X, and generation Y. When were each born and what the size of each cohort.
- Define and understand the difference longitudinal study, time series study, and a cross-sectional study.
- Discuss the changes in child labor over the years.
- Discuss the differences in child labor in the United Stated and globally. Know the percentages of child workers and which part of the globe has the highest percentage of children in the work force.
- Explain what the new slavery is and what the worst forms of child labor include.

Key Terms

Adolescence: a life stage between childhood and adulthood.

Age cohort: group of people who are born within a specific time period and therefore assumed to share both chronological and functional characteristics.

Age norms: distinctive cultural values, pursuits, and pastimes that are culturally prescribed for each age cohort.

Ageism: differential treatment based on age.

Baby-boomers: those born between the years 1945 and 1964.

Chronological age: person's age determined by the actual date of birth.

Confirmation bias: a single case or a few cases of the expected behavior confirm the belief, especially when the behavior is attention getting or widely reported.

Cross-sectional study: comparing different age groups at one moment in time.

Functional age: set of observable characteristics and attributes that are used to categorize people into different age cohorts.

Generation X: generation that followed the baby boom cohort.

Generation Y: those who began to reach young adulthood in the mid-1990s.

Gerontology: scientific study of the biological, psychological, and sociological phenomena associated with old age and aging.

Graying of America: increase in the percentage of the population that is elderly.

Life expectancy: average number of years that people born in a certain year could expect to live.

Life span: division into stages, seasons or age groups.

Longitudinal study: comparing the same group at various points in time as they age.

Midlife crisis: characterized by pressure to make wholesale changes in their work, relationships, and leisure.

Retirement: mark of social status.

Rites of passage: typical experiences for most of us who move through childhood and on to adulthood and beyond.

Sandwich generation: middle-aged adults who are caring for dependent children and aging parents at the same time.

Social Security: begun in 1940 to improve the financial situation of the elderly. The program gave retired workers a monthly stipend based on how much they contributed to the program through their lives.

Time-series study: involves tracking the variable rather than the cohort.

Twixters: new term invented by the media to refer to people in their twenties, years pat their high school or college graduation but still culturally adolescent.

Key People

Robert Butler: coined the term "ageism" in 1969.

Elisabeth Kubler-Ross: counseled many people with incurable diseases and concluded that people faced with imminent death go through five stages.

Robert Lynd: did a study of a typical American community, *Middletown*.

Additional Learning with MySocLab

Read

Life at Age 100 is Surprisingly Healthy (pg 358)
Until recently, very few people lived to be more than 100. But with the number of centenarian rocketing upward, statisticians and scientists have begun studying them — and challenging some of the conventional wisdom about the very old.

Power of Positive Thinking Extends, It Seems, to Aging (pg 360)
A growing body of evidence suggests that positive people may live longer. Recent studies have correlated long life with optimism, with positive thinking, and with a lack of hostility, anxiety and depression.

A Crackdown on the Traffic of Humans (pg 376)
The Bush administration has more than doubled the number of prosecutions of people suspected of trafficking in human beings since 2001, but the problem of foreigners exploited for sex or labor continues to grow, officials said today.

Explore

World Wide Life Expectancy (pg 358)
The map presents the life expectancy of people for each country. It illustrates which countries have higher life expectancy than others.

Is Ageism Increasing in America? (pg 364)
This activity asks questions about the elderly sharing a home with their children and about social security. After answer the questions compare your answers to the answer in the 1998 General Social Survey.

Listen

Alzheimer's (pg 359)
NPR reports about the elderly staying mentally active making them less likely to suffer from Alzheimer's or small strokes.

Watch

Age Myths (pg 359)
This video clip discusses one woman who became a producer of a program for elderly, dispelling the myths that when people get older they have nothing to do or are alone.

Visualize

An Ageing Population (pg 357)
The map illustrates which counties and states in the country have a high percentage of people 65 and older living in them. The site also allows for you to see a ranking of states by percentage of elderly living in them and the age distribution by sex.

Population: Proportion of the Population Under 15, Worldwide (pg 371)
The interactive map allows the use to see which countries have higher or lower proportions of their population under the age of 15.

Practice Test

After completing the practice test, check your answers in the Answer Key of this Study Guide.

Multiple Choice Questions

1. Middle age refer to people who are:
   a. people in their 20s.
   b. people in their 30s.
   c. people in their 40s.
   d. people in their 50s.

2. _____ refers to a person's age that is determined by the actual date of birth.
   a. functional age
   b. age cohort
   c. chronological age
   d. natural age

3. The cause in the increase in the percentage of elderly people include:
   a. a declining birth rate.
   b. the baby boomers are approaching old age
   c. increasing life expectancy
   d. All of the above

4. The "oldest old" refer to people in what age category?
   a. 50-65
   b. 65-75
   c. 75-85
   d. 85 and older

5. In global terms, life expectancy is:
   a. highest in the highest-income countries.
   b. highest in the lowest-income countries.
   c. about the same in all countries.
   d. higher for men than women.

6. Which of the following is correct about the living arrangement of the elderly?
   a. Most live in nursing homes
   b. More elderly men live alone than elderly women
   c. All of the elderly develop a mental disorder
   d. More elderly men than women live with their spouse

7. Which of the following is not a stage in Elisabeth Kubler-Ross's five stages?
   a. Anger
   b. Depression
   c. Accountability
   d. Acceptability

8. There are many myths about the elderly in American society. Which of the following is Not true?
   a. The elderly do not always lose their mental abilities
   b. Most elderly maintain their own homes and apartments
   c. All of the elderly experience social isolation
   d. Middle class elderly have nothing to do with their time

9. What is the poverty rate among the elderly?
    a. Above the national average
    b. Below the national average
    c. About the same as the national average
    d. Almost 0 percent

10. Which group of people is least likely to have health insurance?
    a. Those between the ages of 35 and 44
    b. Those between the ages of 18 and 21
    c. Those between the ages of 60 and 75
    d. Those between the ages of 45 and 54

11. The "sandwich generation" includes those who:
    a. Take care of dependent children.
    b. Care for aging parents.
    c. Care for both dependent children and aging parents.
    d. Care for both dependent children and grandchildren.

12. In the final stage of dying, people come to the stage of:
    a. Denial.
    b. Anger.
    c. Depression.
    d. Acceptance.

13. The birth rate declining and the life expectancy growing has been referred to as the:
    a. aging revolution.
    b. geriatric generation
    c. graying of America
    d. new old generation

14. People who are born at the same time and are assumed to share the chronological and function characteristics are known as:
    a. age cohorts.
    b. peer cohorts.
    c. age groups.
    d. chronological cohorts.

15. Those who are between the ages of 45 and 55 fallen into which stage?
    a. Adolescence
    b. Young adulthood
    c. Young middle age
    d. Middle age

16. In the year 2000, which region has the highest percentage of people 80 years and older?
    a. Europe
    b. Middle East
    c. North America
    d. Oceania

17. What is the sociological reason for women living longer than men in industrialized nations?
    a. Women have higher levels of good cholesterol
    b. Men's hearts weaken more rapidly as they age
    c. Women exercise more than men
    d. Men are more likely to die at a younger age due to accidents and crime.

18. At what stage during the dying process do people acknowledge that they will die but see their death as unjust?
    a. Anger
    b. Negotiation
    c. Depression
    d. Acceptance

19. Elderly people's status started declining:
    a. when the Industrial Revolution came about.
    b. when social norms began to change every few years.
    c. when scientific knowledge began to advance rapidly
    d. all of the above

20. What program improved the financial situation of the elderly?
    a. AARP
    b. Social Security
    c. Welfare
    d. Medicaid

21. What type of study allows a researcher to compare the same people over time?
    a. Cross-section study
    b. Time-series study
    c. Longitudinal study
    d. Secondary analysis study

22. Which racial group has the highest number of children living in poverty?
    a. Caucasian
    b. Asian
    c. Hispanic
    d. African American

23. All except one of the following has lead to an increase in the life expectancy of people in the United States and Western Europe. Which one did not increase the life expectancy?
    a. Performing regular physical fitness
    b. Improved sanitation
    c. Better nutrition
    d. An increase in medical knowledge

24. _____ refers to the distinctive cultural values, pursuits, and pastimes that are culturally prescribed for each age cohort.
    a. Life span
    b. Age cohort
    c. Age norms
    d. None of the above

25. There are many rites of passage that people go through during the life course. Which of the following would not be considered one of them?
    a. Graduating high school
    b. Getting a driver's license
    c. Being allowed to vote
    d. Learning to cook

True/False Questions

True   False   1. The elderly population in the United States has decreased dramatically over the last few decades.

True   False   2. The terms life span and life expectancy generally mean the same thing.

True   False   3. Adolescence is the stage in life that marks the beginning of our olives as fully functioning members of society.

True   False   4. The "old old" refer to those who are between the ages of 75 and 85.

True   False   5. Life expectancy does not vary from one country to another.

True   False   6. Social isolation is a greater problem for the elderly than it is for younger people.

True   False   7. Ageism refers to the idea that the elderly are treated differently based upon their age.

True   False   8. When the elderly disengage from society they gradually withdraw from their communities and the wider world.

True   False   9. Generation X is the largest cohort of people in the last century.

True   False   10. A cross-sectional study examines different age groups at one moment in time.

Fill-in-the-Blank Questions

1. Elisabeth Kubler-Ross claimed that _____ is the last stage that people face when dying.

2. People who are born within a specific time period and are assumed to share both chronological and functional characteristic are considered a(n) _____.

3. _____ is the scientific study of the biological, psychological, and sociological phenomena associated with old age.

4. Robert Butler coined the term _____ in 1969 to refer to differential treatment based on age.

5. Generation _____ has a sizeable minority population and is the first to fully experience the transformation of American households

6. _____ is the life stage between childhood and adulthood.

7. High-status professionals, mangers, and sales workers are less likely to _____ because their jobs are less physically demanding than laborers.

8. As the first wave of baby boomers passed though their adolescence around 1960, America shifted its emphasis from _____ to adolescence.

9. The decline in birthrate plus extended life expectancy has _____ the elderly proportion of the American population and _____ the young proportion.

10. _____ transports people far from their homes for forced, bonded, and illegitimate labor.

Essay Questions

1. Explain why age is socially constructed.

2. Discuss the different life stages that people go through.

3. What are the myths about growing old and what is the actual reality?

4. Define and give an example of ageism.

5. In what ways does inequality manifest among the young?

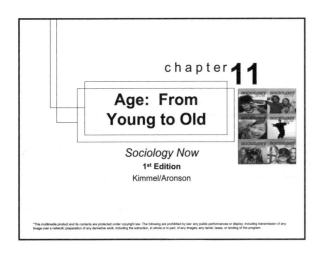

chapter **11**

Age: From Young to Old

Sociology Now
1st Edition
Kimmel/Aronson

Age and Identity

*"The Graying of Youth
Obsessed America"*

– age as social construction
– today people tend to postpone adulthood until halfway through their lives
– age → *identity and inequality*
 • **chronological age**
 • **functional age**
 • **age cohort**
 • **gerontology**

Age and Identity

• **The Stages of Life**
 – **life span**
 – **life expectancy**
 • *how long one can expect to live*
 – new stages of life were coined to accommodate the changes in life expectancy
 • *adolescence today*
 • *teenager 1940s*
 • *teen-age 1920s*

Age and Identity

- the stages of Life (Adulthood)
  - **25-35:** young adulthood
  - **35-45:** "young" middle age
  - **45-55:** middle age
  - **55-65:** "old" middle age
  - **65-75:** "young" old age
  - **75-85:** "old" old age
  - **85 and over** "old" old age

Age and Identity

- **Childhood**
  - children as "miniature" adults
  - impact of Industrial Revolution
    - time of freedom and innocence
    - gender differences
  - "children growing up too fast" these days

Age and Identity

- **Adolescence**

- **Young Adulthood**
  - 18 to 25 to 30
  - *milestones that define adulthood*
    1) living away from parents
    2) full-time job
    3) married
    4) completion of education
    5) having children

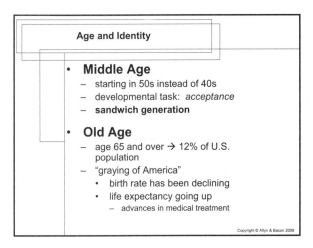

Age and Identity

- **Middle Age**
  - starting in 50s instead of 40s
  - developmental task: *acceptance*
  - **sandwich generation**
- **Old Age**
  - age 65 and over → 12% of U.S. population
  - "graying of America"
    - birth rate has been declining
    - life expectancy going up
      - advances in medical treatment

Copyright © Allyn & Bacon 2009

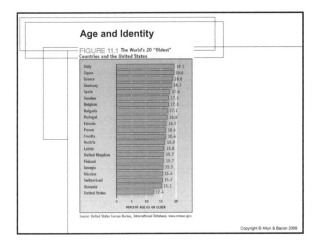

Age and Identity

FIGURE 11.1 The World's 20 "Oldest" Countries and the United States

Copyright © Allyn & Bacon 2009

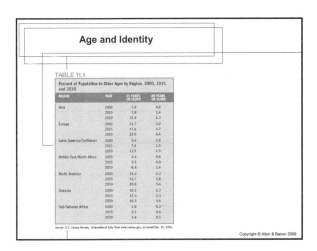

Age and Identity

TABLE 11.1

Copyright © Allyn & Bacon 2009

Age and Identity

- **Aging and Dying**
  - fears of growing old
    - *Living in a nursing home*
    - *Losing mental abilities*
    - *Being alone*
    - *Having nothing to do*
  - *"dying"* as number one fear
  - leading causes of death in U.S.
    - heart disease
    - cancer
    - stroke
    - emphysema

"Most scholars believe that the upper limit of life expectancy is 100, though a small percentage . . . *could* live to see 120."

Copyright © Allyn & Bacon 2009

Age and Identity

  - death
    - individual event
    - sociological phenomenon
  - Elisabeth Kübler-Ross: Stage Theory of Imminent Death
    - *Denial*
    - *Anger*
    - *Negotiation*
    - *Depression*
    - *Acceptance*

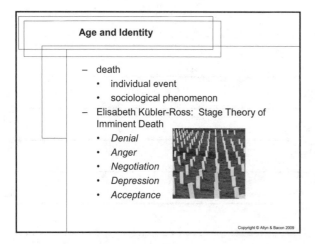

Copyright © Allyn & Bacon 2009

Age and Inequality

  - "old" → term of respect
  - "old" → feeble, fragile, worn out, outdated
  - **ageism**
    - *differential treatment*
    - *most adversely affects elderly*
  - declining status of the aged is *not* universal

- **Age and Poverty**
  - aged are more affluent than ever before
  - many elderly people are still poor
  - **Social Security (1940)**

Copyright © Allyn & Bacon 2009

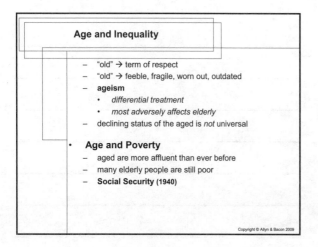

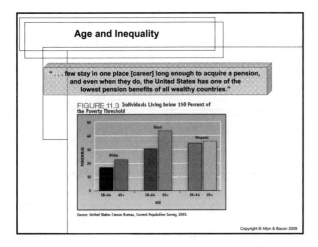

Age and Inequality

"... few stay in one place [career] long enough to acquire a pension, and even when they do, the United States has one of the lowest pension benefits of all wealthy countries."

FIGURE 11.3 Individuals Living below 150 Percent of the Poverty Threshold

Source: United States Census Bureau, Current Population Survey, 2003.

Copyright © Allyn & Bacon 2009

Age and Inequality

- **Social Isolation**
  - Limited regular interaction with family, friends, and acquaintances
  - Retirement closes off work as a source of interaction
  - *Social disengagement*

- **Retirement**
  - mark of social status

- **Elder Care**

Copyright © Allyn & Bacon 2009

Boomers, Busters, and Boomlets: The Generations of Youth

- post WWII baby boom (1945 – 1964)
- "now" generation (1960)
- "me" generation (1980)

- **Generation X (Baby Busters)**
  - followed the baby boomers
  - worse off economically than parents
  - decline in educational opportunity and attainments

Copyright © Allyn & Bacon 2009

**Boomers, Busters, and Boomlets:
The Generations of Youth**

- **Generation Y (A Baby Boomlet)**
  - 1975 – 1995 "echo boom"
  - three times the size of generation X
  - "the millennial generation"
  - homes of working parents and single mothers
  - PC-literate; "plugged in"

- **Global Youth–A Dying Breed**

Youth and Inequality

  - the elderly are more organized
  - aging population has political power
- **Youth and Poverty**
- **Health Care**
- **Child Labor**
  - The New Slavery
  - The Worst Forms of Child Labor

- **Getting Older *and* Getting Better? Youth and Age in the 21st Century**

What Does America Think?

11.1 **Teen Sex**
This is actual survey data from the General Social Survey, 2004.

1. For those in their early teens, 14 to 16 years old, sex before marriage is: always wrong according to 70 percent of all respondents in 2004. Women were more likely than men to report thinking it was always wrong. Another 17 percent of respondents thought it was almost always wrong. Ten percent thought it was sometimes wrong, and almost 4 percent thought it was not wrong at all. Middle-class respondents seemed to be more conservative in their views on teen sex, while upper-class respondents seemed to be the most liberal.

CRITICAL THINKING | DISCUSSION QUESTIONS
1. Why do you think women are more conservative in their views toward teen sex than men?
2. How do you explain the social class differences in responses about attitudes toward teen sex?

What Does America Think?

11.2 Adult Children and Older Parents: The Sandwich Generation

This is actual survey data from the General Social Survey, 2004.

As you know, many older people share a home with their grown children. Do you think this is generally a good idea or a bad idea? According to 2004 GSS survey results, almost half of respondents thought it was a good idea, and almost half thought it was a bad idea. About one-fifth said it depends. There was very little difference among responses when separated by class or gender, but there was significant disparity when separated by race. White respondents were least likely to think it was a good idea and most likely to think it was a bad idea. About half of Black respondents thought it was a good idea. The category of "other" had the highest percentage of respondents thinking it was a good idea.

CRITICAL THINKING | DISCUSSION QUESTION

1. How would you account for the racial differences in responses? The largest numbers of individuals in the category of "other" are of Hispanic or Asian descent. Can you think of any cultural explanations for the disparity? Why do you think there was very little difference based on gender or social class?

What Does America Think?

▶ Go to this website to look further at the data. You can run your own statistics and crosstabs here: http://sda.berkeley.edu/cgi-bin/hsda?harcsda+gss04

REFERENCES: Davis, James A., Tom W. Smith, and Peter V. Marsden. General Social Surveys 1972–2004: [Cumulative file] [Computer file]. 2nd ICPSR version. Chicago, IL: National Opinion Research Center [producer], 2005; Storrs, CT: Roper Center for Public Opinion Research, University of Connecticut; Ann Arbor, MI: Inter-University Consortium for Political and Social Research; Berkeley, CA: Computer-Assisted Survey Methods Program, University of California [distributors], 2005.

Chapter 12
The Family

Chapter Outline

I. The Family Tree
   a. Families as Kinship Systems
      i. Family
         1. The basic unit in society traditionally consisting of two parents rearing their children.
         2. Any of various social units differing from but regarded as equivalent to the traditional family.
         3. Those related to you through blood or marriage, extended back through generations.
      ii. Kinship systems are cultural forms that locate individual sin the culture by reference to their families.
      iii. Line of descent:
         1. Matrilineal
         2. Patrilineal
         3. Bilineal
   b. Culture and Forms of the Family
      i. Families ensure the regular transfer of property and establish lines of succession.
         1. Families restrict the number of people you can have sex with.
         2. To ensure legitimacy every type of society has established a type of marriage.
      ii. Monogamy is the marriage between two people.
      iii. Polygamy is the marriage between three or more people.
      iv. Poygyny is one man with two or more women.
      v. Polyandry is one woman with two or more men.
      vi. Group marriage is the marriage of two or more men and two or more women.
   c. The Family Unit
      i. Family of origin is the family that you are born into.
      ii. Family of procreation is the family you choose to belong to in order to reproduce.
   d. The Development of the Family
      i. Families evolve to socialize children, transmit property, ensure legitimacy, and regulate sexuality.
      ii. They also evolved as economic units.
      iii. In agrarian societies the household has been the basic economic unit.
         1. Production occurred within the household.
         2. Everyone participated in growing and eating the crops.
      iv. There was no distinction between family and society.
      v. The most common model in the premodern era was the extended family.
   e. The Origins of the Nuclear Family
      i. Marriage developed far more functions than simple sexual regulations, ensuring that parents and children know who each other is.
         1. Marriage also validate a gentleman's claim to nobility and establish that a boy had become a man.
         2. It could form a social tie between two families.
      ii. Marriage has also come to represent a distinctive emotional bond between two people.
         1. Compassionate marriage in which individuals choose their marriage partners based on emotional ties and love.
         2. Industrialization and modernization meant that social and economic needs could no longer be met by kin.

     iii. The nuclear family is highly "gendered."
       1. Women were seen as morally superior to men and the homes they made as nurturing and supportive.
       2. The husband became the "breadwinner."
  II. Family and Ethnicity
    a. The European American Family
      i. The European American family took on characteristics from each of the large immigrant groups.
      ii. Contemporary family is the result of deliberate social policies.
      iii. The end of World War II saw the largest infusion of government funding toward the promotion of the new nuclear family.
      iv. The family that finally emerged in the 1950s was far less a naturally emergent evolutionary adaptation and far more the anomalous result of deliberate social planning.
    ii. The Native American Family
      a. Prior to the arrival of Europeans, most Native Americans lived in small villages where extended families dominated.
      b. Family and kinship systems were developed to provide for people's fundamental needs.
      c. Families did not develop primarily out of people's desire for love but out of the desire to survive.
    iii. The African American Family
      a. Before slavery was abolished, most slaves were prohibited from legal marriages.
      b. Since the 1970s, economic changes have resulted in a massive loss of blue-collar jobs and as a result the nuclear family model has become less common.
      c. African American communities have adopted the convention of "fictive kinship" which stretches the boundaries of kinship to include non-blood relations, friends, neighbors, and co-workers.
    iv. The Asian American Family
      a. Chinese and Japanese American families emphasize the family as a unit rather than a group of individuals.
      b. They have families that are more hierarchical.
    v. The Hispanic Family
      a. Most are nuclear families but they do have characteristics of extended families.
      b. They tend to be hierarchical by gender and age.
  III. Forming Families
    a. Courtship and Dating
      i. Courtship was largely unknown in ancient society.
       1. Marriages were arranged.
       2. Children often had a voice in the selection process.
      ii. The custom of dating did not arise until the 1920s.
       1. Started with the working-class.
       2. By the 1930s the custom had spread to the middle class.
       3. By the 1950s parents were eagerly awaiting their child's first date.
    b. Marriage
      i. Marriage is the most common foundation for family formation in the world.
       1. Marriage is also a legal arrangement.
       2. Marriage is not the only living arrangement for people in society.
       3. Multigenerational households consist of adults of more than one generation sharing domestic space.
       4. Marriage itself has changed over time.
      ii. Delayed Marriage
       1. Young people are experiencing longer periods of independent living while working or attending school before marriage.
       2. Significant educational and economic inequalities mean that different groups will continue to vary at age of first marriage.

      iii. Staying single
          1. Singlehood has become the commonplace.
          2. Single women are better educated, are better employed, and have better mental health than single men.
      iv. Cohabitating
          1. Unmarried people in a romantic relationship.
          2. Today cohabitation has become commonplace.
          3. Globally, cohabitation is common in liberal countries
      v. Explanations of Nonmarital Choices
          1. These changes are partially explained by new practices, such as courtship and dating.
          2. These changes tend to be associated with higher levels of education.
          3. These changes are partially explained by changing sexual behaviors and attitudes.

  c. Biracial Marriage
      i. Miscengenation
      ii. Social barriers still place dating, courtship, and marriage within clear racial categories.
      iii. Euro-Americans are least likely to intermarry.
      iv. The most common interracial couple in the United States is a White husband married to an Asian wife.

  d. Same-Sex Marriage
      i. Typical lesbian or gay couples, at least the ones who are open:
          1. They are urban.
          2. They are well educated.
          3. They are less likely to have children.
          4. They are les likely to own their homes than married couples.
          5. They tend to be more egalitarian.
      ii. In the United States they are not allowed to marry.

IV. Parenting
  a. During the past fifty years the answer to the question, "Who should watch the children?" has become more and more narrow.
  b. Gender and Parenting
      i. Domestic work remains women's work.
          1. Women in male-female households do about 2/3 of the housework.
          2. Mothers spend much more time than fathers interacting with their children.
      ii. American fathers are more active and involved parents than ever before.
  c. Single-Parent Families
      i. During the first half of the 20th century, the primary cause of single-parent families was parental death.
          1. By the end of the century, most parents were living, but living elsewhere.
          2. Currently 12.2 million people in the United States are single parents.
      ii. Most people are not single parents by choice.
      iii. Single mothers predominate both because it is easier for a father to become absent during the pregnancy and because mothers are typically granted custody in court cases.
  d. Grandparenting
      i. The number of grandparents raising their grandchildren has grown significantly.
      ii. Grandparents can even legally adopt their grandchildren.
  e. Adoptive Parents
      i. Historically, adoption was considered an option to resolve an unwanted pregnancy.
      ii. Today there are several different types of adoptions:
          1. Foster care adoptions.
          2. Private adoptions.
          3. Inter-country adoptions.
          4. Transracial adoptions.

   iii. Motivations for adoption vary
  f. Not Parenting
   i. In the United States the media are constantly telling us that children are the meaning of life.
   ii. Education is an important predictor of childlessness.
V. Family Transitions
  a. Divorce is the legal dissolution of a marriage.
   i. Grounds of divorce may vary.
   ii. On average men become more content with their marriages over time while women become less.
  b. The Consequences of Divorce
   i. Economically there is clear evidence about who wins and loses.
    1. Women's standards of living decline.
    2. Men's standards of living increase.
   ii. Children are more likely to live with their mothers.
  c. Blended Families
   i. At least half of all children will have a divorced and remarried parent before they turn 18.
   ii. Blended families tend to be far more common among the middle classes.
VI. Violence in Families
  a. Intimate Partner Violence
   i. More than 2 million women are beaten by their partners every year.
   ii. Globally the problem of family violence is widespread.
   iii. There are some differences by class, race, ethnicity, and age.
    1. Poor women experience more violence than wealthier women.
    2. Younger women are far more likely to be a victim than older women.
    3. It is higher in African American families than in White families.
   iv. Gays and lesbians also experience domestic violence.
   v. 85 percent of all victims are female.
  b. Intergenerational and Intragenerational Violence
   i. Intergenerational violence refers to violence between generations.
   ii. Intragenerational violence refers to violence within the same generation.
VII. The Family in the 21st Century: "The Same as it Ever Was"
  a. Families are as old as the human species.
  b. Families have always been changing, adapting to new political, social, economic, and environmental situations.

Chapter Summary

- Families are the basic unit in society traditionally consisting of two parents rearing their children, but also any various social units differing from but regarded as equivalent to the traditional family.

- Families are part of kinship systems, cultural forms that located individuals in the culture by reference to their families and can be matrilineal, patrilineal, or bilineal.

- There are several different forms of the family: monogamy, polygamy, polygyny, polyandry, and group marriage.

- The family unit comes in varied number of types. One family unit is the family or origin- the family you are born into, and the other is the family of procreation- the family you choose to belong to in order to reproduce.

- Families have developed and changed over the course of human history. In agrarian societies the household was the basic economic unit with no distinction between family and society. The most common model in the premodern era was the extended family.

- Marriage has come to represent a distinctive emotional bond between two people and the idea that people should select their own marriage partner, companionate marriage, is a very recent phenomenon.

- The nuclear family emerged in Europe and the United States in the late eighteenth century.

- The nuclear family is highly gendered making the home the woman's sphere and the work world the husband's sphere.

- Racial and ethnic groups exhibit a wide variation in their families. The nuclear family model is most common in European American family while African American families have characteristics of extended families and have developed "fictive kinship" to include non-blood relations, Asian American families view themselves as a unit instead of individuals, and Hispanic families are mostly nuclear but do have characteristics of extended families.

- The formation of families begins with courtship and dating. Dating emerged in the 1920s and was mostly a working-class phenomenon and was extended to the middle class in the 1930s.

- Marriage is the most common foundation for family formation in the world and the marriage of two people- a woman and man- is universal in developed countries, although there are significant variations among different cultures.

- Some people opting for delaying marriage, staying single, and cohabitating. Young people are experiencing longer periods of independent living while working or attending school and singlehood has become commonplace. Cohabitation is also more common now than it was 50 years ago.

- There are numerous explanations as to why people make nonmarital choices including: the courtship and dating practices, higher levels of education, and changing sexual behaviors.

- Two forms of marriage that were illegal in the United States are biracial and same sex marriage.

- Just as children have never been so important in our cultural values, parents have never been considered so important in the lives of their children.

- Women still do the majority of domestic work, although today fathers are more active and involved in the parenting than ever before.

- Single parenting, grandparenting, and adoptive parents have become more commonplace than ever before.

- Divorce is the legal dissolution of a marriage and it may have consequences.

- Intimate partner violence represents violence, lethal or not, experienced by a spouse, ex-spouse, cohabiting partner, boyfriend, girlfriend, ex-boyfriend, ex-girlfriend and can be intergenerational and intragenerational.

Learning Objectives

After completing the reading of Chapter 9, you should be able to answer the following objectives.

- Define family and discuss some of the different ways a family tree can be constructed.
- Discuss the family as a cultural institution and the different types of marriage arrangements.
- Explain the difference between family of origin and family of procreation.
- Discuss the origins of the nuclear family.
- Describe the differences between the European American family, the Native American family, the African American Family, the Asian American family, and the Hispanic family.
- Discuss courtship and dating and how it has changed over the last century.
- Identify and discuss the alternatives to marriage and why people may choose the alternatives.
- Discuss biracial and same-sex marriage in terms of their histories and how prominent they are in society now.
- Talk about the characteristics of single-parent families, grandparenting, adoptive parents, not parenting and what the trends are today.
- Describe how divorce impacts the family in terms of standard of living and the children's well-being.
- Define intimate partner violence, intergenerational violence, and intragenerational violence and discuss the problem in the United States and globally.

Key Terms

Bilineal descent: through both your parents' sides.

Cohabitation: unmarried people in a romantic relationship living in the same residence.

Companionate marriage: individuals choose their marriage partners based on emotional ties and love.

Exogamy

Extended family: two or three generations live under the same roof or at least in the same compound.

Family: the basic unit in society traditionally consisting of two parents rearing their children but also any various social units differing from but regarded as equivalent to the traditional family.

Family of origin: the family you are born into.

Family of procreation: the family you choose to belong to in order to reproduce.

Group marriage: two or more men marrying two or more women.

Intimate partner violence: violence, lethal or nonlethal, experienced by a spouse, ex-spouse, cohabitating partner, boyfriend, girlfriend, ex-boyfriend, or ex-girlfriend.

Kinship system: cultural forms that locate individuals in the culture by reference to their families.

Legitimacy: ensure that men know what children they have produced.

Matrilineal descent: through your mother's side of the family.

Miscegenation: interracial marriage.

Monogamy: marriage between two people.

Multigenerational households: adults of more than one generation sharing domestic space.

Nonmarital sex: sex that is not related to marriage.

Patrilineal descent: through your father's side of the family.

Polyandry: one woman marrying two or more men.

Polygamy: marriage between three or more people.

Polygyny: one man with two or more women.

Key People

Christopher Lasch: suggested the theory of "progressive nucleation" to explain how nuclear families superseded the extended family.

Judith Wallerstein: studied children from divorced families and found that there was a sleeper effect on the children.

Additional Learning with MySocLab
Read

    Staking Out a Place in a House Divided (pg 407)
    Every year in the US nearly one million children experience the divorce of their parents. Studies consistently show that the marital discord prior to the divorce and the divorce itself are very traumatic to these children.
    Study Finds Families Bypassing Marriage (pg 397)
    The number of couples who live together out of wedlock, often with children, is increasing rapidly, a new study reports.
    Personal Health; Planning to Escape from an Abusive Relationship (pg 409)
    A common response of people who learn that a woman is being battered by the man she lives with is: "Why doesn't she leave?

Explore

    Web Activity: Marriage and Family (pg 397)
    Read the articles "More grads delaying marriage" and "Marriage as a Social Contract" to learn about and understand the major transformations of the family in the last 30 years. After reading the articles there is a series of questions to answer.
    Grandparents as Caregivers (pg 404)
    This activity includes a map of the United States showing the percentage of grandparents as caregivers for each county.

Listen

    Fathers Taking More Active Role in Raising Children (pg 402)
    An increasing number of men are trading in briefcases for bibs. It's a bit of a cultural evolution, as more and more fathers find that they enjoy being involved as parents. And the younger the children are when they bond, the stronger the relationship.

Watch

    How is Family Defined? (pg 383)
    Judith Stacey answer the question: Do sociologists agree on how family is defined? The vast majority of sociologists do not bother to ask the question of how to define family.

Visualize

    Cohabitation (pg 395)
    This bar charts illustrates women who have cohabitated with their first husband before marriage and the differences between racial groups, education levels, and religion.

Practice Test

After completing the practice test, check your answers in the Answer Key of this Study Guide.

Multiple Choice Questions

1. If you construct your family tree by tracing your decent through your mother's side of the family, your line of decent is:
    a. matrilineal.
    b. patrilineal.
    c. bilineal.
    d. all of the above.

2. When two or more men marry two or more women this would be considered:
    a. polyandry.
    b. polygamy.
    c. group marriage.
    d. exogamy.

3. The family that you choose to belong to in order to reproduce is:
    a. family of origin.
    b. family of procreation.
    c. kinship system.
    d. family.

4. Which of the following racial or ethnic family tends to be nuclear with a hierarchical system?
    a. European American family
    b. African American family
    c. Hispanic family
    d. Asian American family

5. What percentage of American schoolgirls believe that everyone should be married?
    a. 88 percent
    b. 75 percent
    c. 60 percent
    d. 50 percent

6. What type of relationship consists of two people who are involved romantically and live with each other?
    a. Marriage
    b. Singlehood
    c. Cohabitation
    d. Kinship

7. In which country is the average age of a woman when she gets married approximately 29 years old?
    a. United States
    b. Poland
    c. Iceland
    d. Netherlands

8. What type of family household has decreased the most between 1970 and 2003?
    a. Married couples with children
    b. Married couples without children
    c. Men living alone
    d. Women living alone

9. Which is the most common type of biracial marriage in the United States?
   a. White men and Asian women
   b. White men and African American women
   c. White women and Asian men
   d. White women and African American men

10. Most states have placed restrictions on same-sex marriages. Which of the following states has no restriction at all?
    a. Washington
    b. Maine
    c. Florida
    d. New Mexico

11. Don is married to Nicole and Tammy, what type of marriage is this?
    a. Monogamous
    b. Polygynous
    c. Polyandrous
    d. Group marriage

12. In which racial/ethnic group has the highest percentage of children living in single-parent households?
    a. African American
    b. White
    c. Hispanic
    d. Asian

13. What percentage of U.S. women aged 40 to 44 in the year 2000 did not have any children?
    a. 10
    b. 15
    c. 18
    d. 22

14. Which group of women, who had married between 1990 and 1994, had the highest divorce rates?
    a. Those with master's degree
    b. Those with bachelor's degree
    c. Those with a high school diploma
    d. Those who dropped out of high school

15. A family unit that includes parents, children, grandparents, cousins as well as other kin is called:
    a. a nuclear family.
    b. an extended family.
    c. conjugal family.
    d. group marriage.

16. Which of the following is a cultural universal?
    a. Monogamy
    b. Heterosexual relationships
    c. Incest taboo
    d. Nuclear families

17. What percentage of preschoolers are organized child care facilities?
    a. 90 percent
    b. 75 percent
    c. 40 percent
    d. 25 percent

18. Which category of the U.S. population has the greatest share of female-headed households?
    a. White
    b. African American
    c. Hispanic
    d. Asian American

19. Which group of women would be the least likely to be victims of interpersonal violence?
    a. Higher-income women
    b. Younger women
    c. Unemployed women
    d. Low-income women

20. Looking ahead twenty year in the United States, we can predict that:
    a. most people will remain single.
    b. women will play a smaller role in child rearing.
    c. cohabitation will become the dominant form of family.
    d. family life will be diverse.

21. Exogamy is:
    a. the practice of marrying within one's own group.
    b. the practice of marrying someone within one's own family.
    c. the practice of marrying outside one's group.
    d. none of the above.

22. Polygamy is:
    a. the marriage between two people.
    b. the marriage between three or more people.
    c. the marriage between one man and two or more women.
    d. the marriage between one woman and two or more men.

23. An adoption that includes adopting children from other countries by U.S. couples is refers to as:
    a. Foster care adoption
    b. Private adoption
    c. Inter-country adoption
    d. Transracial adoption

24. Which of the following is not true about the typical openly gay and lesbian couples?
    a. They live in more urban
    b. They are more likely to own their own homes than married couples
    c. They are less likely to have children
    d. They tend to be more egalitarian

25. Which country has the highest age at first marriage for men?
    a. Austria
    b. Poland
    c. United States
    d. Switzerland

True/False Questions

True   False   1. Monogamy is the marriage between three or more people.

True   False   2. Families are the basic unit of society and have traditionally consisted of two parents rearing their children.

True   False   3. Matrilineal decent is traced through both parents' side of the family.

True   False   4. The family of origin is the one people belong to because they are born into it.

True   False   5. Love has always been the basis of two people getting married.

True   False   6. African American families tend to be nuclear families.

True   False   7. The most common reason for single parent homes today is the death of one parent.

True   False   8. Transracial adoption consists of the adoption of a child of a different race from the adopting parents.

True   False   9. Two divorced parents who marry and bring their families into a new family unit become a blended family.

True   False   10. Men and women are equally likely to be victims of intimate partner violence.

Fill-in-the-Blank Questions

1. _____ are cultural forms that locate individuals in the culture by reference to their family.

2. The most common arrangement of marriage is _____, marriage between two people.

3. Sociologists use the term _____ to refer to the stretching of the boundaries of kinship to include non-blood relations.

4. In a _____ marriage individuals are able to choose their marriage partners based on emotional ties and love.

5. The majority of American women, _____ percent, live without a spouse.

6. _____ refers to unmarried people in a romantic relationship living in the same residence.

7. Interracial marriage is also known as _____.

8. _____ is the single major cause of injury to women in the United States.

9. When a sibling physically assault another sibling this is refer to as _____.

10. The number of _____ raising children has grown from 2.2 million in 1970 to nearly 4 million today.

Essay Questions

1. What are the different forms of marriage and give an example of each.

2. Discuss the differences between the European family, African American family, Native American family, Asian family, and Hispanic family. What type of family form is dominant in each and how are they set up hierarchically?

3. What are the alternatives to marriage and why would someone choose these alternatives over marriage?

4. Discuss the consequences of divorce and the impact that it has on the men, women, and children involved.

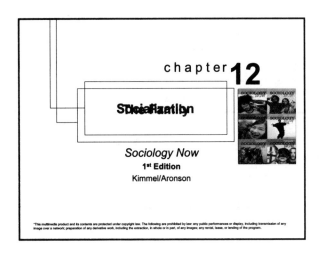

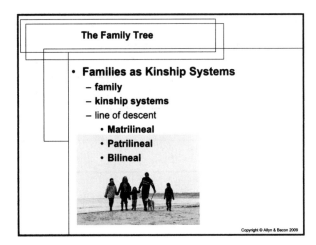

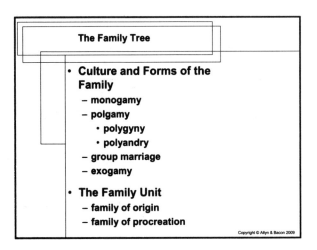

The Family Tree

- **The Development of the Family**
  - agrarian societies → no distinction between family and society
  - family was
    - *A school*
    - *A church*
    - *A hospital*
    - *A day care center*
    - *A police station*
    - *A retirement home*

The Family Tree

- **The Origins of the Nuclear Family**
  - emotional bond between two people
  - **companionate marriage**
  - nuclear as "highly gendered"
  - home as "women's sphere"

Family and Ethnicity

- **European American Family**
- **The Native American Family**
- **The African American Family**
- **The Asian American Family**
- **The Hispanic Family**

Forming Families

- **Courtship and Dating**
  - 1920s → pairs versus group dating

- **Marriage**
  - most common foundation for family formulation in the world
  - legal arrangement
  - **multigenerational households**

Forming Families

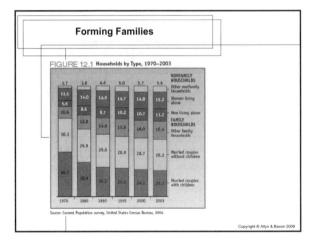

FIGURE 12.1 **Households by Type, 1970–2003**

Source: Current Population survey, United States Census Bureau, 2004.

Forming Families

- **Delayed Marriage**
- **Staying Single**
  - over half of all Americans over 15
- **Cohabiting**
  - **cohabitation**
- **Explanation of Nonmarital Choices**
  - courtship and dating
  - higher levels of education
  - changing sexual behaviors
    - increased acceptance of "premarital sex"
  - **nonmarital sex**

STUDY GUIDE

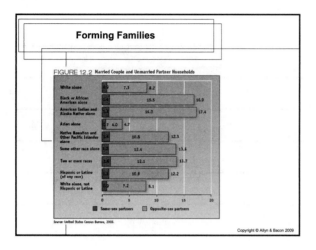

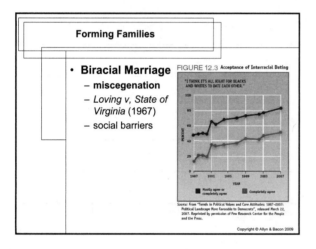

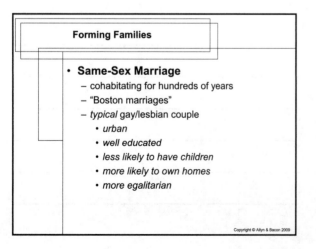

Parenting

- **Gender and Parenting**
- **Single-Parent Families**
- **Grandparenting**
- **Adoptive Parents**
  - *Foster Care*
  - *Private*
  - *Inter-Country*
  - *Transracial*
- **Not Parenting**

Family Transitions

- marriage as lifelong commitment
- divorce
- "divorce divide" based on class and race
- divorce blamed for social ills

- **The Consequences of Divorce**
- **Blended Families**

Family Transitions

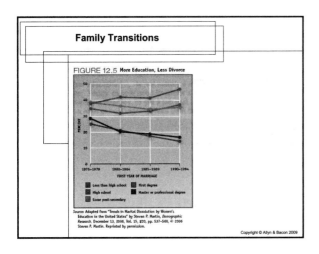

FIGURE 12.5 More Education, Less Divorce

Source: Adapted from "Trends in Marital Dissolution by Women's Education in the United States" by Steven P. Martin, *Demographic Research*, December 13, 2006, Vol. 15, #20, pp. 537–560, © 2006 Steven P. Martin. Reprinted by permission.

Violence in Families

- **Intimate Partner Violence**
  - IPV
  - aka "domestic violence"

FIGURE 12.6 Nonfatal Intimate Partner Victimization Rate by Gender and Race, 1993–2004

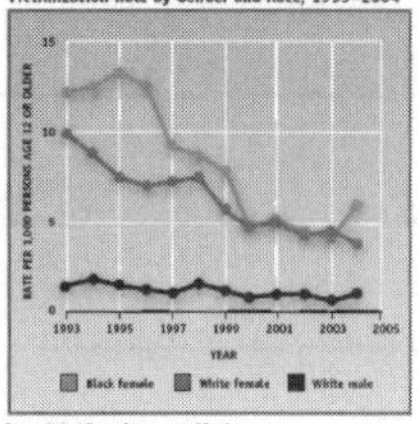

Source: United States Department of Justice.

Copyright © Allyn & Bacon 2009

Violence in Families

- **Intergenerational and Intragenerational Violence in Families**
  - sibling violence
  - violence against parents
  - parental violence against children
    - child abuse
    - child sexual abuse
  - American's more accepting of violence against children then they realize

- **The Family in the 21st Century: "The Same As It Ever Was"**

Copyright © Allyn & Bacon 2009

What Does America Think?

12.1 Racial and Ethnic Family Diversity

These are actual survey data from the General Social Survey.

Do you think there should be laws against marriages between Blacks and Whites? The overwhelming majority of respondents said "no" to this question in the 2002 survey. More Black (95.1 percent) than White (89.6 percent) respondents said "no." The numbers were very different when the question was asked 30 years earlier in 1972, when about 60 percent of respondents said "no." In the 1972 survey, the race categories were limited to "White" (of whom 60.7 said "no") and "other" (of whom 66.7 percent said "no"). Most respondents were White.

CRITICAL THINKING | DISCUSSION QUESTIONS

1. Why do you think almost 10 percent of the population still thinks interracial marriage should be illegal, including 9 percent of black respondents?
2. Part of doing sociology is placing things in historical context. What historical changes have taken place in the past 30 years that might explain how views toward interracial marriage have changed?

Copyright © Allyn & Bacon 2009

What Does America Think?

12.2 Attitudes toward Abortion

These are actual survey data from the General Social Survey, 2004.

1. Do you think it should be possible for a pregnant woman to obtain a legal abortion if the woman's own health is seriously endangered by the pregnancy? In 2004, 86 percent of respondents said "yes," and 14 percent said "no." These results are almost identical to 1972 responses. The percentage of respondents saying "yes" peaked in 1991 at 91.5 percent.

2. Do you think it should be possible for a pregnant woman to obtain a legal abortion if she is married and does not want any more children? In 2004, 41.8 percent of respondents said "yes," and 58.2 percent said "no." The percentage of people saying "yes" peaked 1994 at 48 percent, but otherwise, the data were almost identical to 1972, and attitudes have remained pretty steady since then.

3. Do you think it should be possible for a pregnant woman to obtain a legal abortion if the family has a very low income and cannot afford any more children? The responses from 2004 showed 41 percent of respondents saying "yes" and 59 percent saying "no." The response for those saying "yes" was rather lower than 1972 and again peaked in 1994.

4. Do you think it should be possible for a pregnant woman to obtain a legal abortion if she became pregnant as a result of rape? In 2004, 76.2 percent of respondents said "yes," and 23.8 percent said "no." The response for those saying "yes" was lower than it was in 1972 and peaked in 1991.

CRITICAL THINKING | DISCUSSION QUESTIONS

1. What do you think lies behind the variation of responses in approval toward abortion based on the reason for abortion? The highest approval was for the pregnant woman's health, next for rape victims, lower for married women who do not want children, and lowest for women who want to abort because they are poor. What societal values does this ranking reflect?
2. Why do you think the results break down by gender the way they do?

Copyright © Allyn & Bacon 2009

What Does America Think?

► Go to this website to look further at the data. You can run your own statistics and crosstabs here: http://sda.berkeley.edu/cgi-bin/hsda?harcsda+gss04.

REFERENCES: Davis, James A., Tom W. Smith, and Peter V. Marsden. General Social Surveys 1972–2004: [Cumulative file] [Computer file]. 2nd ICPSR version. Chicago, IL: National Opinion Research Center [producer], 2005; Storrs, CT: Roper Center for Public Opinion Research, University of Connecticut; Ann Arbor, MI: Inter-University Consortium for Political and Social Research, Berkeley, CA: Computer-Assisted Survey Methods Program, University of California [distributors], 2005.

Copyright © Allyn & Bacon 2009

Chapter 13
Economy and Work

Chapter Outline

I. Theories of the Economy
   a. Locke and Hobbes stressed separation, competition and individual isolation as results of rational self-interest.
   b. Adam Smith argued that social life involves more than individuals striving for social gain.
   c. Karl Marx believed that an economic system based on private property divided people into two unequal and competing classes.
      i. Upper class: worked because they achieved satisfaction by owning all the good and services and controlling political and social life.
      ii. Working class: worked because they had to.
   d. Max Weber believed that capitalism originated in a desire for personal spiritual fulfillment and to "make the world a better place."
   e. Emile Durkheim argued that modern societies every person must depend on hundred of others for goods and services.

II. Economic Development
   a. The Agricultural Economy
      i. Grew crops
      ii. No longer nomadic
      iii. Began the exchange of goods and services
   b. The Industrial Economy
      i. The Industrial Revolution- era of the machine, transformed economics, politics, and social life.
      ii. Industrial economies based on factor production differed from agricultural economies in five ways:
         1. Power
         2. Centralization
         3. Specialization
         4. Wage labor
         5. Separation of work and home
   c. Consumption and the Modern Economy
      i. Moved from production (how to get more goods out there) to consumption (how to decide from among the goods available).
      ii. Conspicuous consumption- prestige now based on accumulating as many possessions as possible and showing them off.
   d. The Postindustrial Economy
      i. Jobs are shifting to the service sector.
      ii. Three social changes characterize "post-industrial" economies.
         1. Knowledge work
            a. Knowledge economy less oriented around the actual production of a commodity.
            b. More concerned with the idea of the commodity, it marketing, distribution, and relationship to different groups of consumers.
         2. Rootlessness
            a. Moved workers into the wide world and out of factories.
            b. Time becomes meaningless to postindustrial workers.
         3. Globalization
            a. Globalized production refers to the fact that corporations derive raw materials from all over the world and use manufacturing and assembly plants in many different countries.
            b. Led to outsourcing.

       c. Links owners and manages to an interlocking system of managerial elite.

III. Economic Systems
  a. Capitalism- profit oriented economic system based on the private or corporate ownership of the means of production and distribution.
    i. Classic capitalism has three components:
      1. Private ownership of the means of production
      2. Open market
      3. Profit
    ii. Laissez-Faire Capitalism- property and the means of production should all be privately owned.
    iii. State Capitalism- requires that the government use a heavy hand in regulating and constraining the marketplace.
    iv. Welfare Capitalsim- while there is a market-based economy there are also extensive social welfare programs.
  b. Socialism- economic system in the exact opposite of laissez-faire capitalism
    i. Offers collective ownership
    ii. Collective goals
    iii. Central planning
    iv. Democratic Socialism- have socialist economies, but allow for a degree of entrepreneurship.
  c. Communism- economic system based on collective ownership of the means of production and is administered collectively.

IV. The American Economy
  a. Early American Economic Development
    i. Experienced movement from agricultural to industrial to postindustrial economies.
    ii. U.S. constitution can be read as an economic charter.
  b. The Impact of Industrialization: Displacement and Consolidation
    i. Consolidation
      1. Began in the late 19th century
      2. During the first few decades the government set up regulatory agencies.
      3. New Deal
    ii. World War II
      1. The economy was booming.
      2. Blue-collar workers found themselves in high demand.
  c. The Postindustrial Economy: Technology and Globalization
    i. Technical revolution
    ii. Today, in advanced nations, information technologies have enable companies to race down the information superhighway.
  d. Corporations
    i. Family corporations
    ii. Managerial corporations
    iii. Institutional corporations
  e. Multinational Corporations
    i. No longer clearly located anywhere.
    ii. Globalization has "decoupled" the old win-win relationships between corporate and national interests.
    iii. The world's 40 biggest corporations employ 55 percent of their workfoces in foreign countries.

V. Work, Identity, and Inequality
  a. How we work
    i. In the early days of mass production, the assembly line basically imagined workers as machines.
    ii. The Hawthorne Effect
      1. Workers having input could increase their productivity.
      2. People work better and faster when they feel valued.

          iii.   Theory X and Theory Y
                1.   Theory X assumes that people naturally dislike work, so they will slack off unless they are coerced and threatened.
                2.   Theory Y assumes that people naturally like work, so they will do it if they feel they are a valued part of a team.
          iv.   Manufacturing Consent
                1.   Workers came to embrace a system that also exploited them.
                2.   Manufacturing consent is the production of values and emotions that bind worker to their company:
                    a.   Piece-rate pay system
                    b.   Internal labor market
                    c.   Collective bargaining
    b.   Types of jobs
            i.   White-collar jobs
                 1.   Require considerable education
                2.   Professions can generally be distinguished from other jobs by four characteristics:
                    a.   Theoretical knowledge
                      b.   Self-regulating practices
                      c.   Authority over clients
                      d.   Community orientation
           ii.   Blue-collar jobs
                1.   Jobs involved with production rather than knowledge.
                2.   About 13 percent of American workers have jobs in production.
          iii.   Pink-collar jobs
                 1.   Term coined by Louise Kay Howe in 1977.
                 2.   Many of these jobs are in clerical and sales work.
          iv.   Service work
                1.   Category includes food preparation and service, personal services, and maintenance workers, police officers, and firefighters.
                2.   Lowest paid, least prestigious, and few have health benefits.
    c.   Alternatives to Wage Labor
            i.   Working off the books
                 1.   Informal economy includes several types of activities.
                2.   Informal does not mean unorganized.
                3.   Underground economy comes into play only because the money is undeclared and therefore untaxed.
          ii.   Unpaid work
                1.   Taking care of your own household.
                2.   1920s the idea that unpaid household labor had nothing to do with "real" economy.
                3.   Domestic labor lost he status of "work" and became part of the heterosexual marital bond.
                4.   Near the end of the 20th century, economists began to realize that household labor, or human capital, does make a significant impact to the economy.
          iii.   Self-employment
                1.   Jobs range from blue-collar to white-collar.
                2.   In the past decade women have been leading the way in small businesses.
          iv.   Part-time work
                1.   In 2005, about 25 percent of the American workforce was employed part-time.
                2.   Many chose to work part-time because they want to attend to other commitments.
          v.   Contingent and "On Call Work"
                1.   Replacing permanent employees with employees hired to do a specific project or for a specific time period.

          2. Working only when their services are needed.

          3. Temporary workers are over represented in low-skill, low-paying jobs.

    d. Unemployment

      i. Three types of unemployment:

          1. Seasonal unemployment- changes in demand for workers based on climate or seasonal criteria.

          2. Cyclical unemployment- response to normal business cycles of expansion and contraction.

          3. Structural unemployment- more permanent conditions of the economy.

      ii. Countries measure unemployment by counting people who are actively looking for jobs.

VI. Diversity in the Workplace

    a. Racial Diversity

      i. For every dollar a White man earns, Black and Hispanic men earn 65 cents, Black women 58 cents, and Hispanic women 48 cents.

      ii. With only a few members of a minority group occupy a job, they often believe they were hired as tokens, representatives of their group rather than individuals.

    b. Gender Diversity

      i. In 1900, less than 20 percent of American women worked outside the home.

      ii. Today, over half do.

      iii. Women's unemployment highest in poor countries.

      iv. Pay gap- difference between men and women's earnings.

      v. Work-Family Dynamics

          1. In 2002, for the first time, the majority of married male-female couples in America were dual income.

          2. Household maintenance is still widely assumed to be a woman's job.

    c. Sexual Diversity

      i. Early decisions about wages and benefits assumed a single breadwinner for the entire family- and assumed that he was not only male but heterosexual.

      ii. Corporate culture is built around the assumption of heterosexuality.

      iii. Of the Fortune 500 companies, 253 now offer benefits for same-sex partners, and 410 include sexual orientation in the nondiscrimination policies.

    d. Working Parents

      i. The U.S. ranks 8th among wealthy nations in the percentage of mothers in the labor force.

      ii. For many years, working mothers have been struggling to make corporate culture see children not as "problems" or distractions, but as part of "business as usual."

VII. Work and Economy in the 21st Century

    a. In the future, only a small percentage of workers will do a single job throughout their lives, changing only to move up to positions of greater authority.

    b. Instead they will develop a portfolio or skills that they will use to move horizontally.

Chapter Summary

- The economy is a set of institutions and relationships that manages natural resources, manufactured goods, and professional services which are referred to as capital.

- Several different theories have been used to explain the economy. All of them have some truth: every economic system requires some degree of competition and some degree of cooperation.

- The agricultural economy began the division of labor. No longer did everyone have to be involved in the production of food.

- The Industrial economy is based on factory production and differed from agricultural economies in five different ways.

- As the machines to produce goods became more efficient the emphasis of industrial economies shifted from production to consumption.

- There were three social changes that characterize postindustrial economies: knowledge work, rootlessness, and globalization.

- Capitalism is a profit-oriented economic system based on the private or corporate ownership of the means of production and distribution and has three components: private ownership of the means of production, and open market, and profit as a valuable goal of human enterprise.

- Three different forms of capitalism: Laissez-Faire Capitalism- property and the means of production should all be privately owned; State Capitalism- companies may still be privately owned, but they must meet government-set standards of product quality, worker compensation, and truth in advertising; and Welfare Capitalism- market-based economy for most goods and services, there are also extensive social welfare programs, and the government owns some of the most essential services, such as transportation, health care, and the mass media.

- Socialism is an economic system that is the exact opposite of laissez-faire capitalism. Socialism offers the collective ownership of property, collective goals, and central planning. Socialism differs from communism in the fact that communism is an economic system based on collective ownership of the means of production and is administered collectively, without a political apparatus to ensure equal distribution.

- Democratic socialism allows for a degree of entrepreneurship, some profit, and differences in individual wealth.

- The American economy has shifted from the agricultural to industrial to a postindustrial economy with there also being a shift of jobs to the service sector in the postindustrial economy.

- Corporations is a business that is treated legally as an individual. There are several different types of corporations including: family, managerial, institutional, and multinational.

- Managers have shifted viewing workers as machines to valuing them in terms of their intelligence and creativity.

- Theory X assumes that that people naturally dislike work while Theory Y assumes that people naturally like work.

- The different types of jobs include: white-collar jobs, blue-collar jobs, pink-collar jobs, and service work.

- Although wage labor is predominant form of work, it is not the only form of work. There are alternatives to the wage labor system. Some of these alternatives are working off the books, unpaid labor, self-employment, part-time work, contingent work, and "on call work."

- Unemployment is the measure of people who are actively looking for jobs that do not currently have one. There are three types of unemployment: seasonal unemployment, cyclical unemployment, and structural unemployment.

- Over the last few decades the workplace has become more diverse. Although there is higher representation of racial groups in the workplace, equality in the workplace is still an issue. In terms of gender, today over half of women work outside of the home. Companies have also improved their policies toward homosexuals.

Learning Objectives

After completing the reading of Chapter 13, you should be able to answer the following objectives.

- Know what Locke and Hobbes, Smith, Marx, Weber, and Durkheim believed about the economy.
- Discuss the difference between the Agricultural Economy, Industrial Economy, and Postindustrial economy.
- Distinguish between capitalism, laissez-faire capitalism, state capitalism, and welfare capitalism.
- Define socialism and communism.
- State the differences between capitalism, socialism, and communism and explain why they do not exist in their "pure" form.
- Understand the economic development of the United States and what the impact of the industrialization had on the economy.
- Define corporations and understand the different types of corporations.
- Define multinational corporations and discuss the role they play in the global economy.
- Distinguish between the Hawthorne Effect, Theory X, and Theory Y and what each says about increasing worker productivity.
- Know the different types of jobs, white-collar, blue-collar, pink-collar, and service work and discuss the differences between the four types.
- Identify the six types of alternative to wage labor and what types of jobs would fall into each of these categories.
- Understand the types of unemployment and the differences between them.
- Discuss how the labor force has changed since the 1950s in terms of racial diversity, gender diversity, sexual diversity, and working parents.

Key Terms

Capital: the resources, good, and services.

Capitalism: profit-oriented economic system based on the private or corporate ownership of the means of production and distribution.

Communism: economic system based on the collective ownership of the means of production and is administered collectively, without a political apparatus to ensure equal distribution.

Conspicuous consumption: mark the shift from prestige coming from savings and thrift, to a new form of prestige based on accumulating as many possessions as possible and showing them off.

Consumption: how to decide among the goods available.

Corporations: business that is treated legally as an individual.

Economic system: mechanism that deals with the production, distribution, and consumption of goods and services in a particular society.

Economy: set of institutions and relationships that manages nature resources, manufactured goods, and professional services.

Human Capital: household labor

Industrial Economies: economies based on factory production.

Industrial Revolution: era of the machine, transformed economics, politics, and social life.

Knowledge economy: less oriented around the actual production of a commodity and more concerned with the idea of the commodity.

Labor unions: groups that band together to redress the balance of power through collective bargaining.

Manufacture consent: production of values and emotions that bind workers to their company.

Markets: regular exchanges of good and services.

Mass production: increase in productivity to make products affordable for the majority of the populations.

Multinational corporations: they operate through a network of offices all over the world.

Outsourcing: contracting out to another company work that had once been done internally by your company.

Pay gap: difference between men's and women's earnings.

Postindustrial economies: automated machinery substantially reducing and sometimes eliminating the need for human labor in production.

Production: how to get more good out there.

Race to the bottom: maximizing profits by paying the lowest possible wages.

Socialism: economic system that includes the collective ownership of property, collective goals, and central planning.

Tokens: representatives of their group rather than individuals.

Wage labor: workers receive regular paycheck in exchange for performing a specific task.

Key People

Emile Durkheim: argued that in modern societies, we are all interdependent.

Karl Marx: believed that an economic system based on private property divided people into two unequal and competing classes.

Douglas McGregor: published the book *The Human Side of Enterprise*, about two theories of work: Theory X and Theory Y.

Adam Smith: argued that societies prosper best through individual self-interest.

Max Weber: believed capitalism originated in a desire for personal spiritual fulfillment.

Additional Learning with MySocLab

Read

Western Farmers Fear Third-World Challenge to Subsidies (pg 421)
The article discusses the methods of two farmers in developing nations. Both worry that they will be targets when trade ministers from around the world meet to decide which subsidies to cut back on in the wealthiest nations in order to lessen the damage the subsidies inflict on poor farmers in the developing world.

Explore

Industry and Occupation (pg 439)
The bar chart illustrates the makeup of the American workforce and how it has evolved over the past fifty years as more and more women have sought jobs outside the home.

Web Activity: The Economy (pg 447)
You will visit the Women's Bureau website and read the article "Women in the Labor Force" to better understand the trends of labor force participation among women of various racial and ethnic groups. You will then answer a series of questions relating to the website and article.

Listen

China's Communist (pg 429)
NPR reports on the changing of political leadership in China. The country has shifted from the Communist ideals to a more relax vision with a private sector of the economy.

Watch

Consumption in Society (pg 421)
Discusses the theories from early sociologists and applying them to modern American society and its consumption.

Visualize

The World's Labor Force (pg 439)
The chart illustrates the world's labor force by sector and World Bank stratum.

Practice Test

After completing the practice test, check your answers in the Answer Key of this Study Guide.

Multiple Choice Questions

1. As a social institution, the economy:
    a. manages natural resources.
    b. manages manufactured goods.
    c. manages professional services.
    d. all of the above.

2. The Industrial Revolution was accelerated which invention of James Watt's?
    a. the rotary engine
    b. the steam engine
    c. wind power
    d. electricity

3. The industrial economy is defined by:
    a. computer technology.
    b. small family farms.
    c. factory production.
    d. globalization.

4. Which of the following does not distinguish industrial economies from agricultural economies?
    a. power
    b. separation of work and home
    c. wage labor
    d. decentralization

5. Which term refers to an economy based on computer technology?
    a. Agricultural economy
    b. Service economy
    c. Industrial economy
    d. Postindustrial economy

6. The term global economy refers to:
    a. expanding economic activity that moves across national borders.
    b. the fact that a single nation now produce more than the entire world did a century ago.
    c. the centralization of corporations in one nation.
    d. none of the above.

7. Socialism is an economic system in which there is:
    a. private ownership of the means of production.
    b. government ownership of the means of production.
    c. collective ownership of the means of production.
    d. trans-national ownership of the means of production.

8. A social thinker who celebrated the operation of a laissez-faire capitalist economy was:
    a. Max Weber.
    b. Adam Smith.
    c. Emile Durkheim.
    d. Karl Marx.

9. Which type of economy combines a mostly market-based economy with social welfare programs?
    a. Capitalism
    b. Laissez-Faire Capitalism
    c. State Capitalism
    d. Welfare Capitalism

10. Which is NOT true about communism?
    a. there is a collective ownership of the means of production
    b. goods are administered collectively
    c. the government ensures equal distribution of goods
    d. there is no gap between the owners and workers

11. Franklin D. Roosevelt launched the New Deal, which of the following programs was not part of the New Deal?
    a. Minimum wage
    b. Social Security
    c. Insurance of bank deposit by the government
    d. Deregulation of the stock market

12. Veblem labeled the accumulation of many possessions and then showing them off to enhance social prestige:
    a. prestigious consumption.
    b. conspicuous consumption.
    c. wasteful consumption.
    d. conspicuous prestige.

13. Jointly owning an enterprise, with obligations and liabilities that are legally distinct from those of the owners is:
    a. corporation.
    b. an interlocking director.
    c. an entity.
    d. none of the above.

14. Which type of corporation holds shares in other corporations?
    a. family
    b. managerial
    c. institutional
    d. global

15. Over the last century, union membership:
    a. has increased.
    b. has stayed the same.
    c. has increased only in the private sector.
    d. has declined.

16. Professional can generally be distinguished from other jobs by four characteristic. Which of the following is not one of those characteristics?
    a. theoretical knowledge
    b. self-regulating practices
    c. authority over clients
    d. individual orientation

17. The underground economy includes all of the following except:
    a. gambling.
    b. child care.
    c. drug dealing.
    d. prostitution.

18. According to Figure 13.7, in which state do women have the lowest percentage of earnings compared to men?
    a. Louissiana
    b. Idaho
    c. Washington
    d. Illinois

19. Which global region has the highest female labor force participation?
    a. the Middle East
    b. South Asia
    c. Sub-Saharan Africa
    d. East Asia

20. The pay gap refers to the pay inequality between men and women. Which racial group has the largest pay gap?
    a. White
    b. Black
    c. Hispanic
    d. Asian

21. The _____ is what gay and lesbian employees bump up against when trying to find employment.
    a. glass ceiling
    b. glass escalator
    c. lavender ceiling
    d. homosexual divide

22. Approximately what percentage of mothers with children under the age of one are in the workforce?
    a. 60%
    b. 55%
    c. 53%
    d. 40%

23. Which country has the highest rate of employment for women?
    a. United States
    b. Mozambique
    c. Cambodia
    d. Denmark

24. The response to a normal business cycle of expansion and contraction produces what kind of unemployment?
    a. seasonal
    b. cyclical
    c. structural
    d. it does not produce unemployment

25. Although Business Administration remains the most popular college major, comprising nearly a quarter of all bachelor's degrees awarded in 2005, however, _____ percent of American workers are actually employed in management, business, and financial occupations.
    a. 25%
    b. 21%
    c. 17%
    d. 14%

True/False Questions

True   False   1. The economy organizes the production, distribution, and consumption of goods and services.

True   False   2. Laissez-faire capitalism is also called a socialist economic system.

True   False   3. Combining extensive social welfare programs and market production is called state capitalism.

True   False   4. Compared to communism, capitalism creates greater economic equality.

True   False   5. During the past decade there has been a steady rise of women owned businesses.

True   False   6. Prostitution and the sale of illegal drugs is typically part of the economy that is based on contingent workers.

True   False   7. Adam Smith's idea was that, in a capitalist system, consumers cooperate as much as often as they compete.

True   False   8. Industrial economies are often called global economies.

True   False   9. The global economy rarely pays attention to national borders.

True   False   10. Workers in the United States on average work more hours annually than any other country.

Fill-in-the-Blank Questions

1. _____ is the "hands off" capitalism.

2. Corporations that hold shares in other corporations are known as _____.

3. An _____ is a set of institutions and relationships that manage natural resources, manufactured goods, and professional services.

4. In a _____ economy, jobs shift from the production of goods to services.

5. Socialism is an economic system that promotes collective ownership, _____, and central planning.

6. _____ is the hypothetical economic and political systems in which all members of society are equal and the means of production is collectively owned and administered.

7. Wal-Mart and K-Mart _____ to maximize their profits by paying the lowest wages possible.

8. _____ assumes that people naturally dislike work and will slack off unless they are coerced and threatened.

9. The _____ refers to under-the-table, off-the-books work for income.

10. Women's employment is highest in _____ countries.

Essay Questions

1. How do multinational corporations function?

2. State the defining characteristics of capitalism, socialism, and communism.

3. How has work changed over the last 100 years? Discuss the shift from the agricultural economy to the industrial economy to the postindustrial economy.

4. What are the differences between white-collar jobs, blue-collar jobs, and pink-collar jobs. Specifically how are they defined, what types of jobs are included in these categories, and what percentage of people hold these types of jobs?

5. How has the workplace become more diverse?

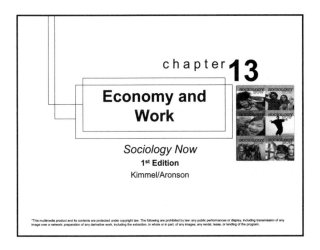

chapter **13**

Economy and Work

Sociology Now
1st Edition
Kimmel/Aronson

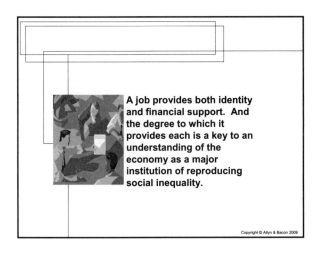

A job provides both identity and financial support. And the degree to which it provides each is a key to an understanding of the economy as a major institution of reproducing social inequality.

Theories of the Economy

- **economy** → *capital*
- Locke and Hobbes
  - resources are limited
  - people must compete with one another
- Marx
- Weber
- Durkheim

Economic Development

– hunters and gatherers

- **The Agricultural Economy**
  – beginnings of *division of labor*
  – **markets**

- **The Industrial Economy**
  – **Industrial Revolution**
  – **Industrial economies**
    - *Power*
    - *Centralization*
    - *Specialization*
    - *Wage labor*
    - *Separation of work and home*

Copyright © Allyn & Bacon 2009

Economic Development

- **Consumption and the Modern Economy**
  – **production**
  – **consumption**
  – **conspicuous consumption** (Veblen)
  – three F's – farming, fishing and forestry comprise 1% of today's workforce

- **The Postindustrial Economy**
  – 2007 – "services" as biggest source of employment
  – **postindustrial economies**

Copyright © Allyn & Bacon 2009

Economic Development

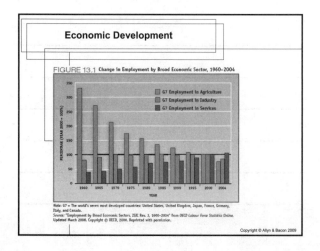

FIGURE 13.1 **Change in Employment by Broad Economic Sector, 1960–2004**

Note: G7 = The world's seven most developed countries: United States, United Kingdom, Japan, France, Germany, Italy, and Canada.
Source: "Employment by Broad Economic Sectors, ISIC Rev. 3, 1960–2004" from OECD Labour Force Statistics Online. Updated March 2006. Copyright © OECD, 2006. Reprinted with permission.

Copyright © Allyn & Bacon 2009

Economic Development

- **Knowledge Work**
  - **knowledge economy**
- **Rootlessness**
- **Globalization**
  - *global economies*
  - **outsourcing**

Economic Systems

- **economic system**
  - production
  - distribution
  - consumption
- **Capitalism**
  - Private ownership
  - Open market
  - Profit
  - **Laissez-Faire Capitalism**
  - **State Capitalism**
  - **Welfare Capitalism**

Economic Systems

- **Socialism**
  - *Marx* – bourgeoisie and proletariat
  - opposite of laissez-faire capitalism
    - *Collective ownership*
    - *Collective goals*
    - *Central Planning*
  - **Democratic Socialism**

- **Communism**
  - collective ownership → w/o political apparatus
  - after years of socialism **(Marx)**

The American Economy

- **Early American Economic Development**
  - The U.S. Constitution can be read as an economic charter

- **The Impact of Industrialization**
  - **Consolidation**
    - Minimum wage
    - Social Security
    - Regulation of stock market (SEC)
    - Insurance of bank deposits (FDIC)

Copyright © Allyn & Bacon 2009

The American Economy

- **The Postindustrial Economy: Technology and Globalization**

- **Corporations**
  - **Family Corporations**
  - **Managerial Corporations**
  - **Institutional Corporations**

- **Multinational Corporations**

Copyright © Allyn & Bacon 2009

Work, Identity, and Inequality

  - we work *both* because we want to and have to

- **How We Work**
  - **The Hawthorne Effect**
  - **Theory X and Theory Y**
  - **Manufacturing Consent**
    - *Piece-rate pay system*
    - *Internal labor market*
    - *Collective bargaining*

Copyright © Allyn & Bacon 2009

Work, Identity, and Inequality

- **Types of Jobs**
  - **White-Collar Jobs**
    - *Theoretical knowledge*
    - *Self-regulating practices*
    - *Authority over clients*
    - *Community orientation*
  - **Blue-Collar Jobs**
  - **Pink-Collar Jobs**
  - **Service Work**

_____

_____

_____

_____

_____

_____

Work, Identity, and Inequality

- **Alternatives to Wage Labor**
  - **Working off the Books**
    - *informal economy*
      - *"underground economy"*
      - *"gray market"*
  - **Unpaid Work**
  - **Self-Employment**
  - **Part-Time Work**
  - **Contingent and "On Call Work"**

_____

_____

_____

_____

_____

_____

Work, Identity, and Inequality

- **Unemployment**
  - *Seasonal unemployment*
  - *Cyclical unemployment*
  - *Structural unemployment*
    - *unemployment compensation*
    - *welfare*

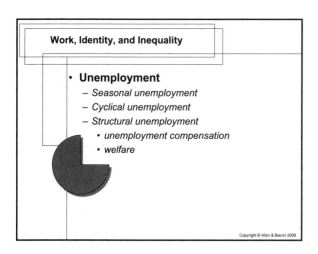

_____

_____

_____

_____

_____

_____

_____

Diversity in the Workplace

- **Racial Diversity**
- **Gender Diversity**
  - pay gap
  - Work-Family Dynamics
- **Sexual Diversity**
- **Working Parents**
- **Work and Economy in the 21st Century**

What Does America Think?

13.1 The Rich and Taxes

This is actual survey data from the General Social Survey, 2002.

Do you think that people with high incomes should pay a larger share of their income in taxes than those with low incomes, the same share, or a smaller share? In the 2002 General Social Survey, 23 percent of respondents said the rich should pay a much larger share of their income in taxes. Almost 44 percent said the rich should pay a larger share. Thirty-one percent thought the current share paid was adequate. When broken down by race, there was a significant difference between Black and White respondents, with Black respondents being much more likely (32 percent) to think that the rich should pay a much larger share of their income in taxes.

CRITICAL THINKING | DISCUSSION QUESTIONS

1. Why do you think the survey responses broke down by race the way they did?
2. How do you think responses might differ if they were broken down by social class? Go to the website and check for yourself. How did your prediction compare to the data?

What Does America Think?

13.2 Women and Work

This is actual survey data from the General Social Survey.

1. Do you approve or disapprove of a married woman earning money in business or industry if she has a husband capable of supporting her? In 1972, 65 percent of respondents approved of a married woman earning money. More women than men approved. In 1998, the numbers were a bit higher, with almost 77 percent of respondents approving and the gender difference in response disappearing.
2. It is much better for everyone involved if the man is the achiever outside the home and the woman takes care of the home and family. In 1977, 18 percent of respondents strongly agreed, with slightly more men than women agreeing. Only 34 percent of respondents disagreed or strongly disagreed. In 2004 the numbers shifted. Only 9 percent of respondents strongly agreed, with no gender difference, and 58 percent disagreed or strongly disagreed.

CRITICAL THINKING | DISCUSSION QUESTION

1. Why do you think a significant number of people still think a woman's place is in her home?
2. What do you make of the lack of variance in the answers by gender?

What Does America Think?

▶ Go to this website to look further at the data. You can run your own statistics and crosstabs here: **http://sda.berkeley.edu/cgi-bin/hsda?harcsda+gss04**

REFERENCES: Davis, James A., Tom W. Smith, and Peter V. Marsden. General Social Surveys 1972–2004: [Cumulative file] [Computer file]. 2nd ICPSR version. Chicago, IL: National Opinion Research Center [producer], 2005; Storrs, CT: Roper Center for Public Opinion Research, University of Connecticut; Ann Arbor, MI: Inter-University Consortium for Political and Social Research; Berkeley, CA: Computer-Assisted Survey Methods Program, University of California [distributors], 2005.

_____

_____

_____

_____

_____

_____

_____

Chapter 14
Politics and Government

Chapter Outline

I.   Politics: Power and Authority
- a. Politics is the art and science of government.
  - i. Government is the organization and administration of the actions of the inhabitants of communities, societies, and states.
  - ii. Power s perceived as legitimate by both power holders and those who are subjected to it.
- b. Class, Status, and Power
  - i. Weber argued that power is not a simple matter of absolutes.
  - ii. Authority is power that is perceived legitimate, by both the holder of power and those subject to it.
- c. Three types of authority
  - i. Traditional Authority- type of power that draws its legitimacy from tradition.
    1. We do things this way because we have always done them that way.
    2. It is very stable, and people can expect to obey the same commands that their ancestors did.
  - ii. Charismatic Authority- type of power in which people obey because of the personal characteristics of the leader.
    1. These leaders are so personally compelling that people follow them even when they have no traditional claim to authority.
    2. It is unstable because it is located in the personality of an individual, not a set of traditions or laws.
  - iii. Ration-legal Authority- leaders are to be obeyed not primarily as representatives of tradition or because of their personal qualities, but because they are voicing a set of rationally derived laws.
    1. Has become the most common form of authority in contemporary societies.
    2. Many argue that modern government would be impossible without it.
- d. Power/Knowledge
  - i. Weber argued that we obey authority because we perceive it to be legitimate.
  - ii. Foucault argued that we obey authority because we cannot conceive of anything else.
  - iii. Power/knowledge does not force us to do things, but it shapes and limits our thoughts and desires until they correspond to the dominant ideologies of our societies.
  - iv. Authorities use three strategies to limit our own power/knowledge and thereby maintain control:
    1. Hierarchical observations
    2. Normalizing judgment
    3. Examination

II.   Political Systems
- a. Authoritarian political systems- power is vested in a single person or small group.
  - i. Monarchy- rule by a single individual.
  - ii. Oligarchy- rule of a small group of people, an elite social class or often a single family.
  - iii. Dictatorship- ruled by one person who has no hereditary claim to rule.
  - iv. Totalitarianism- when political authority is extended over all other aspects of life including: culture, the arts, and social relations.
- b. Democracy- puts legislative decision making into the hands of the people rather than a single individual or a noble class.
  - i. Participatory democracy- every person gets one vote and the majority rules.

       ii.   Representative democracy- citizens elect representatives to make the decisions for them.

      iii.   Illiberal democracy- officials are elected by the people, but they pay so little attention to the constitution and other laws and to the opinions of their constituents that the country might as well be an oligarchy.

  c. Problems of Political Systems

       i.   Democracies are messier than authoritarian systems.

      ii.   Corruption has little to do with whether a country is democratic or not and more to do with whether a country is poor or not.

      iii.   As nations become larger and more complex, more and more levels between the people and the decision making are formed creating bureaucracies.

          1.   In the U.S. most people who run the government are never elected.

          2.   Bureaucracies are inherently antagonistic to democracy.

      iv.   Class, Race, Gender, and Power

          1.   The rich have more political clout than the poor.

          2.   The representation of ethnic minorities in elected offices is tiny.

          3.   Only 15 percent of the 535 seats in Congress are occupied by women.

          4.   Proportional representation is a system where each party would receive a proportion of the legislative seats and thus would be more likely to govern "from the center" and build coalitions.

  d. Citizenship

       i.   To participate in the political process, you must be citizen.

      ii.   Idea of universal citizenship did not take hold until the 19th century.

          1.   When the United States was founded Black were considered 3/5 a person and could not vote.

          2.   Blacks were denied suffrage until 1865 and women until 1920s.

      iii.   By the 20th century most nations recognized two rights to citizenship:

          1.   The right of blood, whereby you become a citizen automatically if your father or mother is a citizen.

          2.   The right of territory, whereby you become a citizen automatically if you are born in a country.

III.   The Political System of the United States

  a. American Political Parties

       i.   Two-Party System

          1.   Federalists led by Alexander Hamilton.

          2.   Republicans led by Thomas Jefferson.

      ii.   Republican and Democrats tend to have different platforms and different ideas about the role of government in the first place.

          1.   Republicans want to stay out of your personal life when you are at work, but when you come home they very much want to intervene.

          2.   Democrats want to stay out of your personal life at home, but you must pay for these freedoms and your privacy by ensuring that others have access to the same freedoms that you have.

  b. Party Affiliation: The Politics of Race, Class, and Gender

       i.   Poor, working class, lower-middle class, and blue collar trade unionists to be Democrats, while the wealthy, upper-middle class, and the white-collar individuals tend to be Republican.

      ii.   Higher education levels go Democratic, the lower go Republican.

      iii.   Most racial minorities vote for Democrats.

      iv.   Women are more likely than men to vote Democratic.

       v.   Voter apathy

          1.   Only about 34 percent f eligible Americans are registered to vote.

          2.   Of registered voters, only 58.3 percent voted in the 2000 presidential election.

  c. Interest Groups

      i. Promote their interests among state and national legislators and often to influence public opinion.
- 1. Protective groups represent only one trade, industry, minority, or subculture.
- 2. Promotional groups claim they represent the interests of the entire society.

      ii. Political action committees
- 1. Lobby groups that work to elect or defeat candidates based on their stance on specific issues.
- 2. Most represent large corporations and there are no poor people's PACs.

IV. Political Change
- a. Social Movements
  - i. Collective attempts to further a common interest or secure a common goal through action outside the sphere of established institutions.
  - ii. They require an educated populace and adequate communication and transportation technology to get the word out.
  - iii. They vary by the types of issues around which they mobilize, their level of organization, and their persistence over time.
- b. Revolutions- attempt to overthrow the existing political order and replace it with a completely new one.
  - i. Immiseration thesis: you get more and more miserable until you lash out.
  - ii. Relative deprivation describes how misery is socially experienced by constantly comparing yourself to others.
  - iii. Political revolution: changes the political group that run the society, but they still draw their strength from the same social groups that supported the old regime.
  - iv. Coup d'etat: replaces one leader with another but often does not bring with it any change.
  - v. Social revolution: changes the social basis of political power.
- c. War and Military
  - i. Worldwide there are 19,670,000 soldiers.
  - ii. The United States spends more money on its military than any country in the world.
    - 1. In 2004, the United States spent $370 billion.
    - 2. In 2004, China spent $67 billion.
  - iii. Quincy Wright identified five factors that serve as the root causes of most war:
    - 1. Perceived threats.
    - 2. Political objectives.
    - 3. "Wag the dog" rationale.
    - 4. Moral objectives.
    - 5. Absence of alternatives.
- d. Terrorism- means using acts of violence and destruction against military of civilian targets as a political strategy.
  - i. Frequently terrorism has no specific political goal; instead it is use to publicize the terrorists' political agenda.
  - ii. Terrorism can be used by the regime in power to ensure continued obedience and to blot out all dissent.
  - iii. Usually we think of it as the actions against he existing regime.
  - iv. Recent technological advances have made weapons easier to acquire or produce and communication among terrorist groups easier.
  - v. Democratic societies reject terrorism in principle, but are vulnerable to it because they afford extensive civil liberties to there people and have less extensive police networks.
  - vi. Terrorism is a matter of definition.
    - 1. One person's terrorist may be another's "freedom fighter."
    - 2. The same group can be labeled terrorist or not, depending on who their foe is.

V. Everyday Politics
- a. Being Political: Social Change

       i.   Carol Hanish- "The Personal is Political, arguing that even the most intimate, personal actions make a political statement.

      ii.   Everyday politics is not a replacement for organized political groups.

    iii.   Groups with little formal power still attempt to resist what they perceive as illegitimate or dictatorial authority.

  b. Civil Society: Declining, Increasing, or Dynamic?

       i.   Civil society includes clubs, churches, fraternal organizations, civic organizations, and other groups that once formed a third "zone" between home and work.

      ii.   In the mid-1970s, two-thirds of the adult American population regularly attended club meetings.

    iii.   Today professionals do all the work and the "members" mail in checks.

    iv.   What are the causes of the decline in civil society?
1. Increased mobility.
2. Mass communication.
3. Commuting.
4. Two-income families.

     v.   In the 21st century, civic engagement by young adults increased.

    vi.   Political activism is taking on new forms.
1. Shift to the marketplace.
2. Preference for hands-on activity.
3. Preference for supportive activities.

VI.   Political Life in the 21st Century

  a. Politics remains a contentious arena, in which people organize together, formally and informally, to fight for their positions and influence the policies, and in turn, influence their lives.

  b. Politics also remains an arena in which we habitually congratulate ourselves for the development and maintenance of a democracy.

STUDY GUIDE

Chapter Summary

- Politics is the art and science of government and is all about authority or power.
- Authority is power that is perceived as legitimate, by both the holder of the power and those subject to it.
- There are three types of authority: traditional, charismatic, and rational-legal. Traditional authority draws its legitimacy from tradition, charismatic from the personal characteristics of the leader, and rational-legal from voicing a set of rationally derived laws.
- Power/knowledge are explicitly connected and they shape and limit our thoughts and desires until hey correspond to the dominant ideologies of society.
- Political systems fall into either authoritarian or democratic. Authoritarian political systems have the power vested in a single person or small group and include monarchies, oligarchies, dictatorships, and totalitarian government. Democratic political systems can be either participatory democracies, in which every single person gets a vote and the majority rules, or they can be representative democracies, in which citizens elect representatives to make decisions for them.
- Some of the problems of political systems are corruption, bureaucracy, racial inequality, gender inequality, and class inequality.
- To participate in the political process you must be a citizen.
- The American political system, citizens are protected as individuals from the exercise of arbitrary control by the government, but individual citizens have little impact of changing the system.
- The two-party system was lead by Alexander Hamilton the leader of the Federalists and Thomas Jefferson the leader of the Republicans.
- Republicans and democrats tend to have different platforms and their affiliates differ in regards to class, education, race, and gender.
- Interest groups promote their interests among state and national legislators and can be classified as protective groups, promotional groups or political action committees.
- Social movements are collective attempts to further a common interest to secure a common goal through action outside the sphere of established institutions. They vary by the types of issues around which they mobilize, their level of organization, and their persistence over time.
- Revolutions are attempts to overthrow the existing political order and replace it with a completely new one.
- According to Quincy Wright perceived threats, political objectives, "wag the dog" rationale, moral objectives, and absence of alternatives are the root causes of most wars.
- Terrorism means using acts of violence and destruction against military or civilian targets as a political strategy.
- The personal is political however everyday politics is not a replacement for organized political groups.
- Civil society is the zone between work and home. It is in a state of decline because of increased mobility, mass communication, commuting, and two-income families.
- Civic engagement by young adults has increased and they are less likely to participate in traditional avenues of political engagement.
- Politics remains an arena in which we habitually congratulate ourselves for the development and maintenance of a democracy, in which we all feel somewhat connect to each other because we are all able to participate in the political process.

Learning Objectives
After completing the reading of Chapter 9, you should be able to answer the following objectives.

- Distinguish between politics, government, power, and authority.
- Describe the three types of authority identified by Weber, and explain how the orderly transfer of authority is achieved under each type.
- Define and give an example of each type of political system: monarchy, oligarchy, dictatorship, totalitarian, participatory democracy, representative democracy, and illiberal democracy.

- Explain the problems with political systems in terms of corruption, bureaucracy, and the inequalities found within them.
- Explain the nature of the two-party system in the United States and discuss the voting patterns for each party.
- Define interest groups and political action committees and how do they influence the political process.
- Discuss social movement, revolutions both political and social.
- Know Quincy Wright's five root causes of most wars.
- Define terrorism and how is it used throughout the world.
- Define civil society and discuss whether it is in decline or not.

Key Terms

Authoritarian political system: power is vested in a single person or small group.

Authority: power that is perceived as legitimate by both the holder of power and those subject to it.

Bureaucracy: more levels between the people and the decision making are formed.

Charismatic authority: type of power in which people obey because of the personal characteristics of the leader.

Civil society: clubs, churches, fraternal organizations, civic organization, and other groups that once formed a third "zone" between home and work.

Coup d'etat: replaces one political leader with another but often does not bring with ti any change in the daily life of the citizens.

Democracy: legislative decision making is by the people rather than a single individual or a noble class.

Dictatorship: ruled by one person who has no hereditary claim to rule.

Government: the organization and administration of the actions of the inhabitants of communities, societies, and states.

Immiseration thesis: the rich would become richer and the poor would get poorer, and eventually the poor would become so poor that they had nothing else to lose, and they would revolt.

Interest groups: promote their interest among state and national legislators and often to influence public opinion.

Illiberal democracies: officials are elected by the people, but they pay so little attention to the constitution and others laws and to the opinions of their constituents that the country might as well be an oligarchy.

Legal-rational authority: leaders are to be obeyed, not primarily as representatives of tradition or because of their personal qualities, but because they are voicing a set of rationally derived laws.

Monarchy: ruled by a single individual.

Oligarchy: rule of a small group of people, an elite social class or often a single family.

Participatory democracy: every person gets one vote and the majority ruling.

Political action committee: lobbying groups that work to elect or defeat candidates based on their stance on specific issues.

Political revolution: changes the political groups that run the society.

Politics: the art and science of government; it is about power, the ability to make people do what you want them to do.

Power: perceived as legitimate by both the holder and those who are subject to it.

Proportional representation: each party would receive a proportion of the legislative seats and thus would be more likely to govern "from the center" ad build coalitions.

Relative deprivation: how misery is socially experienced by constantly comparing yourself to others.

Representative democracy: citizens elect representatives to make the decisions for them.

Revolution: attempt to overthrow the existing political order and replace it with a completely new one.

Social movements: collective attempts to further a common interest or secure a common goal through action outside the sphere of established institutions.

Social revolution: changes the social basis of political power; it changes the social groups or classes that political power rests on.

Suffrage: the right to vote and representation.

Terrorism: using acts of violence and destruction against military or civilian targets as a political strategy.

Totalitarianism: political authority is extended over all other aspects of social life- including culture, the arts, and social relations.

Traditional authority: type of power that draws its legitimacy from tradition.

Two-party system: the federalists, who distrusted the newly enfranchised populace and argued for a stronger centralized government, and the Republicans, who held a more agrarian small-town ideal and argued for a decentralized government with limited power.

Universal suffrage: voting for all adults.

Key People

Michel Foucault: argued that we obey because we cannot conceive of anything else.

Carol Hanish: argued that even the most intimate, personal actions make a political statement.

Robert Michels: argued that all institutions are subject to what he called the "iron law of oligarchy."

Max Weber: argued that power is not a simple matter of absolutes.

Quincy Wright: identified five factors that serve as root causes of most wars.

Additional Learning with MySocLab

Read

A Nation at War: Bringing Combat Home; Telling War's Deadly Story At Just Enough Distance (pg 477)

In the darkness of a conference room at Time magazine last Friday, a war of terrible and beautiful images unfurled on a screen: the steely-eyed marine taking aim, the awe-struck Iraqi pointing to bombers in the sky, the bloodied head of a dead Iraqi with an American soldier standing tall in the background.

Two Years Later: The President; President Urging Wider U.S. Powers in Terrorism Law (pg 479)

President Bush called today for a significant expansion of law enforcement powers under the USA Patriot Act, using the eve of the second anniversary of the Sept. 11 terrorist acts to say that his administration was winning the war on terrorism but that "unreasonable obstacles" in the law impeded the pursuit of terror suspects.

Explore

Web Activity: Politics (pg 470)

This activity explores the affects of gender, immigration, and race on voter participation in the United States. You will read the articles "Gender Gap Persists in the 2004 Election" and "Ethnic Breakdown of Citizenry and Ethnic Voter Participation to learn about how gender, immigration, and race affect voter participation. After reading the articles there is a series of questions to answer.

Web Activity: Collective Behavior and Social Movements (pg 474)

Social movements are collective attempts to further a common interest. You will read the article "Propaganda in Nazi Germany" and visit the website Educators for Social Responsibility to learn what propaganda is and how it was used in Nazi Germany to further the common interest of the Nazi Party.

Listen

The best democracy money can buy (pg 464)

There are at least 40 millionaires in the United States Senate. Political watchdogs say they expect that number to increase because the national political parties are recruiting candidates who are wealthy and willing to spend millions of dollars of their own money to run for office. So-called 'Self-financed" candidates say campaigning with their own money makes them more independent of special interests. But critics worry the trend will make political campaigns more expensive and put public office out of reach for average Americans.

Elections (pg 470)

Experts Debate Impact of Election Day Abstainers. Many critics of the American electoral system focus on the nation's low Election Day turnout, a rate lower here than elsewhere in the free world. Some are now arguing about how big a problem voluntary non-participation poses, and what difference it would make if more people voted.

Watch

Voting (pg 469)

The video clip examines the low voter turnout in Florida and discuss why people are not going to the polls.

Visualize

PACs (pg 473)

The line graph illustrates the number of Political Action Committees between 1976 and 1995.

Practice Test

After completing the practice test, check your answers in the Answer Key of this Study Guide.

Multiple Choice Questions

1. Authority is:
    a. power.
    b. coercion.
    c. legitimate power.
    d. government.

2. Traditional authority is based on:
    a. personality.
    b. custom.
    c. written rules.
    d. all of the above.

3. A leader who is obeyed because of their personal characteristics has what type of authority?
    a. Traditional
    b. Charismatic
    c. Legal-Rational
    d. Power

4. Which of the following is a strategy that is used to limit our power/knowledge?
    a. Examination
    b. Normalizing judgment
    c. Hierarchical observations
    d. All of the above

5. Which type of political system is ruled by one person who has either been elected or appointed?
    a. Monarchy
    b. Oligarchy
    c. Dictatorship
    d. Totalitarian

6. If a small group controls a country it is considered a:
    a. Monarchy
    b. Oligarchy
    c. Dictatorship
    d. Totalitarian

7. Which type of democracy believes that every person should get one vote and the majority rules?
    a. Participatory democracy
    b. Representative democracy
    c. Illiberal democracy
    d. Universal suffrage

8. The idea of universal _____, a person has rights by virtue of birth and residence, did not take hold until the 19th century.
    a. suffrage
    b. citizenship
    c. civil society
    d. power

9. Which type of interest group works to elect or defeat candidates based on their stance on specific issues?
    a. Protective groups
    b. Promotional groups
    c. Political action committees
    d. Lobbyists

10. Politics refers to:
    a. the system of elections.
    b. income distribution.
    c. a formal government.
    d. the art and science of government.

11. _____ refers to the formal organization and administration of the actions of the inhabitants of communities, societies, and states.
    a. Politics
    b. Government
    c. Power
    d. Authority

12. According to Max Weber, the difference between power and authority is that:
    a. authority is rational.
    b. power is perceived as legitimate.
    c. power is less coercive than authority.
    d. authority is perceived as legitimate.

13. Hitler, Ghandi, and John F. Kennedy are all examples of what type of leader?
    a. Traditional
    b. Charismatic
    c. Legal-rational
    d. Dictatorship

14. A totalitarian political system:
    a. encourages citizens to participate in the system.
    b. includes only the elite participating in government.
    c. concentrates all power and regulates people's lives.
    d. is a democracy.

15. In the United States _____ tend to be Democrats while _____ tend to be Republicans.
    a. men; women
    b. upper-class; lower-class
    c. whites; blacks
    d. lower-class; upper-class

16. In the 2000 election how many people who were registered to vote actually voted?
    a. about 58 percent
    b. just less than 50 percent
    c. about 30 percent
    d. only 20 percent

17. Terrorism refers to:
    a. the use of military force to control people.
    b. the claim that all violence is wrong.
    c. the use of diplomacy to fix bad situations.
    d. the use or threat of violence as a political strategy.

18. Which of the following statements is true?
    a. Democracies are especially vulnerable to terrorism.
    b. Terrorism can be used by the regime in power to ensure obedience.
    c. It is a matter of definition if one is considered a 'terrorist" or a "freedom fighter."
    d. All of the above are true.

19. Which country spends the most money on its military?
    a. China
    b. Saudi Arabia
    c. United States
    d. France

20. Rational-legal authority is based on:
    a. custom.
    b. personality.
    c. written laws.
    d. previous authority.

21. Which of the following is not one of the reasons there has been a decline in civil society?
    a. Increased mobility
    b. Commuting
    c. Single-income families
    d. Mass communication

22. Who is most likely to vote republican in federal elections today?
    a. The poor
    b. African Americans
    c. Gays and lesbians
    d. White males

23. What country denied women the right to vote the longest?
    a. Nigeria
    b. South Africa
    c. India
    d. Iran

24. Quincy Wright identified five factors that serve as root causes of most wars. Which of the following is not one of those five causes?
    a. Perceived threat
    b. Political objectives
    c. Moral objectives
    d. Presence of alternative

25. Which type of authoritarian system is ruled by a single individual who has a hereditary claim?
    a. Monarchy
    b. Oligarchy
    c. Dictatorship
    d. Democracy

True/False Questions

True   False   1. Traditional authority draws its legitimacy through the personal characteristics of the leader.

True   False   2. An oligarchy is the rule of a small group of people, an elite social class, or often a single family.

True   False   3. A representative democracy has citizens elect representatives to make decisions for them.

True   False   4. The representation of minorities in elected offices in the United States is large.

True   False   5. Democrats argue that overspending on welfare has made poor people lazy and dependent, unable and unwilling to help themselves.

True   False   6. Poor people tend to vote for democrats more so than republicans in presidential elections.

True   False   7. Protective interest groups claim to represent the interests of the entire society.

True   False   8. A coup d'etat replaces on leader with another and brings significant changes to the political system.

True   False   9. Civil society refers to the zone between work and home.

True   False   10. Political activism is taking on new forms in the 20th century.

Fill-in-the-Blank Questions

1. _____ is power that is perceived as legitimate, by both the holder of power and those subject to it.

2. Leaders that are obeyed because of their person qualities are _____.

3. In an, _____, power is vested in a single person or small group.

4. In _____ democracies officials are elected by the people, but pay little attention to the constitution and other laws and opinions of their constituents.

5. When the United States was founded black men were denied _____ until 1865.

6. _____ is an interest group that lobbies to elect or defeat candidates based on their stance on specific issues.

7. When people seek to effect change they commonly start _____.

8. A _____ revolution changes the political groups that run the society, but they still draw their strength from the same social groups that supported the old regime.

9. Those who feel that most voters are found in the middle ground, there is no need to participate and this leads to _____.

10. The United States is an anomaly among democratic nations in that it has a _____.

STUDY GUIDE

Essay Questions

1. Discuss the five reasons why wars take place.

2. What are the differences between the three types of authority and give examples of each.

3. Discuss the difference between authoritarian political systems and democratic political systems and give examples of each.

4. What are the two parties in the United States, what are their platforms, and who votes for them?

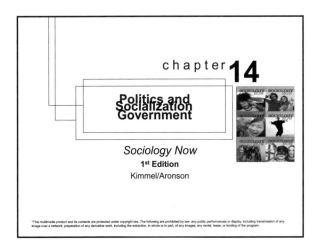

chapter **14**

Politics and Government
Socialization

Sociology Now
1st Edition
Kimmel/Aronson

This multimedia product and its contents are protected under copyright law. The following are prohibited by law: any public performances or display, including transmission of any image over a network; preparation of any derivative work, including the extraction, in whole or in part, of any images; any rental, lease, or lending of the program.

Politics: Power and Authority

- **politics** → *art and science of government*
- **power**

• **Class, Status, and Power**
  - **authority**
  - situational/contextual limits of authority

Copyright © Allyn & Bacon 2009

Politics: Power and Authority

• **Traditional Authority**
  - legitimacy drawn from tradition

• **Charismatic Authority**
  - personal characteristics of leader

• **Legal-Rational Authority**
  - voicing a set of laws

Copyright © Allyn & Bacon 2009

Politics: Power and Authority

- **Power/Knowledge**
  - Strategies used by authorities to limit our own power/knowledge

    - *Hierarchical observation*
    - *Normalizing judgment*
    - *Examination*

Copyright © Allyn & Bacon 2009

Political Systems

- **Authoritarian Systems**
  - **Monarchy**
  - **Oligarchy**
  - **Dictatorship**
  - **Totalitarianism**

- **Democracy**
  - **participatory democracy**
  - **representative democracy**
  - **universal suffrage**
  - **illiberal democracies**

Copyright © Allyn & Bacon 2009

Political Systems

- **Problems of Political Systems**
  - **Corruption**
    - *Outside interests donate large sums of money*
    - *Obey special interest groups instead of the people*
    - *Misuse of government funds for personal gain*
  - **Bureaucracy**
  - **Class, Race, Gender, and Power**

- **Citizenship**

Copyright © Allyn & Bacon 2009

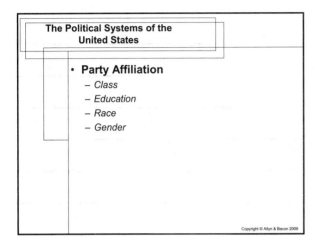

The Political Systems of the United States

- **Party Affiliation**
  - *Class*
  - *Education*
  - *Race*
  - *Gender*

Copyright © Allyn & Bacon 2009

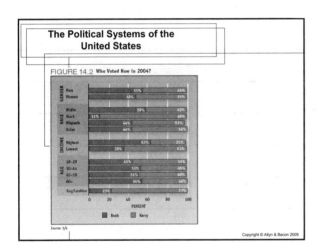

The Political Systems of the United States

FIGURE 14.2 Who Voted How in 2004?

Copyright © Allyn & Bacon 2009

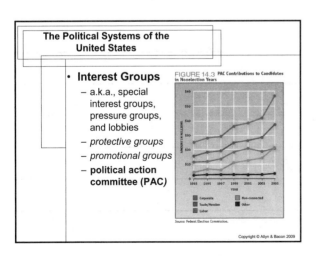

The Political Systems of the United States

- **Interest Groups**
  - a.k.a., special interest groups, pressure groups, and lobbies
  - *protective groups*
  - *promotional groups*
  - **political action committee (PAC)**

FIGURE 14.3 PAC Contributions to Candidates in Nonelection Years

Copyright © Allyn & Bacon 2009

265

Political Change

- **Social Movements**
  - further common interest
  - secure common goal
  - "outside" established institutions

- **Revolutions**
  - overthrow/replace existing social order
  - **immiseration thesis**
  - **relative deprivation**
  - **coup d'etat**
  - political revolution

Copyright © Allyn & Bacon 2009

Political Change

- **War and the Military**
  - root causes of most wars **(Wright)**
    - *Political objectives*
    - *"Wag the dog" rationale*
    - *Perceived threats*
    - *Moral objectives*
    - *Absence of alternatives*

- **Terrorism**

Copyright © Allyn & Bacon 2009

Political Change

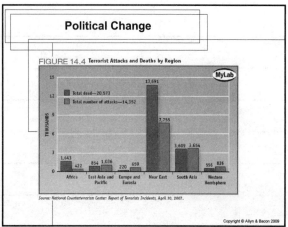

FIGURE 14.4 Terrorist Attacks and Deaths by Region

Source: National Counterterrorism Center: Report of Terrorists Incidents, April 30, 2007.

Copyright © Allyn & Bacon 2009

Everyday Politics

- **Being Political: Social Change**
  - "personal problems are political problems"
    - racism, sexism, and homophobia
    - friendships across social lines
    - social labels
    - support/non support of worker exploitation

Everyday Politics

- **Civil Society: Declining, Increasing or Dynamic?**
  - causes for decline in civil society
    - *Increased mobility*
    - *Mass communication*
    - *Commuting*
    - *Two-income families*

Everyday Politics

  - new forms of political engagement
    - *Shift to the marketplace*
    - *Preference for hands-on activity*
    - *Preference for supportive activity*

- **Political Life in the 21st Century**

STUDY GUIDE

What Does America Think?

14.1 International Organizations and American Governmental Power

These are actual survey data from the General Social Survey, 2004.

International organizations are taking away too much power from the American government. Only 9 percent of respondents in the 2004 General Social Survey strongly agreed with this statement. Another 26 percent agreed. Those from the lower class were most likely to agree (39.1 percent). Thirty percent of respondents disagreed, and only 3 percent strongly disagreed. Those in the upper class were most likely to disagree (53 percent).

CRITICAL THINKING | DISCUSSION QUESTIONS

1. What role, if any, do you think international organizations should play in decisions made by the U.S. government? How would you explain a social class difference in response to this question?
2. Why do you think political party affiliation often correlates with social class? What party-associated values or beliefs might contribute to one's view on the power of international organizations?

What Does America Think?

14.2 Government and Standard of Living

These are actual survey data from the General Social Survey, 2004.

Some people think that the government in Washington should do everything possible to improve the standard of living of all poor Americans; they are at Point 1 on this card. Other people think it is not the government's responsibility and that each person should take care of him- or herself; they are at Point 5. Where would you place yourself on this scale, or haven't you made up your mind on this? Only 17 percent of respondents picked the first choice, government action. There was a huge disparity between those in the lower and upper classes, though. Most respondents agreed that both the government and the individual were responsible for improving the standard of living.

CRITICAL THINKING | DISCUSSION QUESTIONS

1. The disparity between lower- and upper-class respondents with regard to opinions on this question is very large. What do you think explains this disparity?
2. Where do you place yourself on the social class ladder? How does your position inform your own opinion on improving standard of living?

What Does America Think?

▶ Go to this website to look further at the data. You can run your own statistics and crosstabs here: http://sda.berkeley.edu/cgi-bin/hsda?harcsda+gss04

REFERENCES: Davis, James A., Tom W. Smith, and Peter V. Marsden. General Social Surveys 1972–2004: [Cumulative file] [Computer file]. 2nd ICPSR version. Chicago, IL: National Opinion Research Center [producer], 2005; Storrs, CT: Roper Center for Public Opinion Research, University of Connecticut; Ann Arbor, MI: Inter-University Consortium for Political and Social Research, Berkeley, CA: Computer-Assisted Survey Methods Program, University of California [distributors], 2005.

Chapter 15
Religion and Science

Chapter Outline

I.   Comparing Religion and Science
  a. Both are organized and coherent systems of thought that are organized into social institutions.
  b. Religion is the set of beliefs about the origins and meaning of life, usually based on the existence of a supernatural power.
      i.   Acquires its ideas through revelation.
      ii. Distinguishes between the physical world and the spiritual world.
  c. Science is the accumulated systematic knowledge of the physical or material world, which is obtained through experimentation and observation.
      i.   Acquires its ideas through empirical verification.
      ii. Interested in only the physical world.

II. Classical Theories of Religion
  a. Durkheim and Social Cohesion
      i.   Religion serves to integrate society, to create a sense of unity out of the enormously diverse collection of individuals.
      ii. Cultures try to recreate rituals that would remind individuals that they are part of a whole that is greater than its parts.
      iii. Secular societies develop a civil religion.
  b. Marx and Social Control
      i.   Religions kept social change from happening by preventing people from revolting against the miserable conditions of their lives.
      ii. Religion provided a justification for the inequality.
  c. Weber and Social Change
      i.   Argued that religion could be used as a catalyst to change.
      ii. Thought perhaps the Protestant Reformation had feed individuals from constraints and enabled each individual to develop his or her relationship to God directly, without priests or churches as intermediaries.

III. Religious Groups
  a. Cults
      i.   They form around a specific person or idea drawn from an established religion.
      ii. Typically small and composed of deeply fervent believers.
  b. Sects
      i.   Small subculture within an established religious institution.
      ii. They break from traditional practices and remain within the larger institution.
  c. Denominations
      i.   Large-scale, extremely organized religious body.
      ii. It has an established hierarchy, methods for credentialing administrators, and much more social respect than either a cult or sect.
  d. Ecclesiae
      i.   Religion so pervasive that the boundary between state and church is nonexistent.
      ii. Clerical elite serve as political leaders or at least formal advisors to political leaders.

IV. Religions of the World
  a. Western Religions
      i.   They are exclusive: They have one true faith and all others are invalid.
      ii. Judaism
          1. Believes that the covenant between God and Abraham around 2000 BCE.
          2. Flourished in the ancient world.
      iii. Christianity
          1. Founded in 2000 years ago by the disciples of Jesus, who declared him to be the son of God.

2. Christianity is the world's largest religion today with approximately 2.1 billion adherents.

    iv. Islam

        1. Founded around 1400 years ago when God grew displeased with the corruption of the teachings of his earlier prophets and gave his last prophet, Mohammed, a new sacred text, the Koran.

        2. Islam means the "Submission to God."

        3. Approximately 1.3 billion people in the world are Islamic.

    v. Fundamentalism

        1. Claim to be the truest and purest followers of their religion.

        2. Jihad, is a holy war and means to commit acts of terrorism against non-Muslims, are the most fundamentalist in the Islamic religion.

  b. Eastern Religions

    i. Hinduism

        1. Developed from indigenous religions in India around 1500 BCE.

        2. Hinduism is based largely on oral tradition, passed on from one generation to the next by storytellers.

        3. Today there are nearly one billion Hindus mostly in South Asia and in Indian communities around the world.

    ii. Buddhism

        1. Developed as a reaction to the corruption of Hinduism.

        2. Founded by Siddhartha Gautama later called Buddha.

        3. There are 376 million Buddhists mostly in East Asia.

    iii. Confucianism

        1. The official religion of China until the People's Republic officially became atheist in 1949.

        2. Establishes a strict social hierarchy.

  c. Contemporary Religions

    i. Secularization: process of moving away from religious spirituality and toward the worldly.

    ii. The majority of countries in the world, the majority of the global population, are experiencing a religious resurgence.

        1. In Eastern Europe the number of atheists and nonreligious people has been declining steadily since 1990.

        2. In the developing countries, religion continues to hold enormous sway over the society.

V. Religion in the United States

  a. The United States has been a nation of religious immigrants.

    i. As some nations become increasingly secular, those who are religious may seek a haven in the United States.

    ii. American religious institutions have grown as providers of social support and cultural interaction.

  b. The separation of church and state, the prohibitions on school prayer, and the general global trend toward secularization make religiosity something of a rebellion against the dominant culture.

  c. Third Great Awakening

    i. Religious revival that further democratizes spirituality, making a relationship with the sacred attainable to even greater numbers of Americans.

    ii. Americans are deeply religious, but only commit to religious organizations as long as they like them.

  d. Religious experience and Religious Identity

    i. People vary in their level of religious affiliation and in the intensity of their beliefs.

    ii. Most Western religions not only prohibit women from leadership but also condemn homosexuality as contrary to divine law.

    iii. Denominational affiliation and rates of religiosity vary by race and ethnicity.

  e. Religion on Campus

        i. The higher the level of educational attainment, the less devout you will be in practicing religion.

        ii. Church attendance among college students is lower than that of the nation as a whole.

           1. Two-thirds of college students do pray.

           2. Nearly 50 percent of freshman say they are seeking opportunities to grow spiritually.

        iii. Church-affiliated colleges have seen faster enrollment increases than secular colleges.

    f. New Age Religions

        i. New Age is an umbrella term for many different groups and individual practices, is very often call simply "spirituality."

        ii. Believers are often open minded and pluralistic.

    g. Religion as Politics

        i. Manifesting the vision of one's religious beliefs in the political arena is often an essential part of the religion.

        ii. Liberation Theology emerged in 20th century Latin America in response to the ruthless political dictators.

        iii. Most commonly religious mobilization ahs aimed to move society to the political right.

        iv. Common for secular politics to be intolerant of religious diversity.

        v. The separation of church and state was meant to protect liberty and ensure democracy in the United States, it also enabled religion and science to develop and expand separately with sever political debates straining their coexistence.

           1. Evolution and creationism.

           2. School prayer.

           3. Embryonic stem cell research.

VI. Science as an Institution

    a. Types of Science

        i. Biological sciences that study living organisms.

        ii. Physical sciences that study nonliving processes.

        iii. Mathematics provides the quantitative foundation of all other sciences.

        iv. Social sciences concern human beings.

    b. The Norms of Science

        i. Objectivity- judgments are based on empirical verification, not on personal feelings or opinions.

           1. Anyone using the scientific method should be able to arrive at the same conclusions regardless of his or her personal characteristics.

           2. Advocacy research is undertaken to provide the research necessary to support or promote a particular position.

        ii. Common ownership

           1. Research results should be public knowledge.

           2. As scientific projects become increasingly complex, government, universities, and private companies will increasingly share the funding costs and the results.

        iii. Distinterestedness

           1. Scientific research should not be conducted for personal goals, but for the pursuit of scientific truth.

           2. The new partnership between universities and private corporations push scientists away from performing basic research and more toward applied research.

    c. Scientific Networks

        i. Scientists develop rules of conduct, and those who do not accept these rules are excluded form scientific networks.

        ii. Those at the top of the scientific hierarchy are the gatekeepers, making sure that scientific research conforms to what they think is worthy.

      d. Scientific Breakthroughs
- i. Thomas Kuhn believed that scientific progress was not gradual and linear; instead it is erratic and unpredictable.
- ii. Scientists accept prevailing theories as true and organize their experiments within the existing framework, but sometimes cannot explain their finding by existing theories.

      e. The Role of the Scientist and Society
- i. Today scientific research is funded by governments, through grants for research, and by private companies.
- ii. Private enterprise and government fund different aspects of research.
  1. Government funds basic science, scientific research that has no immediate application other than the furtherance of knowledge.
  2. Private companies are interested in developing new products and fund research that has possibilities for commercial application.

VII.   Science and Religion in the 21st Century
- a. As a society we are becoming increasingly scientific.
- b. We are also becoming increasingly religious.
- c. Some scholars predict a long period of tension between religion and science, followed by the triumph of one over the other.

Chapter Summary

- Both religion and science are organized and coherent systems of thought that are organized into social institutions.
- Religion is a set of beliefs about the origins and meaning of life, usually based on the existence of a supernatural power while science is the accumulated systematic knowledge of the physical or material world, which is obtained through experimentation and observation.
- Religion is a cultural universal.
- Durkheim believed that religion served to integrate society, to create a sense of unity out of the enormously diverse collection of individuals; Marx believed that religion served as an ideological "blinder" to the reality of exploitation and kept social change from happening while; Weber argued that religion could be a catalyst to change.
- Cults, sects, denominations, and ecclesiae are all different forms of religious groups.
- Western religions include Judaism, Christianity, and Islam and Eastern religions include Hinduism, Buddhism, and Confucianism.
- Secularization is the process of moving away from religious spirituality and toward the worldly and the secularization thesis has been supported by empirical data however, it turns out that secularization has not occurred.
- There have been many factors as to why religion in the United States has increased instead of decreased and they include: the United States has been more than simply a nation of immigrants, but actually a nation of religious immigrants; the united states has been swept by several waves of increased religious passion; and American religious institutions have grown as providers of social support and cultural interaction.
- Religions do not vary only by denomination; we vary in our level of religious affiliation and in the intensity of our beliefs.
- Denominational affiliation and rates of religiosity vary by gender, race, and sexual orientation.
- On college campuses science and religion most often clash. The higher your level of educational attainment, the less devout you will be in practicing your religion.
- The first national survey on the spiritual lives of college students found that more than two-thirds of college freshman pray and almost 80 percent believe in God.
- New age is an umbrella term for many different groups and individual practices, so is very often called simply "spirituality."
- Religion has always been political.
- Liberation theory within the Catholic Church was a source of popular mobilization against ruthless political dictators.
- In recent years the boundary between religion and science has become blurry, and several political debates currently strain their happy coexistence: evolution and creationism, school prayer, and embryonic stem cell research.
- There are many different types of sciences in the world including: biological sciences, physical sciences, mathematics, and social sciences.
- The norms of society are objectivity, in which judgments are based on empirical verification; common ownership, research results should be public knowledge; and disinterestedness, scientific research should not be conducted for personal goals.
- Scientists develop rules of conduct and those who do not accept these rules are excluded from scientific networks.
- Scientific progress is erratic and often unpredictable.
- Today, scientific research around the world is supported by governments through grants for research, and by private companies, which employ scientists to develop new products and they typically fund different aspects of research.
- Human beings are curious about the world and always want to understand it better; science gives them that opportunity and at the same time we are becoming increasingly religious.

Learning Objectives

After completing the reading of Chapter 9, you should be able to answer the following objectives.

- Define religion and science and how it acquires it ideas.
- Describe how Emile Durkheim, Karl Marx, and Max Weber thought religion served society.
- Define cult, sect, denomination, and ecclesiae and give an example of each.
- Discuss the three Western Religions and the three Eastern religions and explain how they are similar and dissimilar.
- Define secularization and discuss how the world is becoming more or less secularized.
- Explain why the rates of religious beliefs and participation have declined in every other industrialized country but the United States.
- Explain how religious membership in the United States varies by race, gender, and age.
- Discuss whether students on campus are less religious than the nation as a whole.
- Define New Age religions.
- Discuss how religion is involved in the political realm, specifically liberation theology.
- List the political debates that go on between religion and science.
- Know the different types of science.
- Discuss the norms of science: objectivity, commonplace, and disinterestedness.
- Describe scientific networks and how scientific communities are like religious elites.
- Know the role of the scientist and how it has changed since the 16th century.

Key Terms

Advocacy research: provide research necessary to support or promote a particular position.

BCE: time before the coming of Christ.

Buddhism: teaches that enlightenment was possible in this lifetime, through the "Tenfold Path" of physical and spiritual discipline.

CE: time after the coming of Christ.

Charismatic leader: someone who is able to draw people away from established institutions.

Christianity: founded 2,000 years ago by the disciples of Jesus, who declared him to be the son of God.

Civil religion: secular rituals create the intense emotional bonds among people that used to be accomplished through religion.

Confucianism: establishes a strict social hierarchy.

Cult: forms around a specific person or idea drawn from an established religion.

Cultural universals: exists in every single culture.

Denomination: large-scale, extremely organized religious body.

Disinterestedness: research should not be conducted for personal goals but for the pursuit of scientific truth.

Ecclesiae: religion that is so pervasive that the boundary between state and church is nonexistent.

Empirical verification: information is developed, demonstrated, and double-checked using an experimental method.

Fundamentalism: return to the basic precept, the "true word of God," and live exactly according to His precepts.

Hinduism: developed from many indigenous religions in India around 1500 BCE.

Islam: founded about 1,400 years ago when God grew displeased with the corruption of the teachings of his earlier prophets and gave his last prophet a new sacred text.

Jihad: holy war.

Judaism: believes that the covenant between God and Abraham become the foundation of Jewish law.

Liberation theology: focuses on Jesus not only as savior but specifically as the savior of the poor and oppressed and emphasizes the Christina mission of bringing justice to the poor.

New Age: umbrella term for many different groups and individual practices, so is very often called simply "spirituality."

Objectivity: judgments are based on empirical verification, not on personal feelings or opinions.

Profane: secular, everyday lives.

Religion: set of beliefs about the origins and meaning of life.

Religiosity: the extent of one's religious beliefs, typically measured by attendance at religious observances or maintaining religious practices.

Revelation: God, spirits, prophets, or sacred books give us the answers to the questions of existence.

Rituals: solemn reenactments of the sacred events.

Sacred: holy or divine

Science: accumulated systematic knowledge of the physical or material world.

Sect: small subculture within an established religious institution.

Secularization: the process of moving away from religious spirituality and toward the worldly.

Syncretic religions: perfectly acceptable to practice Buddhism, Hinduism, Confucianism, Taoism, and any other religion you want, all at the same time.

Third Great Awakening: religious revival that further democratizes spirituality, making a relationship with the sacred attainable to even greater numbers of Americans.

World Religions: religions wit a long history, well-established traditions, and the flexibility to adapt to many different cultures.

Key People

Emile Durkheim: religion served to integrate society, to create a sense of unity our of the enormously diverse collection of individuals.

Martin Luther: led people away from Catholicism to Protestantism.

Karl Marx: believed that religion kept social change from happening by preventing people from revolting against the miserable conditions of their lives.

Max Weber: argued that religion could be a catalyst to change.

Additional Learning with MySocLab

Read

Visions of Doom Endure in Queens; Prophecy, and a Rift, at a Shrine (pg 489)
One recent Saturday evening, several hundred Roman Catholics wearing white gloves and clutching rosary beads gathered in Flushing Meadows-Corona Park in Queens for a candlelight vigil.
This Is a Religious War (pg 496)
Most of the people of the world live in societies with religious institutions. Current estimates suggest that two billion are Christians, one billion are Muslims, hundreds of millions are Hindus, hundreds of millions more are: Jewish, Buddhists, Shintos, Confucianists, Taoists, and many, many more denominations.

Explore

Are Believers Happier? (pg 501)
This activity examines whether those who are religious are happier than those who are not. Tables are presented with data from the 1998 General Social Survey for believers and nonbelievers who are happy and by affiliation.

Listen

Freethinkers (pg 498)
Freethinkers, the latest book from author Susan Jacoby, explores the history of American secularism.
Teens and Wicca (pg 501)
Wicca one of the fastest growing religions for high school and college aged individuals. The dominant faiths in America today include the Roman Catholic Church, Protestant Christianity, Judaism, Islam and Buddhism. But an incredibly diverse range of smaller, less-known religions are flourishing, too.

Watch

Approaches to Religion (pg 510)
The topic of this video discusses how the sociological approach to religion differs from a theological approach. As sociologists we cannot presuppose that Christianity is correct.

Visualize

Religious Organizations (pg 493)
The chart lists the different types of religious organizations and gives a brief summary of each.
Religions of the World (pg 498)
The map illustrates the percentage of religions for the different nations of the world.

Practice Test

After completing the practice test, check your answers in the Answer Key of this Study Guide.

Multiple Choice Questions

1. What institution believes that the origins and the meaning of life are based on the existence of a supernatural power?
    a. Science
    b. Religion
    c. Education
    d. Spirituality

2. Which theorists argued that religion could be a catalyst to change?
    a. Emile Durkheim
    b. Karl Marx
    c. Max Weber
    d. Georg Simmel

3. Karl Marx believed that religion:
    a. is a major cause for the rise of capitalism.
    b. focuses life on the present rather than the future.
    c. treats the existing society as corrupt.
    d. undermines the power of the government.

4. A ritual is a matter of:
    a. who you socialize with.
    b. song and dance.
    c. the holy and divine.
    d. formal, ceremonial behavior.

5. What type of religious organization is formed around a specific person or idea drawn from an established religion?
    a. Cult
    b. Sect
    c. Denomination
    d. Ecclesiae

6. A sect is best defined as a:
    a. a group that has deeply fervent believers.
    b. a new or different religion.
    c. a small subculture within an established religion..
    d. a large-scale, extremely organize religious body.

7. State churches that are established in society are also called:
    a. Cult
    b. Sect
    c. Denomination
    d. Ecclesiae

8. Which of the following is not true about Western religions?
    a. They are exclusive
    b. They are evangelistic
    c. There is a sacred book
    d. There are no regular worship services

9. Which religion is the single largest religion in the world today?
     a. Judaism
     b. Christianity
     c. Islam
     d. Budhism

10. Which is not one of the three major Western religions?
     a. Christianity
     b. Judaism
     c. Islam
     d. Buddhism

11. _____ is process of moving away from religious spirituality an toward the worldly.
     a. Fundamentalism
     b. Ecclesia
     c. Secularization
     d. Protestant ethic

12. Jehovah's Witnesses would be considered a:
     a. Cult
     b. Sect
     c. Denomination
     d. Ecclesiae

13. Where are the majority of Hindus located?
     a. South Asia
     b. South Africa
     c. Easter Europe
     d. Central America

14. Which is not one of the top ten religions in the United States?
     a. Christianity
     b. Judaism
     c. Wicca
     d. Confucianism

15. Which Great Awakening made a relationship with the sacred attainable to even greater numbers of Americans, with even less effort or religious discipline?
     a. First
     b. Second
     c. Third
     d. Fourth

16. Which racial/ethnic group has the highest percentage of Catholics?
     a. White
     c. Hispanic
     d. Black
     c. Asian

17. Which of the following would not be considered a trait of a fundamentalist religious group?
     a. accepting religious pluralism
     b. interpreting religious texts literally
     c. endorsing conservative political goals
     d. they claim they are the purest followers of religion

18. Liberation theology includes all but one of the following ideas. Which one is not consistent with this theory?
   a. God's natural order includes human suffering
   b. Jesus is the savior of the poor
   c. Religion should help people strive to end suffering
   d. Justice should be brought to the poor

19. Which of the following is not a norm of science?
   a. Objectivity
   b. Common ownership
   c. Disinterestedness
   d. Secularization

20. Which group of people has the highest percentage employed in science and engineering?
   a. White women
   b. White men
   c. Black men
   d. Black women

21. Thomas Kuhn proposed that science changes in a _____ way.
   a. Linear
   b. Gradual
   c. Erratic
   d. Unstable

22. If one is to make a judgment based on empirical evidence they would be considered what kind of scientist.
   a. Subjective
   b. Objective
   c. Disinterested
   d. Advocate

23. Which of is not a type of science?
   a. Biological
   b. Social
   c. Physical
   d. Linguistics

24. There are several debates that are ongoing between church and state that have strained their coexistence. Which of the following is not one of them?
   a. Evolution and creationism
   b. School prayer
   c. Embryonic stem cell research
   d. Church doctrine on politics

25. What type of research would provide the research necessary to support or promote a particular position.
   a. Advocacy research
   b. Objective research
   c. Subjective research
   d. None of the above

STUDY GUIDE

True/False Questions

True False 1. Religion is a cultural universal.

True False 2. Weber believed that religion provided a justification for social inequalities.

True False 3. Cults forms around a specific person or idea drawn from an established religion.

True False 4. A denomination is a religion that is so pervasive that the boundary between state and church is nonexistent.

True False 5. Judaism was founded 2,000 year ago by the disciples of Jesus, who declared him to be the son of God.

True False 6. Islam is one of the three major Eastern religions.

True False 7. The majority of countries in the world are experiencing an increase in religiosity not in secularization.

True False 8. The Third Great Awakening in American history has made a relationship with the sacred attainable to even greater numbers of Americans, with even less effort.

True False 9. Most western religions prohibit women and homosexuals from leadership positions.

True False 10. Church-affiliated colleges have seen a significant decrease in their enrollment because students are attending secular colleges.

Fill-in-the-Blank Questions

1. Science acquires its knowledge through _____: information is developed, demonstrated, and double-checked using an experimental method.

2. While we are alive, we can experience the _____, that which is holy or divine.

3. _____ are solemn reenactments of the sacred events.

4. Marx called religion the _____ of the masses.

5. _____ have an established hierarchy, methods for credentialing administrators, and more social respect than either a cult or a sect.

6. A _____ is a small subculture within an established religious institution.

7. The "corruption of Hinduism lead to the development of _____.

8. _____ is the process of moving away from religious spirituality and toward the worldly.

9. In twentieth-century Latin America, _____ within the Catholic Church was a source of popular mobilization against ruthless political dictators.

10. The most important norm of science is _____, in which judgments are based on empirical verification, not on personal feelings or opinions.

Essay Questions

1. What is religion and science and how does each acquire its ideas?

2. Discuss the various types of religious organizations: cults, sects, denominations, and ecclesiae. How are they different and how do they come into being?

3. Compare and contrast the six major world religions. What do they have in common, how do they differ, and what is the general difference between Western and Eastern religions?

4. As an institution how does science function in terms of its norms, scientific networks, and the inequality found within it?

chapter **15**

Religion and Science

Sociology Now
1st Edition
Kimmel/Aronson

*This multimedia product and its contents are protected under copyright law. The following are prohibited by law: any public performances or display, including transmission of any image over a network; preparation of any derivative work, including the extraction, in whole or in part, of any images; any rental, lease, or lending of the program.

Comparing Religion and Science

- **religion** → beliefs
  - revelation
  - prophet/charismatic leadership

- **science** → systematic knowledge
  - empirical verification\physical world

Copyright © Allyn & Bacon 2009

Classical Theories of Religion

- cultural universal
- **Durkheim and Social Cohesion**
  - "social glue"
  - civil religion
- **Marx and Social Control**
  - justified inequality
  - "the opiate of the masses"
- **Weber and Social Change**
  - catalyst to change

Copyright © Allyn & Bacon 2009

Religious Groups

- **Cults**
  - smallest/simplest form of religion
  - deeply fervent believers
  - social marginality

- **Sects**
  - subculture within an established religious institution
  - short lived versus "established" sects

Copyright © Allyn & Bacon 2009

Religious Groups

- **Denominations**
  - large-scale, extremely organized
  - most adopt religion of parents

- **Ecclesiae**
  - nonexistent boundary between church and state
  - merging of politics and religion

Copyright © Allyn & Bacon 2009

Religions of the World

- **Western Religions**
  - *exclusive*
  - **Judaism**
  - **Christianity**   • denominations and sects
  - **Islam**   • **fundamentalism**

- **Eastern Religions**
  - *syncretic*
  - **Hinduism**
  - **Buddhism**
    - Hinayana
    - Mahayana
  - **Confucianism**

Copyright © Allyn & Bacon 2009

Religions of the World

- **Contemporary Religion: Secularization or Resurgence?**
  - secularization
  - religion has *not* declined as predicted
  - global religious resurgence

  " . . . religion offers an alternative to modern society, which people may regard as corrupt – and corrupting."

Religions of the United States

  - religion still strong in U.S.
    - *U.S. haven for religious immigrants*
    - *waves of increased religious passion*
    - *social support and cultural interaction*
    - *separation from political life*
  - **Third Great Awakening**

Religions of the United States

- **Religious Experience and Religious Identity**
  - religious variation (race, gender, etc.)
  - women more religions than men
  - Western religions
    - *condemn homosexuality*
    - *differential treatment of women*

- **Religion on Campus**
  - college student religiosity and race

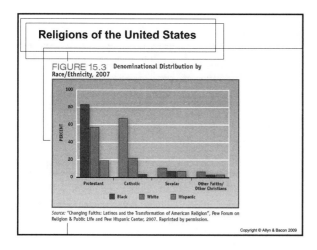

Religions of the United States

FIGURE 15.3 Denominational Distribution by Race/Ethnicity, 2007

Source: "Changing Faiths: Latinos and the Transformation of American Religion", Pew Forum on Religion & Public Life and Pew Hispanic Center, 2007. Reprinted by permission.

Copyright © Allyn & Bacon 2009

Religions of the United States

- **New Age Religions**
  - draws from other religions
  - open minded and pluralistic

- **Religion as Politics**
  - liberation theology
  - church or state?
    - *Evolution and creationism*
    - *School prayer*
    - *Embryonic stem cell research*

Copyright © Allyn & Bacon 2009

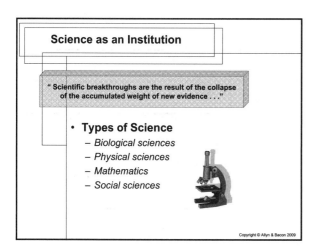

Science as an Institution

" Scientific breakthroughs are the result of the collapse of the accumulated weight of new evidence . . ."

- **Types of Science**
  - *Biological sciences*
  - *Physical sciences*
  - *Mathematics*
  - *Social sciences*

Copyright © Allyn & Bacon 2009

Science as an Institution

- **The Norms of Science**
  - Objectivity
    - Advocacy Research
  - Common Ownership
  - Disinterestedness

- **Scientific Networks**
  - science is a collaborative effort
  - women underrepresented in top ranks

Science as an Institution

- **Scientific Breakthroughs**

- **The Role of the Scientist and Society**

- **Science and Religion in the 21st Century**

What Does America Think?

15.1 What Is the Bible?

These are actual survey data from the General Social Survey, 1998.

Which of these statements comes closest to describing your feelings about the Bible? Thirty percent of respondents felt that the Bible was the literal word of God. Almost half believed it was God inspired, and 17 percent thought it was a book of fables. Social class differences were significant; the higher one's social status the less likely one was to believe the Bible was the word of God.

CRITICAL THINKING | DISCUSSION QUESTION

1. Why do you think social class differences were so striking? What might lead someone from the lower class, for example, to have stronger views on the Bible being literal than someone from the upper class?

What Does America Think?

15.2 Prayer in Schools

These are actual survey data from the General Social Survey, 2004.

The U.S. Supreme Court has ruled that no state or local government may require the reading of the Lord's Prayer or Bible verses in public schools. What are your views on this—do you approve or disapprove of the Court ruling? Overall, almost 37 percent of respondents approved of the ruling, while 63 percent disapproved of the ruling. Men were more likely than women to approve of the ruling.

CRITICAL THINKING | DISCUSSION QUESTION

1. Why do you think men were more likely than women to approve of the ruling?

What Does America Think?

▶ Go to this website to look further at the data. You can run your own statistics and crosstabs here: **http://sda.berkeley.edu/cgi-bin/hsda?harcsda+gss04**

REFERENCES: Davis, James A., Tom W. Smith, and Peter V. Marsden. General Social Surveys 1972–2004: [Cumulative file] [Computer file]. 2nd ICPSR version. Chicago, IL: National Opinion Research Center [producer], 2005; Storrs, CT: Roper Center for Public Opinion Research, University of Connecticut; Ann Arbor, MI: Inter-University Consortium for Political and Social Research; Berkeley, CA: Computer-Assisted Survey Methods Program, University of California [distributors], 2005.

Chapter 16
The Body and Society: Health and Illness

Chapter Outline

I. The Social Construction of the Body
    a. The Sociology of Beauty
        i. What we think of as beautiful is less a matter of individual perceptions and more about every-shifting cultural standards.
        ii. Weight and Height
            1. The body shape and weight that is considered ideal also varies enormously.
            2. Wealthy countries worry about obesity while poor countries worry about malnutrition and starvation.
            3. The United States is by far the fattest country.
            4. Globally obesity is a growing health problem.
                a. There are now as many overnourished people as undernourished.
                b. Obesity is couples with starvation and malnutrition in many developing societies as well.
        iii. Feeding and Starving the Female Body
            1. Anorexia nervosa involves chronic and dangerous starvation dieting and obsessive exercise.
            2. Bulimia typically involves binging and purging.
            3. Anorexia and bulimia rates are higher in the United States than in any other country.
                a. Estimates in the United States calculate that 3.7 percent of American women suffer from anorexia at some point in their lifetime.
                b. Up to 4.2 percent struggle with bulimia at some point in life.
        iv. Pumping up and the Male Body
            1. Men have become increasingly concerned with their bodies, especially fitness and weight.
            2. Many men experience what some researchers have labeled muscle dysmorphia, a belief that one is too small.
            3. Adonis complex is the belief that men must look like Greek Gods.
            4. Increasing numbers of men are also exhibiting eating disorders.
            5. Steroids enable men to build muscle mass quickly and dramatically, so that one looks incredible big.
        v. Embodying Identity
            1. Virtually all of us spend some time and energy in some forms of bodily transformation.
            2. Tattoos: Inking Identity
                a. Today tattoos are quite common.
                b. Tattoos are seen as a way people can design and project a desired self-image.
            3. Cosmetic Surgery
                a. This is one of the fastest-growing methods of bodily transformation.
                b. Though women continue to be the primary consumers of cosmetic surgery, male patients now comprise 20 percent of all procedures.
                c. The popularity of different procedures differs by county.
            4. Changing Identity by Changing the Gendered Body: Transgenderism
                a. Transgenderism is an umbrella term that describes a variety of people, behaviors, and groups whose identities depart from normative gender ideals of masculinity or femininity.

        b. Transgenderism is typically experienced as a general discomfort that becomes increasingly intense during puberty.

        c. Transgenderism enables us to dissolve what is experienced as an arbitrary privileging of the body-at-birth and give more weight to who we feel we are, bringing us close to a world in which we can choose our gender.

     vi. The "Disabled" Body

1. A disability is a physical or mental impairment that substantially limits one or more major life activities.
2. Disabilities are not always visible, nor are they necessarily "disabilities," in that many disabled people could live full and normal lives if only the larger society would cooperate.
3. Nearly 20 percent of all Americans have one or more disabilities.
4. The number of Americans with a physical or mental disability has increased in recent years.
5. Disabilities are unevenly distributed by race and class within the United States.

II. Healthy Bodies, Sick Bodies

  a. The World Health Organization defines health as a state of complete mental, physical, and social well-being, not simply the absence of disease.

  b. Health and Inequality

      i. Epidemiology is the study of the causes and distribution of disease and disability.

     ii. Social epidemiology focuses on the social and behavior factors.

    iii. Mortality rate is the death rate as a percentage of the population.

    iv. Morbidity rate indicates the rates of new infections from disease.

     v. Measures of health care include;

1. Life Expectancy.
2. Infant mortality rate.
3. Maternal mortality rate.
4. Chronic diseases.
5. Acute diseases.
6. Infectious diseases.

     vi. Age and Health

1. Our health changes as we age.
2. Breakthroughs in medical technologies and treatments mean that life expectancy will continue to increase at roughly the same rate as today.

    vii. Race, Class, and Health

1. The wealthier you are the healthier you are.
2. Poor urban Blacks have the worst health of any ethnic group in the United States, with the possible exception of Native Americans.
3. Those who need health care the most actually have the least access and the poorest care.

   viii. Gender and Health

1. Through the 20th century women have been increasingly outliving men.
2. The women's health movement has brought increasing awareness to certain illnesses such as breast cancer that overwhelmingly affect women.

  c. The Global Distribution of Health and Illness

      i. The wealthier the country, the healthier the population.

     ii. The cause of death for most people in the developed world is chronic diseases.

  d. Sickness and Stigma

      i. The Sick Role

1. According to Parson's the individual is not responsible for getting sick.
2. Elliot Freidson specified three different types of sick roles:
    a. Conditional sick role.
    b. Unconditionally legitimate sick role.
    c. Illegitimate sick role.

           3.   Corbin and Strauss identified three types o work that individuals do to manage their illnesses within an overall context of identity management.

               a.   Illness work.

               b.   Everyday work.

               c.   Biographical work.

    ii.   Mental Illness

           1.   Any of the various psychiatric disorders or diseases, usually characterized by impairment of thought, mood, or behavior.

           2.   Definition is strongly affected by social construction.

           3.   The mentally ill continue to suffer prejudice.

    iii.   Drugs, Alcohol, and Tobacco

           1.   Alcohol and tobacco additions are considered treatable medical conditions.

           2.   Drug addiction is understood to be a treatable medical condition, but it receives so much social disapproval that its treatment is often ignored in favor of being dealt with in another institution: prison.

           3.   A drug is any substance that, when ingested into the body, changes the body's functioning in some way.

               a.   The most extensively used illegal drug in the United States is marijuana.

               b.   Alcohol is a drug that is used recreationally by the overwhelming majority of the adult population.

               c.   Tobacco consumption varies widely by race, class, and gender.

    iv.   HIV/AIDS

           1.   Since it was first diagnosed in 1981, the social epidemiology of it has changed dramatically.

               a.   Initially it was so localized among urban gay men in the Unites States that it was called gay-related immune deficiency.

               b.   It gradually merged among people who had received blood transfusions with infected blood supplies or those sharing intravenous drug paraphernalia.

           2.   AIDS is the greatest health crisis in human history.

               a.   There were 4.3 million new infections and three million deaths in 2006 alone.

               b.   Today the epicenter of the disease is sub-Saharan Africa.

III.   Health as an Institution

   a.   Health care is a big business.

      i.   The United States has both the most advanced health care delivery system in the world and one of the most inequitable and expensive among industrial nations.

      ii.   Many of the problems in the American health care system derive from its scale and size.

   b.   Conventional and Alternative Health Care

      i.   Alternative medicine involves the diagnoses and treatment of health problems using unconventional treatment strategies, drawn instead from other cultural practices or different theoretical traditions.

      ii.   Industrial societies tend to see illnesses as being manifest through physical symptoms and are to be treated through medical interventions.

   c.   Health Care Reform

      i.   Efforts to reform the health care system have been shaped by the powerful lobbying efforts by the health insurance companies, the pharmaceutical companies, and the professional associations of doctors.

      ii.   Health care analysts calculate that nearly one-third of all health care spending consists of profit and waste.

IV.   Health in the 21st Century

   a.   The debate about reforming the health care system often comes down to a moral debate.

      i.   Is health care a right that should be guaranteed by the government to every citizen?

      ii.   Should it be bought and sold like any other commodity in the marketplace?

b. The way we present our bodies is a form of social interaction, and our social institutions use and shape those embodied selves.

Chapter Summary

- What we think of as beautiful is less a matter of individual perception and more about every-shifting cultural standards like body shape and weight.
- The United States is by far the fattest county but the weight gain is unevenly distributes by race, gender, and class.
- The current standards of beauty for women combine dramatically thin and also muscular and buxom, which are virtually impossible to accomplish and as a result an increasing number of young women are diagnose with either anorexia nervosa or bulimia every year.
- Men have increasingly become concerned with their bodies and suffer from muscle dysmorphia, a belief that one is insufficiently muscular, or the Adonis complex, the belief that men must look like Greek Gods.
- Body piercing, tattoos, cosmetic surgery, and transgenderism are all ways in which people transform their bodies.
- A disability is a physical or mental impairment that substantially limits one or more major life activities however they are not always visible.
- The World Health Organization defines health as a state of complete mental, physical, and social well-being. The study of the causes and distribution of disease and disability is called epidemiology while the focus on these social and behavior factors that effect the causes and distribution of disease is call social epidemiology.
- Our health is affected by age, gender, race, and class.
- The problem of health and inequality is an enormous issue globally in that the wealthier countries have healthier populations while poor countries have high rates of infectious diseases, malnutrition, and starvation.
- Talcott Parsons uses the term sick role to describe how we learn to be sick and Elliot Freidson expanded on this idea to incorporate three different types of sick roles: conditional, unconditionally legitimate, and the illegitimate.
- Those who suffer from mental illness, alcohol or drug addiction, physical or mental disability, or HIV also suffer from a stigmatized identity, however the trend now is to deinstitutionalize these people and reintegrate them back into society.
- A mental illness includes any type of psychiatric disorder or disease and is affected by social construction.
- A drug is any substance that, when ingested into the body, changes the body's functioning in some way. Marijuana, alcohol, cocaine, and heroine are all examples of recreational drugs.
- HIV/AIDS used to be called the gay-related immune deficiency however, the disease has spread to all different types of people and is considered the greatest health crisis in human history according to the Untied Nations.
- A crucial sociological aspect off health and illness is the set of institutions that are concerned with health care such as, medical professionals, hospitals, medical insurance companies, and pharmaceutical companies.
- The health care industry reflects inequalities of race, ethnicity, and gender in our society.
- Alternative medicine involves the diagnoses and treatment of health problems using unconventional treatment strategies and draw from cultural practices or different theoretical traditions instead of following the Western model of health and illness.
- The health care system in the United States has been shaped by the powerful lobbying efforts of the health insurance companies, the pharmaceutical companies, and the professional associations of doctors and their efforts have expended the privatization of health care which has led to disparities in health care between rich and poor.
- The debate now is whether health care is a right or a privilege.

Learning Objectives
After completing the reading of Chapter 9, you should be able to answer the following objectives.

- Discuss how beauty is socially constructed.
- Understand how socioeconomic status affects one's body shape and weight.

- Define anorexia nervosa, bulimia, muscle dysmorphia, and the Adonis complex and how has society influenced these.
- Discuss the different types of bodily transformations and who uses each of these.
- Define disability and discuss the distribution of disabilities in the United States and globally.
- Define epidemiology and social epidemiology.
- List the measures of health care.
- Know how age, race, class, and gender affect health and illness.
- Discuss the global problem of health and inequality.
- Define sick role and describe the three different types of sick roles specified by Elliot Freidson.
- Discuss how some illnesses have become deinstitutionalized and how other natural processes have become medicalized.
- Define mental illness and how it is socially constructed.
- Explain how drugs, alcohol, and tobacco have become medicalized and deinstitutionalized.
- Discuss HIV/AIDS in terms of what it is, who is susceptible to it, and how it is distributed globally.
- Discuss the health care industry in the United States and who has access to it.
- Understand alternative medicine.
- Discuss how the health care system has been shaped by lobbyists and what sates have begun to do to improve health care.

Key Terms

Adonis complex: the belief that men must look like Greek gods, with perfect chins, thick hair, rippling muscles, and washboard abdominals.

Alternative medicine: involves the diagnosis and treatment of health problems using unconventional treatment strategies, drawn instead from other cultural practices or different theoretical traditions.

Anorexia nervosa: involves chronic and dangerous starvation dieting and obsessive exercise.

Bulimia: binging and purging.

Deinstitutionalization: reintegration of the sick back into society/

Disability: physical or mental impairment that substantially limits one or more major life activities.

Drug: any substance, that when ingested into the body, changes the body's functioning in some way.

Epidemiology: study of the causes and distribution of disease and disability.

Health: state of complete mental, physical, and social well-being.

Medicalization: is the way that medical treatments have supplanted other options for the healthy and the ill.

Mental illness: any of the various psychiatric disorders or diseases, usually characterized by impairment of thought, mood, or behavior.

Morbidity rate: rates of new infections from disease.

Mortality rate: death rate as a percentage of the population.

Muscle dysmorphia: belief that one is to small, insufficiently muscular.

Secondhand smoke: the smoke that is inhaled by nonsmokers as a result of other people smoking.

Sick role: how we learn to be sick.

Social epidemiology: focus on social and behavioral factors.

Stigmatized identity: perception that they are somehow responsible for their illness and that it is their fault.

Transgenderism: umbrella term that describes a variety of people, behaviors, and groups whose identities depart from normative gender ideals of masculinity or femininity.

Key People

Juliet Corbon and Anselm Strauss: identified three types of work that individuals do to mange their illnesses within an overall context of identity management.

Elliot Freidson: specified three different types of sick roles.

Talcott Parsons: the origins of illness come from outside the individual's control

Additional Learning with MySocLab

Read

> **If You Have a Ticket and a Wheelchair, What Next? (pg 531)**
> LISA CORCORAN loves going out on the town. She likes Broadway musicals and movies -- and she usually can get there, with the help of a special map of the county that she relies on.
>
> **In a Battered Taxi, a Nurse to India's Poorest (pg 536)**
> In the less developed regions of the world, hunger persists, death and birth rates are highest, overall quality of life is lowest. The poorest regions of the world comprise eighty percent of the world's population today and they are growing.wed him to school from his family's 100-acre dairy farm in southern Massachusetts.
>
> **Decade After Health Care Crisis, Soaring Costs Bring New Strains (pg 547)**
> The single most successful type of small business in the US has been and continues to be the private medical practice. Medical doctors average five times the annual income of the average US worker.

Explore

> **Web Activity: Health and Medicine (pg 544)**
> For this activity you will visit the World Bank Group website and read the article "AIDS in Developing Countries" to learn about AIDS and other life threatening diseases that plague less developed countries. After reading the article and visiting the website there is a series of questions to answer.

Listen

> **Racial Disparity Found in Health Care (pg 534)**
> New research on racial disparities in health care shows a dramatic difference in the quality of care received by black Medicare patients versus white patients.

Watch

> **Health Care for the Poor (pg 535)**
> The video clip explores how the nation's health care system does not work for low income people.
>
> **Health Care Reform (pg548)**
> The video clip examines a couple who started a provider network to include alternative medicine providers.

Visualize

> **Cost of Medical Care: The Soaring Costs of Medical Care: What the Average American Pays Each Year (pg 534)**
> This chart illustrates the soaring costs of medical care since the 1960s, exemplifies why poor people cannot afford to see a doctor.
>
> **AIDS: A Global Glimpse, How Many People get Infected with HIV/AIDS per year (pg 544)**
> The bar chart illustrates how many people get infected with HIV/AIDS per year and where the epidemic is most severe.

Practice Test

After completing the practice test, check your answers in the Answer Key of this Study Guide.

Multiple Choice Questions

1. Which is not one of the five states with the highest levels of obesity?
   a.   Alabama
   b.   West Virginia
   c.   Louisiana
   d.   Illinois

2. The World Health Organization claims that the number of overnourished people is _____ than the number of undernourished people.
   a.   Less
   b.   About the same
   c.   More
   d.   None of the above

3. If a person starves themselves and is involved in obsessively exercising they would be considered an:
   a.   Anorexic
   b.   Bulimic
   c.   Dysmorphic
   d.   Normal

4. When one believes that they are too small and have insufficient muscle mass they are suffering from:
   a.   the Adonis complex.
   b.   muscle dysmorphia.
   c.   anxiety.
   d.   None of the above.

5. In 2006, what percentage of the U.S. population is obese?
   a. 11.3 percent
   b. 20 percent
   c. 32 percent
   d. 40 percent

6. Which country has the highest rate of obesity for females in 2005?
   a. United States
   b. Saudi Arabia
   c. France
   d. Brazil

7. What is the percentage of men who suffer from eating disorders?
   a.   3 percent
   b.   5 percent
   c.   10 percent
   d.   20 percent

8. Which of the following is not a form of body transformation discussed in the chapter?
   a.   Tattooing
   b.   Cosmetic surgery
   c.   Transgenderism
   d.   Dieting

9. A disability is:
    a. a mental impairment that limits activity.
    b. a physical impairment that limits activity.
    c. not always visible.
    d. all of the above.

10. What percentage of the disable population are boys between the ages of 5 and 15?
    a. 7 percent
    b. 4 percent
    c. 43 percent
    d. 40 percent

11. Which of the following is not a measure of health care?
    a. Life expectancy
    b. Infant mortality rates
    c. Acute diseases
    d. Fertility rates

12. Compared to people in poor countries those who live in wealthier countries:
    a. have poor health.
    b. live shorter lives.
    c. live longer lives.
    d. have fewer health insurance benefits.

13. What was revealed in the Tuskegee experiment?
    a. Black men contracted syphilis at higher rates than white men.
    b. That penicillin was an effective method for treating syphilis.
    c. That racism existed within the public health care system.
    d. None of the above.

14. In countries that have high rates of poverty they also have high rates of:
    a. infectious diseases.
    b. malnutrition.
    c. starvation.
    d. all of the above.

15. Talcott Parson's used the term "sick role" to describe:
    a. how we get sick.
    b. how we learn to be sick.
    c. how the sick play their role.
    d. how the sick improve their situation.

16. Tuberculosis is most prevalent in which of the following nations?
    a. Australia
    b. Sudan
    c. South Africa
    d. India

17. When a mentally ill person is reintegrated back into society they are being:
    a. medicalized.
    b. deinstitutionalized..
    c. stigmatized.
    d. epidemiologized.

18. Alcohol, tobacco, and marijuana are all considered:
    a. toxins.
    b. socially acceptable
    c. drugs
    d. recreational

19. Which of the following is the drug of choice among college students?
    a. Cocaine
    b. Methamphetamines
    c. Marijuana
    d. Alcohol

20. What type of medical model is prominent in the industrial countries?
    a. alternative medicine
    b. holistic
    c. spiritual
    d. biomedical

21. In 2006, 40 million people were infected with HIV/AIDS and the country with the highest number of cases is:
    a. United States
    b. Tunisia
    c. South Africa
    d. Russia

22. Someone who has schizophrenia, bipolar disorder, or dementia would be considered:
    a. ill.
    b. mentally ill.
    c. deinstitutionalized.
    d. stigmatized.

23. In developing nations people are more likely to die from what type of disease?
    a. Infectious
    b. Heart
    c. Kidney
    d. Lung

24. Which group in the United States has the worst health?
    a. Poor urban Hispanics
    b. Poor rural Whites
    c. Poor rural Blacks
    d. Poor urban Blacks

25. A disease that strikes suddenly and may cause severe illness, incapacitation, or even death is a:
    a. Chronic disease
    b. Infectious disease
    c. Incurable disease
    d. Acute disease

True/False Questions

True   False   1. Weight that is considered ideal is standard across cultures.

True   False   2. Men are more likely to have muscle dysmorphia than are women.

True   False   3. Cosmetic surgery is one of the fastest-growing method of bodily transformation.

True   False   4. Transgenderism describes a variety of people, behaviors, and groups whose identities do not depart from normative gender ideals of masculinity and femininity.

True   False   5. The World Health Organization includes mental, physical, and social well-being in their definition of health.

True   False   6. In the United States and across the globe, the wealthier you are, the healthier you are.

True   False   7. According to Elliot Freidson the most typical type of sick role is the conditional sick role.

True   False   8. Marijuana is the drug that is used recreationally by the overwhelming majority of the adult population.

True   False   9. The epicenter of AIDS is southeast Asia.

True   False   10. Alternative medicine involves the diagnoses and treatment of health problems using unconventional treatment strategies that draw from cultural practices or different theoretical traditions.

Fill-in-the-Blank Questions

1. In the United States women feel trapped by what feminist writer Naomi Wolf called the _____, a nearly unreachable cultural ideal of feminine beauty.

2. _____ involves chronic and dangerous starvation dieting and obsessive exercise.

3. The _____ is the belief that men must look like Greek gods, with perfect chins, thick hair, rippling muscles, and washboard abs.

4. In cultures becoming increasingly image oriented, _____ is conscious identity work.

5. The World Health Organization defines _____ as a state of complete mental, physical, and social well-being, not simply the absence of disease.

6. The study of the causes and distribution of disease and disability is called _____.

7. _____ refers to the way that medical treatments have supplanted other options for both the healthy and the ill.

8. A substance that changes the body's functioning in some way when ingested into the body is called a _____.

9. _____ involves the diagnoses and treatment of health problems using unconventional treatment strategies, drawn instead from other cultural practices or different theoretical traditions.

10. Schizophrenia, dementia, and bipolar disorder are all considered _____.

Essay Questions

1. How is beauty socially constructed?

2. Discuss the how the current beauty standards affect men and women in terms of weight and body shape?

3. What are three different types of body transformations discussed in the chapter? What part of the population uses these methods to transform their bodies and why?

4. Discuss how age, race, class, and gender affect people's health in the United States and Globally?

5. Discuss the HIV/AIDS epidemic. Who is most effected by the disease, how have medical breakthroughs transformed the disease, and why is the transmission of it more prevalent in the developing world?

chapter **16**

**The Body and Society:
Health and Illness**

Sociology Now
1st Edition
Kimmel/Aronson

*This multimedia product and its contents are protected under copyright law. The following are prohibited by law: any public performances or display, including transmission of any image over a network; preparation of any derivative work, including the extraction, in whole or in part, of any images; any rental, lease, or lending of the program.

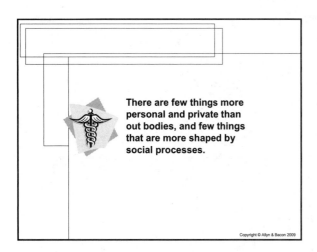

There are few things more
personal and private than
out bodies, and few things
that are more shaped by
social processes.

Copyright © Allyn & Bacon 2009

The Social Construction of the Body

- **The Sociology of Beauty**
  - ever-shifting cultural standards
  - varies from culture to culture
  - varies between race, ethnicity, class, etc.
  - "beauty myth"

  - **Weight and Height**
    - advantages to being tall
    - weight & socio-economic factors
    - poor more likely to be obese
    - starvation and obesity

Copyright © Allyn & Bacon 2009

The Social Construction of the Body

– **Feeding and Starving the Female Body**
  • **Anorexia nervosa**
    – chronic starvation
  • **bulimia**
    – "binging and purging"

– **Pumping up the Male Body**
  • **muscle dysmorphia**
  • **Adonis complex**

  • GI Joe and Barbie

Copyright © Allyn & Bacon 2009

The Social Construction of the Body

• **Embodying Identity**
  – body piercing (beyond the ears)
    • tongue, eyebrows, navel, nose, lips, nipples and genitals

– **Tattoos: Inking Identity**
  • 24% of Americans between 18 and 50 have at least one tattoo
  • tattoos sexually charged
    – *design*
    – *size*
    – *placement*

Copyright © Allyn & Bacon 2009

The Social Construction of the Body

– **Cosmetic Surgery**
    – breast augmentation/reduction
    – rhinoplasty
    – liposuction
    – eyelid surgery
    – Botox injections
    – facelifts
  • globalization of Western aesthetic

Copyright © Allyn & Bacon 2009

The Social Construction of the Body

– **Changing Identity by Changing the Gendered Body: Transgenderism**
  • continuum of femininity and masculinity
  • biological sense doesn't match internal gender identity
  • implications of sex reassignment surgery are enormous

The Social Construction of the Body

• **The "Disabled" Body**
  – physical or mental impairment
  – limits one or more major life activities
  – 20 % of Americans
  – numbers of disabled has increased
    • advances in medicine: birth
    • advances in medicine: survival
    • life expectancy has increased

"Disabilities do not reside in the bodies of the person but rather emerge through a realtionship with the society."

Healthy Bodies, Sick Bodies

– **health** (WHO)
  • physical, mental, and social well-being – not just the absence of disease

• Health and Inequality
  – **epidemiology**
  – **social epidemiology**
  – **mortality rate**
  – **morbidity rate**

  – *incidence and prevalence*

Healthy Bodies, Sick Bodies

– measures of health care
- *Life expectancy*
- *Infant mortality rate*
- *Maternal mortality rate*
- *Chronic diseases*
- *Acute diseases*
- *Infectious diseases*

– **Age and Health**
– **Race, Class, and Health**
– **Gender and Health**

Copyright © Allyn & Bacon 2009

Healthy Bodies, Sick Bodies

• **The Global Distribution of Health and Illness**
– chronic diseases cause most deaths in the developed world

• **Sickness and Stigma**
– **The Sick Role**
  • *conditional*
  • *unconditionally legitimate*
  • *illegitimate*

Copyright © Allyn & Bacon 2009

Healthy Bodies, Sick Bodies

– illness management "work" **(Corbin/Strauss**

– *illness work*
– *everyday work*
– *biographical work*

• **stigmatized identity**
• **deinstitutionalization**
• **medicalization**

Copyright © Allyn & Bacon 2009

Healthy Bodies, Sick Bodies

- **Mental Illness**
  - definition of any illness is strongly affected by social construction
  - prejudice continues

- **Drugs, Alcohol, and Tobacco**
  - **drug**
  - *therapeutic or recreational use*
  - Marijuana
  - Alcohol
    - "binge drinking"

Copyright © Allyn & Bacon 2009

Healthy Bodies, Sick Bodies

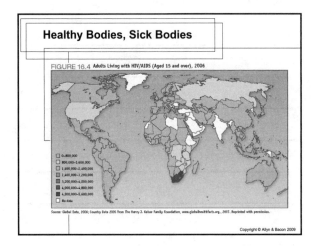

FIGURE 16.4 Adults Living with HIV/AIDS (Aged 15 and over), 2006

Source: Global Data, 2006; Country Data 2005 from The Henry J. Kaiser Family Foundation, www.globalhealthfacts.org., 2007. Reprinted with permission.

Copyright © Allyn & Bacon 2009

Health as an Institution

- health care industry reflects inequalities of race, ethnicity, and gender
- patients more likely to trust doctors who share their race or ethnicity

TABLE 16.4

Copyright © Allyn & Bacon 2009

Health as an Institution

- **Conventional and Alternative Health Care**
  - **alternative medicine**
    - *biomedical* versus *holistic*
    - *"naturopathic"*
    - *curanderismo*
    - chiropractic

Copyright © Allyn & Bacon 2009

Health as an Institution

- **Health Care Reform**

- **Health in the 21st Century: Living Longer – and Healthier?**

Copyright © Allyn & Bacon 2009

What Does America Think?

16.1 Emotional Problems

These are actual survey data from the General Social Survey, 2000.

1. Say you went to treatment for an emotional health problem, such as feeling depressed or anxious, that affects your work and other daily activities so that you accomplish less than you would like. Would you definitely expect, probably expect, probably not expect, or definitely not expect to feel better about yourself as a person? Forty percent of respondents said they would definitely expect to feel better about themselves, and another 46 percent said they would probably expect to feel better about themselves. Gender differences were not large.

2. Would you definitely expect, probably expect, probably not expect, or definitely not expect your overall quality of life to improve? Slightly more than 30 percent of respondents said they would definitely expect their quality of life to improve, and another 50 percent said they probably would expect their life to improve. Women were slightly more optimistic than men.

3. Would you definitely expect, probably expect, probably not expect, or definitely not expect to be cured? Almost 27 percent of respondents said they would definitely expect to be cured, and another 43 percent said they probably would expect to be cured.

CRITICAL THINKING | DISCUSSION QUESTIONS

1. When it comes to feeling better about oneself and improving the quality of one's life, women seem to be more optimistic than men. However, when it comes to being cured, men are slightly more optimistic than women. How might you explain that?

2. How might social class play a role in acknowledging and seeking treatment for emotional problems?

Copyright © Allyn & Bacon 2009

305

What Does America Think?

16.2 Genetic Testing

These are actual survey data from the General Social Survey, 2004.

1. Some people say that genetic screening may cause trouble. Others think it is a wonderful medical advance. Based on what you know, do you think genetic screening will do more harm than good or more good than harm? Slightly more than 70 percent of respondents in 2004 said genetic testing did more good than harm. White respondents were significantly more likely to say that, as were respondents in the middle and upper classes.

2. If you or your partner was pregnant, would you want her to have a test to find out if the baby had any serious genetic defects? Sixty-six percent of respondents said they would have genetic testing done on their fetus. White respondents were more likely than Black respondents to say so. Social class differences were not large, but those in the lower class and the upper class were more likely to say they would have their fetus tested.

CRITICAL THINKING | DISCUSSION QUESTIONS

1. White respondents were more likely than Black respondents to say genetic testing does more good than harm, yet Black respondents were more likely to say they would have their fetus tested for genetic abnormalities. What might explain this apparent discrepancy?

2. Social class differences in responses were striking. Like the responses broken down by race, the social class differences do not seem to make sense on the surface. How do you explain them?

What Does America Think?

▶ Go to this website to look further at the data. You can run your own statistics and crosstabs here: http://sda.berkeley.edu/cgi-bin/hsda?harcsda+gss04

REFERENCES: Davis, James A., Tom W. Smith, and Peter V. Marsden. General Social Surveys 1972–2004: [Cumulative file] [Computer file]. 2nd ICPSR version. Chicago, IL: National Opinion Research Center [producer], 2005; Storrs, CT: Roper Center for Public Opinion Research, University of Connecticut; Ann Arbor, MI: Inter-University Consortium for Political and Social Research; Berkeley, CA: Computer-Assisted Survey Methods Program, University of California [distributors], 2005.

Chapter 17
Education

Chapter Outline

I. The Sociology of Education
    a. Education as a Social Institution
        i. Education is a social institution through which society provides its member with important knowledge.
        ii. It teaches both a subject and a hidden curriculum.
        iii. The United States is a credential society in which you need diplomas, degrees, and certificates to quality for jobs.
    b. The History of Education
        i. For most of human history there were no schools.
        ii. In many cultures schools developed out of a need to train religious leaders.
        iii. European schools developed in connection with monasteries or cathedrals to teach priests and other religious workers necessary subjects.
        iv. The United States was among the first countries in the world to set a goal of education for all of its citizens, under the theory that an educated citizenry was necessary for a democratic society to function.
        v. Some groups have consistently enjoyed more educational success than others.

II. Education and Globalization
    a. Education is closely tied to economic success.
        i. Globally there is considerable inequality in education opportunity.
        ii. A child's family background or socioeconomic status is a strong predictor of participation in secondary education.
        iii. Gender also determines education opportunity.
            1. Among Arab states 19.8 percent of men and 41.1 percent of women are not literate.
            2. One in three children world-wide live in a country that does not ensure equal access to education for boys and girls.
    b. Intelligence(s) and Literacy
        i. Tests we have devised to measure the intelligence quotient are highly correlated with success in school.
            1. Some scholars contend that hey are measuring the social, economic, and ethnic differences that correlate with success rather than intelligence itself.
            2. Few scholars believe that different levels of success in school among different ethnic groups is not due to bias or inequality after all.
        ii. Howard Gardner argues that intelligence is not a single characteristic.
    c. Cultural Literacy
        i. E.D. Hirsch Jr. argued that the modern school curriculum, with its emphasis on diversity, is depriving children of the background that they need to be effective American citizens.
        ii. Scientific literacy is the knowledge and understanding of the scientific concepts and processes required for personal decision making, participation in civic and cultural affairs, and economic productivity.

III. Education and Inequality
    a. Education and Mobility
        i. Most of us believe that education is the ticket to social mobility.
            1. Education is also one of the primary vehicles by which society reinforces social inequalities based on race, ethnicity, class, and gender
            2. As long as we believe that education is a strict meritocracy we believe that different educational outcomes are based on characteristics of those individuals or those groups.

ii. Sociologists study the hidden curriculum.
1. Education not only creates social inequalities but makes them seem natural, normal, and inevitable.
2. The most important lessons take place outside of the classroom.

b. Inequality and the Structure of Education
i. Private versus Public Schools
1. Today one in nine American children attend private schools.
2. Nearly three-fourths of the private schools are run by religious bodies.
3. Many people believe that a private school provides better education.
ii. Wealthy versus Poor School Districts
1. Schools in wealthy districts can afford state-of-the-art labs and libraries.
2. In the poor neighborhoods that have the crumbling buildings, overcrowded classrooms, and overworked, underpaid teachers.
iii. Racial Segregation
1. Segregation requires that White and non-White students attend different schools.
2. Integration began with busing students which balanced school's ethnic distribution.
3. Integration began to reverse when the 1991 Supreme Court ruling allowed the return of neighborhood schools.

c. Bilingual Education
i. In 1968 Congress passed the Bilingual Education Act, asserting that children's native language was not English were being denied equal access to education and that school districts should take affirmative steps to rectify the language deficiency.
ii. Critics argue that these programs are costly and inefficient.
iii. Many researchers have concluded that bilingual education helps students to learn English.

d. Tracking
i. Grouping students according to their ability.
ii. Strong labeling of students develops through tracking.
iii. Funds go mostly toward the educational needs of the high-track students, the low-track students receive poorer classes, textbooks, supplies, and teachers.

e. Gender Inequality in Schools
i. Education reproduces gender stereotypes.
ii. Class materials used often reflect stereotyped differences between women and men, boys and girls.
iii. The visible and successful campaign for gender equality in school has produced a backlash.
iv. There is evidence that from elementary schools to college, boys perform worse than girls.

f. School for Gender Identity
i. One of the lessons taught in school is what it means to be a man or a woman.
1. Gender conformity is carefully scrutinized.
2. It is most significantly taught by peers, who act a as a sort of "gender police," enforcing the rules.
ii. Gay-baiting has little to do with sexual orientation.
iii. The constant teasing and bullying that occur in middle and high schools have become national problems.
1. Bullying is not one single thing but a continuum stretching from hurtful language through shoving and hitting to criminal assault and school shootings.
2. Harmful teasing and bullying happen to more than 1 million school children a year.

g. School Reform
i. Schools are one of the major ways in which people hope to move up in the social hierarchy.

          ii. At the same time schools are one of the major ways that social inequalities are reproduced and legitimized.

    h. Privatization

        i. Voucher system uses taxpayer funds to pay for students' tuition at private schools

        ii. Charter schools are publicly funded elementary or secondary schools that set forth in their founding document goals they intend to meet in terms of student achievement.

    i. Homeschooling

        i. The most important reason cited for homeschooling was concern about the environment of traditional schools.

        ii. Homeschooling is a phenomenon largely of the political far left and far rights.

    j. No Child Left Behind

        i. Law outlines a top-down approach to school performance with a number of revolutionary provisions:

        ii. The cost of enforcing this law is immense.

            1. Department of Education budget increased from $14 billion to $22.4 billion to handle it.

            2. Teachers complain that the program does not target the students who need the most help and even forces them to dumb down accountability measures that were already in place.

IV. Sociology of Higher Education

    a. Preparing for College

        i. Among industrialized countries, American 15-year-olds rank 24 out of 29 on math literacy and problem-solving ability.

        ii. Because they are unprepared for college, it is understandable that they are not prepared to graduate within the traditional four years.

    b. Higher Education and Inequality

        i. The class barrier to higher education is actually increasing.

        ii. Colleges are drawing more members form upper-income households and fewer from average or below-average income households.

        iii. Poorer students are priced out of the market for higher education by soaring tuition increases.

    c. Student Life

        i. Schools offer several different cultures, all competing and colliding with each other.

        ii. Cathy's Smalls study on college students found that they were amazingly busy.

            1. Most worked at part-time jobs, juggled 5 courses, and try to join campus activities to pad their college resumes to gain a competitive advantage in the job market.

            2. The biggest differences between campus life today and that in the 1970s was the virtual lack of any free time in the lives of her students, the absence of a sense of campus "community," and the absence of any impact by faculty on the lives of students.

V. Education, Inc.

    a. For-Profit Universities

        i. The cost is comparatively low, the university rather than the professor owns the curriculum, and students can graduate relatively quickly.

        ii. The University of Phoenix is the largest for-profit university in the United States.

        iii. As institutions of higher learning, for-profits strip the university of its other functions.

    b. The Marketization of Higher Education

        i. Public universities have shifted from state institutions to state-supported institutions to state-assisted institutions.

        ii. As universities transform themselves into competitive commercial operations, they increasingly ask the "clients" to pay "fees," particularly when they are out of state and foreign students.

    c. McSchool

       i. There has been significant publicity concerning the food industry's takeover of school lunch programs.

      ii. To keep strapped school districts functioning amid increasing enrollments and widening budget deficits, to pay for unfunded government mandates, to subsidize sports and other enrichment programs, elementary and high schools are opening their doors to hundreds of thousands of dollars in corporate money annually.

          1. In 2004, a New Jersey elementary school became the first school in the country to sell naming rights to a corporate sponsor.

          2. Across the United States, corporate sponsors' logos appear on sports fields, gyms, libraries, playgrounds, and classrooms.

VI.   Education in the 21st Century

    a. American shave always had the optimistic faith that education leads to a secure future, to happiness, to success.

    b. Like every social institution, education is always gong to be both a tool of liberation and a tool of oppression.

Chapter Summary

- Sociologists define education as a social institution through which society provides its members with important knowledge like basic facts, job skills, and cultural norms and values.
- Education teaches both a subject and a hidden curriculum in which people learn individualism and competition, conformity to mainstream norms, obedience to authority, passive consumption of ideas, and acceptance of social inequality.
- For most of human history there were no schools, instead parents taught their children the necessary skills, however some cultural developed schools to train their religious leaders. The United States was among the first countries to set a goal of education for all of its citizens and the free public education movement began in 1848.
- Education is closely tied with economic success and a number of developing nations have begun intensive efforts to improve education.
- The primary goal of education is to make people smarter and the IQ test was designed to predict success in school, but to some the test seems highly biased.
- E.D. Hirsch Jr. believed that the modern school curriculum, with its emphasis on diversity, deprives children of the background that they need to be an effective American citizen because what they are learning is trivia rather than a sound core curriculum.
- Scientific literacy is the knowledge and understanding of the scientific concepts and processes required for personal decision making, participation in civic and cultural affairs, and economic productivity.
- Most of us believe that education is a ticket to social mobility and while this is partly true, sociologists also study the hidden curriculum through which education not only creates social inequalities but makes them seem natural, normal, and inevitable.
- There are different types of schools including private and public, and there is uneven distribution of resources for school that result in often dramatic differences in student achievement.
- Segregation requires White and non-White students living in the same district to attend separate schools but busing decreased segregation however, when the 1991 Supreme Court ruling allowed the return of neighborhood schools, school districts began to resegregate.
- Tracking, or grouping students according to their ability is common in American schools, but can lead to individuals being labeled as dumb by both teachers and other students.
- The term self-fulfilling prophecy was coined by Merton for a curious phenomenon: When you expect something to happen, it usually does so by labeling students as dumb they usually will fulfill that role.
- School teaches boys and girls what it means to be a man or a woman and gender conformity is carefully scrutinized.
- One of the most popular types of school reform during the last few decades has been privatization. Two types of privatization include the voucher system and charter schools.
- The No Child Left Behind act was signed in 2002 and had a number of sweeping provisions including: students in elementary school must take annual tests to ensure that they have met minimal standards of competency in reading and math, students in schools that are falling behind can transfer to better schools on the government's tab, and every child should learn to read and write English by the end of third grade.
- Higher education is becoming a necessity for middle-class and even working-class lives but the class barrier to education is increasing. Those who come from upper=income families attend elite schools and poorer students are priced out of the market for higher education by soaring tuition increases.
- Student life has generally been seen as revolving around drinking, partying, playing video games, and watching sports however a study conducted by Cathy Small showed that students have amazingly busy lives because most work part time, juggle five courses, and try to join campus activities to pad their college resumes to gain a competitive advantage in the job market.
- An increasing number of for-profit organizations have arisen in recent year and have advantages over traditional universities.
- Public institutions have shifted from state-supported to state-assisted institutions and have transformed into a business.
- Marketing has spread to elementary and secondary schools with the food industry taking over school lunch programs and selling naming rights to a corporate sponsor.
- Education is always going to be both a tool of liberation and a tool of oppression.

Learning Objectives
After completing the reading of Chapter 9, you should be able to answer the following objectives.

- Define education and know what the hidden curriculum in the educational system is.
- Understand how the educational system has changed throughout history.
- Discuss the global inequality in educational opportunities in terms of gender and socioeconomic status.
- Know what IQ tests where designed to measure and what the eight types of intelligence are according to Howard Gardner.
- Understand the difference between cultural literacy and scientific literacy.
- Understand how education affects people's social mobility.
- Discuss the differences between private and public schools.
- Understand how education reinforces social inequalities.
- Describe how school teaches people gender conformity.
- Understand the privatization of schools and the two types: voucher system and charter schools.
- Know what the No Child Left Behind Act is and some of the provisions in it.
- Describe the inequalities in the higher education system.
- Define for-profit universities and what their advantages are over traditional universities.
- Discuss the trend of "marketization" and how this has transformed public universities.
- Understand the term McSchool.

Key Terms

Charter schools: publicly funded elementary or secondary schools that set forth in their founding document goals they intend to meet in terms of student achievement.

Credential schools: you need diplomas, degrees, and certificates to qualify for some jobs.

Education: social institution through which society provides its members with important knowledge- basic facts, job skills, and cultural norms and values

For-profit universities: proprietary schools.

Hidden curriculum: individualism and competition, conformity to mainstream norms, obedience to authority, passive consumption ideas, and acceptance of social inequality.

Integration: the school's ethnic distribution is more balanced.

Scientific literacy: the knowledge and understanding of the scientific concepts and processes required for personal decision making, participation in civic and cultural affairs, and economic productivity.

Segregation: requiring White and non-White students living in the same district to attend separate schools.

Self-fulfilling prophecy: when you expect something to happen, it usually does.

Tracking: grouping students according to their ability.

Voucher system: uses taxpayer funds to pay for students' tuition at private schools.

Key People

John Dewey: proponent of "progressive education."

Frederick Douglass: stated that learning to read and write would be the "road to liberation" for oppressed minorities.

Howard Gardner: argued that intelligence is not a single characteristic.

E.D. Hirsch Jr.: argued that modern school curriculum, with its emphasis on diversity, is depriving children of the background that they need to be effective American citizens.

Horace Mann: believed that education could be "the great equalizer" eliminating class and other social inequalities.

Robert K. Merton: coined the term "self-fulfilling prophecy."

Additional Learning with MySocLab

Read

With the Apples Arriving by E-Mail, Teachers Adapt (pg 558)
The article discusses how technology has transformed the classroom over the years.

Teach Your Children, Virtually (pg 574)
This article discusses children learning through virtual academies. A mother who wanted to home school her children but did not think she was capable of doing it herself enrolled them in a virtual school.

Explore

Web Activity: Education (pg 574)
Read the articles "The Pros and Cons of Homeschooling" and "Number of Homeschooled Student in Michigan Unclear" to learn about the pros and cons of homeschooling and the efforts of monitoring homeschooled children. After reading the articles there is a series of questions to answer.

Listen

States Defend School Funding Laws in Court (pg 566)
A Texas state judge ruled that the Texas system for funding education is unconstitutional. The state is expected to appeal the case, but *Education Week* reporter David Hoff tells NPR's Jennifer Ludden there is litigation over school funding in more than half of the states.

Watch

School Inclusion (pg 569)
The video discusses the inclusion of children with learning disabilities in regular and special education classes. Experts believe that this can greatly benefit them rather than tracking them into special education classes only.

Visualize

SATs: National Results of the Scholastic Assessment Test (pg 563)
The graph shows the changes in verbal and math SAT scores from 1967 to 2005

"Race, Ethnicity, and Education": The Funneling Effects of Education (pg 570)
The graph illustrates the racial divide in education from high school through college.

Practice Test

After completing the practice test, check your answers in the Answer Key of this Study Guide.

Multiple Choice Questions

1. Education is the social institution by which society provides people with knowledge of:
   a. job skills.
   b. basic facts.
   c. cultural norms and values.
   d. all ob the above.

2. The hidden curriculum teaches children:
   a. active consumption of ideas.
   b. conformity to mainstream norms.
   c. rejection of social inequalities.
   d. cooperation.

3. Which state has the highest high school graduation rate?
   a. South Carolina.
   b. Georgia
   c. Iowa
   d. Florida

4. The majority of high school dropouts come from:
   a. high income families.
   b. middle income families.
   c. low-income families.
   d. none of the above.

5. Approximately what percentage of children live in countries that do not ensure equal access to education for boys and girls?
   a. 50 percent
   b. 45 percent
   c. 38 percent
   d. 33 percent

6. Which of the following is not one of Gardner's eight types of intelligence?
   a. Linguistic
   b. Spatial
   c. Interpersonal
   d. Scientific

7. Which group has the highest median income?
   a. Female high school graduates
   b. Males with an associates degree
   c. Females with a master's degree
   d. Males with a Bachelor's degree

8. Approximately what percentage of those attending public schools are Black?
   a. 17 percent
   b. 10 percent
   c. 15 percent
   d. 20 percent

9. The term hidden curriculum refers to:
    a. the subtle presentations of political and cultural ideas in the classroom.
    b. the idea that college is available only to those who can afford it.
    c. the important role of parents being involved in the schooling process.
    d. the process of tracking students by race, class, and gender.

10. One major problem with tracking is that:
    a. schools do not consider the student's social background when assigning tracks.
    b. students do not get to study what they are interested in.
    c. it reinforces existing inequalities for average or poor students.
    d. most of the funds go toward the educational needs of the low-track students.

11. Which of the following is a latent function of schooling?
    a. Learning to write
    b. Ensuring some common culture
    c. Teaches about the U.S. way of life
    d. Teaching job skills

12. The most crucial factor affecting access to college in the United States is:
    a. money.
    b. gender.
    c. personal achievement.
    d. athletic ability.

13. Across the United States, which region has the highest dropout rate?
    a. The East Coast
    b. The West Coast
    c. The Midwest
    d. The South

14. Which of Gardner's eight types of intelligence measures the skill of perceiving and understanding other individuals' moods, desires, and motivations?
    a. Linguistic
    b. Interpersonal
    c. Intrapersonal
    d. Naturalist

15. Which region of the world has the lowest percentage of girls' aged 10-14 currently attending school?
    a. South America
    b. Western/Middle Africa
    c. Eastern/Southern Africa
    d. South Central Asia

16. The problem of literacy means that:
    a. many old people have forgotten what they learned in school.
    b. when people cannot read or write they cannot compete in the global market.
    c. a significant portion of the population does not attend college.
    d. many teachers are unable to teach the basic skills.

17. Charter schools are:
    a. private schools that typically enroll low-income students.
    b. private schools that have a religious curriculum.
    c. public schools that have the freedom to try new programs.
    d. public schools that are run by a private company.

18. Which of the following is not a provision in the No Child Left Behind Act?
    a. Students in elementary school must take annual tests to ensure they meet minimum standards
    b. Students in schools that are falling behind can transfer to better schools
    c. School must provide a wide variety of classes
    d. Every child should learn to read and write English by the end of the third grade.

19. How many states are debating whether to drop out of participating in the Elementary and Secondary School act and forgo federal funding for education?
    a. 20
    b. 30
    c. 40
    d. 50

20. On average SAT scores of high school seniors has _____ since 1976.
    a. increased
    b. decreased
    c. stayed the same
    d. none of the above

21. Cathy Small's research on college students found that:
    a. most students work part-time jobs.
    b. they take five classes.
    c. they try to join campus activities.
    d. all of the above.

22. What is the biggest reason for the decline in lucrative student enrollment?
    a. Many are now getting jobs right out of high school.
    b. Foreign competition
    c. Students are now choosing on line programs.
    d. High school students are choosing to attend community colleges.

23. Elementary and high schools have started subsidizing their yearly budget by:
    a. asking the federal government for more money.
    b. raising tuition.
    c. selling naming rights to corporate sponsors.
    d. none of the above.

24. For-profit schools refer to:
    a. private schools that typically enroll high-income students.
    b. public schools that are run by private companies.
    c. public schools that have the freedom to try new programs and policies.
    d. private school that have a religious curriculum.

25. Which state has the highest high school drop out rate?
    a. Maine
    b. Minnesota
    c. Arkansas
    d. Mississippi

True/False Questions

True   False   1. In many cultures, schools developed out of a need to train religious leaders.

True   False   2. Gender does not determine educational opportunities around the world.

True   False   3. Jon D. Miller's research revealed that most American adults do not understand what molecules are.

True   False   4. Women who have a Master's degree earn more than men with a Bachelor's degree.

True   False   5. Hispanics are more likely to attend public schools than private schools.

True   False   6. Segregation requires that White and non-White students be evenly distributed in schools.

True   False   7. In reality it is the reverse discrimination that has led boys to do worse in school than girls.

True   False   8. The voucher system are publicly funded elementary or secondary schools that set forth in their founding document goals they intend to meet in terms of student achievement.

True   False   9. Most parents who home school their children do so because of their concerns about the environment of other schools.

True   False   10. The United States has a larger number of foreign students attending universities than any other country.

Fill-in-the-Blank Questions

1. _____ is a social institution through which society provides its members with important knowledge.

2. Abolitionist _____ stated that learning to read and write would be the "road to liberation" for oppressed minorities.

3. Knowledge and understanding of the scientific process required for personal decision making, participation in civic and cultural affairs, and economic productivity is knows as _____.

4. For African Americans, about _____ percent graduate from high school.

5. Busing programs decrease segregation in favor of _____, in which the school's ethnic distribution is more balanced.

6. _____ groups students according to their ability.

7. The _____ uses taxpayer funds to pay for students' tuition at private schools.

8. The law that was signed in January 2002 by President George W. Bush that outlined a top-down approach to school performance was the _____ act.

9. The marketing success of for-profit universities has led to a trend to _____ in traditional universities.

10. Although the research shows that _____ education helps students learn English, it is not widespread or widely supported.

Essay Questions

1. What is education and what are its manifest and latent functions?

2. Explain the inequity in educational opportunities across the world. How does socioeconomic status and gender influence one's educational opportunities?

3. What is tracking in schools and how can it be harmful to students?

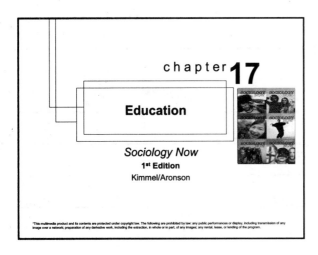

chapter **17**

Education

Sociology Now
1ˢᵗ Edition
Kimmel/Aronson

*This multimedia product and its contents are protected under copyright law. The following are prohibited by law: any public performances or display, including transmission of any image over a network; preparation of any derivative work, including the extraction, in whole or in part, of any images; any rental, lease, or lending of the program.

The Sociology of Education

- **The Sociology of Education**
  - **education**
  - *manifest* versus *latent* functions
  - **hidden curriculum**
  - **credential society**

- The History of Education
  - most of human history – no schools
  - tutors, ex. Aristotle
  - educated citizenry and democracy – U.S. education system

Copyright © Allyn & Bacon 2009

The Sociology of Education

  - 1918 – mandatory education until the age of 16
  - industry-driven occupational differentiation
  - "progressive education" (Dewey)
  - 1980s/1990s – "back to basics"
  - "road to liberation" (Douglass)
  - "the great equalizer" (Mann)

Copyright © Allyn & Bacon 2009

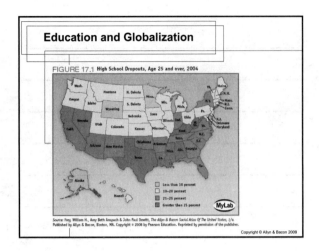

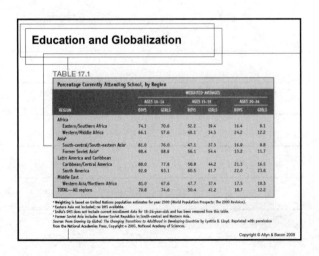

Education and Globalization

- **Intelligence(s) and Literacy**
  - The **I.Q.** score: being smart" versus success in school
    - bias of educational system
    - social and cultural differences
  - eight types of intelligence **(Gardner)**

- **Cultural Literacy**
  - Hirsch
  - **scientific literacy**

Education and Globalization

TABLE 17.2

Gardner's Eight Types of Intelligence

- **Linguistic**—sensitivity to meaning and order of words
- **Logical-mathematical**—the ability in mathematics and other complex logical systems
- **Spatial**—the ability to "think in pictures," to perceive the visual world accurately, and recreate (or alter) it in the mind or on paper
- **Musical**—the ability to understand and create music
- **Bodily-kinesthetic**—the ability to use one's body in a skilled way, for self-expression or toward a goal
- **Interpersonal**—the ability to perceive and understand other individuals' moods, desires, motivations
- **Intrapersonal**—the understanding of one's own emotions
- **Naturalist**—the ability to recognize and classify plants, minerals, animals

Source: Gardner, 1997.

Education and Inequality

- **Education and Mobility**
  - social mobility
  - creation of social inequalities
  - hidden curriculum
    - *learned social roles*
    - *dominant and subordinate*
    - *gender and racial hierarchies*

Education and Inequality

- **Inequality and the Structure of Education**
  - Private versus Public Schools
  - Wealthy versus Poor School Districts
  - Racial Segregation
    - segregation
    - integration

Education and Inequality

- **Bilingual Education**
  - Bilingual Education Act of 1968
    - equal access
    - rectify language deficiency
  - melting pot versus multiculturalism
  - U.S. language education remains weak

- **Tracking**
  - tracking
  - self-fulfilling prophecy (Merton)
  - reinforces inequality

Education and Inequality

- **Gender Inequality in School**
  - "Math class is tough!" – *Barbie*
  - gender stereotypes
  - differential treatment of girls and boys in the classroom
  - *Title IX legislation*

- **Schooling for Gender Identity**
  - gender conformity→ peers
  - "gay" = insufficiently masculine
  - bullying

Education and Inequality

- **School Reform**

- **Privatization**
  - voucher system
  - charter schools

- **Homeschooling**
  - response to concerns about the environment of traditional schools

Copyright © Allyn & Bacon 2009

Education and Inequality

- **No Child Left Behind**
  - 670-page law outlines a top-down approach to school performance
    - *competency testing*
    - *tuition assistance*
    - *every child should learn to read and write English by end of 3rd grade*
  - highly controversial

Copyright © Allyn & Bacon 2009

The Sociology of Higher Education

"[Higher education] . . . is not merely a matter if intellectual interests: Today, people need bachelor's degrees, and some-times master's degrees, to get a job that would have required a high school diploma less than 50 years ago"

- **Preparing for College**
  - low student readiness/achievement
  - little over 50 % of college students earn a bachelor's within six years of enrolling
  - tests scores holding steady since 1970s

Copyright © Allyn & Bacon 2009

The Sociology of Higher Education

- **Higher Education and Inequality**
  - high school graduation→ *rim of funnel* of educational privilege
  - class barrier increasing
  - high tuition and scholarships: *being smart is not a replacement for having money*

Copyright © Allyn & Bacon 2009

The Sociology of Higher Education

- **Student Life**
  - different cultures
    - *professional/academic*
    - *social: drinking, partying, etc.*
  - pursuit of "fun" **(Moffatt)**
  - lack of free time **(Small)**

TABLE 17.6

Student Life by the Numbers

In 2005, the National Survey of Student Engagement, administered by the Center for Postsecondary Education and Indiana University surveyed more than 48,000 college seniors. Here's how they spend their time (the numbers indicate percentages of students)

ACTIVITY	0 HOURS/WEEK	1–5	6–10	11 OR MORE
Studying and preparing for class	0	20	25	55
Working for pay	56	6	9	29
Activities outside of class (organizations, publications, student government, sports)	43	30	12	15
Relaxing and socializing	2	33	29	35

Source: National Survey of Student Engagement, 2006.

Copyright © Allyn & Bacon 2009

Education, Inc.

- **For-Profit Universities**
  - a.k.a. proprietary
  - market niche
  - University of Phoenix
  - separation and (or) elimination of other *dimensions of higher education*
    - *no labs*
    - *no research*
    - *no tenure or other forms of academic freedom*

Copyright © Allyn & Bacon 2009

Education, Inc.

- **The Marketization of Higher Education**
  - state-supported vs. state-assisted
  - "fees"
  - declining foreign student enrollment as a result of foreign competition

FIGURE 17.5 Distribution of Foreign Students by Host Country/Territory, 2002–2003

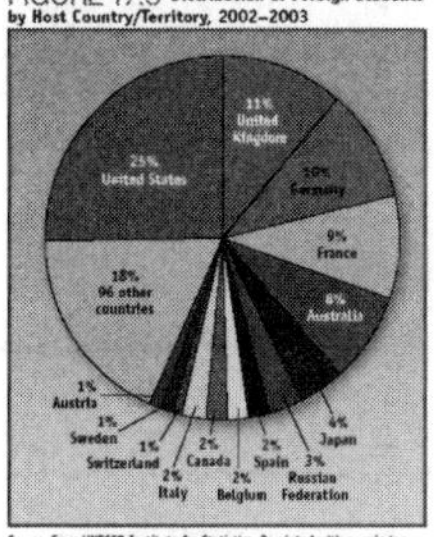

Source: From UNESCO Institute for Statistics. Reprinted with permission.

Copyright © Allyn & Bacon 2009

Education, Inc.

- **The Marketization of Higher Education**
  - state-supported versus state-assisted
  - "fees"
  - declining foreign student enrollment as a result of foreign competition

- **McSchool**

- **Education in the 21st Century**

Copyright © Allyn & Bacon 2009

What Does America Think?

17.1 Complete Formal Schooling

These are actual survey data from the General Social Survey, 2002.

How important is it that young people should complete formal schooling? Almost three-quarters of respondents in 2002 said it was extremely important that the young complete formal education. Another 18 percent thought it was quite important. Only about 3 percent thought it was not too important or not at all important. Social class differences were not large, but those in the working class were among the most likely (71.7 percent) to think it was extremely important for young people to finish school, while 82.7 percent of the upper class agreed.

CRITICAL THINKING | DISCUSSION QUESTION

1. Although the social class differences in responses are small, they are interesting. Why do you think those in the lower class and the upper class are more likely to say formal schooling is extremely important?

Copyright © Allyn & Bacon 2009

What Does America Think?

17.2 Confidence in Education

These are actual survey data from the General Social Survey, 2004.

As far as the people running the education system are concerned, would you say you have a great deal of confidence, only some confidence, or hardly any confidence at all in them? Data from 2004 show that over half of all respondents have only some confidence in the education system. Slightly more than 30 percent have a great deal of confidence, and 13 percent have hardly any. Differences by race were significant and interesting. Black respondents were far more likely than White respondents to have confidence in the education system. These differences have remained steady since the 1970s.

CRITICAL THINKING | DISCUSSION QUESTIONS

1. The differences in survey response by race were striking. Why do you think that Black respondents were dramatically more likely to have a great deal of confidence in the education system than were White respondents, particularly because Black students have generally and historically been underserved by the educational system?

2. Conversely, why do you think White respondents were so pessimistic about the educational system?

Copyright © Allyn & Bacon 2009

What Does America Think?

► Go to this website to look further at the data. You can run your own statistics and crosstabs here: http://sda.berkeley.edu/cgi-bin/hsda?harcsda+gss04

REFERENCES: Davis, James A., Tom W. Smith, and Peter V. Marsden. General Social Surveys 1972–2004: [Cumulative File] [Computer File]. 2nd ICPSR version. Chicago, IL: National Opinion Research Center [producer], 2005; Storrs, CT: Roper Center for Public Opinion Research, University of Connecticut; Ann Arbor, MI: Inter-University Consortium for Political and Social Research; Berkeley, CA: Computer-Assisted Survey Methods Program, University of California [distributors], 2005.

Copyright © Allyn & Bacon 2009

Chapter 18
Mass Media

Chapter Outline

I. What are the Mass Media?
   a. Media are the ways that we communicate with each other.
   b. Mass media are the ways to communicate with a vast number of people at the same time, usually over great distances.
   c. Types of Mass Media
      i. Print Media
         1. Printing press appeared in China in the eighth century and Europe in the fifteenth.
         2. During the 1800s most people owned only two or three books.
         3. The newspaper and magazine were originally vehicles for general interest readers.
            a. Today 13,000 magazines are published in the United States.
            b. The number of newspapers over the past century has shrunk.
         4. Globally one can discern the differences between rich and poor nations by their newspaper circulation.
      ii. Blogs: Online Print Journals
         1. It is essentially an online personal journal or diary where an author can air his or her opinion directly to audiences.
         2. There are approximately 12 million of them.
      iii. Radio, Movies, and Television
         1. Radio was born with Thomas Edison's gramophone.
         2. Moves were born with a 12-minute clip in 1903.
         3. The television was the most popular form of mass media in the United States between 1955 and 1985.
            a. Today the average household has more television sets than people.
            b. Today viewers can choose from among hundreds of channels.
      iv. Games, Gambling, and Porn: Guy Media
         1. Worldwide more than 300 million people play video games.
         2. Young males are the primary players of online poker.
         3. Pornography is a massive media category worldwide.
            a. In the United States, gross sales of all pornographic media range between $10 and $14 billion a year.
            b. Adult bookstores outnumber McDonald's restaurants.
         4. Parents are concerned with the time boys spend using these media.
      v. The Internet
         1. By 2007, every country in the world, with a very few exceptions, was online.
         2. As of 2007, the internet was access by 76 percent of the population of Sweden, 70 percent of the population of the United States, and 67 percent of Japan.
         3. The internet has not only transformed mass media but is a new form of mass media in its own right.
         4. The internet has been accused of facilitating increased isolation.
   d. Saturation and Convergence: The Sociology of Media
      i. The average American home today has 3 television sets, 1.8 VCRs, 3.1 radios, 2.6 tape players, 2.1 CD players,, 1.4 video game players, and at least one computer.
      ii. Now all forms of technology are digital.
II. Media Production and Consumption
   a. For years there was a division between production and consumption.

      i. This boundary is being increasingly blurred.

      ii. Media producers are all consumers themselves.

b. Cultural Industries

      i. Mass media are characterized by industrial patterns such as hierarchy and bureaucracy.

      ii. Cultural industries are the mass production of cultural products that are offered for consumption.

          1. Instead of crafting an individual work of creative genius, move studies and radio stations are like assembly line, producing cultural products as if they were loaves of bread.

          2. They may recycle the same tired images and themes over and over again because they are cheap and have been successful in the past.

      iii. Media production and media consumption are more complex than the kind of "hypodermic need" idea.

          1. Producers cannot churn out exactly the same old images audiences have seen before.

          2. Media consumers are not passive zombies.

              a. Audiences are active and participate in process of making meaning out of our media.

              b. We actively interpret media text.

              c. Encoding/decoding is used to describe the dynamic relationship between how media texts construct messages for us and how people actively and creatively make sense of what they see, hear, or read.

c. Multicultural Voices

      i. Mass media can be more democratic, spreading ownership and consumption of media to more and more people enabling previously voiceless minorities access to connection and visibility.

      ii. Ethnic media markets have grown robustly in the United States in the 21st century.

d. Media Consolidation

      i. Increased control of an increasing variety of media by a smaller and smaller number of companies.

      ii. During the past two decades, media ownership ahs rapidly become concentrated in fewer and fewer hands.

          1. Time and Warner Brothers merged into the world's biggest media company in 1989.

          2. Media consolidation raises fears about the access to the diverse sources of news and opinions that citizen in a democracy need to make informed decisions about how to vote and how to live.

          3. Journalistic integrity is another concern stemming from corporate media conglomeration.

e. The importance of Advertising

      i. The purpose of advertising is to convince prospective consumers that they want or need a product.

      ii. Advertising is an engine of media production; most media depend on advertising to survive and profit.

f. Celebrities

      i. Actors and singers are among the most common mass media products.

      ii. Mass media created celebrity.

          1. Celebrities are not necessarily famous because of their talent or accomplishments, but because they appear so often in mass media texts that audiences feel that they know them personally.

          2. Celebrities are neither friend nor stranger, they are "intimate strangers."

III. Consuming Media, Creating Identity

a. Consumers have five broad goals in consumption.

      i. Surveillance, to find out what the world is like.

    ii. Decision making, to acquire enough information on a subject to make a decision.

    iii. Aesthetics.

    iv. Diversion.

    v. Identity.

  b. There is no single, definitive meaning in media texts.

    i. Readers and viewers interpret what they see in different ways.

    ii. John Fiske suggests three possible types of readings.

      1. Dominant/hegemonic.

      2. Ironic.

      3. Oppositional/resistant.

  c. We never consume media in a vacuum.

    i. We consume media texts within an interpretative community.

    ii. Your friends, school, and family all represent interpretative communities.

    iii. These communities produce fans.

      1. A fan is someone who finds significant personal meaning through allegiance to a larger social group.

      2. Fandom is a public affiliation, not just a private love.

IV. Regulating Media

  a. The fact that the media can be both more and less democratic at the same time means that eventually media will encounter government regulation.

    i. Currently there are laws that attempt to prevent the concentration of media in one company's hands.

    ii. The other way in which the media is regulated has to do with the effects of media consumption on consumers.

      1. Violence.

      2. Sexually explicit acts.

    iii. Worries about media consumption by children has come in two forms.

      1. One argument is that media incite or create violence because children are presumed to be highly impressionable.

      2. The other is that children are not constitutionally ably to handle "mature" themes.

    iv. All media are censored- the question is not whether or not there is censorship, but rather what should be censored and why.

    v. With each new medium, there is renewed concern about controlling the harmful effects of its content.

V. Globalization of the Media

  a. American movies were being shown around the world as early as the 1920s.

    i. The Simpsons is broadcast is Central and South America, Europe, South Africa, Israel, Turkey, Japan, South Asia, and Australia.

    ii. In China the most popular programs are Friends and Seinfeld.

  b. The mass media have become truly global n nature.

    i. CNN broadcast via 23 satellites to more than 212 countries and territories in all corners of the globe.

    ii. The Internet is growing more global every day, allowing millions of users from all over the world to come online to seek and share information, post opinions, and shop for items previously available only to those who physically traveled to other countries.

    iii. Global village is the term used to describe an environment in which people everywhere could make their voices hear to one another.

  c. What is Media Globalization?

    i. Media globalization has two main concerns.

      1. There is the technological innovation that allows us to communicate instantaneously over vast distance.

      2. There are also concerns about the cultural products that are available around the world.

      ii.   Both media production and consumption are strongly oriented toward the wealthier members of the world's population.

   d. Cultural Imperialism

      i.   Imperialism is the economic control of one country by another.

      ii.   Cultural imperialism is cultural control of one country by another.

          1.   The overwhelming majority of music in the global marketplace is sung in English.

          2.   The cultural imperialism thesis holds that this kind of Western media dominance will shape all the cultures of the world and ensure their Westernization.

VI.   Media in the 21 Century: New Media, New Voices

   a. Developments such as satellite TV and the Internet have allowed local groups to develop a voice that they never had before.

   b. New media today are helping other cultures to preserve the local and help "alternative" voices to be heard.

   c. Media both unite and fragment us; they both marginalize and free us.

Chapter Summary

- Media are the way that we communicate with each other and mass media are ways to communicate with a vast number of people at the same time, usually over a great distance.
- There are several different types of mass media including print media, magazines and newspapers, blogs, radios, movies, televisions, video games, and the internet.
- We now live in a society that is saturated by the media.
- Mass media are characterized by industrial patterns such as hierarchy and bureaucracy.
- Cultural industries are the mass production of cultural products that are offered for consumption making movie studios and radio stations like assembly lines.
- Media consumers are not passive zombies; instead audiences are active and participate in the process of making meaning out of our media.
- Stuart Hall coined the term encoding/decoding to capture this dynamic relationship between how media texts construct messages for us and how, at the same time, people actively and creatively make sense of what they see, hear, and read.
- Mass media enables people who were previously voiceless to access to connection and visibility.
- Media consolidation refers to the increase control of an increasing variety of media by a smaller and smaller number of companies and now huge conglomerates own or hold large stakes in a variety of media today.
- Advertising is an important aspect of media since most media depend on it to survive and profit.
- Mass media created celebrity because it now brings people into our homes every week making people famous not because of their talent or accomplishments, but because they appear so often in mass media texts that audiences feel that they know them personally.
- It is largely through our media consumption that we know who we are and were we fit in society.
- There are five broad goals in consumption: surveillance, decision making, aesthetics, diversion, and identity.
- We do not consume media in a vacuum; instead we consume it within an interpretive community that guides our interpretation and convey the preferred meanings of mass media texts.
- Currently there are laws that attempt to prevent the concentration of media in one company's hands and the other way in which the media is regulated has to do with the effects of media consumption on consumers.
- The mass media has become global in nature and there are two main concerns about this: 1) the technological innovation that allows us to communicate instantaneously over vast distance and 2) the cultural products that are available around the world.
- Cultural imperialism is the cultural control of one country by another and this thesis holds that Western media dominance, driven by the relentless desire for profits, will shape all the cultures of the world and ensure their Westernization.
- Developments such as satellite TV and the Internet have allowed local groups to develop a voice that hey never had before, no matter how strictly local governments may control media access.

Learning Objectives

After completing the reading of Chapter 9, you should be able to answer the following objectives.

- Define media and mass media.
- Know the different types of media and their history.
- Understand the convergence of media.
- Discuss media production and consumption.
- Know what cultural industries are and how they promote old-fashioned, oppressive ideologies.
- Explain how mass media has become a voice for minorities.
- Define media consolidation and give an example.
- Know why advertising is important to the mass media.
- Discuss how the mass media created celebrities and know why celebrities are famous.
- List the five broad goals for media consumption.
- Discuss the three possible types of readings of media: dominant/hegemonic, ironic, oppositional/resistant.

- Define interpretive community and discuss how they guide our interpretations of mass media texts.
- Discuss fans and how they show allegiance.
- Explain how the government regulates media in terms of the concentration of media in one company's hands and the effects of media consumption on consumers.
- Know what media globalization is.
- Define cultural imperialism and discuss why the cultural imperialism thesis is concerned with Western dominance.

Key Terms

Blog: an online personal journal or diary where an author can air his or her opinions directly to audiences.

Cultural imperialism: the cultural control of one country by another.

Culture industries: mass production of cultural products that are offered for consumption.

Encoding/Decoding: the dynamic relationship between how media texts construct messages for use and how, at the same time, people actively and creatively make sense of what they see, hear, and read.

Fan: someone who finds significant personal meaning through allegiance to a larger social group.

Global village: describes the environment in which people everywhere could make their voices heard to one another.

Interpretive community: the social groups that we understand media within and with whom we share certain strategies for interpreting and using media content.

Mass media: ways to communicate with vast numbers of people at the same time, usually over great distances.

Media: the ways that we communicate with each other.

Media text: words, images, and/or sounds.

Media consolidation: increased control of an increasing variety of media by a smaller and smaller number of companies.

Key People

John Fiske: suggested three possible types of readings of media texts.

Stuart Hall: coined the term encoding/decoding.

Additional Learning with MySocLab

Read

Trying to Elude The Google Grasp (pg 607)

The computer chip, monitor, and keyboard have become iconic symbols of the post-industrial economy. So much of our daily lives depends upon and often revolves around the use of computer technology.

Dear Campaign Diary: Seizing the Day, Online (pg 591)

The article discusses the internet and blogs used during the Gubernatorial race in California after the recall of governor Gray Davis.

Explore

Ownership of Television sets worldwide (pg 592)

The map gives a visual representation of the number of television sets owned per 1,000 people.

Listen

Social Life vs. Cyber Life (pg 595)

Host Bob Edwards talks with NPR's Brooke Gladstone about a new Stanford University study finding that some people are spending more time online and less time interacting with people.

Love Billboard: by Jim Henslin (pg 610)

Discusses how Western ideas are starting to infiltrate India's culture through the media.

Practice Test

After completing the practice test, check your answers in the Answer Key of this Study Guide.

Multiple Choice Questions

1. What is the term used to refer to the ways we communicate with a vast number of people at the same time?
   a. Media
   b. Mass media
   c. Print media
   d. Telecommunications

2. What was the first type of mass media?
   a. Print
   b. Blogs
   c. Radio
   d. Internet

3. Which country has the largest movie industry?
   a. United States
   b. Japan
   c. Nigeria
   d. South Africa

4. What percentage of people in Columbia access the internet?
   a. 70 percent
   b. 16 percent
   c. 11 percent
   d. 7 percent

5. The term used to describe a small number of companies control virtually all of the media is:
   a. media consolidation.
   b. media conglomeration.
   c. media industry.
   d. media production

6. Which of the following is not a reason as to why advertising is so important to the media?
   a. It allows the media to make a profit
   b. Ads pay for the cost of production
   c. The media depend on ads to survive
   d. Advertisers reproduce cultural values

7. Celebrities become famous because:
   a. of their talent.
   b. they have accomplished great things.
   c. they appear often in media texts.
   d. people become friends with them.

8. Which is not included in one of the five broad goals of consumers when viewing media?
   a. Surveillance
   b. Diversion
   c. Regularity
   d. Aesthetics

9. Viewers interpret what they see in different ways. Which of the following is not one of those according to John Fiske?
    a. Dominant/hegemonic
    b. Ironic
    c. Oppositional/resistant
    d. Fondness/flexibility

10. In what type of community do we consume media texts within?
    a. Consolidated
    b. Interpretive
    c. Personal
    d. Private

11. A fan is someone who:
    a. attends pep rallies.
    b. spends all of their money on fan clubs and their idols merchandise.
    c. knows all the personal details about another person in the media.
    d. finds significant personal meaning through allegiance to a larger social group.

12. When did American movies start being shown around the world?
    a. 1990s
    b. 1970s
    c. 1940s
    d. 1920s

13. Which of the following is a major concern of media globalization?
    a. Imperialism
    b. Consolidation
    c. Cultural Imperialism
    d. Conglomeration

14. Which country between 1990 and 1995 important the highest percentage of movies?
    a. Russia
    b. Japan
    c. Sweden
    d. Ethiopia

15. Which print media has been hardest hit by the development of new media?
    a. Books
    b. Newspapers
    c. Magazines
    d. Comic books

16. _____ is the language that is most often used in blogs.
    a. English
    b. Japanese
    c. Chinese
    d. Spanish

17. How many television sets does the average American home have today?
    a. 4
    b. 3
    c. 2
    d. 1

18. When media appear simultaneously together we say that media are:
    a. consolidating.
    b. integrating.
    c. converging.
    d. combining.

19. Which racial/ethnic still makes up the majority of prime time characters?
    a. Asian American
    b. Hispanic
    c. African American
    d. White

20. When minorities are shown in media text, they are presented:
    a. in ways that sometimes reinforce negative stereotypes.
    b. in high status positions.
    c. more positively than white characters.
    d. in ways that always reinforce negative stereotypes.

21. What concept is helpful in explaining why mass media promote old-fashioned, even oppressive ideology?
    a. Culture oppression
    b. Culture diversity
    c. Culture industries
    d. Culture relativism

22. Which of the following is not a concern of consolidation of the media?
    a. Homogenized content
    b. Journalistic integrity
    c. The separation of news
    d. What gets produced

23. Marshall McLuhan coined the term _____ to describe an environment in which people everywhere could make their voices heard to one another.
    a. Global economy
    b. Global village
    c. Global world
    d. Global imperialism

24. Research shows that the attitudes and behaviors of men were changed when they viewed which of the following?
    a. Violent media
    b. Pornographic media
    c. Both violent and pornographic media together
    d. Motocross racing media

25. Recent consolidation of media ownership has caused:
    a. diversification of information available to the general public.
    b. a more balanced and fair reporting system on news programs.
    c. profit sharing in all sectors of media.
    d. a narrowing of attitudes and opinions available to the general public.

True/False Questions

True   False   1. Mass media allows us to communicate with a vast number of people at the same time over a great distance.

True   False   2. Young males are the primary players of online poker.

True   False   3. The media represents all ethnic groups proportionately.

True   False   4. Media consumers participate in the process of making meaning out of media.

True   False   5. During the past two decades, media ownership has become less concentrated with more owners of different types of media.

True   False   6. Celebrities gain their fame through their talents and accomplishments.

True   False   7. Watching violence in the media increases people's tendencies towards violence.

True   False   8. Censorship laws reflect the interests of who is in power to declare them.

True   False   9. Cultural imperialism is the economic control of one country by another.

True   False   10. The cultural imperialism thesis holds that Western media dominance will shape all the cultures of the world and ensure their Westernization.

Fill-in-the-Blank Questions

1. The _____ has not only transformed mass media but is a new form of mass media in its own right.

2. We actively interpret the words, images, and/or sounds that are referred to as the _____.

3. An _____ is a group that guide interpretation and convey the preferred meaning of mass media texts.

4. Someone who finds significant personal meaning through allegiance to a larger social group is called a _____.

5. Today, the average American home has more _____ than people.

6. _____ mass produce cultural products that are offered for consumption.

7. People who are famous not because of their talent or accomplishments, but because they appear so often in mass media texts that audiences feel that they know them personally are _____.

8. _____ is cultural control of one country by another.

9. Marshall McLuhan coined the term _____ to describes the environment in which people everywhere could make their voices heard to one another.

10. We refer to the increased control of an increasing variety of media by a smaller and smaller number of companies as _____.

Essay Questions

1. What are the different types of mass media and how have they changed throughout history?

2. What are the five broad goals in media consumption? Describe in detail.

3. What is media globalization and why is cultural imperialism a concern?

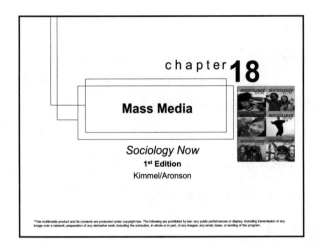

chapter **18**

Mass Media

Sociology Now
1st Edition
Kimmel/Aronson

This multimedia product and its contents are protected under copyright law. The following are prohibited by law: any public performances or display, including transmission of any image over a network; preparation of any derivative work, including the extraction, in whole or in part, of any images; any rental, lease, or lending of the program.

What Are the Mass Media?

- **media** (plural of medium)
  - ways of communicating with each other
- **mass media**
  - press, radio, television, computer

- Types of Mass Media
  - **Print Media**
    - printing press – 8th century China, 15th century Europe
    - newspapers and magazines

Copyright © Allyn & Bacon 2009

What Are the Mass Media?

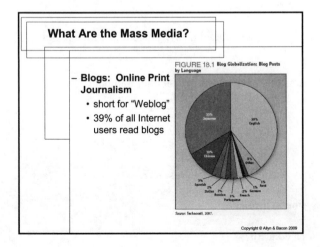

- **Blogs: Online Print Journalism**
  - short for "Weblog"
  - 39% of all Internet users read blogs

FIGURE 18.1 **Blog Globalization: Blog Posts by Language**

Source: Technorati, 2007.

Copyright © Allyn & Bacon 2009

What Are the Mass Media?

- **Radio, Movies and Television**
  - average U.S. households has more television sets than people
  - world is brought closer tog

- **Games, Gambling, and Porn: Guy Media**
  - replacement of social interaction (boys) *versus*
  - changing patterns of social interaction with others)

Copyright © Allyn & Bacon 2009

What Are the Mass Media?

- **The Internet**
  - change from computer as business tool to mass medium
  - Internet has transformed mass media and is a new form
  - increased social isolation or new form of "community"?

Copyright © Allyn & Bacon 2009

What Are the Mass Media?

- **Saturation and Convergence: The Sociology of Media**
  - the average American has:
    - 3 TVs
    - 1.8 VCRs
    - 3.1 radios
    - 2.6 tape players
    - 2.1 CD players
    - 1.4 video game players
  - analysts believe we are moving towards one machine that will serve as reception point for all media

Copyright © Allyn & Bacon 2009

Media Production and Consumption

- How do the media produce what they produce?
- For Whom?
- What is the relationship between the producers and the audience?
- How are audiences created and maintained?

- **Culture Industries**
  - hierarchy and bureaucracy
  - aesthetical sensibility
  - **culture industries**

Media Production and Consumption

- "the logic of safety" (Gitlin)
- some mass media producers do have artistic vision, challenge preconceptions, stereotypes, and ideologies
- **media text**
- **encoding/decoding**

- **Multicultural Voices**
  - mass media as tool to pass along cultural traditions
  - gay youth connections

Media Production and Consumption

- **Media Consolidation**
  - **media consolidation**
    - smaller number of companies
    - huge conglomerates
    - concern over journalistic integrity

- **The Importance of Advertising**
  - association with product and desirable qualities/activities
  - engine of media production
  - relationship between producers and consumers?

Media Production and Consumption

- **Celebrities**
  - celebrity stories sell magazines and products
  - mass media created celebrity
  - paradoxical relationship between celebrity and audience

Consuming Media, Creating Identity

- goals of consumption of media
  - *Surveillance*
  - *Decision making*
  - *Aesthetics*
  - *Diversion*
  - *Identity*

  - reading media texts (**Fiske**)
    - *Dominant/hegemonic*
    - *Ironic*
    - *Oppositional/resistant*
  - **interpretive community**
  - **fan**

Regulating Media

  - media creates access AND concentrates power
  - no causal link between violent media and long-term violent behavior
  - can children handle "mature" themes?
  - censorship raises questions about context more so than content

Globalization and the Media

- – global village
- **What is Media Globalization?**
  - – instant communication over vast distances
  - – availability of cultural products
- **Cultural Imperialism**
  - – cultural control of one country over another
- **Media in the 21st Century: New Media, New Voices**

Globalization and the Media

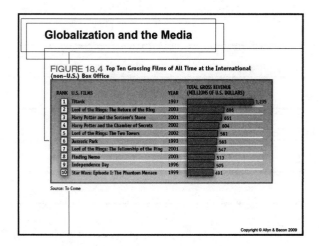

FIGURE 18.4 Top Ten Grossing Films of All Time at the International (non–U.S.) Box Office

RANK	U.S. FILMS	YEAR	TOTAL GROSS REVENUE (MILLIONS OF U.S. DOLLARS)
1	Titanic	1997	1,235
2	Lord of the Rings: The Return of the King	2003	696
3	Harry Potter and the Sorcerer's Stone	2001	651
4	Harry Potter and the Chamber of Secrets	2002	604
5	Lord of the Rings: The Two Towers	2002	581
6	Jurassic Park	1993	563
7	Lord of the Rings: The Fellowship of the Ring	2001	547
8	Finding Nemo	2003	513
9	Independence Day	1996	505
10	Star Wars: Episode I: The Phantom Menace	1999	491

Source: To Come

What Does America Think?

18.1 **Confidence in Press**

These are actual survey data from the General Social Survey, 2004.

As far as the people running the press are concerned, would you say you have a great deal of confidence, only some confidence, or hardly any confidence at all in them? The GSS survey results for 2004 indicate that almost 44 percent of the population has hardly any confidence in the press. Almost half of respondents had only some confidence in the press. Those in the upper class were most likely to reporting having a great deal of confidence in the press and at the same time were also the group most likely to report having very little confidence in the press. The percentage of respondents reporting confidence in the press has steadily declined since 1972 for all social class categories.

CRITICAL THINKING | DISCUSSION QUESTION

1. Take a good look at the social class differences in responses. They are complex. How do you explain them?

What Does America Think?

18.2 Free Press

These are actual survey data from the General Social Survey, 2002.

Which of these three statements comes closest to your feelings about balancing freedom of the press and the right to privacy? In the 2000 General Social Survey, just over 20 percent of respondents felt there should complete freedom of the press, even if the press sometimes invades the privacy of public figures. Sixty-four percent of the respondents felt the press should develop a code of ethics to keep it from invading the privacy of public figures. Almost 15 percent of respondents thought the government should keep the press from printing stories that invade the privacy of public figures. Respondents who identified as lower class were least likely to support complete freedom of the press.

CRITICAL THINKING | DISCUSSION QUESTION

1. Respondents in the middle class were least likely to favor government censoring of the press, while those in the lower class were most likely to favor it. How do you explain these social class differences?

What Does America Think?

➤ Go to this website to look further at the data. You can run your own statistics and crosstabs here: **http://sda.berkeley.edu/cgi-bin/hsda?harcsda+gss04**

REFERENCES: Davis, James A., Tom W. Smith, and Peter V. Marsden. General Social Surveys 1972–2004: [Cumulative file] [Computer file]. 2nd ICPSR version. Chicago, IL: National Opinion Research Center [producer], 2005; Storrs, CT: Roper Center for Public Opinion Research, University of Connecticut; Ann Arbor, MI: Inter-University Consortium for Political and Social Research; Berkeley, CA: Computer-Assisted Survey Methods Program, University of California [distributors], 2005.

Chapter 19
Sociology of Environments: The Natural, Physical, and Human Worlds

Chapter Outline

   I.   The Human Environment
- a. Humans are a social species.
- b. Demography is the scientific study of human populations and one of the oldest and most popular branches of sociology.
- c. Being Born
  - i. Demographers use two birth measurements.
    1. Fertility- the number of children that a woman has.
    2. Fecundity- the maximum number of children that she could possibly have.
  - ii. Fertility rate is the number of children that would be born to each woman if she lived through her childbearing years with the average fertility of her age group.
    1. Poor countries usually have a fertility rate of four or more.
    2. Rich countries usually have a fertility rate of less than two.
- d. Dying
  - i. The mortality rate is the number of deaths per year for every thousand people.
    1. In the United States the mortality rate is 8.25.
    2. Poor nations can have either higher or lower mortality rates.
  - ii. Life expectancy is the average number of years a person can expect to live.
  - iii. The infant mortality rate is the number of deaths per year in each thousand infants up to one year old.
    1. It is extremely low in high-income nations.
    2. The infant mortality rate serves as a proxy for the overall health of the country.
- e. Moving In, Moving Out
  - i. Demographers are interested in physical movements, as people emigrate and immigrate.
    1. Most wealthy countries have sizeable populations of voluntary immigrants.
    2. Over 46 million people living today emigrated form their home territory involuntarily.
    3. Voluntary migrants usually have two sets of motives for their move.
       - a. Reasons they want to leave their home territory in the first place.
       - b. Reasons they want to settle in this particular territory.
  - ii. There have been four major flows of immigration in modern history.
    1. Between 1500 and 1800 Europeans began to establish colonial empires around the world.
    2. About the same time Europeans transported over 11,000,000 East and West Africans to their New World colonies in North and South America and the Caribbean to work as slaves.
    3. Beginning about 1800, East Asians emigrate from China to major cities in the United States, Latin America, Africa, and the Middle East.
    4. Between 1880 and 1920, millions of Southern and Eastern Europeans emigrated as they faced increasing political and economic strife as their countries modernized.
- f. Studying Immigration
  - i. Immigration rate is the number of people entering a territory each year for every thousand of the population.
  - ii. Emigration rate is the number of people leaving per thousand.
  - iii. Internal migration means moving from one region to another within a territory.
- g. Population Composition
  - i. This is the comparative numbers of men and women and various age groups.

1. The male to female ration is never 50:50.
2. After birth, the ratio of men to women decreases in every age group because men are more likely to die in accidents, warfare, and of certain diseases.
    ii. The distribution of people of different age groups can be best represented by a graph called a population pyramid.
    1. Poor countries have expansive pyramids.
    2. Rich countries have constrictive pyramids.
    3. A few countries have stationary pyramids.
    iii. Demographers use population blocks to determine current and future social service needs of society.
II. Population Growth
    a. Cities and countries can grow or shrink for a variety of reasons: natural population increase, immigration and emigration, and changing boundary lines when territories are annexed of lost.
    b. How High Can It Go?
        i. Malthusian theory held that the population would increase by geometric progression, doubling in each generation.
        ii. Zero population growth is where the number of births does not exceed the number of deaths.
    c. Demographic Transition
        i. Demographic Transition theory holds that population and technology spur each other's development.
        1. Initial stage.
        2. Transitional growth stage.
        3. Incipient decline stage.
        ii. This theory has been criticized for two reasons.
        1. It always works in the same direction.
        2. It is not technology that causes a decrease in mortality rate, but rather the changes in personal and public health practices.
    d. Decreasing the Rate of Flow
        i. A number of organizations and nations have come together to try to decrease the population explosion.
        ii. Several countries have started protocols intended to decrease population.
III. The Urban Environment
    a. The City: Ancient to Modern
        i. Most ancient cities grew up along major rivers, where enough food could be produced to feed a large nonfarming population.
        ii. The number of large cities stayed about the same throughout the Middle Ages and Renaissance.
        iii. When the Industrial Revolution began around 1750, agricultural productivity increased exponentially.
        iv. Where urbanization is high, people moving from rural areas have their choice of many cities, but where urbanization is low, there are fewer choices.
        1. Poor countries with a high rural population are more likely to have megacities.
        2. Over half of the world's 40 megacities are located in poor nations.
        v. Population density is a measure of how crowded a city feels.
        1. Older cities will have a larger population density, because they were constructed before the automobile allowed cities to spread out.
        2. The more recently the city was founded the lower the population density.
    b. The Countryside
        i. The U.S. Census Bureau used to define urban as living in an incorporated area with a population of 2,500 or more.
        1. So many people live in unincorporated areas adjacent to big cities or small town that have been engulfed by big cities, that many demographers suggest a change from a simple dichotomy to a rural-urban continuum.

        2.   By using the continuum, 93.9 percent of the U.S. population was rural in 1800, 60.4 percent in 1900, and 19 percent in 2000.

     ii.   The decline of the rural population can be attributed to the decline of farm jobs, a move into the cities, and an expansion of the cities.

    iii.   Globalization increasingly impoverishes the countryside.

  c.   Suburbs

      i.   The White middle class began moving out of the cities altogether, into outlying areas called suburbs, where their houses were separate from the others, with front and back years, just like upper-class estates.

     ii.   The first mass-produced suburb opened in an unincorporated area on Long Island in 1951.

        1.   During the 1960s suburbs grew four times faster than cities due to "white flight."

        2.   Once suburban areas had their own jobs and amenities, they were no longer simply "bedroom communities."

  d.   The Sociology of Commuting: Separate and Unequal

      i.   In 1900 the rich and poor walked to work.

        1.   The automobile arrived and quickly engulfed every other mode of transportation.

        2.   If you were middle class or working class, you drove.

        3.   If you were poor, you took the bus.

     ii.   As more and more jobs moved out of the cities into the suburbs middle-class suburbanites found their commute easier.

  e.   Revitalizing Downtown

      i.   During the 1980s and 1990s, many cities fought back, trying to revitalize their downtowns.

        1.   Somtimes they take over whole downtown neighborhoods, raising the property values so much that poor and even middle-class people could no longer afford to live there.

        2.   Cities annexed the suburbs so they could charge property tax.

     ii.   Suburbs and edge cities are increasing difficult to distinguish from inner cities.

    iii.   As suburbs expanded outward, it was inevitable that hey would meet the suburbs of adjacent cities, until they all combined into one gigantic city, a megalopolis.

        1.   They have enormous structural problems.

        2.   Sociologists worry about the loss of social identity in a megalopolis.

IV.   Sociology and the City

  a.   Many early sociologists were fascinated and appalled by life in cities.

      i.   Ferdinand Töennies theorized that families, village, and perhaps neighborhoods in cities form through gemeinschaft, or commonality.

        1.   They shared common norms, values, and beliefs.

        2.   Cities and states formed through gesellschaft, or "business company."

     ii.   Emile Durkheim took his own look at village and cities and theorized that village life was so much nicer because there was little division of labor.

        1.   Mechanical solidarity- connection based on similarity; they shared norms and values.

        2.   In cities everyone was different and what held them together was organic solidarity- the connection based on interdependence.

    iii.   Georg Simmel worried about the overstimulation of the city environment.

    iv.   Urban analyst Jane Jacobs found that busy streets were not a source of overstimulation.

        1.   Children played there, neighbors sat on stoops to gossip with each other, there was a sense of solidarity and belonging.

        2.   In the suburbs no one knew anyone else and the streets were deserted expect for people hurrying from their cars into their houses.

  b.   Human Ecology

     i. A discipline of the social sciences that looks at he interrelations of human beings within a shared social environment.

     ii. Urbanization

         1. Louis Wirth argued that people lose their kinship ties when they move from villages to cities.

         2. With no kinship ties there is no consensus about what norms should be followed, and even when an act occurs that most people agree is deviant, they cannot rely on informal networks to maintain social control.

     iii. The Urban Village

         1. Herbert Gans found that social networks are about the same size in both the city and the small town.

         2. Gans found five types of people in the city

             a. Cosmopolitans.

             b. Young, single professionals.

             c. Ethnic villagers.

             d. The deprived.

             e. The trapped.

     iv. Concentric Zones

         1. Robert Park and Ernest Burgess studied how human ecology affected the use of urban space in the city.

         2. Cities developed according to "concentric zones" of activity.

c. Global Urbanization

     i. In 2000, 75 percent of the population of Latin American lived in urban areas.

     ii. The gap between rich and poor is more noticeable in these urban centers than anywhere else in the world.

     iii. Many cities around the world have global rather than local ties.

         1. They are command centers not only of their own countries but also of the global economy.

         2. They are more interdependent on each other than on the countries where they happen to be located.

V. The Natural Environment

a. Ecosystems are interdependent systems of organisms and their environment.

     i. Early sociologists often theorized that the social world was a subcategory of the natural world.

     ii. Herbert Spencer argued that biological, social, and psychological, and moral systems are all interrelated.

     iii. After the first few decades of sociological thought, social sciences tended to ignore the environment.

         1. During the 1970s people began to envision Earth not as an infinite space, but as a small, fragile community.

         2. Some sociologists began to criticize the discipline for being too anthropocentric.

b. Energy

     i. The United States is by far the world's largest energy consumer.

     ii. Americans are 5 percent of the world's population but consume at least 25 percent of every type of energy.

c. Vanishing Resources

     i. Globally, forest are being depleted at the rate of one acre per second, depriving the world of a gigantic natural storage capacity for harmful carbon dioxide.

     ii. Deforestation results in the loss of top soil because the cleared land is quick to erode.

     iii. Desertification means that the world is quickly losing ground water.

d. Environmental Threats

     i. The natural environment is not only natural; it is "social" in that here is a constant interaction between the natural and the built environments, between nature and culture.

     ii. Pollution- domestic waste, industrial waste, and agricultural runoff.

        iii. Garbage
            1. In the United States 54.5 percent of our municipal solid waste went into garbage dumps.
            2. Landfills pose two major problems.
                a. Most garbage is not biodegradable.
                b. When the garbage is biodegradable, it degrades into toxic chemicals, which seep into the groundwater and increase water pollution.
        iv. Global Warming
            1. Since the 19th century, the global temperature has increase by about 1.08 degrees Fahrenheit.
            2. Sociologists attempt to calculate the social ramifications of such climate shifts.
    e. The Sociology of Disaster
        i. A disaster is a sudden environmental change that results in a major loss of life and property.
        ii. Kai T. Erikson looked at the human response to a dam that burst and flooded Buffalo Creek in Logan County, West Virginia.
        iii. Eric Klineberg investigated the social conditions that led to and compounded the disaster in 1995, during the week-long heat wave in Chicago that was responsible for over 700 deaths.
VI.   Environments in the 21st Century
    a. If Katrina and its aftermath have taught us anything, it is that we should be prepared.
    b. The connections between the natural world, social life, and the ways that technology shape and transforms both arenas is the heart of sociological investigation.
    c. Nature is nurture- the natural world does not exist expect in relationship to the social and built worlds.

Chapter Summary

- Demography is the scientific study of human populations.
- Demographers are interested in studying fertility, fecundity, fertility rate, mortality rate, life expectancy, emigration, and immigration.
- The immigration rate is the number of people entering a territory for every thousand of the population while the emigration rate is the number of people leaving per thousand. Demographers usually study the changing population by examining the net migration rate.
- The population composition is the comparative number of men and women and various age groups and is represented by population pyramids which can either be expansive pyramids, constrictive pyramids, or stationary pyramids.
- Population growth can be caused by natural population increase, immigration and emigration, and changing boundary lines when territories are annexed or lost.
- The Malthusian theory holds that the population would increase by geometric progression, doubling in each generation, however it fails to foresee cultural trends.
- Demographic transition theory holds that population and technology spur each other's development and there are three stages: initial stage, transitional growth stage, and incipient decline stage.
- The city expanded after the Industrial Revolution, which manufacturing more important than farming and thus the rural population began to decline. Suburbs did not appear until the 1950s when the white middle-class started moving out of the city.
- Töennies theorized that families, villages, and neighborhoods in the city formed through gemeinschaft while cities and states formed through gesellschaft while Durkheim theorized that village life was held together by mechanical solidarity white cities were held together by organic solidarity.
- Human ecology arose as a discipline that looks at the interrelations of human being within a shared social environment.
- Louis Wirth argued that people lose their kinship ties when they move from villages to cities, but Herbert Gans disagreed and found that social networks are about the same size in both the city and the small town.
- Global urbanization was considered a sign of development, a sure sign that the nation was becoming richer and more prosperous, but the gap between the rich is more noticeable in these urban centers than anywhere else in the world.
- Resources are be depleted all the time: forests are being depleted at the rate of one acre per second, deforestation accounts for about 25 percent of all human-made emissions of carbon dioxide, desertification is becoming common in many places, and animal and plant species are endangered or extinct.
- The environmental threats include pollution, garbage, and global warming.
- The connections between the natural world, social life, and the ways that technology shapes and transforms both arenas are at the heart of sociological investigation.

Learning Objectives
After completing the reading of Chapter 9, you should be able to answer the following objectives.

- Understand what demographers study and are primarily concerned with.
- Know what fertility, fecundity, fertility rate, mortality rate, life expectancy, and infant mortality rate are.
- Discuss the differences between emigration and immigration and the reasons for migrating.
- Define immigration rate, emigration rate, net migration rate, and internal migration.
- Understand population composition and how the different types of population pyramids illustrate the population.
- Explain how cities and countries' populations grow or shrink.
- Explain the Malthusian theory and how it failed to foresee the cultural trends that would influence population growth.
- Discuss the demographic transition theory and its three stages.
- Discuss the differences between the city, countryside, and suburbs.
- Define gentrification and megalopolis.
- Discuss Töennies gemeischaft and gesellschaft and Durkheim's mechanical and organic solidarity.

- Define human ecology.
- Explain why Louis Wirth though that people would lose kinship ties when they moved to cities.
- List the different types of people Herbert Gans found that live in the city.
- Know the five concentric zones of the city proposed by Robert Park and Ernest Burgess and who resides in each.
- Discuss global urbanization and its impact on poverty.
- Define ecosystems.
- Know the different vanishing resources and why they are vanishing.
- Discuss the threats to the environment: pollution, garbage, and global warming.
- Understand what the sociology of disaster studies.

Key Terms

Demographic transition theory: the population and technology spur each other's development

Demography: scientific study of human population and one of the oldest and most popular branches of sociology.

Ecosystems: interdependent systems of organisms and their environment.

Emigration rate: the number of people leaving a territory each year for every thousand of the population.

Fecundity: maximum number of children that a woman could possibly have.

Fertility: the number of children that a woman has.

Fertility rate: number of children that would be born to each woman if she lived through her childbearing years with the average fertility of her age group.

Gentrification: a population taking over whole neighborhoods, raising the property values so much that poor and even middle-class people can no longer afford to live there.

Human ecology: discipline of the social science that looks at the interrelations of human beings within a shared social environment.

Immigration rate: the number of people entering a territory each year for every thousand of the population.

Infant mortality rate: the number of death per year in each thousand infants up to one year old.

Internal migration: moving from one region to another within a territory.

Life expectancy: the average number of years a person can expect to live.

Malthusian theory: the population would increase by geometric progression, doubling in each generation.

Mechanical solidarity: connection based on similarities.

Megalopolis: suburban expansion that would meet up with suburbs of adjacent cities, until they all combine into one gigantic city.

Mortality rate: the number of deaths per year for every thousand people.

Natural population increase: the number of births every year subtracted by the number of deaths.

Net migration rate: the difference between the immigration and emigration rates in a given year.

Organic solidarity: connections based on interdependence.

Population composition: comparative numbers of men and women and various age groups.

Population density: number of people per square mile or kilometer.

Population pyramid: distribution of people of different age groups in which five- or ten-year age groups are shown as different-sized bars.

Suburbs: houses are separate from others, with front and back yards.

Zero population growth: the number of births every year is the same as the number of deaths.

Key People

Emile Durkheim: used the term mechanic solidarity and organic solidarity to compare cities and villages.

Paul Ehrlich: argued that even a moderate percent population increase would soon spin out of control

Herbert Gans: found five types of people living in the city.

Frank Notestein: argued that population growth is tied to technological development.

Ferdinand Töennies: used the term gemeinschaft to describe how families, villages, and neighborhoods formed and gesellschaft to describe how cities and states formed.

Additional Learning with MySoc Lab

Read:

Meager Harvests in Africa Leave Millions at the Edge of Starvation (pg 641)
The anti-natalist perspective on population growth suggests that populations grow faster than a society's ability to grow food. Swarns discusses the problems in Malawi's food shortages.
Pataki Orders Strict Controls on Pollution in Rebuilding (pg 644)
For centuries, the surge of industrialization and modernization has left environmental destruction in its wake. Not until recently have politicians, business leaders, and citizens made environmental balance their priority.

Explore

Population Growth (pg 625)
The chart illustrates the population growth for the United States and discusses the population distribution and change.
Web Activity: Social Change and the Environment (pg 645)
Read the article "Greenhouse gases are air pollutants under the Clean Air Act" and "Consequences of Global Warming" to learn more about global warming and it affects. You will then answer a series of questions relating to both articles.
Hazardous Waste Sites (pg 646)
The interactive map allows the user to see which states have the highest number of hazardous waste sites.

Listen

Global Warming (pg 644)
A new study says soot from fires, smokestacks and diesel engines may account for as much as a quarter of all global warming. The study also suggests soot has hastened the melting of glaciers and ice throughout the northern hemisphere. The findings suggest climate change might be slowed through relatively simple measures.

Visualize

Suburban Growth (pg 633)

The chart lays out the factors that promote suburban growth.

Largest Cities (pg 639)

The interactive map allows the user to see where the ten largest cities in the world are located.

Energy (pg 642)

The table shows the United States and World Energy Consumption between 1960 and 1994.

Practice Test

After completing the practice test, check your answers in the Answer Key of this Study Guide.

Multiple Choice Questions

1. Which region of the world has the highest infant mortality rate?
    a. North America
    b. Sub-Saharan Africa
    c. Australia
    d. Eastern Europe

2. Poor countries tend to have what type of population pyramid?
    a. Expansive
    b. Constrictive
    c. Stationary
    d. None of the above

3. The Demographic transition theory has three stages, which is not one of them?
    a. Initial stage
    b. Transitional growth stage
    c. Incipient decline stage
    d. Gentrification stage

4. According to Park and Burgess, cities developed according to concentric zones. Which of these zones consisted of the middle and upper-class residential areas?
    a. Zone 1
    b. Zone 2
    c. Zone 3
    d. Zone 4

5. Which environmental threat is concentrated in urban areas as the result of carbon monoxide, sulfur dioxide, and nitrogen oxide form cars, heater, and industrial processes?
    a. Domestic waste
    b. Air pollution
    c. Agricultural runoff
    d. Industrial waste.

6. Of the following, which may contribute to higher mortality rates?
    a. War
    b. Famine
    c. Disease
    d. All of the above

7. What is the scientific study of human populations?
    a. Demography
    b. Fertility
    c. Immigration
    d. Population composition

8. What percentage of the population growth is taking place in poor countries?
    a. 50 percent
    b. 63 percent
    c. 85percent
    d. 96 percent

9. In which country do women have to apply for "pregnancy permits?"
    a. India
    b. United States
    c. China
    d. Somalia

10. The three stage historical process of population growth is known as:
    a. the Malthusian theory.
    b. the demographic transition theory.
    c. the growth curve theory.
    d. the demographic transition theory.

11. The annual number of deaths per 1,000 population is the:
    a. life expectancy rate.
    b. fertility rate.
    c. mortality rate.
    d. fecundity rate.

12. What factor may contribute to someone's decision to emigrate?
    a. A good economy
    b. Civil stability
    c. Educational opportunities
    d. Political oppression

13. What is a megacity?
    a. A city of 10 million or more
    b. A city of 5 million or more
    c. A city that is at the center of a megalopolis
    d. A central city with at least 50,000 people and the urbanized area linked to it.

14. Which of the following is not a factor in the declining rural population?
    a. The decline of farming jobs
    b. Immigration to the cities for better economic opportunities
    c. The expansion of cities into the countryside
    d. The strong communities and kinships that are offered in the city.

15. Who first proposed the terms mechanical and organic solidarity?
    a. Emile Durkheim
    b. Ferdinand Töennies
    c. Robert Redfield
    d. Georg Simmel

16. Louis Wirth argued that cities undermine:
    a. economy and politics.
    b. religion.
    c. kinship ties.
    d. crime rates.

17. Georg Simmel worried about the oversimulation of the city environment that would cause people to:
    a. pay attention to everything going on in the city.
    b. pay attention to only those things which you thought were important.
    c. pay attention to the strangers passing on the street.
    d. pay attention to nothing going on in the city.

18. Which is not one of the types of people Herbert Gans found that lived in the city?
    a. Ethnic villagers
    b. The trapped
    c. Cosmopolitans
    d. The privileged

19. What is global urbanization?
    a. Movement from the countryside to major metropolitan areas in the United States.
    b. Large cities in the world are command centers not only of their own countries but also of the global economy.
    c. Movement of people from the United States oversees to megacities.
    d. The movement of people from the cities to the suburbs.

20. _____ are interdependent systems of organisms and their environment.
    a. Ecology
    b. Ecosystems
    c. Global cities
    d. Environmentalism

21. Which country is the world's largest energy consumer?
    a. United States
    b. Great Britain
    c. Norway
    d. Kuwait

22. In general, what is the relationship between average income level and population increase for countries in the world?
    a. The higher the average income, the faster the population increases
    b. All nations are increasing at about the same rate
    c. The lower the average income, the faster the population increases
    d. There is no clear pattern

23. In the initial stage of demographic transition theory, population:
    a. increase slowly due to high birth and death rates..
    b. increase rapidly due to better medical care.
    c. increase rapidly due to high birth rates and low death rates.
    d. decrease slowly due to high death rates.

24. What percent of the world's megacities are located in poor nations?
    a. less than 10 percent
    b. approximately 30 percent
    c. 40 percent
    d. more than 50 percent

25. Which high-income nation has the highest number of births per 1,000 population?
    a. Germany
    b. Italy
    c. United States
    d. Britain

True/False Questions

True   False   1. Fertility refers to the maximum number of children a woman could possibly have.

True   False   2. AIDS is a cause of significant decline in population growth in many low-income nations.

True   False   3. The emigration rate is the number of people leaving a territory each year for every thousand of the population.

True   False   4. The male to female ratio is never 50:50.

True   False   5. Population pyramids can only be expansive pyramids.

True   False   6. The Malthusian theory holds that the population and technology spur each other's development.

True   False   7. Demographers have suggested using a rural-urban continuum instead of the simple urban/rural dichotomy use in their research.

True   False   8. Gentrification happens when people take over whole downtown neighborhoods and raise property values so much that poor and even middle-class people can no longer afford to live there.

True   False   9. Mechanical solidarity refers to a connection that is based on similarities.

True   False   10. Urbanization has shown that nations were becoming richer and more prosperous.

Fill-in-the-Blank Questions

1. _____ is the number of children that would be born to each woman if she lived through her childbearing years with the average fertility of her age group.

2. The _____ rate is the number of people entering a territory each year for every thousand of the population.

3. The distribution of people of different age groups can best be represented by a graph called a _____ .

4. According to the _____ , the population and technology spur each other's development.

5. According to Emile Durkheim, cities are held together by _____ .

6. _____ has caused the Earth's temperature to rise about 1.08 degrees Fahrenheit since the 19th century.

7. The natural environment is not only natural, it is _____ in that there is constant interaction between the natural and the built environment.

8. Families, villages, and neighborhoods in cities are formed through _____ , or commonality according to Ferdinand Töennies.

9. Where the number of births does not exceed the number of deaths there is _____ .

10. _____ is the average number of years a person can expect to live.

Essay Questions

1. State the position of the Malthusian theory and the Demographic transition theory. Discuss which view you thin is more accurate, based on the information provided about each theory.

2. What were the four major flows of immigration in modern history? Where were the immigrants from, where did the move to, and what were their reasons for immigrating?

3. How is the natural environment threatened by human-created problems?

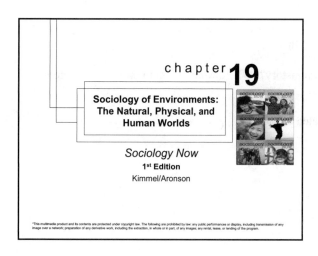

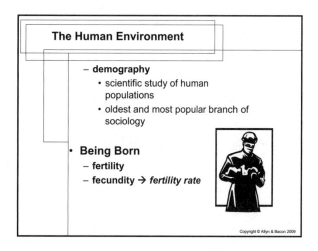

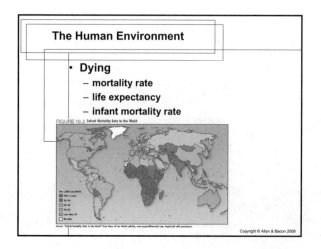

The Human Environment

- **Moving In, Moving Out**
  - *emigrating* → leaving
  - *immigrating* → arriving
    - Involuntary
    - Voluntary
      - *Push*
      - *Pull*

Copyright © Allyn & Bacon 2009

Population Growth

- **Studying Immigration**
  - **immigration** and **emigration rate**
  - **internal migration**
    - average American moves 11 times during his or her life
    - city, county, state, region

TABLE 19.1   – "Rust Belt" to "Sun Belt"

Biggest Population Gains and Losses, 2000–2004			
GAINS		LOSSES	
Riverside–San Bernardino, CA	325,842	New York, NY	−844,058
Phoenix, AZ	194,392	Los Angeles, CA	−471,118
Las Vegas, NV	168,463	Chicago, IL	−252,997
Tampa, FL	145,580	San Francisco, CA	−243,934
Atlanta, GA	126,106	San Jose, CA	−174,295

Note: Los Angeles is second in losses, but adjacent counties are first in gains—these changes may simply be a matter of people moving to the suburbs and just outside city limits
Source: Frey, 2005. MSAs or PMSAs listed rather than city

Copyright © Allyn & Bacon 2009

Population Growth

- **Population Composition**
  - **population composition**
  - comparisons by age and gender
  - ratio of men to women
  - **population pyramid**
    - "expansive"
    - "constrictive"
    - "stationary"

Copyright © Allyn & Bacon 2009

Population Growth

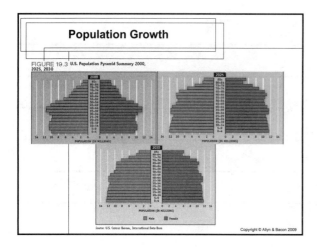

FIGURE 19.3 U.S. Population Pyramid Summary 2000, 2025, 2030

Source: U.S. Census Bureau, International Data Base

Copyright © Allyn & Bacon 2009

Population Growth

- natural population increase

• **How High Can It Go?**
- **Malthusian theory**
- starvation: more people than food
  • population→ *geometric progression*
  • food production → arithmetic progression
- **Marx→** unequal distribution of resources
- **Ehrlich →** *the Population Bomb*
  • **zero population growth**

Copyright © Allyn & Bacon 2009

Population Growth

• **Demographic Transition**
- **demographic transition theory**
- population and technology spur each other's development
  • *Initial stage*
  • *Transitional growth*
  • *Incipient decline stage*

• **Decreasing the Rate of Flow**
- compromising personal freedom?

Copyright © Allyn & Bacon 2009

The Urban Environment

- **The City: Ancient to Modern**
  - Çatalhöyük – oldest city
  - cities grew along major rivers
  - impact of Industrial Revolution
  - 1900 – London most populous city
  - **population density**

TABLE 19.3

World's Largest Cities (Urban Agglomerations), 2007		
Tokyo	Japan	33,400,000
Seoul	South Korea	23,200,000
Mexico City	Mexico	22,100,000
New York	USA	21,800,000
Mumbai	India	21,300,000

Source: www.citypopulation.de/World.html

Copyright © Allyn & Bacon 2009

The Urban Environment

- **The Countryside**
  - rural-urban continuum – 9 levels
  - rural "antipathy" to progress
  - many small towns and cities are being repopulated

- **Suburbs**
  - "detached" housing
  - "man's home is his castle"
  - *bedroom communities → edge cities*

Copyright © Allyn & Bacon 2009

The Urban Environment

- **The Sociology of Commuting: Separate and Unequal**
  - cars
  - public transportation
    - cities
    - suburbs

- **Revitalizing Downtown**
  - **gentrification**
  - **megalopolis**

Copyright © Allyn & Bacon 2009

Sociology and the City

- – Durkheim
  - **mechanical solidarity**
  - **organic solidarity**
- **Human Ecology**
  - **human ecology**
  - **Urbanization**
  - **The Urban Village** (Gans)
    - *Cosmopolites*
    - *Yuppies*
    - *Ethnic villagers*
    - *The deprived*
    - *The trapped*

Sociology and the City

- – **Concentric Zones**
  - **Zone 1** – central city
  - **Zone 2** – manufacturing/wholesale
  - **Zone 3** – working-class residential
  - **Zone 4** – middle/upper middle class residential
  - **Zone 5** – commuter

- **Global Urbanization**

The Natural Environment

- – **ecosystems**
- – social world as subcategory of the natural world **(Spencer)**
- – significance of the impact of social life n the natural world **(Huntington)**
- – **1970s →** *Spaceship Earth*
  - conservation
  - avoiding depletion of natural resources
  - avoiding "fouling our nest"

The Natural Environment

- **Energy**
- **Vanishing Resources**
- **Environmental Threats**
  - **Pollution**
  - **Garbage**
  - **Global Warming**
- **The Sociology of Disaster**
- **Environments in he 21st Century**

Copyright © Allyn & Bacon 2009

The Natural Environment

FIGURE 19.5 World Temperature Increases, 2001–2005

Temperature Increase, 2001–2005

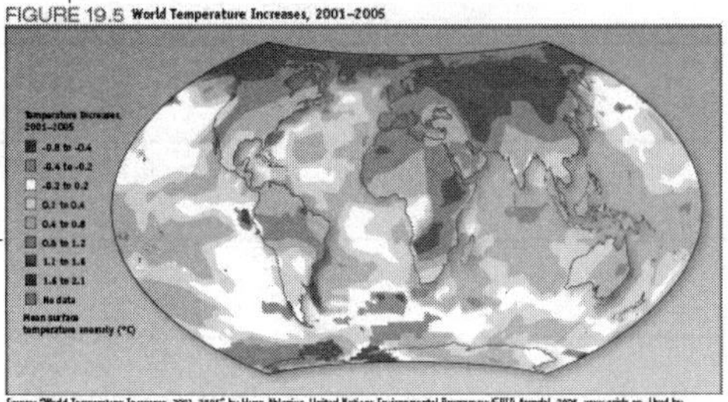

Source: "World Temperature Increases, 2001–2005" by Hugo Ahlenius, United Nations Environment Programme/GRID-Arendal, 2006. www.grida.no. Used by permission.

Copyright © Allyn & Bacon 2009

What Does America Think?

19.1   Environmental Threats and Science

These are actual survey data from the General Social Survey, 2000.

Many of the claims about environmental threats are greatly exaggerated. Less than 30 percent of respondents agreed or strongly agreed with this statement, and almost 43 percent disagreed or strongly disagreed. Those in the middle and upper classes were more likely to disagree, while those in the lower class were most likely to agree. Age and race differences were not significant.

Modern science will solve our environmental problems with little change to our way of life. Almost 50 percent of respondents disagreed or strongly disagreed with this statement, while only 22 percent agreed or strongly agreed. Those in the upper class were most likely to disagree.

CRITICAL THINKING | DISCUSSION QUESTION

1. Why do you think there are social class differences in the survey responses?

Copyright © Allyn & Bacon 2009

What Does America Think?

19.2   What Are We Willing to Do?

These are actual survey data from the General Social Survey, 2000.

How often do you make a special effort to sort glass or cans or plastic or papers and so on for recycling? Almost 33 percent of respondents said they always recycle, while 24 percent said they often recycle. Those in the upper class were much more likely to say they always recycle (50 percent), and those in the lower class were more likely to say they never recycle (16.2 percent), although that percentage was still relatively low.

CRITICAL THINKING | DISCUSSION QUESTION

1. What do you think explains the social class differences in responses?

Copyright © Allyn & Bacon 2009

What Does America Think?

▶ Go to this website to look further at the data. You can run your own statistics and crosstabs here: http://sda.berkeley.edu/cgi-bin/hsda?harcsda+gss04

REFERENCES: Davis, James A., Tom W. Smith, and Peter V. Marsden. General Social Surveys 1972–2004: [Cumulative File] [Computer file]. 2nd ICPSR version. Chicago, IL: National Opinion Research Center [producer], 2005; Storrs, CT: Roper Center for Public Opinion Research, University of Connecticut; Ann Arbor, MI: Inter-University Consortium for Political and Social Research; Berkeley, CA: Computer-Assisted Survey Methods Program, University of California [distributors], 2005.

Copyright © Allyn & Bacon 2009

Chapter One Answers
What is Sociology?

ANSWER KEY

Multiple Choice

1. d (pg 5)	6. b (pg 17)	11. d (pg 27)	16. b (pg 13)	21. c (pg 22)
2. b (pg 4)	7. d (pg 18)	12. a (pg 17)	17. c (pg 12)	22. c (pg 26)
3. c (pg 13)	8. b (pg 21)	13. b (pg 29)	18. d (pg 13)	23.d (pg 25)
4. c (pg 15)	9. b (pg 24)	14. c (pg 4)	19. a (pg 14)	24. d (pg 26)
5. a (pg 16)	10. c (pg 25)	15. a (pg 4)	20. c (pg 32)	25. a (pg 25)

True/False

1. true (pg 11)	6. true (pg 21)
2. true (pg 9)	7. false (pg 24)
3. false (pg 33)	8. true (pg 31)
4. false (pg 17)	9. false (pg 33)
5. true (pg 14)	10. true (pg 20)

Fill-in-the-Blank

1. forms (pg 19)	6. postmodernism (pg 33)
2. John Locke (pg 13)	7. Thorstein Veblen (pg 20)
3. solidarity (pg 18)	8. status and party (pg 18)
4. manifest (pg 25)	9. multiculturalism (pg 27)
5. structural functionalism (pg 24)	10. paradigm (pg 24)

Essays

1. Pages 24-27

The three major sociological perspectives include: symbolic interactionism, structural functionalism, and conflict theories. Symbolic interactionism examines how an individual's interaction with his or her environment- other people, institutions, ideas- help people develop a sense of "self." The "symbolic" part was the way we use symbol systems to navigate the social world. This is a micro level perspective. Structural functionalism is a theory that social life consisted of several distinct integrated levels that enable the world to find stability, order, and meaning. Structural functionalism is a macro level analysis. Conflict theories suggest that the dynamics of society, both of social order and social resistance, were the result of the conflict among different groups. They believe that those who had power sought to maintain it; those who did not have power sought to change the system to get it. Conflict theories are also a macro analysis.

2. Pages 14-23

Classical figures from the history of sociology include Auguste Comte, Alexis de Tocqueville, Karl Marx, Emile Durkheim, Max Weber, and Georg Simmel.

Auguste Comte believed that each society passed through three stages of development based on the form of knowledge that provided its foundation: religious, metaphysical, and scientific. In the religious stage supernatural forces are understood to control the world. In the metaphysical stage, abstract forces and "destiny" are perceived to be the prime movers of history. In the scientific, or "positive", stage events are explained through the scientific method of observation, experimentation, and analytic comparison. He believed that, like the physical sciences, sociology must rely on science to explain social facts and saw two basic facts to be explained: "statics," the study of order, persistence, and organization; and "dynamics," the study of the processes of social change. He believed that sociology would become the "queen of sciences," shedding light on earlier sciences and providing knowledge about the natural world with a science of the social world and sociology would reveal the principles and laws that affected the function of all societies. Sociologists have never abandoned his questions: the question of order and disorder, persistence and change.

Alexis de Tocqueville is known for studies of American democracy and the French Revolution. He saw the United States as the embodiment of democracy. His greatest insight is that democracy can either enhance or erode individual liberty. On the one hand, democracy promises increasing equality of conditions and increasingly uniform standards of living. On the other hand, it also concentrates power at the top and weakens traditional sources of liberty, like religion or the aristocracy. Democracies can lead to mass society, in which individuals feel powerless, and are easily manipulated by the media. As a result, democratic societies are faced with two possible outcomes, free institutions or desportism.

Karl Marx was the most important of all socialist thinkers. Marx's great intellectual and political breakthrough came in 1848. With Engels, he wrote *The Communist Manifesto*. Asserting that all history had "hitherto been the history of class struggles," the Manifesto linked the victory of the proletariat to the development of capitalism itself, which dissolved traditional bonds, like family and community, and replaced them with the naked ties of self-interest. His central work *Capitalism* laid out a theory of how capitalism worked as a system. His central insight was that the exchange of money and services between capital and labor is unequal. Because of competition, capitalists must try to increase the rate of surplus value and to do this capitalist replace human labor with machines, lower wages until the workers can not afford even to consume the very products they are producing, and by centralizing their production until the system reaches a crisis. Eventually it would all come tumbling down. Marx believed that the "laws of motion of capitalism would bring about its own destruction as the rich got so rich and the poor got so poor that they would revolt against the obvious inequity of the system. Then workers would rise up and overthrow the unequal capitalist system and institution communism- the collective ownership of all property.

Emile Durkheim searched for distinctly social origins of even the most individual and personal of issues. His greatest work *Suicide* is a class example of his sociological imagination. On the surface, suicide appears to be the ultimate individual act, yet Durkheim argued that suicide is profoundly social, an illustration of how connected and individual feels to others. Durkheim's study of suicide illustrated his central insight: that society is held together by "solidarity," moral bonds that connect us tot eh social collectivity. Social order cannot be accounted for by the pursuit of individual self-interest; solidarity is emotional, moral, and non-rational.

Max Weber had an interest in rationality in the modern world. His major insights were that rationality was the foundation of modern society and that while rationality organized society in more formal, legal, and predictable ways, it also trapped us an "iron cage" of bureaucracy and meaninglessness. Weber's interpretive sociology understands social relationships by showing the sense they make to those who are involved in them. He also insisted that experts separate their personal evaluations from their scientific pronouncements because such value judgments cannot be logically deduced from facts. His most famous work, *The Protestant Ethic and the Spirit of Capitalism*, was a study of the relationship of religious idea to economic activity. Weber believed that the modern capitalist order brought out the worst in us. Weber added the idea of status and party to the class division among people.

Georg Simmel was in quest of a subject matter for sociology that would distinguish it from other social sciences and the humanistic disciplines. The special task of sociology is to study the forms of social interaction apart from their content. Simmel assumes that the same social forms could contain quite different content, and the same social content could be embodied indifferent forms. What mattered to Simmel was the ways that these forms of domination or competition had specific, distinctive properties. Simmel's major concern was really about individualism. His work is always animated by the question of what the social conditions are that make it easier for persons to discover and express their individuality.

The American Sociological thinkers included Thorstein Veblen, Lester Ward, and George Herbert Mead.

Thorstein Veblen is best known for his bitingly satirical work, *The Theory of the Leisure Class*, in which he argued that America was split in tow, between the "productive"- those who work- and the "pecuniary"- those who have the money. He divided Americans into workers and owners and argued that the wealthy were not productive. They lived off the labor of others, like parasites. They spent their time engaged in competitive displays of wealth and prestige, which he called "conspicuous consumption"- consumption that is done because it is visible and because it invites a certain social evaluation of "worth." He also saw a tension between the benevolent forces of technology and the profit system that distorts them. It was not a matter of the technology but of its ownership and control and the uses to which it was put.

Lester Ward was the first to free sociology from the biological fetters of the Darwinian model of social change. Ward stressed the need for social planning and reform. His greatest theoretical achievement, call the theory of "social Telesis," was to refute social Darwinism, which held that those who ruled deserved to do so because they had adapted best to social conditions.

George Herbert Mead studied the development of individual identity through social processes. He argued that what gave us our identity was the product of our interaction with ourselves and with others, which is based on the distinctly human capacity for self-reflection. He distinguished between the "I," the part of us that is inherent and biological, from the "me," the part of us that is self-conscious and created by observing ourselves in interaction. The "me" is created by managing the generalized other, by which he meant a person's notion of the common values, norms, and expectations of other people in society. Mead developed a distinctly social theory of the self- on that doe not bubble up from one's biology alone but a self that takes shape only through interaction with society.

The "Other" Cannon includes Mary Wollstonecraft, Margaret Fuller, Frederick Douglass, W.E.B. Du Bois, and Charlotte Perkins Gilman.

Mary Wollstonecraft has been called the first major feminist. Many of her ideas such as equal education for the sexes, the opening of the professions to women, and her critique of marriage as a form of legal prostitution, were shocking to her contemporaries but have proven remarkably visionary. She argued that society could not progress if half its members are kept backward, and she proposed broad education changes for both boys and girls.

Margaret Fuller wrote the book *Woman in the Nineteenth Century* which became the intellectual foundation of the American women's movement. The book is a bracing call for complete freedom and equality. Fuller calls on women to become self-reliant and not expect help from men and introduces the concept of sisterhood. She also calls for the end of to sexual stereotyping and the sexual double standard.

Frederick Douglass was the most important African American intellectual of the nineteenth century. Douglass's work stands as an impassioned testament to the cruelty and illogic of slavery, claiming that all human beings were equally capable of being full individuals. His principle theme was that slaveholding is learned behavior and presumably can be unlearned.

W.E. B. Du Bois mast the most articulate, original, and widely read spokesman for the civil rights of black people for a period of over 30 years. He wrote nineteen books and hundreds of articles, edited four periodicals, and was the founder of the NAACP and the Pan-African movement. His work forms a bridge between the nineteenth century and the Civil Rights movement of the 1960s. He believed that race was the defining feature of American society and the most significant contribution he could make toward achieving racial justice would be a series of scientific studies of the Negro. In 1899, he wrote *The Philadelphia Negro*, he planned an ambitious set of volumes that would together finally understand the experiences of the American Negro. His work defines a 'moment in history when the American Negro began to reject the idea of the world belonging to white people."

Charlotte Perkins Gilman is best known for her groundbreaking *Women and Economics*, a book in which she explores the origin of women's subordination and its function in evolution. Women make a living by marriage, not by the work she does, and so man becomes her economic environment. As a consequence her female qualities dominate her human ones, because it is the female traits through which she earns her living. Gilman was one of the first to see the need for innovation in child rearing and home maintenance that would ease the burdens of working women.

3. Pages 27-29
Societies across the globe are becoming increasingly connected through globalization and multiculturalism. Globalization is the interconnections among different groups of people al over the world, the dynamic webs

that connect us to one another and the ways these connections also create cleavages among different groups of people. Multiculturalism is the understanding of many different culture, we come to understand the very different ways that different groups of people approach issues, construct identities, and crate institutions that express their needs. Globalization of the media industries allows books, magazines, movies, television programs, and music from almost every country to be consumed all over the world. Proponents of globalization claim that it allows poor countries and their citizens to develop economically and raises their standards of living. Opponents argue that the creation of an unfettered international free market has benefits multinational corporations in the Western world at the expense of local enterprise, local cultures, and common people.

Chapter Two Answers
Culture and Society

ANSWER KEY

Multiple Choice

1. d (pg 41)	6. b (pg 52)	11. c (pg 52)	16. d (pg 56)	21. b (pg 42)
2. d (pg 41)	7. c (pg 50)	12. c (pg 50)	17. d (pg 56)	22. b (pg 43)
3. b (pg 41)	8. a (pg 57)	13. a (pg 46)	18. b (pg 60)	23. a (pg 51)
4. c (pg 41)	9. a (pg 42)	14. d (pg 50)	19. c (pg 63)	24. d (pg 52)
5. c (pg 61)	10. d (pg 56)	15. a (pg 51)	20. c (pg 62)	25. c (pg 57)

True/False

1. true (pg 45)	6. false (pg 43)
2. true (pg 56)	7. true (pg 42)
3. false (pg 41)	8. false (pg 57)
4. false (pg 46)	9. false (pg 50)
5. true (pg 53)	10. true (pg 62)

Fill-in-the-Blank

1. subcultures (pg 42)	6. laws (pg 50)
2. counterculture (pg 43)	7. fads (pg 21)
3. culture (pg 40)	8. symbols (pg 62)
4. language (pg 46)	9. cultural diffusion (pg 63)
5. rituals (pg 47)	10. real culture (pg 51)

Essays

1. Page 43

Subcultures are a group of people within a culture who share some distinguishing characteristic, beliefs, values, or attributes that set them apart from the dominant culture while countercultures identify themselves through their difference and opposition to the dominant culture. Subcultures are communities that constitute themselves through a relationship of difference to the dominant culture. Countercultures offer an important grounding for identity, but they do so in opposition to the dominant culture. Countercultures demand a lot of conformity from members because they define themselves in opposition.

2. Pages 48-50

Norms are the rules a culture develops that define how people should act and the consequences of failure to act in the specific ways. A mores is a stronger norm that is informally enforced while a folkway is a relatively weak and informal norm that is a result of patterns of action. A law is a norm that that has been organized and written down. An example of a norm would include faithfulness in a marriage, an example of a mores is wearing flip-flops to a job interview with a fortune five hundred company, an example of a folkway is wearing a white dress to a wedding if you are not the bride, and an example of a law would be homicide.

3. Page 48

Norms are the rules a culture develops that define how people should act and the consequences of failure to act in the specific ways while values are the ethical foundations of a culture, its ideas about right and wrong, good and bad. Norms prescribe behavior within the culture, and values explain to us what the culture has determined is right and wrong. Norms tell us how to behave while values tell us why. Both not only guide our own goals and actions but also inform our judgments of others.

4. Page 52

Achievement and success. Americans highly value personal achievement such as succeeding at work and at school, gaining wealth, power prestige, and successfully competing with others.
Individualism. The individual is the centerpiece of American life. Individuals take all credit and all responsibility for their lives.
Activity and work. Americans believe one should work hard and play hard. One should always be active. Americans work longer hours with fewer vacations than any other industrial society, and this gap is growing. We believe that hard work pays off in upward mobility.
Efficiency and practicality. Americans value efficient activity and practicality. Being practical is more highly valued than being intellectual.
Science and technology. We are a nation that relies daily on scientific breakthroughs, supporting research into the furthest recesses of outer space and infinitesimal subatomic particles for clues about our existence and tiny genetic markers for cures for illness.
Progress. Americans believe in constant and rapid progress, that everything should constantly be "new and improved."
Material comfort. Americans value living large. We believe that "living well is the best revenge."
Humanitarianism. We believe in helping our neighbors, especially during crises, and value personal kindness and charity.
Freedom. Americans believe that freedom is both the means and the end of a great society. We resist any limitations on our freedom and believe that the desire for freedom is a basic human need, which may even justify imposing freedom on others.
Democracy. Americans believe in a "government of the people, by the people, and for the people," a government that represents them. Democracy also entails the right to express your own opinion.
Equality. Americans believe that everyone is created equal and entitled to the same rights that everyone else enjoys.
Racism and group superiority. We believe in equality of opportunity, we also believe that some people are superior to others. Usually, we assume that "our" group is superior to the others. Historically, the dominant group has assumed it was superior.

5. Page 61

Cultural imperialism is the deliberate imposition of one's country's culture on another. The global spread of American fashion, media, and language is often seen as an imposition of American values and ideas as well as products. Cultural imperialism is not imposed by government instead it is cultural in that these products become associated with a lifestyle to which citizens of many countries aspire. Cultural transfer is not one directional. There are many cultural trends among Americans that originate in other countries. Imported luxury cars, wine, beer, and food fads all originate in other countries and become associated with exotic lifestyles elsewhere.

Chapter Three Answers
Society: Interactions, Groups, and Organizations

ANSWER KEY

Multiple Choice

1. d (pg 77)	6. a (pg 82)	11. a (pg 91)	16. a (pg 80)	21. c (pg 74)
2. c (pg 78)	7. c (pg 84)	12. c (pg 95)	17. a (pg 80)	22. b (pg 83)
3. c (pg 79)	8. b (pg 83)	13. a (pg 81)	18. d (pg 75)	23. d (pg 87)
4. b (pg 72)	9. d (pg 86)	14. b (pg 87)	19. b (pg 75)	24. d (pg 89)
5. b (pg 81)	10. d (pg 91)	15. c (pg 78)	20. c (pg 72)	25. d (pg 97)

True/False

1. F (pg 77)	6. T (pg 91)
2. T (pg 78)	7. T (pg 95)
3. T (pg 72)	8. F (pg 96)
4. F (pg 84)	9. F (pg 76)
5. F (pg 84)	10. T (pg 74)

Fill-in-the-Blank

1. primary group (pg 82)	6. status (pg 77)
2. reference (pg 83)	7. expectations and performances (pg 79)
3. looking-glass self (pg 72)	8. stereotype (pg 87)
4. impression management (pg 73)	9. network (pg 88)
5. nonverbal (pg 74)	10. bureaucratic personality (pg 97)

Essays

1. Pages 72-74

We construct social reality through social interaction. Cooley proposed the concept of the looking-glass self to describe the process by which our identity develops. He argued that we develop our looking-glass self in three different stages. The first stage is that we imagine how we appear to others around us. We think people see us as smart or stupid. If a teacher yells at me for not knowing the answer, I will believe that I am not smart. The conclusion does not need to be accurate, but misinterpretations can be just as powerful as accurate evaluations. In the second stage we draw general conclusions based on the reactions of others. If I imagine that many people think that I am not smart, then I will conclude that indeed I am not smart. In the third stage we develop our sense of personal identity based on our evaluations of others' reactions. That is, I imagine that many people think that I am not smart, so I become stupid or hide my intelligence. Erving Goffman believed that hour selves change not only because of other people's reaction but also because of the way we actively try to present ourselves to other people. We learn to modify our behavior in accordance with what particular people expect of us. We all take part in impression management, where we are actively trying to control how others perceive us by changing our behaviors to correspond to an ideal of what they will find most appealing. Goffman called his theory dramaturgy. Social life is like a stage play, with our performances changing according to the characters on stage at the moment. We all try to give our best performances possible, to convince other characters that they are corresponding to an ideal of the best role that is being played.

2. Pages 91-93

The three most common types of organizations are normative, coercive, and utilitarian. Normative organizations are typically voluntary organizations. Members receive no monetary rewards and often have to pay to join. They participate because they believe in the goals of the organization. An example of a normative organization would include: Sierra Club, Kiwanis, Red Cross, AARP, NRA, etc. Coercive organizations are organizations in which membership is not voluntary. Prisons, reform schools, and mental institutions are all examples of coercive organizations. They tend to have very elaborate formal rules and severe sanctions for those seeking to exit voluntarily. The also tend to have elaborate informal cultures, as individuals try to create something that makes their experience a little bit more palatable. Utilitarian organizations are those to which we belong for a specific, instrumental purpose, a tangible material reward. Material rewards are the primary motivation for joining this type of organization. We remain in the organization as long as the material rewards we seek are available. Examples of these types of organizations include: universities and corporations.

3. Page 95
According to Max Weber the ideal bureaucracy would have a division of labor, hierarchy of authority, rules and regulations, impersonality, career ladders, and efficiency. Each person in a bureaucratic organization has some specific role to play. People often become specialists, able to perform a few functions exceptionally well, but they might be unable to do what their colleagues or co-workers do. The hierarchy of authority is the idea that positions in a bureaucracy are arranged vertically, with a clear reporting structure, so that each person is under the supervision of another person. Those at the top have power over those below them, all along what is often called the chain of command. The chain is often impersonal. Those in the hierarchy do not exert power on a whim. Everyone follows clearly defined rules and regulations that govern the conduct of each specific position in the organization and define the appropriate procedures for the function of each unit and the organization as a whole. The rules and regulations are formalizes and written down, which further reduces the individual discretion supervisors may have and increases the formal procedures of the organization. Formal and codified rules and regulations and a hierarchy of positions lead to a very impersonal system. Members of bureaucratic organizations are detached and impersonal, and interactions are to be guided by instrumental criteria not how a particular decision might make you feel. Bureaucratic organizations have clearly marked paths for advancement, so that members who occupy lower positions on the hierarchy are aware of the formal requirements to advance. They thus are more likely to see their participation as careers rather than as jobs and further commit themselves tot eh smooth functioning of the organization. Formal criteria govern promotion and hiring; incumbents cannot leave their positions to their offspring. Efficiency is the last characteristic of the ideal bureaucracy. The formality of the rules, the overarching logic of rationality, the clear chain of command, and the impersonal networks enable bureaucracies to be extremely efficient, coordinating the activities of a large number of people.

Chapter Four Answers
How Do We Know What We Know? The Methods of the Sociologist

ANSWER KEY

Multiple Choice

1. a (pg 109)	6. d (pg 124)	11. a (pg 126)	16. d (pg 105)	21. d (pg 123)
2. c (pg 117)	7. b (pg 117)	12. b (pg 110)	17. b (pg 116)	22. c (pg 130)
3. b (pg 110)	8. c (pg 118)	13. c (pg 112)	18. c (pg 115)	23. a (pg 131)
4. a (pg 106)	9. c (pg 124)	14. d (pg 114)	19. a (pg 115)	24. c (pg 134)
5. d (pg 107)	10. d (pg 117)	15. b (pg 133)	20. b (pg 110)	25. d (pg 124)

True/False

1. T (pg 104)	6. T (pg 119)
2. T (pg 111)	7. T (pg 122)
3. F (pg 112)	8. T (pg 114)
4. F (pg 114)	9. F (pg 130)
5. F (pg 127)	10. T (pg 133)

Fill-in-the-Blank

1. Research method (pg 111)	6. Cluster sample (pg 119)
2. Sample (pg 119)	7. Secondary analysis of data (pg 122)
3. Control (pg 112)	8. Causally (pg 129)

Essays

1. Pages 112-124.

The different types of research methods include: experiments, participant observation, ethnography, interviews, surveys, content analysis and secondary analysis of existing data. The first step in doing research is to pick a topic. For the purpose of this essay we will use domestic violence. You could do a survey, developing a questionnaire that would include either closed-ended or open-ended questions, and then discuss what type of sampling procedure you would use. You would discuss some of the issues in trying to define domestic violence and the problems that you would encounter in attempting to draw your sample. Some of the positive aspects to using a survey are that you could survey many victims of domestic violence at a relatively low cost. However, gaining access to this population is difficult since many victims never come forward. Another problem with using a survey is that you cannot go into detail about their experiences as a victim. Using in-depth interviews may be a more appropriate way of obtaining information from domestic violence victims. To fully understand their experiences questions may need to be asked that require answers to long to answer in a survey format. This method may be more expensive and will probably require that you have a smaller sample size. As you formulate your essay you may want to think about the other types of methods that you could use. The methods that may be difficult to apply to this topic are the experiment and content analysis. In your conclusion summarize the factors that influenced you to choose the method that you did.

2. Pages 109-111

The research topic that will be chosen for this essay question is that of fear of crime. Fear of crime is a very broad category that needs to be narrowed down. First you will need to define the problem. The question should be refined so that it is more manageable. Instead of looking at the broad question of fear of crime one could ask what are the gender differences in fear of crime. After narrowing your topic a literature review is necessary to identify the research that has already been conducted on this topic. After reviewing all of the possible literature you must then formulate a hypothesis. One hypothesis for the gender differences in fear of crime could be: women are more likely to have higher levels of fear of crime than are men. In this hypothesis gender is the independent variable while fear is the dependent variable. After identifying your variables you need to design a project. For this project there are numerous data sets that could be used for secondary data analysis. Quantitative methods would be most appropriate since there are large data sets already out there measuring fear of crime (International Crime Victimization Survey, National Crime Victimization Survey). Next you will need to collect data. If you are using secondary data analysis the data has already been collected you will need to figure out how to get a hold of it. If you are conducting your own survey, you will need to come up with questions pertaining to your topic and select your sampling method. After collecting all of the data it is time to analyze it. The technique you use to analyze your data will depend on the type of method you have chosen to use. Using surveys one could analyze their data using the appropriate statistical method. After analyzing your data you need to figure out how to report your findings. For most students papers written for class or a class presentation would be most appropriate. For more advanced people in the profession a professional conference or journal would be most appropriate.

3. Pages 133-134

It is necessary to have an Institutional Review Board to ensure that human subjects are not harmed in any way. Erich Goode did not use the IRB at his university because he felt that his research did not harm his subjects in any way. In all research you must take into consideration the rights of your subjects to not endure any physical or psychological harm. The IRB was set up so that researchers would have to obtain informed consent. Subjects must be notified of the nature of the project and if there are any potential risks to participating in the research. Subjects must also be informed that at any point in time they can withdraw their participation for any reason. The researcher must maintain confidentiality at all times and the test subjects are to be anonymous. Subjects are also not to be deceived unless it is absolutely necessary and they must be free from harm. There are several protected groups including children, college students, prisoners, the mentally ill, and other groups because they cannot really give consent.

Chapter Five Answers
Socialization

ANSWER KEY

Multiple Choice

1. c (pg 141)	6. b (pg 147)	11. b (pg 145)	16. d (pg 161)	21. a (pg 148)
2. b (pg 143)	7. b (pg 145)	12. d (pg 149)	17. a (pg 158)	22. d (pg 145)
3. a (pg 145)	8. c (pg 146)	13. a (pg 151)	18. d (pg 156)	23. a (pg 140)
4. d (pg 141)	9. d (pg 147)	14. c (pg 159)	19. b (pg 154)	24. d (pg 143)
5. d (pg 144)	10. b (pg 144)	15. d (pg 160)	20. c (pg 151)	25. c (pg 145)

True/False

1. T (pg 144)	6. T (pg 152)
2. F (pg 144)	7. F (pg 158)
3. F (pg 146)	8. F (pg 161)
4. T (pg 148)	9. T (pg 149)
5. F (pg 150)	10. T (pg 149)

Fill-in-the-Blank

1. generalized other (pg 144)	6. sensorimotor (pg 145)
2. id and superego (pg 147)	7. conventional (pg 146)
3. resocialization (pg 149)	8. secondary socialization (pg 150)
4. adulthood (pg 159)	9. mass media (pg 154)
5. 60 (pg 160)	10. initiation rituals (pg 158)

Essays

1. Pages 145-146

Piaget studied children of different ages to see how they solve problems. The four stages of development include sensorimotor, preoperational, concrete operational, and formal operational. From birth until about 2 years of age children are in the sensorimotor stage. In this stage the can understand only what they see, hear, or touch. From ages 2-7 children move into the preoperational stage in which they are now capable of understanding and articulating speech and symbols, but are not yet able to understand common concepts like weight. From ages 7-12 children are in the concrete operational stage. In this stage causal relationships are understood, and they understand common concepts, but are yet unable to reach conclusions through general principles. Children can learn specific rules but are not able to reach conclusions based on general principles. Children reach the formal operational stage at about age 12. They are now able to think abstractly and critically. They can talk about general concepts like truth and can reach conclusions based on general principles.

2. Page 140-141, 144-145, 147-148

Nature refers to our physical makeup while nurture refers to how we grow up. Nature and nurture both play a role in who we are. Before the Enlightenment nature was supreme: our identities were created by God along with the natural world and could not be changed by mere circumstances. Nurture played virtually no part at all. Jean-Jacques Rousseau argued that human being do inherit identities however, their environment can also change them. In the nineteenth century the nature side of the debate got a boost when Charles Darwin observed that animal species evolve over time. Growing up in different environments changes our ideas about who we are and where we belong. The type of environment does not determine what sort of human nature you will think you have, but the environment plays a part in calculating it. The choice is not nature or nurture, it is both.

It could be argued that both Mead and Freud believe that nurture plays a significant role in our development.

3. Pages 151-156

Different sorts of families socialize their children in different ways. Depending on the class status of your family, you may be raised to value certain ideas over others. Children in working class families are primarily interested in teaching the importance of outward conformity while middle-class families focus on developing children's curiosity and creativity. How children see themselves depends largely on what happens at home during the first few years of their lives. The education system also socializes children. Education instills social norms and values, such as the importance of competition. Education socializes us into class, race, gender, and sexual identity statuses. Peers groups have an enormous socializing influence, especially during middle and late childhood. They provide an enclave where we can learn the skills of social interaction and the importance of group loyalty. They teach social interaction through encouragement as well as through coercion and humiliation. Most often peer groups reinforce the socialization that children receive elsewhere. Most people are immersed in mass media every day. Children spend five and a half hours a day consuming media and are influenced by the messages portrayed. The media present messages concerning gender, race, class, and sexuality. People spend about one-third of their lives in the workplace and often we define ourselves by our jobs. Workplaces are similar to schools in that there are supervisors and peer groups with expectations that we are supposed to follow. We learn how to be "professional."

4. Pages 157-160

The first stage of the human life course is childhood. During this period of time children do not work and they are considered to be fragile and innocent. Children are seen as innocents, needing protection and guidance. Without their parents they would not grow up to be healthy adults. Children enter adolescents at about the age of 11 or12. During this time, they have a great deal of freedom to make their own choices about their friends and activities, and they often explore political, social, sexual, and religious identities. They do not have the responsibilities of adults, nor do they enjoy many adult privileges. Adolescences is also a very recent phenomenon. After adolescence is adulthood. Adulthood is marked by completing your education, getting a job, getting married, leaving your parents' home, and having a baby. Young adulthood occurs during the late teens until about the age of 30. This is when people usually attend college and are not settled down into permanent careers, residence, or families. From young adulthood one passes into middle age, roughly from age 30 to 60. Above age 60 is considered old age. In society today older people tend to move into retirement communities or nursing homes and must make social connections all over again.

Chapter Six Answers
Deviance and Crime

ANSWER KEY

Multiple Choice

1. c (pg 168)	6. b (pg 175)	11. a (pg 179)	16. c (pg 181)	21. a (pg 191)
2. a (pg 170)	7. d (pg 176)	12. d (pg 182)	17. d (pg 190)	22. b (pg 194)
3. d (pg 170)	8. a (pg 176)	13. b (pg 183)	18. c (pg 186)	23. c (pg 195)
4. b (pg 171)	9. d (pg 177)	14. d (pg 179)	19. b (pg 188)	24. b (pg 196)
5. d (pg 174)	10. b (pg 178)	15. a (pg 179)	20. d (pg 189)	25. d (pg 181)

True/False

1. F (pg 168)	6. F (pg 179)
2. T (pg 170)	7. T (pg 183)
3. T (pg 174)	8. F (pg 196)
4. T (pg 175)	9. F (pg 191)
5. F (pg 178)	10. T (pg 183)

Fill-in-the-Blank

1. deviance (pg 168)
2. primary deviance (pg 177)
3. broken windows theory (pg 180)
4. hate (pg 186)
5. anomie (pg 179)
6. learning (pg 181)
7. folkways (pg 170)
8. control theories (pg 176)
9. white-collar crimes (pg 183)
10. weakest (pg 188)

Essays

1. Pages 190-191 and 197

In this essay use the facts from the chapter to support your answer. The sample essay will answer why the criminal justice system is biased.

The criminal justice system is biased. African Americans are arrested at much higher rates that are white. They comprise 12.5 percent of the population, but are 54.5 percent of arrests for robber, 48.5 percent for murder, 33.3 percent for rape, and 32.6 percent for drug use. Latinos are also overrepresented in the criminal justice system as well. They make up 13 percent of the U.S. population but are 31 percent of those incarcerated in the federal system. Latino defendants are imprisoned three times as often as white and are detained before trial for first-time offenses almost twice as often as Whites, despite the fact that they are the least likely of all ethnic groups to have a criminal history. Latinos are also disproportionately charged with nonviolent drug offenses and represent the vast majority of those arrested for immigration violations. Also, within the criminal justice system the majority of police officers and judges are white. Minority representation has increased among local officers. Bias remains in both arrest and prosecution. Race also plays a part in who gets the death penalty. Black convicted of murdering Whites are most likely to get the death penalty and Whites convicted of murdering Blacks are least likely.

2. Page 168 and 178

Deviance is the breaking of a social rule or refusing to follow one whereas crime is defined as any act that violates a formal normative code that has been enacted by a legally constituted body. Deviance is only considered a crime when you violate a formal code. You can commit a crime and not bee seen as deviant if other people see your act as acceptable. An example of a deviant act would be organizing a hate group, picking your nose, yelling explicatives while in church, while an example of a crime could be rape, assault, theft, etc.

3. Page 170

The three types of social controls are folkways, mores, and taboos. Folkways are routine, usually unspoken conventions of behavior. Breaking these makes others in the group uncomfortable and violators might be laughed at, frowned on, or scolded. They are rarely made into laws. Folkways would include facing the back wall in an elevator or going into great detail when someone asks you how you are doing. Mores are norms with a strong moral significance and are viewed as essential to the proper functioning of a group. We absolutely should r should not behave this way. Examples of mores include yelling at someone or assaulting someone. The last type of social control is taboos. These are prohibitions viewed as essential to the well-being of humanity. To break a taboo is unthinkable, beyond comprehension. Taboos are always made into laws. Examples would include incest and cannibalism.

4. Page 182

Control theory suggests that deviants/delinquents are often individuals who have low levels of self-control as a result of inadequate socialization. People are rational so they decide whether or not to engage in an act by weighing the potential outcome. If a person knows that there is no punishment they would be likely to do a great many things that they would never dream otherwise. People are constrained by the fear of punishment. People take part in the cost-benefit analysis to determine how much punishment is worth a degree of satisfaction or prestige. You weight the respective costs of doing something against the benefits of doing it. People who have very little to lose are most likely to become rule-breakers. We often fail to break rules even when the benefits would be great and the punishment minimal. The outer control that keep people from performing deviant acts include our families, social institutions, and authority figures while the inner controls include our self-perceptions as "good" people, religious principles, and internalized socialization.

The dominant class produces deviance by making and enforcing laws that protect its own interest and oppress the subordinate class.

\

Chapter Seven Answers
Stratification and Social Class

ANSWER KEY

Multiple Choice

1. b (pg 207)	6. b (pg 223)	11. b (pg 213)	16. c (pg 232)	21. d (pg 221)
2. c (pg 22)	7. c (pg 206)	12. d (pg 221)	17. d (pg 234)	22. d (pg 208)
3. a (pg 220)	8. d (pg 207)	13. c (pg 224)	18. d (pg 235)	23. c (pg 209)
4. d (pg 221)	9. c (pg 207)	14. d (pg 210)	19. a (pg 236)	24. a (pg 211)
5. d (pg 221)	10. a (pg 209)	15. b (pg 230)	20. b (pg 214)	25. b (pg 212)

True/False

1. F (pg 208)	6. F (pg 221)
2. F (pg 210)	7. F (pg 223)
3. T (pg 214)	8. T (pg 226)
4. F (pg 219)	9. T (pg 229)
5. T (pg 214)	10. T (pg 230)

Fill-in-the-Blank

1. class, status, and power (pg 210)	6. social mobility (pg 226)
2. mode of production (pg 210)	7. middle-income (pg 232)
3. socioeconomic status (pg 212)	8. modernization theory (pg 233)
4. widening (pg 217)	9. core (pg 235)
5. culture of poverty (pg 223)	10. women (pg 221)

Essays

1. Pages 206-209

Social stratification is the system of structured social inequality and the structure of mobility in a society. The three different types of stratification systems are caste systems, class systems, and feudal systems. In a caste system your position is permanent and fixed. You are assigned your position at birth, without the ability to get out of it. These systems are often found in traditional agricultural societies that divide people by occupation. Like the caste system, the feudal system is also a fixed system and permanent. If you were born a lord or a serf, you stayed there your whole life. Serfs were considered the property of the lords and could not seek outside employment. Feudalism began to disappear as the class of free men in the cities grew larger and more prosperous, and the center of society began to shift from the rural manor to the urban factory. Industrial society dispensed with feudal rankings and ushered in the modern class system. The class system is based on economic position- a person's occupation, income, or possessions. The class systems are the most open and permit the greatest amount of social mobility, which is the ability to move up- or down- in the rankings. Class systems are systems of stratification based on economic position and people are ranked according to achieved status.

2. Pages 210-212

Karl Marx argued that human survival depends on producing things. He argued that it has always been the case that some people own the means of production and everyone else works for them. Capitalists or the bourgeoisie owned the means of production and the lower classes or the proletariat were forced to become wage-laborers or go hungry. They received no share of the profits and lived in perpetual poverty. Marx believed that society was stratified into two classes, one that owned the means of production and the other did not. Max Weber argued that there were three components to social class: economic, social, and political. Class position was determined based on whether you were an owner or a worker, how much money you made, your property, and how much money you had in the bank. Status was based on your relationship to consumption. People see what you have and how you live and make judgments about how much wealth and power you have. Power is the ability to do what you want to do. This may mean a certain amount of control over your own working situation. Weber's system of stratification is more complex because your class is not only dependent on whether or not you own the means of production, but what your job title is, what your relationship to consumption is, and your ability to do what you want to do. In Weber's system there can be multiple classes not just the bourgeoisie and the proletariat, people can fall somewhere in between.

3. Pages 223-224

The three explanations of poverty are the individual, cultural, and structural. One common explanation is that people are poor because they lack something. This explanation believes that people are lazy and unmotivated and that is why they are poor. Most Americans believe that the vast majority of poor people are "undeserving" poor. The cultural explanation of poverty argues that poverty is not a result of individual inadequacies but of larger social and cultural factors. Poor children are socialized into believing that they have nothing to strive for, that there is no point in working to improve their conditions. As adults, they are resigned to a life of poverty, and they socialize their children the same way. Therefore poverty is transmitted from one generation to another. The structural explanation says that poverty is not necessary resigned to their situation, they face structural disadvantages that are nearly impossible to overcome. They would like to lift themselves out poverty and lead better lives, but they suffer from poor education, higher rates of chronic diseases, poor or nonexistent health care, inferior housing, and a greater likelihood of being victimized by crime and a greater likelihood of being labeled criminals.

4. Page 233-234

Rostow's modernization theory focuses on the conditions necessary for a low-income country to develop economically. He argued that a nation's poverty is largely due to the cultural failings of its people. They lack a work ethic that stresses thrift and hard work; they would rather consume today than invest in the future. Such failings are reinforced by government policies that set wages, control prices, and generally interfere with the operation of the economy. They can develop economically only if they give up their backward way of life and adopt modern Western economic institutions, technologies, and cultural values that emphasize savings and productive investment. The four stages that countries desiring to break out of poverty must go through are the traditional economy, takeoff to economic growth, drive to technological maturity, and high mass consumption.

5. Page 235-236

Core countries include Western Europe, the United States, Australia, New Zealand, Japan, and South Africa. These are the most advanced industrial countries and they take a large share of profits in the world economic system. Goods flow into these countries. Peripheral countries include countries in sub-Saharan Africa, Latin America, East and Southeast Asia, and Oceania. These countries are low income, largely agricultural, and often manipulated by core countries. Goods, services, and people tend to flow away from the periphery. The most profitable activities in the commodity chain are likely to be done in the core countries, while the least profitable activities are likely to be done in peripheral countries. Peripheral countries are dependent on core countries because a huge percentage of the peripheral state's economy is based on a few products or even just one product for export to the core states. If the core states decrease their demand by only a little, the economy is ruined. Peripheral states lack major industries, so they sell their raw material inexpensively to the core states. Peripheral countries sell their raw materials at low cost to the core countries, the core countries manufacture the product and then turn around and sell the product back to the peripheral countries at high prices. Since the peripheral countries are unable to manufacture their raw materials into usable goods, they are dependent on core countries for this. Then they are forced to buy expensive manufactured goods back from them. The unequal trade patterns keep peripheral states constantly in debt to core states.

Chapter Eight Answers
Race and Ethnicity

ANSWER KEY

Multiple Choice

1. b (pg 244)	6. d (pg 271)	11. c (pg 247)	16. d (pg 255)	21. d (pg 254)
2. d (pg 248)	7. a (pg 243)	12. d (pg 251)	17. b (pg 257)	22. c (pg 272)
3. a (pg 272)	8. b (pg 246)	13. d (pg 271)	18. a (pg 259)	23. b (pg 264)
4. c (pg 251)	9. d (pg 248)	14. b (pg 252)	19. c (pg 261)	24. d (pg 265)
5. d (pg 259)	10. a (pg 249)	15. c (pg 253)	20. c (pg 272)	25. c (pg 267)

True/False

1. T (pg 244)	6. F (pg 252)
2. F (pg 244)	7. T (pg 253)
3. F (pg 248)	8. F (pg 257)
4. F (pg 251)	9. F (pg 264)
5. T (pg 251)	10. T (pg 33)

Fill-in-the-Blank

1. attitude (pg 251)	6. Hate groups (pg 257)
2. cultural traits (pg 244)	7. Native Americans (pg 22)
3. Identifiability (pg 248)	8. Model (pg 268)
4. Racism (pg 252)	9. Pluralism (pg 272)
5. Fair-weathered liberals (pg 253)	10. Hispanics (pg 265)

Essays

1. Pages 259-260

The primordial theory suggests that a conflict exists between in-groups and out-groups, but does not explain how some groups come to be classified as out-groups. People become prejudice through a natural process. According to this theory we chose naturally to want to be around people who are like us in terms of personality and physical attributes. According to the frustration-aggression theory, people are goal directed, and when they can not reach their goals, they become angry and frustrated. If they can not find the source of their frustration, or if these sources are too powerful to challenge, they will direct their aggression toward a scapegoat, a weak, convenient, and socially approved target. Sometimes people may become convinced that their scapegoat is actually the cause of their frustration, but often they are just lashing out at someone convenient. Conflict theory suggests that prejudice is a tool used by the elites, people at the top of the social hierarchy to "divide and conquer" those at the bottom, making them easier to control and manipulate. Racial and ethnic stereotypes are used to legitimate systemic inequality. Feminist theory considers how the category of race overlaps with other social categories, especially gender but also sexual orientation, social class, religion, age, and ability status. Stereotypes about stigmatized groups in all of these categories are remarkable similar. They almost always are illogical, emotional, primitive, potentially violent, and sexually suspect. These taken together form a matrix of domination, which is an interlocking system of control in which each type of inequality reinforces the others so that the impact of one cannot be fully understood without also consider the others.

2. Page 248

The four traits that a group needs to be classified as a minority group are: differential power; identifiability; ascribe status; and solidarity and group awareness. There must be a significant difference in access to economic, social, and political resources for one group to be considered a minority group. The minority group members may hold fewer professional positions, have a higher rate of poverty, a lower median household income, greater incidence of disease, higher incarceration rates, or a lower life expectancy. All of these patterns point to the lifelong pattern of discrimination and social inequality. Minority group members also share physical or cultural traits that distinguish them from the dominant group. These traits may be skin color or ethnic heritage. Also, minorities have an ascribed status. People are members of minority groups because they are born with the trait and membership is not voluntary. Affiliation in many ethnic groups may be a matter of choice, but one cannot decide that they want to be Hispanic. There must be an awareness of membership so that there are clearly defined "us" and "them."

3. Page 263-271

Native Americans were the original inhabitants of North America. Some of these groups were nomadic hunter-gatherers, but many were settled agrarian, living in villages as large and prosperous as any villages among the European settlers. The Europeans approached the Native Americans with stereotypes of them as "noble savages" or as "wild savages." Native Americans were systematically deprived of their land and put on reservations and some were outright killed. The threat of Native Americans being savages was contrived as the excuse to appropriate Native American land and natural resources, and to clear a path for the transcontinental railroad. The stereotype of Native American as uncivilized is still intact today, though it is has changed from violent to intuitive. About half of all Native Americans today live in rural areas, mostly on reservations, and the rest are concentrated in big cities. The history between the Europeans and Native Americans left many tribes destroyed and displaced onto reservations. Native Americans are worse off today than any other minority group in many measures of institutional discrimination.

Latinos and Latinas make up 12.5 percent of the U.S. population. They are now the largest ethnic minority group in the United States due to both immigration and higher birth rates. Latinos come from various countries of origin including: Mexico, Central America, South America, Cuba, the Dominican Republic, and Puerto Rico. They are not only the fastest growing minority group in the United States; they are also the fastest-growing affluence. The social status of Latinos varies depending on the country of origin. Those who are from South America and Cuba tend to have higher education levels and belong to the middle class, while Central Americans, Dominican Republic and Puerto Ricans have high rates of poverty.

In the 2000 census, 12.5 percent of the U.S. population was identified as Black or African American, with ancestry in sub-Saharan Africa. African American is an ethnicity, referring to the descendants of Black Africans who came to North America as slaves between 1500 and 1820. African Americans are the only group to immigrate to the United States against their will. Today, African Americans have achieved some measure of political and economic success. There is a sizeable Black middle-class overall however, their social status is by far lower than Whites.

About 3.6 percent of the population traces its ancestry to East, Southeast, or South Asia. These groups include China, the Philippines, India, Korea, Vietnam, and Japan. Most of these are recent immigrants. They are often depicted as the "model minority." Asian American have the highest college graduation rate of any ethnic group and even though they are only 5 percent of the total population they comprise 15 percent of all U.S. physicians and surgeons, 15 percent of all computer and mathematical occupation, 10 percent of all engineers, and 16 percent of the student body at Ivy League colleges. The success of Asian Americans is attributed to their incredible work ethic.

About 2 million people in the United States trace their history to the Middle East or North Africa. Most of them are recent immigrants who have arrived since 1970. They come from Iran, Turkey, Israel, and other countries. Those who immigrated between 1880 and 1920 were refugees from the failing Ottoman Empire and were mostly working class and poor. After the 1970s many who immigrated were middle class. They are the most well-educated ethnic group in the Unites States. Over half of them have college degrees and their median salary is slightly higher than the national mean. Prejudice and discrimination against them has increased since the World Trade Center attacks.

4. Page 272-273

When people assimilate they are abandoning their cultural traditions altogether and embrace the dominant culture. Only a few of the minority groups' traditions enter the "melting pot," most are left behind. Pluralism maintains that a stable society need not contain just one ethnic, cultural, or religious group, instead these groups can treat each other with mutual respect and not compete and try to dominant each other. With pluralism comes multiculturalism and cultural groups exist not only side by side but equally. With assimilation the dominant group forces people to leave their traits behind and take on the dominant groups traditions.

Chapter Nine Answers
Sex and Gender

ANSWER KEY

Multiple Choice

1. b (pg 280)	6. d (pg 297)	11. a (pg 295)	16. d (pg 300)	21. a (pg 301)
2. b (pg 281)	7. d (pg 288)	12. c (pg 298)	17. c (pg 308)	22. c (pg 299)
3. a (pg 286)	8. b (pg 291)	13. b (pg 302)	18. a (pg 309)	23. d (pg 282)
4. d (pg 282)	9. c (pg 292)	14. c (pg 300)	19. b (pg 310)	24. b (pg 287)
5. c (pg 283)	10. d (pg 291)	15. a (pg 302)	20. c (pg 300)	25. c (pg 308)

True/False

1. F (pg 280)	6. F (pg 309)
2. F (pg 284)	7. T (pg 301)
3. T (pg 282)	8. F (pg 295)
4. F (pg 298)	9. T (pg 291)
5. T (pg 302)	10. F (pg 289)

Fill-in-the-Blank

1. gender (pg 280)	6. sex segregation (pg 299)
2. sex hormones (pg 283)	7. glass ceiling (pg 301)
3. primary (pg 284)	8. 70 cents (pg 301)
4. gender socialization (pg 290)	9. hidden curriculum (pg 304)
5. socially constructed (pg 291)	10. multicultural feminism (pg 310)

Essays

1. pg 286

Margaret Mead concluded that gender varies by culture. The three South Sea cultures that she had studied had remarkable different ideas about what it meant to be a man or a woman. In two of the cultures, women and men were seen as similar. Among the Arapesh both men and women were kind, gentle, and emotionally warm. Among the Mundugamor women and men were equally violent and aggressive. The Tchambuli were more like the people in the United States. One sex was charming and graceful while the others were dominant and energetic economic providers. The different though was in that culture the men were the charming and graceful people while the women were dominant and energetic economic providers. Mead argued that developed cultural explanations that claim that their way is the natural way to do things, but all arrangements are equally culturally based.

2. Pages290-292

Gender socialization is the process by which males and females are taught the appropriate behaviors, attitudes, and traits for their biological sex. From birth on males and females are treated differently. Girls are held closer they get pick clothing; boys are held at arms length and get blue clothing. Throughout childhood boys and girls are given gender appropriate toys. They are dressed differently, taught to play differently, and read different books. Girls are awarded for physical attractiveness and boys are rewarded for physical activity. Girls who cross over to the boys' side are labeled "tomboys" and boys who cross over to the girls' side are labeled "sissies." They learn gender differences and gender inequality.

3. Pages 307-308
The first wave of feminism took place is the nineteenth century. The women involved in this movement were concerned with women's entry into the public sphere. The issues that were important to the women of this era were the ability for women to vote, go to college, to serve on juries, to go to law school or medical school, or to join a profession had largely succeeded by the middle of the twentieth century. In the 1960s and 1970s the second wave of feminism developed. They were determined to continue the struggle to eliminate obstacles to women's advancement but were also equally determined to investing the ways that gender inequality is also part of personal life, which included their relationships with men. They also focused on men's violence against women, rape, and the denigration of women in the media, women's sexuality, and lesbian rights. Their motto was, "The personal is political." The third wave of feminism is occurring today. They share the outrage at institutional discrimination and interpersonal violence, they also have a more playful relationship with mass media and consumerism. They insist on the ability to be friends and lovers with men. They are also more multicultural and seek to explore and challenge the intersections of gender inequality with other forms of inequality such as class, race, ethnicity, and sexual orientation. They feel more empowered than their predecessors. Their motto is, "Girls rule!"

4. pg 298-301
In the United States people have very definitive ideas of what sorts of occupations are appropriate for women and which are appropriate for men. Women who are successful are often though to be "less than" real women, while men who are successful are seen as "real men." These ideologies translate into the practice of women being paid less, promoted less, excluded from some positions, and are assigned to specific jobs deemed more appropriate for them. Gender discrimination in the workplace was far more direct than it is now. Women used to be discouraged from taking jobs away from men or might have been asked in a job interview if they were going to have children or get married. Gender inequality is also sustained in the workforce through sex segregation. Men and women are concentrated into different occupations, industries, jobs, and levels in workplace hierarchies. Women also earn less than men and this is magnified at the management level.

Chapter Ten Answers
Sexuality

ANSWER KEY

Multiple Choice
1. c (pg 316)   6. d (pg 328)   11. d (pg 334) 16. d (pg 339)   21. c (pg 340)
2. d (pg 317)   7. b (pg 322)   12. b (pg 335) 17. c (pg 332)   22. d (pg 341)
3. b (pg 318)   8. a (pg 330)   13. c (pg 337) 18. b (pg 329)   23. a (pg 342)
4. b (pg 328)   9. d (pg 331)   14. d (pg 337) 19. b (pg 335)   24. b (pg 324)
5. a (pg 322)   10. c (pg 332) 15. a (pg 340) 20. a (pg 340)   25. c (pg 323)

True/False
1. F (pg 316)   6. T (pg 329)
2. F (pg 319)   7. T (pg 332)
3. T (pg 322)   8. T (pg 333)
4. T (pg 323)   9. F (pg 335)
5. F (pg 328)   10. F (pg 340)

Fill-in-the-Blank
1. behavior (pg 317)   6. homophobic (pg 335)
2. initiators, resistant (pg 319)   7. sex tourism (pg 339)
3. same sex (pg 324)   8. nonprofit organizations (pg 342)
4. asexual (pg 325)   9. sexuality (pg 316)
5. hooking up (pg 332)   10. Kinsey (pg 328)

Essays

1. Pages 316-317

There are four ways in which sexuality can be seen as socially constructed. These include sexuality varying enormously from one culture to the next, sexuality varying within any one culture over time, sexuality varying among different groups in society, and sexual behaviors changing over the course of your life. Anthropologists have catalogued a wide variety of sexual attitudes and behaviors around the world and historians have pointed out the ways in which Victorian sexual morality developed in the nineteenth century and the ways it has been challenged. Race, ethnicity, age, religion, and gender all construct our sexualities. Sexual behaviors and attitudes vary by race or by whether you come from a big city or a small town. Also, what one find erotic as a teenager may not be a preview of your eventual sexual tendencies since sexual tastes develop, mature, and change over time.

2. Page 322 and 336-338

Homosexuality is the sexual desires or behaviors with members of one's own gender. Homosexuals have been discriminated against and they often band together, both to find suitable partners and to escape the hostility of the mainstream society. As early as the nineteenth century, there were gay neighborhoods in some large cities, but most people with same-sex interests believed that hey were alone. During World War II, gay and lesbian soldiers found each other and realized that there were many more than anyone thought. In the 1950s gay men and lesbians began forming organizations to petition for the end of police harassment. The 1969 Stonewall riots led to the formation of the
Gay liberation front. More gay rights groups followed, until by 1975, there were hundred. They were not apologetic instead they were loud, in-your-face, shouting rather than whispering, demanding rather than asking. They were extremely successful. During the next few years sodomy laws were thrown out in half of the U.S. states and the American Psychiatric Association removed homosexuality from its list of disorders.

3. Pages 339-340

Sex tourism represents the globalization of prostitution. Well-organized groups direct the flow of the consumer to the commodities. The tourists seem to be men and women who are being friendly and flirtatious, but the locals are usually victims of kidnapping and violence. In some Eastern European countries and new nations of the former Soviet union, as well as Africa, young girls and boys are abducted or lured to European cities to serve as virtual sex slaves, paying off debts incurred in transporting them to their new homes. Some countries, such as Thailand, have become destinations of choice for sex tourists and have well-developed sex tourism industries. Proprietors take advantage of high unemployment and traditional attitudes about women to ensure a steady supply and use the exoticism of the Orient and traditional stereotypes about docile and compliant Asian women to ensure a steady demand from their heterosexual counterparts. There are countries who sell sex and countries who can buy it. Men, women, and children from Latin America, Asia, Eastern Europe, and Africa are moved to the United States. The high-income nations are purchasing the sex, while the low income nations are selling the sex.

Chapter Eleven Answers
Age: From Young to Old

ANSWER KEY

Multiple Choice

1. d (pg 354)	6. d (pg 359)	11. c (pg 356)	16. c (pg 358)	21. c (pg 371)
2. c (pg 348)	7. c (pg 361)	12. d (pg 361)	17. d (pg 360)	22. d (pg 373)
3. d (pg 357)	8. c (pg 358)	13. c (pg 357)	18. a (pg 361)	23. a (pg 349)
4. d (pg 358)	9. b (pg 372)	14. a (pg 349)	19. d (pg 363)	24. c (pg 349)
5. a (pg 357)	10. b (pg 373)	15. d (pg 349)	20. b (pg 364)	25. d (pg 350)

True/False

1. false (pg 356)   6. true (pg 365)
2. false (pg 349)   7. true (pg 363)
3. false(pg 352)   8. true (pg 365)
4. true (pg 358)   9. false (pg 368)
5. false (pg 357)   10. true (pg 371)

Fill-in-the-Blank

1. acceptance (pg 361)   6. adolescence (pg 349)
2. age cohort (pg 348)   7. retirement (pg 365)
3. gerontology (pg 348)   8. childhood (pg 367)
4. ageism (pg 363)   9. increased; decreased (pg 371)
5. Y (pg 369)   10. Global trafficking (pg 375)

Essays

1. Page 348

Sociologists argue that age is less a biological condition than a social construction. Depending on the norms of your society different activities may be seen as appropriate for different age groups. Prior to the twentieth century, people became adults astonishingly early. Today, people postpone adulthood until halfway through their lives. There has been so much change and redefinition of age. In some societies 15 year-olds may play soccer and go to school while in another fight in a real war. It is not the passing of years but the social environment that determines the characteristics of age. The norms of society are constantly changing. In earlier years children were expected to act as little adults and work on the farm, today there is a childhood and children are to be carefree and naïve.

2. Pages 350-358

Childhood is the first stage of life that people go through. The Western concept of childhood did not arise as a distinct stage of life until the Industrial Revolution of the eighteenth century. Now most children would require training outside the home before they could go to work, so schools and apprenticeships were designed to train children in adult social norms. One of the major elements in our beliefs about childhood as a stage of life is that it is "innocent." Children's actions do not carry the same consequences as those of adults and we also believe that children must be shielded from information about sex and death. After childhood, people moved into adolescence. In this stage people were no longer considered children, but they have yet to enter the adult world. They had to go to high school because the more labor became specialized they required more specialized training. People then pass into young adulthood. This marks the beginning of our lives as fully functioning members of society. There are five milestones that define adulthood: establishing a household separate from our parents; getting a full-time job so we are no longer financially dependent; getting married; completing our education; and having children. Major structural changes in the economy have pushed the age at which we complete these from about 22 to close to 30. Middle age follows young adulthood. In this stage people are usually in their 50s. In middle age one must accept one's life as it is. After middle age comes old age. There are three stages in old age: "young old," ages 65-75, who are likely to enjoy relative good health and financial security and tend to live independently; "old old," ages 75-85, suffer many more health and financial problems; the "oldest old," ages 85 and higher, suffer the most health and financial problems.

3. Pages 358-359

One myth of growing old is that they live in a nursing home. The vast majority of elderly people maintain their own homes and apartments, and a large percentage live with relatives. Only about 5 percent live in continuous long-term care facilities or nursing homes. The fear is really about losing independence, and it is true that about 20 percent of people over age 70 are unable to care for themselves without assistance. The second myth is that people lose their mental abilities. Alzheimer's is one of several different root causes of senility. However, less than 5 percent of the elderly develops any of the types. Some decline in learning and memory does occur after 70, but usually it is more of a nuisance than a tragedy. The third myth is that the elderly are along. Some degree of loneliness is inevitable as long-term family and friends die or move away, but 71 percent of elderly men and 44 percent of elderly women live with a spouse or romantic partner and a sizeable percentage lives with relatives other than their spouses. The fourth myth is that the elderly have nothing to do. This is usually a characteristic of income rather than age. The poor are likely to have nothing to do regardless of their age, but middle-class and affluent elderly tend to be more active in sports, hobbies, and religious and community groups than the middle-aged who are busy with their children and careers.

4. Page 363
Ageism is the differential treatment of people based on their age. It usually affects the elderly but can have an impact on younger people as well. An example of this might be a housing developer near his home in Washington D.C. and did not allow people over 65 to buy homes. Another example would be a job refusing to hire someone over the age of 60 because they know that the person is close to retirement.

5. Pages 371-373
Young people are virtually powerless in our society. They come from single-parent, disadvantaged families with little political influence and no control over public resources. Children cannot vote and there are few activist groups for them to get involved in. Older generations are better off economically and have more political clout. The poverty rate for children under 18 in the United States in 2006 was 21.9 percent. They by far have the highest poverty rate of any age group. Also, 12 percent of these children have no health care. In 1999, 52.9 percent of Americans age 18 through 21 had no health insurance at all. About 33 percent of Americans under that age of 35 spent the whole year in 2002 with no health insurance.

Chapter Twelve Answers
The Family

ANSWER KEY

Multiple Choice

1. a (pg 383)	6. c (pg 395)	11. b (pg 383)	16. c (pg 384)	21. b (pg 384)
2. c (pg 384)	7. d (pg 395)	12. a (pg 403)	17. d (pg 401)	22. b (pg 383)
3. b (pg 385)	8. a (pg 394)	13. c (pg 405)	18. b (pg 390)	23. c (pg 404)
4. d (pg 391)	9. a (pg 399)	14. d (pg 406)	19. a (pg 410)	24. b (pg 400)
5. b (pg 393)	10. d (pg 401)	15. b (pg 386)	20. d (pg 413)	25. d (pg 395)

True/False

1. F (pg 383)	6. F (pg 390)
2. T (pg 382)	7. F (pg 402)
3. F (pg 383)	8. T (pg 404)
4. T (pg 384)	9. T (pg 408)
5. F (pg 386)	10. F (pg 410)

Fill-in-the-Blank

1. kinship systems (pg 382)	6. cohabitation (pg 395)
2. monogamy (pg 383)	7. miscegenation (pg 398)
3. fictive kinship (pg 390)	8. interpersonal violence (pg 409)
4. companionate (pg 387)	9. intergenerational violence (pg 410)
5. 51 (pg 395)	10. grandparents (pg 404)

Essays

1. Pages 383-384
The different types of marriages include monogamy, polygamy, polygyny, polyandry, and group marriage. Monogamy is the marriage between two people. In the United States all legal marriages are monogamous and almost always between one man and one women. Polygamy is the marriage between three or more people. The most common form of polygamy is polygyny, one man marries two or more women. An

example of this could be the Mormons in Utah who still practice this outlawed form of marriage. Polyandry is when one woman marries two or more men. This is the most rare form of marriage but it has been documented in Tibet and a few other places where men are absent for sexual months of the year.

2. Pages 389-391

The European family has been transformed into a nuclear family. At the end of World War II there was a large infusion of government funding toward the promotion of this new nuclear family. The Native American family and kinship systems were developed to provide for people's fundamental needs and are formed out of the desire to survive. The extended family model of the tribal society is common only on reservations; most who reside in cities follow the nuclear family structure. The African American family today consists of only one parent, usually the mother, making the nuclear family model even less common. Fictive kinship stretches the boundaries of kinship to include nonblood relations, friends, neighbors, and co-workers which is unique to the African American family. The Asian family is fairly similar to the European family. Asian families are nuclear families although the families from China tend to be more collective than Euro-American families. Euro-American families tend to be more democratic while Asian families are more authoritarian. Hispanics families fall somewhat between Euro-American and African American families. Most are nuclear families, but they do have characteristics of extended families, with grandparents, aunts, uncles, and more distant relatives living close together. The families tend to be hierarchical by age and gender.

3. Pages 394-398

The types of alternative marriages include: delayed marriage, staying single, and cohabitation. In the United States, young people experience longer periods of independent living while working or attending school before marriage. A 25-year old man is far more likely to be single and childless today than he would have been 50 years ago. Men and women are more likely to put off marriage because of educational or economic opportunities. Staying single has increased dramatically since the 1970s. The proportion of white adults who had never married rose from 16 percent in 1970 to 20 percent in 2000, 19 percent to 28 percent for Hispanics, and 21 to 39 percent for African Americans. Women are more likely to be single than men. The majority of American women are living without a spouse. Single women are better educated, better employed, and have better mental health than single men. Singles have financial independence, but they also have sole financial responsibility for their lives and futures. Cohabitation refers to unmarried people in a romantic relationship living in the same residence. A few decades ago, when non-marital sex was illegal in most states, cohabitation was virtually impossible. Today cohabitation has become commonplace, largely lacking in social disapproval. Almost half the people 25 to 40 years of age in the United States have cohabitated. Some people cohabitate because of financial need. The changes in the alternative marriages are partially explained by new practices, such as courtship and dating. These changes are associated with higher levels of education. The higher the level of education, the later people get married. These changes are also partially explained by changing sexual behaviors and attitudes.

4. Pages 407-408

Economically, there is evidence about losses and gains. In a large majority of divorces, women's standards of living decline while men's standards of living go up. The men who are used to being the primary breadwinner may suddenly find that they are supporting one on a salary that used to support the whole family. Those women who are more accustomed to being in charge of the household may suddenly find that their income must stretch from being a helpful supplement to supplying most of the family's necessities. After the divorce, children are more likely to live with the mothers, while the father visits on specified days. Children who live with their mothers after divorce have higher rates of poverty since the father is the major breadwinner. Judith Wallerstein found a sleeper effect in the children of divorced couples. She found that later, their parent's divorce affected the children's relationships. Research has consistently found, contrary to Wallerstein's findings, that children are more resilient and adapt successfully to their parents' divorces. Mavis Hetherington found that 75 to 80 percent of children cope reasonably well with divorce.

Chapter Thirteen Answers
Economy and Work

ANSWER KEY

Multiple Choice

1. d (page 418)	6. a (page 423)	11 d (page 431)	16. d (page 437)	21. c (page 449)
2. b (page 419)	7. c (page 427)	12. b (page 420)	17. b (page 441)	22. c (page 450)
3. c (page 419)	8. b (page 426)	13. a (page 431)	18. a (page 447)	23. b (page 447)
4. d (page 420)	9. d (page 426)	14. c (page 432)	19. d (page 446)	24. b (page 444)
5. d (page 421)	10. c (page 428)	15. d (page 438)	20. a (page 449)	25. d (page 437)

True/False

1. True (page 418)	6. False (page 441)
2. False (page 426)	7. True (page 418)
3. False (page 426)	8. False (page 423)
4. False (page 428)	9. True (page 423)
5. True (page 443)	10. False (page 434)

Fill-in-the-Blank

1. Laissez-Faire (pg 426)	6. Communism (pg 428)
2. Institutional corporations (pg 432)	7. Race to the bottom (pg 433)
3. Economy (pg 418)	8. Theory X (pg 435)
4. Postindustrial economy (pg 421)	9. Informal Economy (pg 440)
5. Collective goals (pg 427)	10. Poor (pg 447)

Essays

1. Pages 432-434

Multinational corporations are no longer located anywhere. They operate globally and are transnational. The products of multinational corporations do not really "come from" anywhere. A designer may live in one country, while the parts are outsourced to another, and the factories are located in yet another country, and the assembly occurs in a different country. These corporations outsource to countries where wages are much lower than in the United States. Multinational companies are not attached to a home country any more, so they do not put their profits back into it in the form of more hiring or better benefits. The threat of further outsourcing continues to keep wages down at home.

2. Pages 9-13

Capitalism is a profit-oriented economic system based on the private or corporate ownership of the means of production and distribution. Individual companies compete with each other for customers and profits with no government interference. The three components of classical capitalism include the private ownership of the means of production, and open market with no government interference, and profit as a valuable goal of human enterprise. There are three different types of capitalism: laissez-faire capitalism, state capitalism, and welfare capitalism. Laissez-faire capitalism believes that property and the means of production should all be privately owned. Markets should be able to compete freely to sell goods, acquire raw materials, and hire labor with no government interference. State capitalism requires that the government use a heavy hand in regulating and constraining the marketplace. Companies may still be privately owned, but they must also meet government-set standards of product quality, worker compensation, and truth in advertising. Welfare capitalism gives the government even more control over private investors that state capitalism. While there is a market-based economy for most goods and services, there are also extensive social welfare programs, and the government owns some of the most essential services, such as transportation. Socialism is the economic system is the exact opposite of laissez-faire capitalism. In a socialist economy there is collective ownership, collective goals, and central planning. With a socialist economy there is strong government control. Communist economies are based on collective ownership of the means of production and the goods are administered collectively, without a

386

political apparatus to ensure equal distribution. Socialism requires strong government intervention, but in a communist state, government is abolished. With communism, social inequalities will disappear, along with crime, hunger, and political strife.

3. Pages 429-431

Work in the United States has changed drastically over the last 100 years. The United States was formed as an agricultural economy. By 1860, 16 percent of the population lived in urban areas. With the Industrial Revolution came a new type of economy. Colonial America was a nation of small businessmen, farmers or shopkeepers, but industrialization meant consolidation. In the late nineteenth century there were a few that managed to accumulate huge fortunes almost overnight because there were no federal regulations to limit price fixing, underpaying and overworking employees, or establishing monopolies. At one point Rockefeller controlled 90 percent of the oil reserves in American. Americans began to embrace money making as a virtue. Many people moved from working on the farm to cities where they would work in factors and mills. Small farms could no longer compete with big business. By 1956, the number of white-collar workers in the U.S. was greater than the number of blue-collar workers. This is when the postindustrial economy began. It was not until the 1980s when the high-tech industries made technology cheap enough for everyday use, that the production of knowledge surpassed the production of goods. The shift between the industrial economy and the postindustrial economy is marked by the shift in production of goods to the production of knowledge.

4. Pages 436-438

White collar jobs are knowledge-based jobs, with the day being spent on manipulating symbols: talking speaking, reading, writing, and calculating. Most white-collar jobs require considerable education and offer the highest salaries and the most opportunity for advancement. White-collar jobs include professors, lawyers, doctors, and librarians. Less than 14 percent work in management, business, and financial occupations. Sales are considered a white collar job and seventeen percent of American workers are in sales. Blue collar jobs involve production rather than knowledge. Today, less than a fourth of the population has blue-collar jobs. Examples of blue-collar jobs include factory workers, construction workers, plumbers, and farmers. The third category of jobs is called pink-collar jobs. These are jobs that are often held by women and are the lowest paying and lowest prestige jobs. Many of the most dominant pink-collar jobs are in clerical and sales work. They are typists, file clerks, receptionists, and secretaries. Today 26 percent of the working population is working in pink-collar occupations.

5. Pages 446-451

The workplace has become more diverse in terms of race although there are still many inequalities that racial and ethnic minorities face. Today, over half of women work outside the home. Women comprise more than half of all managers and professional. Although more and more women are working they still face discrimination at work. In 2002 the majority of married male-female couples in America were dual income. Women now make up 39 percent of America's top wealth holders. The workplace originated in a heterosexual division of labor. Employers used to be able to not hire or fire at anytime a homosexual. Through the efforts of gay and lesbian workplace activists homosexuals have changed the workplace. Of the Fortune 500 companies, 253 now offer benefits for same-sex partners and 410 include sexual orientation in their nondiscrimination policies. For many years, working mothers have been struggling to make corporate culture see children not as "problems" or distractions, but as part of "business as usual." Sixty percent of all mothers and 53.3 percent of mothers with children under 1 year old are in the workforce. Employers now have to deal with both men and women wanting to spend time with their families.

Chapter Fourteen Answers
Politics and Government

ANSWER KEY

Multiple Choice

1. c (pg 457)	6. b (pg 460)	11. b (pg 456)	16. a (pg 471)	21. c (pg 481)
2. b (pg 457)	7. a (pg 462)	12. d (pg 457)	17. d (pg 477)	22. d (pg 470)
3. b (pg 458)	8. b (pg 467)	13. b (pg 458)	18. d (pg 478)	23. a (pg 468)
4. d (pg 459)	9. c (pg 473)	14. c (pg 461)	19. c (pg 477)	24. d (pg 477)
5. c (pg 461)	10. d (pg 456)	15. d (pg 470)	20. c (pg 458)	25. a (pg 460)

True/False

1. F (pg 457)	6. T (pg 470)
2. T (pg 460)	7. F (pg 472)
3. T (pg 462)	8. F (pg 476)
4. F (pg 466)	9. T (pg 480)
5. F (pg 469)	10. T (pg 482)

Fill-in-the-Blank

1. authority (pg 457)	6. political action committees (pg 473)
2. charismatic (pg 458)	7. social movements (pg 474)
3. authoritarian political system (pg 460)	8. political (pg 476)
4. illiberal (pg 463)	9. voter apathy (pg 471)
5. suffrage (pg 467)	10. two-party system (pg 469)

Essays

1. Page 477

There are five factors that serve as root causes of most wars. The first is that there are perceived threats. Societies mobilize in response to threats to their people, territory, or culture. If threats are not real they can always be manufactured. When the United States was attacked on 9/11 there was a perceived threat to the people and territory. The second cause is political objectives. War is often a political strategy. Societies go to war to end foreign domination, enhance their political stature in the global arena, and increase their wealth and power. The third cause is the "wag the dog" rationale. When internal problems create widespread unrest at home, a government may wage war to divert public attention and unify the country behind a common, external enemy. The fourth cause is moral objectives. Leaders often infuse military campaigns with moral urgency, rallying people around visions of freedom rather than admitting they fight to increase their wealth or power. Morality and religion are mobilized for the cause. The final cause of war is the absence of alternatives. Sometimes there is no choice. When your country is invaded by another, it is hard to see how one would avoid a war. The United States had adopted a strictly isolationist policy during World War II, but had to do something when Pearl Harbor was attacked.

2. Pages 457-459

Traditional authority is a type of power that draws it legitimacy from tradition. Those in power derive it from who they are. This type of authority is very stable, and people can expect to obey the same commands that heir ancestors did. An example of this type of authority would be when the kings and queens rules England. The second type of authority is charismatic. Charismatic authority is a type of power in which people obey because of personal characteristics of the leader. These leaders are so personally compelling that people follow them even when they have no traditional claims to authority. They are often religious prophets. Charisma is morally neutral. Charismatic leaders can change societies, leading people away from the traditional rules and toward a more personal experience of authority. Charisma is very unstable since it is located in the personality of the individual, not a set of traditions or laws. Examples of charismatic leaders include Gandhi, Hitler, Kennedy, and Nelson Mandela. The third type of authority is the legal-rational. In this type of authority leaders are to be obeyed, not primarily as representatives of tradition or because of their personal qualities, but because they are voicing a set of rationally derived laws. Examples of this type would include George W. Bush and George Washington.

3. Pages 460-463
Authoritarian political systems vest the power in a single person or small group. The person holds power through heredity and sometimes through force or terror. A monarchy is a political system that is ruled by a single individual. An example would be Saudi Arabia where the king receives no direct input from the people and there are no political parties or elections. An oligarchy is the rule of a small group of people, an elite social class or often a single family. An example of this would be the Maggior Consiglio in Italy. Dictatorships are another type of authoritarian political system. A dictatorship is ruled by one person who has no hereditary claim to rule. They may acquire power through a military takeover, or they may be elected or appointed. Examples of this type of political system would include Hitler and Mussolini. Totalitarianism is when political authority is extended over all other aspects of social life including culture, arts, and social relations. The best example of this is the North Korean leader, Kim Jon-il. There are pictures of him posted all over the country and political messages are broadcast over loudspeakers constantly reminding citizens that they owe allegiance to the state. Democracies put legislative decision making into the hands of the people rather than a single individual or noble class. Participatory democracy gives every person one vote and the majority rules. Representative democracies have citizens elect representatives to make the decisions for them. Illiberal democracies have elected officials that pay little attention to the constitution and other laws and to the opinions of their constituents that the country might as well be an oligarchy. An example of an illiberal democracy is Singapore. Participatory democracies are almost impossible to have and existed in ancient Greece where only a small number of people could legally participate. Representative democracies can be found in Western Europe and North America.

4. Page 469-471
The United States original two-party system consisted of the Federalists and the Republicans. Today the parties are called Republican and Democrat. The Republicans run against government, claiming that government's job should be to get out of the way of individuals and off the back of the average taxpayer. Democrats believe that only with active government intervention can social problems like poverty and discrimination be solved. Republicans want to stay out of your personal life when you are at work. They want to lower taxes, enable you to keep more of what you ear, but when you come home they very much want to intervene. They want to tell you what gender you may love and marry, they want to control your decisions about pregnancy and birth control, and they want to control what you can even know about sex. The Democrats on the other had want to leave you alone when you are in the privacy of your own home, believing you should be able to make decisions about when, how, and with whom you make love. They trust that you can make good decisions about what books you read, but that you must pay for these freedoms and your privacy by ensuring that other shave access to the same freedoms that you have. The poor, working-class, lower-middle class, and blue-collar trade unionists ten to be Democrats while the wealthy, upper-middle class, white-collar individuals tend to be Republicans. Generally the higher educational levels vote Democrat and the lower Republican. Racial and ethnic minorities have historically been Democrats and that is still true today even though the percentages are somewhat lower. Women are more likely to vote Democratic than men.

Chapter Fifteen Answers
Religion and Science

ANSWER KEY

Multiple Choice

1. b (pg 488)	6. c (pg 492)	11. c (pg 498)	16. b (pg 503)	21. c (pg 514)
2. c (pg 490)	7. d (pg 493)	12. b (pg 492)	17. a (pg 496)	22. b (pg 511)
3. b (pg 490)	8. d (pg 495)	13. a (pg 497)	18. a (pg 508)	23. d (pg 510)
4. d (pg 490)	9. b (pg 495)	14. d (pg 501)	19. d (pg 511)	24. d (pg 510)
5. a (g 491)	10. d (pg 495)	15. c (pg501)	20. b (pg 514)	25. a (pg 511)

True/False

1. T (pg 489)	6. F (pg 497)
2. F (pg 490)	7. T (pg 499)
3. T (pg 491)	8. T (pg 501)
4. F (pg 493)	9. T (pg 503)
5. F (pg 495)	10. F (pg 506)

Fill-in-the-Blank

1. empirical verification (pg 488)	6. sect (pg 492)
2. sacred (pg 489)	7. Buddhism (pg 497)
3. rituals (pg 490)	8. Secularization (pg 498)
4. opiate (pg 490)	9. liberation theology (pg 508)
5. denomination (pg 493)	10. objectivity (pg 511)

Essays

1. Page 488

Religion is a set of beliefs about the origins and meaning of life, usually based on the existence of a supernatural power. The big questions for religion involve existence. Religion acquires its ideas through revelations. God, spirits, prophets, or sacred books give us the answers to the questions of existence. Science is the accumulated systematic knowledge of the physical or material world, which is obtained through experimentation and observation. Science deals with the questions of classification or processes. Science acquires its knowledge through empirical verification. Information is developed, demonstrated, and double-checked using an experimental method. Science basis its claims on what has been shown this way, rather than asking you to believe something on faith.

2. Page 491-494

Cults are formed around a specific person or idea drawn from an established religion. They are often formed by splitting off from the main branch of the religion. They are typically small and are composed of deeply fervent believers. An example of a cult would be the Branch Davidians in the 1980s. Sects are small subcultures within an established religious institution. They break from traditional practices, but remain within the larger institutions. They typically arise when some members of an established religious institution believes that the institution is drifting from its true mission. Sects seek to remain true to the initial mission by demanding more of its members than does the established institution. Many are short lived. An example of a sect would be the Amish. Denominations are large-scale, extremely organized religious body. It has an established hierarchy, methods for credentialing administrators, and much more social respect than either a cult or a sect. An example of a denomination is Roman-Catholic. Ecclesiaes is a religion that is so pervasive that the boundary between church and state is nonexistent. In these societies, the clerical elite often serve as political leaders or at least formal advisors to political leaders. Everyone in the society belongs to that religion. Today and example would be Muslim in Saudi Arabia.

3. Page 494-498

The six major world religions can be divided into the Western religions and the Eastern religions. The Western religions include Judaism, Christianity, and Islam. Judaism believes that the covenant between God and Abraham around 2000 bce become the foundation of Jewish law. Today there are three branches: Orthodox, who follow traditional Jewish law very strictly; Reformed, who attempt to modernize dress, dietary laws, and worship practices; and Conservative, who rebelled against the over modernization of the Reformed branch. Christianity was founded 2,000 year ago by the disciples of Jesus, who declared him to be the son of God. There are three main branches, Roman Catholic, Eastern Orthodoxy, and Protestantism. Islam was founded about 1,400 years ago when God grew displeased with the corruption of the teachings of his earlier prophets and gave his last prophet, Mohammed, a new sacred text. Islam is far more communal than Christianity and requires the fusion of religion and government. Only a Muslim government is seen as legitimate. There are two main branches, Shi'ite and Sunni, which differ in the number of beliefs and practices. Eastern religions consist of Hinduism, Buddhism, and Confucianism. Hinduism developed from the indigenous religions in India around 1500 bce. It is based largely on oral tradition, passed from one generation to the next by storytellers. Buddhism developed as a reaction to the corruption of Hinduism. While Hinduism taught that enlightenment could come only after countless lifetimes of reincarnation, Buddhism taught that enlightenment was possible in this lifetime. There are two main branches today, Hinayana and Mahayana. Confucianism was the official religion of China until the People's Republic of China became atheist in 1949. This religion does not have much to say about gods or the afterlife, instead, it establishes a strict social hierarchy. It sees Heaven and Earth as linked realms that are constantly in touch with each other. Eastern religions tend to be somewhat more tolerant of other religions that Western religions.

4. Page 511-513

Like all institutions, science has norms on how to govern interactions among scientists and relationships between scientists and the rest of society. The most important norm of science is objectivity. Judgments are based on empirical verification, not on personal feelings or opinions. Scientists are to check their personal lives at the door and differences in class, race, or gender should not make a difference in procedure or results. A second norm is common ownership. Research results should be open to everyone, public knowledge. Disinterestedness is another norm of science. Scientific research should not be conducted for personal goals, but for the pursuit of scientific truth. These norms are to be followed by scientists to preserve the integrity of the work. Scientific networks are social relationships between scientists working in given fields or in all fields. Scientists develop rules of conduct, and those who do not accept them are excluded from the networks. Established scientists control research by acting as gatekeepers and if you do not do science by their rules, you do not get to do science. The scientific networks the inequality in our nation. The majority of scientists are white males. They get to make the rules and others have to abide by them. In terms of income, minorities and women consistently make less money reinforcing the unequal system in America.

Chapter Sixteen Answers
The Body and Society: Health and Illness

ANSWER KEY

Multiple Choice

1. d (pg 525)	6. b (pg 524)	11. d (pg 534)	16. d (pg 538)	21. c (pg 545)
2. b (pg 525)	7. c (pg 528)	12. c (pg 534)	17. b (pg 539)	22. b (pg 539)
3. a (pg 526)	8. d (pg 530)	13. c (pg 535)	18. c (pg 542)	23. a (pg 536)
4. b (pg 527)	9. d (pg 531)	14. d (pg 536)	19. d (pg 543)	24. d (pg 534)
5. c (pg 524)	10. a (pg 532)	15. b (pg 537)	20. d (pg 548)	25. d (pg 534)

True/False

1. F (pg 523)	6. T (pg 534)
2. T (pg 527)	7. T (pg 537)
3. T (pg 529)	8. F (pg 542)
4. F (pg 530)	9. F (pg 545)
5. T (pg 533)	10. T (pg 547)

Fill-in-the-Blank

1. beauty myth (pg 523)	6. Epidemiology (pg 533)
2. anorexia nervosa (pg 526)	7. Medicalization (pg 539)
3. Adonis complex (pg 527)	8. Drug (pg 542)
4. Tattooing (pg 529)	9. Alternative medicine (pg 547)
5. Health (pg 533)	10. Mental illnesses (pg 540)

Essays

1. Pages 522-523

Beauty is less a matter of individual perception and more about cultural standards. Standards of women's beauty vary depending on economic trends and the status of women. We construct our identity through out bodies: what we think is beautiful or the ways we adorn and transform them to fit with cultural norms. Body shape and weight that are considered ideal change over time. When the economy goes up, women's standards become increasingly feminine, exaggerating biological differences to suggest that male breadwinners can afford to have their wives stay at home. It is not individual women who want to become increasingly feminine; it is the culture that persuades what is considered beautiful

2. Pages 526-528

Weight and height ideal varies enormously and the standards are becoming more difficult to achieve. In 1975, the average female fashion model weighed about 8 percent less than the average woman; by 1990 the disparity had grown to 23 percent. Almost half of 9-11 year olds are on diets and by college the percentage has nearly doubled. In America we are both fatter and thinner. Poor people are less likely to eat healthy and exercise than are rich people. Obesity is now a major health problem in America even though the idea body shape is thin. The current beauty standards of thinness are opposite of what Americans really are. In 2006, 32 percent of people were obese. Current standards of beauty for women combine two images- dramatically thin and muscular and buxom. These are virtually impossible to accomplish. Increasing numbers of women are being diagnosed with anorexia and bulimia. Males who are pressured by the American beauty standard may experience muscle dsymorphia and the Adonis complex. Men may think they are not muscular enough. Men today are taught to see their bodies as women see their, as ongoing works-in-progress. The standards for men and women are increasingly impossible to attain and both are now at risk for developing disorders related to weight and body shape.

3. Pages 529-531

The three types of body transformations discussed in this chapter include tattoos, cosmetic surgery, and transgenderism. Tattoos have long been a way to decorate the body among people. Today tattoos are quite common. About 24 percent of all Americans between the ages of 18 and 50 have at least one tattoo. Tattoos are increasingly seen to symbolize traits valued by peers, including environmental awareness, athletic ability, artistic talent, and academic achievement. Gangs and other marginalized groups use them as specific markers of identity. Cosmetic surgery is one of the fastest growing methods of bodily transformation. The total number of cosmetic procedures in 2006 was 11.5 million. Though women continue to be the primary consumers of cosmetic surgery, male patients now comprise 20 percent of all procedures. The body may be seen as the last arena left hat we can make perfect and over which we can exercise control in an age of declining fortunes and downward mobility. Transgenderism describes a variety of people, behaviors, and groups whose identities depart from normative gender ideals of masculinity and femininity. They develop a gender identity that is different from the biological sex of their birth. Some people feel constrained by gender role expectations and seek to expand these by changing their behavior. Some feel as if their biological sex does not match their internal sense of gender identity. Transgenderism remains relatively uncommon in society.

4. Pages 534-536

Our health changes as we age. As we age our general health declines. Also, the wealthier you are the healthier you will be. Being poor is a good predictor of being ill. Lower-class people work in more hazardous jobs, they have fewer health insurance benefits, and often times live in neighborhoods or in housing that endangers their health. Women with a family income under $10,000 pr year are three times more likely to die of heart disease and nearly three times more likely to die of diabetes than those with income above $25,000. Women are more likely to be in poverty than are men. Race plays into this since it is racial minorities who have higher poverty rates than whites. Latinos die of several leading causes of death at far higher rates than do Whites, including liver disease, diabetes, and HIV. Racism also is harmful to health. In developed countries women outlive men by about five to eight years, but they outlive men by less than three years in the developing world. The norms of masculinity often encourage men to take more health risks and then discourage them from seeking health care services. Globally, the health problem is enormous. The wealthier the country is the healthier its population will be. The cause of death for most people in the developed world is chronic diseases, such as heart attacks and cancers, but in the developing world over one-half of all deaths are the result of infectious diseases or complications during pregnancy and childbirth.

5. Pages 544-545

HIV is a sexually transmitted disease and is also transmitted with the exchange of other body fluids, like blood. Initially the disease was localized in the gay population but soon emerged among people who had received blood transfusions with infected blood supplies or those sharing intravenous drug paraphernalia. Blacks make up 12 percent of the U.S. population but account for half of all new reported HIV infections. AIDS is also a gendered disease with men accounting for 85 percent of the cases in 2003. In the developing world, HIV/AIDS affects women and men in equal numbers. In 2006, 40 million people were infected with HIV worldwide with the epicenter of the disease being located in Sub-Saharan Africa. There, a 15-year-old boy or girl faces a 50-50 chance that he or she will contract HIV/AIDS. Medical breakthroughs since the 1990s transformed the disease from an almost universal likelihood of death to a chronic disease that can be managed with a combination of drug therapies. In poor countries though these drugs are not affordable and the governments do not have enough money to subsidize them. The transmission in the developing world is more prevalent people of cultural and religious beliefs that make campaigns to reduce risk very difficult. In Africa people believe that HIV is a Western "import" and infects only gay men. Some men in southern Africa have begun to seek out young girls who are virgins as sex partners, on the assumption that they could not possible be infected with the disease and as a result many of these young girls are becoming infected because they men were HIV-positive and were unaware of it.

Chapter Seventeen Answers
Education

ANSWER KEY

Multiple Choice

1. d (pg 556)	6. d (pg 563)	11. b (pg 556)	16. b (pg 561)	21. d (pg 579)
2. b (pg 556)	7. d (pg 565)	12. a (pg 577)	17. d (pg 574)	22. b (pg 581)
3. c (pg 559)	8. a (pg 566)	13. d (pg 559)	18. c (pg 575)	23. c (pg 582)
4. c (pg 559)	9. a (pg 556)	14. b (pg 563)	19. a (pg 575)	24. b (pg 580)
5. d (pg 560)	10. c (pg 569)	15. b (pg 561)	20. c (pg 577)	25. d (pg 559)

True/False

1. T (pg 557)	6. F (pg 567)
2. F (pg 560)	7. F (pg 571)
3. T (pg 564)	8. F (pg 574)
4. F (pg 565)	9. T (pg 575)
5. T (pg 566)	10. T (pg 582)

Fill-in-the-Blank

1. education (pg 556)	6. tracking (pg 568)
2. Frederick Douglas (pg 558)	7. voucher system (pg 573)
3. scientific literacy (pg 564)	8. No Child Left Behind (pg 575)
4. 56 (pg 559)	9. marketization (pg 581)
5. integration (pg 567)	10. bilingual education (pg 568)

Essays

1. Pages 556-557

Education is a social institution through which society provides its members with important knowledge-basic facts, job skills, and cultural norms and values. It provides socialization, cultural innovation, and social integration. Education has both manifest, clearly apparent, and latent, potential or hidden, functions.

The manifest functions include the subjects that we are taught. We learn to read and write in grade school and then learn job skills such as accounting in college. Latent functions are by-products of the education process, the norms, values, and goals that accrue because we are immersed in a specific social environment. The latent functions include learning individualism and competition, conformity to mainstream norms, obedience to authority, passive consumption of ideas, and acceptance of social inequality.

2. Pages 560-562

Globally, there are considerable amounts of inequality in educational opportunities. A child in a high-performing nation can expect far more education than a child residing in a poor country. It is important to note that a child's socioeconomic status is a strong predictor of participation in secondary education. In the developing nations children from higher status families receive far more education than children from poor families. Gender also determines educational opportunities. Many children live in countries that do not offer equal access to education for boys and girls. Gender disparity is widespread at the secondary level and the magnitude of inequity increases by educational level. While disadvantages for girls in secondary education are common in low-income countries, girls tend to outnumber boys in high-income countries.

3. Pages 568-569

Tracking is grouping students according to their ability and it commonplace in American schools. Some schools do not have formal tracking, but virtually all have mechanisms for sorting students into groups that seem to be alike in ability and achievement. Labeling of students occurs in tracking systems whether the system is formal or informal. Individuals who are placed in the low-achievement, non-college-preparatory classes maybe labeled as dumb by teachers and by other students. They are not only labeled, they are treated as if they are dumb, which in turn affects their self-image and ultimately their achievement in a self-fulfilling prophecy. The negative impact of tracking mostly affects minority students. The term self-fulfilling prophecy is the term used to describe a curious phenomenon: When you expect something to happen, it usually does. Also, the resources available usually go to the needs of the high-track students so that leaves the low-track students with poorer classes, textbooks, supplies, and teachers. Tracking reinforces previously existing inequalities for average or poor students but has positive benefits for advanced students.

Chapter Eighteen Answers
Mass Media

ANSWER KEY

Multiple Choice

1. b (pg 588)	6. d (pg 602)	11. d (pg 606)	16. a (pg 591)	21. c (pg 599)
2. a (pg 589)	7. c (pg 603)	12. d (pg 609)	17. b (pg 595)	22. c (pg 601)
3. c (pg 592)	8. c (pg 605)	13. c (pg 611)	18. c (pg 597)	23. b (pg 610)
4. b (g 594)	9. d (pg 605)	14. d (pg 612)	19. d (pg 598)	24. c (pg 593)
5. a (pg 601)	10. b (pg 606)	15. b (pg 590)	20. a (pg 598)	25. d (pg 601)

True/False

1. T (pg 588)	6. F (pg 603)
2. T (pg 593)	7. F (pg 608)
3. F (pg 598)	8. T (pg 609)
4. T (pg 599)	9. F (pg 611)
5. F (pg 601)	10. T (pg 611)

Fill-in-the-Blank

1. internet (pg 595)	6. cultural industries (pg 599)
2. media texts (pg 599)	7. celebrities (pg 603)
3. interpretive community (pg 606)	8. cultural imperialism (pg 611)

4. fan (pg 606)   9. global village (pg 610)
5. televisions (pg 592)   10. media consolidation (pg 601)

Essays

1. Pages 589-595

The different types of mass media include print media, online print journalism, radio, movies, and television, video games, and the internet. Print media includes books, magazines, and newspapers. During the 1800s, most people owned only two or three books. In the first decades of the twentieth century, reading became a middle-class activity. Newspapers and magazines were originally made for general interest readers and in the nineteenth century, both flourished. Newspapers became a staple of middle-class life in the developed world. Today there are thousands of specialized magazine publications; however the number of newspapers has decreased over time. The increase in print media over time was due to the fact that populations were becoming more literate. Blogs have become an increasingly popular form of online media. About 57 million Americans read blogs. Blogs are one of the most recent types of media. In the early nineteenth century the gramophone was a staple of American life and entrepreneurs sought to harness the power of transmitting sound via invisible "radio waves." In 1923, 7 percent of American households had radio receivers and by 1935, 65 percent. Movies were born with a 12-minute clip in 1903 changing the media world forever. By the mid-1930s over half of the U.S. population went to the movies every week. The television was introduced in the late 1940s. Between 1955 and 1985 television was the most popular form of mass media in the United States. Virtually everyone was watching the same channels since there were only three national networks. Today the average American home has more televisions than people. Television viewing changed though with the invention of cable. American homes were not all tuning into the same channel, now they had many channels to choose from. Worldwide, there are more than 300 million people who play video games. Three-fifths of Americans age 6 and older play video games regularly. The home computer was on the market as far back as 1975, but personal computers were a business tool not a mass medium. With the development of the World Wide Web in the 1980s the computer transformed the world yet again. Online usage grew 300,000 percent per year. By 2007, virtually every country in the world was online. In poor countries, internet access remains an overwhelmingly elite activity. The internet has become so integral to middle-class lives. It is a new form of mass media. Information is scattered across hundreds of sites in dozens of countries.

2. Pages 604-605

The five broad goals of media consumption are surveillance, decision making, aesthetics, diversion, and identity. Surveillance is important so that people can find out what the world is like. Surveillance is the main reason that we consume news and information programs, nonfiction books, magazines, and newspapers. When we consume media we make decisions and we use the media to acquire enough information about a subject to make a decision. We also consume media for aesthetic purposes. Media object are also works of art because they create a particular vision of reality. Media is consumed also to divert our attention. If we are being entertained, the reasoning goes, we are not engaged in big, important, useful work. By stepping outside of everyday reality for a moment, we are refreshed and better prepared to think about that big, important, useful work. Finally, consuming mass media texts allows us to create and maintain a group identity.

3. Pages 610-612

Media globalization is the ability to communicate instantaneously over vast distances and inform people all over the world about the cultural products that are available. Cultural imperialism is the cultural control of one country by another. This is a concern because with media globalization the United States has invaded other cultures. Western and American media products have been imported into poor countries and dominating their culture. The overwhelming majority of music in the global marketplace is sung in English, of the top-grossing films of all time at the international box office all of the top ten were American films. The cultural imperialism thesis holds that this kind of Western media dominance, driven by the relentless desire for profits, will shape all the cultures of the world and ensure their Westernization. The media dominance will substitute American values like individualism and consumerism for the local values of countries where media products are sold. Eventually, cultural distinctiveness will be eroded, threatening national and cultural identity. Other nations will be so thoroughly indoctrinated with U.S. cultural, political, and economic images and ideals that hey will forget who they are.

Chapter Nineteen Answers
Sociology of Environments: The Natural, Physical, and Human Worlds

ANSWER KEY

Multiple Choice

1. b (pg 620)	6. d (pg 619)	11. c (pg 619)	16. c (pg 638)	21. a (pg 642)
2. a (pg 624)	7. a (pg 618)	12. d (pg 621)	17. d (pg 637)	22. c (pg 627)
3. d (pg 628)	8. d (pg 627)	13. b (pg 631)	18. d (pg 638)	23. a (pg 628)
4. d (pg 639)	9. c (pg 629)	14. d (pg 632)	19. b (pg 639)	24. d (pg 631)
5. b (pg 644)	10. d (pg 626)	15. a (pg 636)	20. b (pg 640)	25. c (pg 619)

True/False

1. F (pg 618)	6. F (pg 628)
2. T (pg 619)	7. T (pg 632)
3. T (pg 622)	8. T (pg 635)
4. T (pg 624)	9. T (pg 636)
5. F (pg 624)	10. F (pg 639)

Fill-in-the-Blank

1. fertility rate (pg 619)	6. global warming (pg 645)
2. immigration (pg 622)	7. social (pg 643)
3. population pyramid (pg 624)	8. gemeinschaft (pg 636)
4. Demographic transition theory (pg 628)	9. zero population growth (pg 628)
5. organic solidarity (pg 637)	10. life expectancy (pg 619)

Essay

1. Pages 627-628

The Malthusian theory holds that the population would increase by geometric progression, doubling in each generation. The demographic transition theory holds that the population and technology spur each other's development. This theory has three stages: initial stage, transitional growth stage, and the incipient decline stage. In the initial stage society has both a high birth rate and a high death rate, so the population size remains stable or else grows very slowly. In the transitional growth stage industrialization leads to a better food supply, better medical care, and better sanitation, all resulting in a decrease in mortality at all age levels. The social prestige of large families has not decreased, so the birth rate remains high, and the population explodes. In the incipient decline stage social forces and cultural beliefs catch up with technology. Both the birth and death rates are low, so population growth returns to minimal levels. Zero population growth is rare, but many industrialized countries like Germany are coming close. It seems as if the Demographic transition theory is more accurate than the Malthusian theory. The Malthusian theory is incorporated in the second stage of the demographic transition theory, making the demographic transition theory more expansive.

2. Pages 621-622

The four major flows of immigration in modern history were between 1500 and 1800, the beginning of the nineteenth century, and between 1880 and 1920. Between 1500 and 1800 Europeans began to establish colonial empires around the world. Millions of English, Spanish, French, and Portuguese citizens emigrated to the sparsely settled regions of North and South America, South Africa, and Oceania. Some of these people were forced to leave as punishment for a crime, but most chose to leave because they were drawn by the promise of wealth or political freedom. At the same time, Europeans transported thousands of East and West Africans to their new colonies to work as slaves. These people did not immigrant by choice; instead they were forced to leave their homeland for the new colonies. Beginning in about 1800, East Asians began to emigrate from Chine and other countries. They immigrated to major cities in the United States, Latin America, Africa, and the Middle East. Between 1880 and 1920, millions of Southern and Eastern Europeans emigrated as they faced increasing political and economic strife as their countries modernized.

3. Pages 643-646
There is constant interaction between the natural and the built environment, between people and the places where they live, and between nature and culture. The environment is threatened by several human –created problems. Pollution is one major environmental problem that has been created by humans. There are three major sources of water pollution: domestic waste, industrial waste, and agricultural runoff. Water pollution can cause a huge number of unspecified health problems in humans and destroys organisms that reside in our lakes, streams, and oceans. Air pollution is concentrated in urban areas. Carbon monoxide, sulfur dioxide, and nitrogen oxide have a profound impact on the lungs and circulatory system. These gases also have negative effects on the animals trying to breathe the same air. Garbage is another environmental problem that has been created by humans. In the United States in 2003, we produce 236,000,000 metric tons of municipal solid waste. Most of it ends up in garbage dumps. Landfills have two major problems. First, most of the garbage is not biodegradable and when the landfills are full there will be no place to put the garbage. Secondly, when garbage is biodegradable it degrades into toxic chemicals which seeps into the groundwater and increases water pollution or into the air to increase air pollution. A third environmental problem created by humans is that of global warming. Since the nineteenth century global temperatures have been on the rise primarily because carbon dioxide, aerosols, and other gases released by human technology are prohibiting heat from escaping. This results in a greenhouse effect. Ninety percent of the world's glaciers are in threat. Other possible effects include a proliferation of hurricanes and extreme weather events, droughts and desertification, and the extinction of species (polar bears) as their ecosystems are destroyed.

NOTES

NOTES

NOTES

NOTES